HAKLUYT'S PROMISE

HAKLUYT'S PROMISE

An Elizabethan's Obsession for an
English America

PETER C. MANCALL

Yale University Press
New Haven & London

Published with assistance from the foundation established in memory of Oliver Bay Cunningham of the Class of 1917, Yale College, and from the Annie Burr Lewis Fund.

Set in Adobe Caslon type by Keystone Typesetting, Inc., Orwigsburg, Pennsylvania.
Printed in the United States of America by Vail-Ballou Press.

The Library of Congress has cataloged the hardcover edition as follows:

Mancall, Peter C.
  Hakluyt's promise : an Elizabethan's obsession for an English America /
Peter C. Mancall.
    p. cm.
  Includes bibliographical references and index.
  ISBN-13: 978-0-300-11054-8 (clothbound : alk. paper)
  ISBN-10: 0-300-11054-5 (clothbound : alk. paper)

  1. Hakluyt, Richard, 1552?–1616. 2. Travel writers—England—Biography. 3. Clergy—England—Biography. 4. Discoveries in geography—English. 5. Voyages and travels—Early works to 1800.
6. North America—Discovery and exploration—English—Early works to 1800. I. Title.
  G69.H2M27 2007
  910.92—dc22
  [B]   2006022826

A catalogue record for this book is available from the British Library.

  ISBN 978-0-300-16422-0 (pbk.)

10 9 8 7 6 5 4 3 2 1

For Lisa, as promised

Contents

A Note on the Text

Punctuation and spelling have been silently corrected in places to clarify meaning. When modernized, quotations follow the guidelines presented in Frank Friedel, ed., *Harvard Guide to American History*, rev. ed. (Cambridge, Mass., 1974), 1:27–36.

Hakluyt's Promise

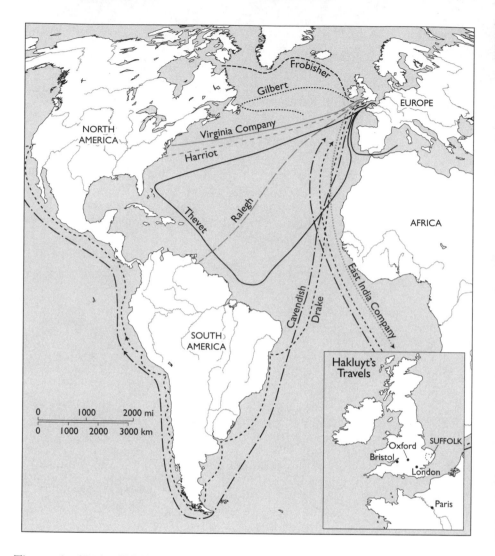

The travels of Richard Hakluyt and his contemporaries.

London, c. 1592
Woodson's Tusk

When Richard Hakluyt was forty years old, he sat one day in his study in London with a walrus tusk in his hands. The year was 1591 or 1592. Hakluyt's friend Alexander Woodson had sent the foot-and-half-long tusk to Hakluyt from his home in Bristol, about one hundred miles west of London. Though Hakluyt neglected to mention its origin, the tusk came from the North Atlantic, quite possibly from Iceland, a frozen wasteland surrounded by dangerous beasts. Woodson, a physician and mathematician, thought that the tusk could be ground down and used in medicines for his patients. He believed that its powder was as effective as any unicorn's horn in treating victims of poison.[1]

That idea, and the tusk itself, might have seemed odd to many in London. But not to Hakluyt, an expert on natural phenomena, who had read about walruses in the French explorer Jacques Cartier's account of his journey to modern-day Canada in 1534. These were "beasts as great as oxen, which have two great teeth in their mouthes like unto Elephants teeth, and also live in the sea." Hakluyt could testify from his own experience about the size of these creatures. The hides he had seen have been "as big as any Oxe hide, and being dressed I have yet a piece of one thicker then any two Oxe or Buls hides in England. The Leatherdressers take them to be excellent good to make light targets against the arrowes of the Savages; and I hold them farre better then the light leather targets which the Moores use in Barbarie against arrowes and lances, whereof I have seene divers in her Majesties stately Armorie in the towre of London." The teeth alone were "a foote and some times more in length." English comb- and knife-makers purchased them to use in their shops. Even before he grasped the tusk in his fingers, Hakluyt might have known what a walrus looked like, yet another benefit of being an avid reader

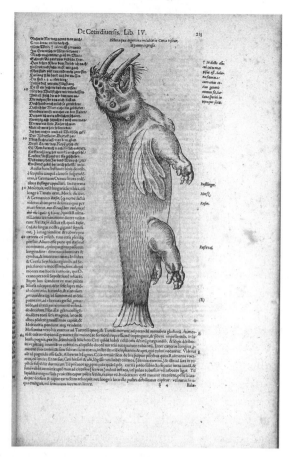

Knowledge of the walrus, or "morse," as Hakluyt termed it, had been available in Europe since the mid-sixteenth century. From Conrad Gesner, *Historiae Animalium Lib. IV* (Frankfurt, 1620)

and collector of travel accounts and maps. The tusk was but one of the precious commodities to be harvested in the Americas.[2]

The year 1592 was like many others in Elizabethan London, at least judging from the chronicles where contemporaries kept track of annual events. Printers promised the usual assortment of sermons, ballads, catechisms, news reports, and books on such typical subjects as the capture of a foreign galley, a notable case of witchcraft, and the importance of snaring rabbits. Chroniclers reported that public officials had maimed or killed a variety of felons. A

Catholic priest who refused to accept the tenets of reformed (Protestant) religion was executed on the west side of the church grounds at St. Paul's, not far from Hakluyt's dwelling in Westminster. Men convicted of capital crimes were hanged, but two women who poisoned their husbands were burned. One woman who claimed she was the daughter of King Philip II of Spain was whipped in the streets when an investigation revealed that her father was actually a butcher in East Cheape. This story was so remarkable that a printer planned to publish a ballad about it.[3]

The chroniclers also recorded catastrophes and natural wonders. The disastrous sinking of a boat that left Gravesend but foundered near Greenwich attracted substantial attention. Many on board drowned, a scene that terrified the queen, who witnessed the tragedy. Calamities came in different guises. Drought had spread across the land that year, killing livestock, which had no way to slake their ceaseless thirst. The most remarkable event echoed a memorable scene from the book of Exodus: on Wednesday, September 6, "very boysterous" winds, to use the words of one chronicler, had blown the fresh water out of the Thames and held back salt water from the sea, which made the riverbed so shallow that "men in divers places might goe 200 paces over." The drought and the full moon of the equinox, which "sea-faring men have observed" produced the most substantial tides in the Thames, possibly caused the bizarre phenomenon. One collier took advantage of the freakish scene by riding a mare back and forth on each side of London Bridge "without danger of drowning."[4]

Hakluyt mentioned none of these things in his writings. He was more concerned with Woodson's gift.

By the time the tusk arrived in London, Hakluyt had become famous as an editor of travel accounts. Born six years before Queen Elizabeth I acceded to the throne in 1558, he rose to prominence less on his connections than on his indefatigable industry. He was a talented child who in the 1560s won a scholarship to the prestigious Westminster School on London's outskirts. From there he received the support he needed to attend Christ Church in Oxford during the 1570s, where he studied theology and the emerging discipline of geography. In the 1580s he became a source of information and inspiration for England's policy makers, including the queen. By the end of that decade he had achieved international acclaim as one of Europe's greatest authorities on overseas exploration. By century's end Hakluyt had solidified his position as the most important promoter of the English settlement of

North America. His efforts helped to keep the idea of colonization alive in the face of repeated English disappointments during the sixteenth century. Yet as the new century began Hakluyt turned his attention more directly to the next most promising arena for English mercantile action: the Spice Islands in the southwest Pacific.

Hakluyt's training for the ministry shaped his understanding of the world he inhabited. Like his queen, he feared the Catholic Church and loathed the fact that the teachings of Rome were already spreading in the western hemisphere. (His antipathy toward the Roman church did not stop him from modeling his intellectual work after one Venetian Catholic and befriending one of the closest advisers of the Catholic king of France.) To advance the cause of reformed religion and simultaneously enrich the realm, Hakluyt launched a campaign to encourage Elizabeth to support the colonization of eastern North America. Yet Hakluyt never joined an expedition across the ocean. Instead, he spent virtually his entire life in England, reading books, talking to survivors of journeys abroad, and writing about the exploits of travelers.

A life spent reading and writing had many rewards. Yet such a life was available in Hakluyt's England only for the leisured rich or those who knew how to attract wealthy individuals or merchant companies to support their ventures. Early in his life, perhaps by the time he left college, Hakluyt had relied on the support of one group of merchants while he learned Latin, Greek, Spanish, French, Portuguese, and Italian. Those linguistic talents were necessary for him to keep up with the ever-growing body of travel accounts that streamed out of printing shops. But reading books in these languages brought him anxiety as well as pleasure. Turning the pages of books produced on the Continent, Hakluyt realized that the Spanish and Portuguese had been making substantial profits from a century of overseas ventures in the East as well as the West. Even the French, hardly a maritime power in the sixteenth century, managed to claim parts of North America based on the discoveries of Cartier in the 1530s.

But what did the English have to show for their efforts? Fishing crews had been sailing west from Bristol for generations, hauling back the cod that swam in uncountable numbers on the shelf of the North American continent. Yet none of these sailors had left any indication that they had followed John and Sebastian Cabot to the coasts of North America. Nor had any of them laid claim to America itself, although crews had landed there to refresh their supplies. It was not just the fishermen who disappointed. English explorers could not find the Northwest Passage, which they believed provided a direct route north of the American landmass to East Asia. Most distressing, the only real effort to establish a colony abroad had collapsed with the disappearance of the Roanoke settlers on the coast of modern-day North Carolina in the mid-1580s. Failure, failure, failure—it was hardly a record that elicited pride.

For Hakluyt, these missed opportunities cut deeply. The Spanish, Portuguese, and French often took missionaries with them. Most of these men (with the notable exception of French Huguenots such as Jean de Léry, who went to Brazil in the mid-sixteenth century) planned to convince the indigenous peoples of the Americas, Africa, and Asia of the benefits of Roman Catholicism. The spread of that religion, heretical to the Protestant English since the age of Henry VIII, aroused anxieties about the growing power of the Catholic Church. Hakluyt understood those fears and played on them in his writings. He knew that spreading reformed Christianity might keep the English in the colonization business despite the earlier failures. He knew, too, that colonies could be profitable ventures, especially if English settlers abroad sent home valuable commodities.

But travel carried enormous risks in the sixteenth century. One did not need to sail across the ocean to recognize its myriad threats. Hakluyt knew that every journey meant an encounter with danger. Storms could swamp any vessel. Slack winds left boats drifting in becalmed waters while those on board starved or sank into the misery caused by scurvy. Enormous creatures lurked in the deep, ready to devour humans and ships alike. Monsters lurked at the edges of the known world, and occasionally within Europe. Sebastian Münster, one of the most famous encyclopedists of the century, produced a widely reprinted cosmography that illustrated these menaces and others, including monsters to be found on land and at sea.

Woodson's walrus tusk was one of many souvenirs that came to England from those desperate waters in the sixteenth century, but it was not the only thing that Hakluyt collected. By the time he died in 1616 his possessions included income-producing clerical sinecures, a manor in rural Suffolk, a house in London, and two shares in the Virginia Company. He also kept a small mountain of manuscripts and books, though it is possible he gave many of them away before his death. There is no inventory of Hakluyt's library, though in 1592 he undoubtedly possessed such volumes as *Americae Tertia Pars*, published that year by the Flemish engraver Theodor de Bry, who had worked with Hakluyt two years earlier. That book, and others in de Bry's *America* series, testified to both the dangers and the wonders of what could be

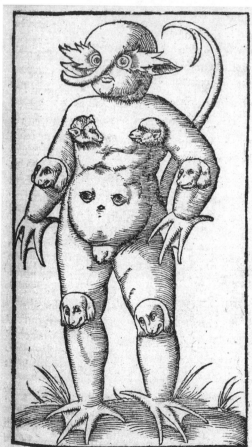

The dangers of the world: monsters inhabiting the edges of civilization and in the oceans. From Sebastian Münster, *Cosmographiæ Universalis Lib. VI* ([Basel, 1552]).
(HUNTINGTON LIBRARY)

found in the oceans and in the western hemisphere. Among the marvels were schools of flying fish, which offered their bodies to starving passengers on the journey across the Atlantic. Of course, surviving the crossing would mean little if English travelers fell victim to cannibals, who appeared repeatedly in de Bry's book on Brazil.[5]

Poring over his papers and books had allowed Hakluyt to earn the distinction of knowing more about what lay beyond Europe's shores than any other person in England. He had gained that intellectual prize, like all his treasures, not by traveling—he never went farther than Paris—but by reading and listening and then gathering details from travelers into his own books. By the time he was finished, he had printed more pages than his contemporary William Shakespeare.

The available evidence suggests that Hakluyt was not a man who indulged in much introspection. Most of his correspondence has disappeared over the centuries. He tucked the most important surviving documents about himself into the books he edited. He left few clues about his personal life, his relationship to either of his wives or his son, or any place that he lived. At his death he was famous enough to be buried in England's most distinguished church, yet the location of his body remains unknown. He has consistently eluded biographers. If he had been given to similes, a device he only occasionally employed, he might have written that the traces of his life were as impermanent as footsteps left along the shores of the seas he studied with such care. The sea and the shore can be found. Hakluyt has vanished.

CHAPTER 2

—————————— ◆ • ◆ ——————————

London, 1568
The Visit

W hen he was sixteen, Richard Hakluyt went to visit his older cousin, also named Richard Hakluyt, who was then living at the Middle Temple in London. (For the rest of this book I will refer to the cousin as the lawyer.) The year was 1568, and Hakluyt, the son of a member of the Skinners' Guild in London, was one of forty scholarship students at Westminster School, which was then lodged in an ancient monastery. The Middle Temple, marked simply as "The Temple" on contemporary maps, was one of the Inns of Court, a place where young men dreamed and older men schemed. Set on the banks of the Thames, the Temple housed some of Elizabethan England's political elite and eventually welcomed to its ranks Sir Walter Ralegh (Raleigh) and possibly Sir Francis Drake.[1]

If Hakluyt wrote about his visit to the lawyer in any depth, no record of such an account has survived the four centuries since his death in 1616. But twenty-one years after he made the visit, he described it in the dedication of one of his books. As he knew then, what happened that day made as deep an impression on him as anything that would occur later in his life.

In the late 1560s, the Middle Temple, along with its neighbor the Inner Temple, had become one of the principal residences for better law students in Elizabethan London. They were not the only places to study law; students could also attend the other Inns of Court, Gray's Inn and Lincoln's Inn, as well as institutions known as the Inns of Chancery. Together the inns could house approximately one thousand students, making London one of Europe's preeminent cities for future jurists.

It is difficult to appreciate what the Temple looked like to Hakluyt when he visited. Contemporary maps placed it at the far edge of London, near the boundary between the crowded streets of the city and the relatively open spaces to the west. It was close to the old walled city, but not in it. The Thames flowed nearby, beyond the Temple Gardens, a small park filled with mature trees that ran almost the entire distance between the docks at the Temple and those at White Friars. Though the city within the walls was densely settled, the Temple marked a boundary of sorts. Near the river, buildings had not yet crowded out ancient fields. The neighborhood was less crowded than precincts within the walls, and perhaps less noisy than blocks near the bull- and bearbaiting rings on the opposite side of the Thames. Livestock browsed in fields only a few blocks north of the river. The students at the Temple shared access to the site's most impressive building, the Temple Church, as well as a history of that edifice beginning with the formation of the Templar order sometime around 1118, or about four and a half centuries before Hakluyt paid his cousin the visit. The church rose on the spot there in about 1185. With its five-foot thick walls, it was built to last.[2]

If Hakluyt entered the church he might have seen the gray marble cenotaphs of some of the most prominent Templars. Eleven knights were entombed there. Eight bore arms. Five lay with their legs crossed at the ankles to signify their oath to protect the Holy Land "against the infidels and unbeleeving Jewes," as one contemporary put it; the other three lay with legs straight. The oldest remains belonged to William Marshall, Earl of Pembroke—the "flower of chivalry" as the eminent historian Georges Duby once called the man who controlled much of England and Ireland—who had died in 1219. Two of his sons lay nearby, having fallen in battle in 1231 and 1241. But memories of even the elite fade over time, and the most astute sixteenth-century chronicler could recall the name of only one more of the knights; the identities of the rest had faded into oblivion. Their names had disappeared, but not their imposing edifices, which can still be found in the church.[3]

When Hakluyt arrived, the Temple's other prominent building, the hall, was still under construction after six years. After it opened three years later it became the principal meeting place for the Temple's residents, and by 1575 it featured what one later commentator called "the best Elizabethan roof in London." Shakespeare's *Twelfth Night* premiered there, with the queen in attendance and (so legend has it) the playwright himself on stage. The building's interior today resembles other surviving sixteenth-century rooms. Dark paneled walls give the hall a somber feeling, though lit by candles, lanterns,

This detail from Ralph Agas's large and highly detailed contemporary map of Elizabethan London shows the Temple and its environs on the northern edge of the Thames, with three boats docked at the pier there. From Agas, *Civitas Londinum* (facsimile published London, 1874).

and bustling residents and students it was quite possibly the cheeriest part of the place. But it is impossible to know exactly what it looked like in Elizabeth's time because the Temple was bombed in the Blitz. What remains is a copy. Photographs hanging in a galley overlooking the hall testify to the destructive horrors of twentieth-century hatreds.[4]

In the late sixteenth century the Temple stood out against the humdrum architecture of the city. The vast majority of London's buildings then were made from lumber cut in English woods, though even then those forests were growing sparse. Europe's best cartographers no longer crowded their maps of the realm with trees signifying dense woods, as they still did for other parts of the Continent. Eventually the thinning of English forests would mean much to Hakluyt and would change the city. Brick and stone would replace wood as the major building material. But that was a problem for a later day. This was a city made of wood. In Elizabeth's England, only the most substantial churches or private palaces were built with stone.[5]

Walls laid down over the years by unnamed stonemasons, many of them presumably drawn from the army of casual laborers or underemployed who clogged the streets of the crowded city, gave the Temple its imposing edifice. But strong walls provided only a measure of protection, as the residents of the Temple discovered in 1381 when rebels from Kent and Essex descended on the institution. Those rebels tore down the dwellings of the Temple's occupants. They stole records and books from the church and burned them in the street. The rebuilding took years, and many of the records were never found again. Even as late as the reign of Henry VIII stonemasons worked to finish the gatehouse. But there were no other threats to the building's occupants or records after the fourteenth-century violence. In the two centuries that followed, the Temple rose in prominence and attracted the talented to its rooms. Inside their elegant chambers, some of the realm's intellectual elite laid plans for the expansion of the nation's economy. Rising near the Thames, residents could watch the ships that often crowded the river. Nearby the hospital of St. John's of Jerusalem generated sufficient funds to pay the sinecures of the Temple church's master, four priests, and one clerk who jointly took responsibility for tending to the religious needs of the parish.[6]

Hakluyt never mentioned the exact date of his visit to the lawyer. If he had come in June or July, perhaps the room was lit either directly from the sun or in that endless half-light of a London summer evening. But if he arrived in January, the Temple and its occupants would have had unobstructed daylight for only a few hours each day. They would have had fires burning in each room, and candles or lanterns to provide the light necessary for reading. But the sun rose late and set early, shrouding the city in the almost perpetual dark of a winter's eve. Hakluyt might have approached the Temple through streets clogged with fog (a common phenomenon, given the Temple's location almost on the banks of the Thames) or the smoke from countless fires burning everywhere to fend off the chill. Coal had not yet replaced wood as the prime heating material, so the skies would have not been filled with particles of coal dust that later dirtied every surface and shortened so many lives.

The Temple stood within walking distance of Westminster, where

Hakluyt had attended school since 1564, the year he turned twelve. The school had been refounded four years earlier, after the Reformation, in the old monastery there. Though funded by the queen, the school was less distinguished then; as one of its historians has noted, from 1563 to 1572, which included the time that Hakluyt attended, "there were three Head Masters, but no one of them was a man of mark." Still, being a queen's scholar there was a significant measure of any boy's potential, or at least his connections. The less talented students (called "town boys") had to pay their own way.[7]

Hakluyt's stroll from Westminster to the Temple took him past well-established houses and cheap shanties, often located cheek-by-jowl along the city's increasingly crowded streets. If the winds blew in the right direction, he would have smelled the decaying flesh of discarded carcasses in Butcher's Row. The stench of offal had been plaguing the neighborhood since at least the mid-fourteenth century. The aroma of human waste was also becoming a problem in the city, which lacked adequate means for removing it. That waste fouled local water supplies and cut short the lives of countless residents of the city, many of them infants who in the first year of life were particularly vulnerable to waterborne contagion. Had Hakluyt walked along the banks of the Thames, he might very well have spotted the effluvia of the city floating on the river's surface, but he would have paid it no mind. Despite periodic efforts over the years to keep the Thames clean, the modern sensibility about pollution had not yet become fixed among the residents of England (or any other place in Europe). Only noxious smells from dead animals and butchers dripping blood in the streets when they hauled carcasses to the river for disposal elicited complaints.[8]

London was becoming a booming metropolis, but it had not yet arrived. The Royal Exchange, which facilitated merchants' activities and helped propel the city's business elite forward, did not open until 1571, so there was at the time of Hakluyt's visit no centralized institution for investment activities. But even by 1568 the city's population had already begun its meteoric increase; by the early seventeenth century it would rank as one of the five largest cities in Europe. The city's demographic growth came at an astonishing human cost, especially when its denizens had no adequate means to cope with unusual ecological circumstances. The city's population doubled from 1550, when approximately 70,000 people lived there, to 1603, the year that Elizabeth died and the city's residents numbered 140,000. When Hakluyt went to see the lawyer, London had at least 85,000 occupants, a remarkable rise from mid-century, especially given that an outbreak of bubonic plague five years earlier had killed approximately 17,500 in the metropolis. The antiquarian William Camden, an associate of Hakluyt, later estimated that the disease killed 130,000, an impossible number of victims in the city in 1563.[9]

Hakluyt left no record of what London was like during those years he attended Westminster School, but the antiquarian and chronicler John Stow did. Born around 1525, Stow had already become one of the capital's most important preservers of its memories by the time Hakluyt arrived. He was also perhaps the most astute observer of London during those years. Three centuries later his biographer for the *Dictionary of National Biography* called him "the most accurate and business-like of English annalists or chroniclers of the sixteenth century," an assessment that would have enraged his competitor Richard Grafton, who thought that Stow's works were inadequate. (Stow, in response, wrote in the preface of one of his works in the 1570s that he had "laboured for the truth, more then some others.")[10] Like many chroniclers, he paid attention to politics and to wars. But he also studied civil pageants, unusual weather, and other notable occurrences. Through his words we can imagine the city that Hakluyt saw.

Stow took note of epic events, such as the epidemic of 1563, recalling that "the poore Citizens of London" suffered "a three-fold plague[:] pestilence, scarcitie of money, and dearth of victuals." That apocalyptic visitation fell hardest on the poor, since the rich fled into the countryside. The disease led to the suspension of the academic calendar for months, though at Westminster students were back at their work by the Easter term of 1564. By autumn of that year nature's wrath returned. The Thames flooded so severely that cattle drowned. On December 21, winter's eve, the temperature fell so low that the Thames froze. Hakluyt, new to Westminster that year, might have joined others on a sheet of ice that ran from there to London Bridge. Some played football on the frozen surface while more men and women walked on it than on any street in the city. But the freeze was brief, and by the first week of the new year none of the ice remained. Still, its impact was just beginning to be felt. The flood that followed the thaw tore down bridges and drowned those who could not escape the water's rush.[11]

In 1566, the year that Hakluyt turned fourteen, the queen traveled from London to Oxford, where she stayed in Christ Church, which would become Hakluyt's college when he arrived in that ancient university town four years later. The students had been looking forward to her visit for two years, so her arrival at the end of August was cause for celebration. In her honor they engaged in the kinds of academic exercises that the queen had seen at

Cambridge two years earlier. They staged both comedies and dramas to entertain her. The festivities did not go as well as the students had hoped. The students mounted a production of a comedy called *Palemon* and another play entitled *Arcer* that had "such tragicall successe as was lamentable," Stow wrote, "for at that time by the fall of a wall, and a paire of staires and great presse of the multitude, three men were slaine." The tragedy of the nighttime performance did not stop the queen from delivering a Latin oration the next day, an address that was "so wise and pithy" that the nation, Stow recommended, should celebrate the fact of her talents and the university rejoice at having such a noble patroness.[12]

The year 1568, when Hakluyt visited the lawyer, was hardly the best of times in London. A vicious windstorm had raced up the Thames on March 28 and capsized boats, drowning an unknown number of those on board. The summer was dry and the winter that followed harsh. Shortages of hay and fodder forced prices upward, and some farmers could not afford to purchase what their flocks needed. "There followed also a great death of cattell," Stow wrote, "especially of horse and sheepe."[13]

Such disasters often spelled trouble, especially in a city in which uncounted thousands had no regular income or adequate housing. Yet the capital always lured immigrants who continued to flock there; had they not, the excess of deaths over births would have led to a decrease in its population. Those who lived there found ways to survive, importing what they needed from the countryside or the Continent. The local elites funded a conduit to bring water from the Thames to Walbrooke Corner (near Downgate), a public works project necessary to cope with the city's growth. By the end of the century, the queen actually forbade new construction within the city, one of the earliest Western responses to the problems of urban sprawl. Those crowded precincts would eventually become a reservoir of men, women, and children who would take a chance on a one-way journey across the Atlantic rather than waste away among the crowds in the streets or the desperate who filled the prisons.[14]

Stow's publishing career stretched from 1561, when he printed an edition of a medieval manuscript, to almost his death in 1605. When he was seventy-eight he published a survey of the city that had been his home for decades. It included a long description of the then-separate city of Westminster and remains the most detailed description of the urban landscape that Hakluyt inhabited. Given Stow's penchant for historical research, his survey also included the details about particular buildings, streets, and neighborhoods that give life to otherwise inanimate objects. He also described the route from Westminster to the Temple, mapping the neighborhood that Hakluyt probably walked through on that fateful day.

Hakluyt's journey began at Westminster, where he was attending a school that he fondly remembered as "that fruitfull nurserie" for the benefits it had provided. The church succeeded a monastery founded by a seventh-century king of the East Saxons named Sebert, who had been encouraged to undertake the project by King Ethelbert of Kent. Ethelbert was himself a convert to Christianity, having been baptized by Bishop Melitus of London. To show the world that he was, as Stow put it, "a christian indeed," he built his own church in honor of St. Peter and God. The church rose outside the boundaries of the walled city of London in a place so overgrown that the Saxons called it "Thorney." Like other churches built to demonstrate fealty to Christianity, this one also rose on a spot that had already been holy: a Roman temple dedicated to Apollo had once graced those lands. Sebert and his wife, Athelgoda, were perhaps the first to be entombed in the church, though their bodies were later translated to a new church during the reign of Richard II in the fourteenth century. In the mid-tenth century, King Edgar repaired the already ailing monastery.[15]

According to a medieval chronicler named T[homas?] Clifford, the monastery had fallen on hard times. It was occupied by a few Benedictine monks, who were devoted to service but suffered in their poverty. Edward decided to convert the monastery into his sepulcher. The location seemed right for such a place because, as Clifford wrote, "it was neare to the famous Cittie of London and the River of Thames, that brought in all kinde of Marchandizes from all partes of the worlde." The king demanded that a tenth of all the rents he received be devoted to constructing the new church to make it suitable to honor St. Peter. Soon after he ordered the construction of St. Margaret's church to save the monks the trouble of getting to Westminster from their old church.[16]

In the mid-thirteenth century King Henry III followed a more ambitious building plan at the site, eventually tearing down Edward's walls in order to enlarge the church. In 1246 he ordered that a market fair be set up nearby for fifteen days; during this time he forbade any other commerce in the city. The work finished in 1285. Only fourteen years later much of the church burned when a fire broke out at the adjacent royal palace. The flames destroyed the palace and many nearby houses, including the monastery. In later

years two of England's best-known builders set to work on repairing Westminster. Later monarchs also became involved, including Henry VII, who
decided to tear down a chapel and nearby tavern called the White Rose to
construct a new chapel. The stone for the new chapel came from Hud-
dlestone Quarry in Yorkshire, which partly explained the extraordinary cost
of fourteen thousand pounds. Henry VII, proud of his efforts, chose to have
himself entombed there. In order to ensure that his memorial was sufficiently
worthy, the king's executors paid a Florentine painter a thousand pounds to
create a suitable interior. Perhaps Hakluyt caught a glimpse there of the
sculpture of Empress Helena reading a book;[17] years later, when he set down
to record the achievements of the nation, her story was among the oldest in
his book. Henry VIII, whose religious reforms altered the nation, maintained
Westminster's special status. By then it had already become the only place for
coronations of the realm's monarchs.

When Hakluyt was in school, Westminster's most famous residents were
its dead, who included many members of England's royal families. The East
Saxons Sebert and Athelgoda were there, as was Harold I, the first King of
England interred in the Abbey. Edward the Confessor lay there, his tomb at
one point covered with gold and silver. Henry III's shrine was decorated with
jasper imported from France at the order of his son Edward I. Eleanor of
England, consort of Edward I and daughter of King Ferdinand III of Castile,
was interred there in December 1290, with a tomb soon marked by an elegant
bronze effigy (curiously not noted by Stow in his survey). Of course, fashions
for the dead change like those for the living. After being buried in the Lady
Chapel in 1438, Henry V's wife, Catherine, was disinterred in the reign of
Henry VII to lay a new foundation. They never reburied her, preferring
instead to put her remains in a wooden coffin aboveground, tucked behind
the eastern end of the presbytery. Throughout the sixteenth century monarchs found their final resting places in various niches within Westminster.
None could match the finery of Henry VII's sepulcher and chapel. His granddaughter and Elizabeth's predecessor Queen Mary eventually came to rest
nearby but without any notable monument.

Most of the dead arrived at Westminster thanks to connections to various
monarchs or because they brought with them gifts of landed estates. But not
all had royal blood or had married into the nobility. As Stow, a collector of
Chaucer, was proud to note, the "most famous Poet of England," who died in
1400, also made it to the cloister. Though he did not know it, the young
Hakluyt who paraded by these shrines was walking through the building that

This statue of the Empress Helena, who later played a crucial role in Hakluyt's understanding of English history, might have caught his eye when he walked past the chapel of Henry VII in Westminster

(NATIONAL MONUMENTS RECORD, ENGLISH HERITAGE)

would in the second decade of the seventeenth century become his final resting place, too.[18]

As he made his way from Westminster to the Middle Temple, Hakluyt saw a cross-section of Elizabethan London. Perhaps he passed Thieving Lane, which ran from the Close to the monastery's gatehouse and was used to eject the undesirables who clustered in Westminster seeking sanctuary. If he followed the route that Stow later described from Westminster to Temple Bar, he would have walked up Cannon Row, a street dominated by the stately urban residences of some of England's aristocratic families. That way led to a bridge over Long Ditch and into King's Street, past Whitehall. Bowling alleys and tennis courts were there, and even a pit for fighting cocks constructed for King Henry VIII. Though the walled city of London was densely settled, the city of Westminster still had sufficient open spaces for gardens, orchards, and parks. Henry had also built a "sumptuous Gallery," as Stow called it, for the nobility to look down upon a green for jousts and military exercises.[19]

Eventually the way toward the Temple led past St. James Park, two hospitals, and a hermitage built near Charing Cross, where Edward I had raised a memorial to his lost queen. The Hospital of Ste. Marie Rouncivall had been inhabited at one point by a fraternity of monks, but the order was suppressed in the Reformation and the building turned into dwellings. The Hospital of St. James, just west of Charing Cross, had been founded by the city's residents in some ancient time—Stow claimed that no one recalled the circumstances—and had become a home to fourteen leprous nuns who lived a chaste life there. All who passed by would have noticed the bishop of Norwich's palace. By Hakluyt's time the mansion had long since been confiscated from the Church by Henry VIII and become the residence of the keepers of the Great Seal of the nation. Further on sat the king's mews, which had been the lodging place of the monarch's falcons (and resident falconer) but became by the latter decades of the century a royal stables instead. Beyond the stalls and the hay bales sat a house for the lunatic and distraught. Legend had it that the residence had been ordered by some ancient king who did not like the sight of such people and so ordered them to the house near Charing Cross.[20]

The approach to the Temple brought a stroller past the beautiful house of William Cecil, Lord Burleigh, constructed with brick and lumber by one of Edward VI's knights, Sir Thomas Palmer. The building was "very large and spacious," and Cecil, the lord treasurer, expanded it still more. Beyond lay "diverse faire buildings, Hosteries, and houses for Gentlemen, and men of honor," though Stow never noted if these were in fact occupied by any of the hundreds of men who had business in the Temple. As he neared his destination Hakluyt turned down Temple Bar, which became Fleet Street farther east. If he had strayed slightly northward or gone farther than he needed, he would have passed the Inns of Chancery, the first notice in the landscape that the journey from medieval monastery to the modern study of law had been accomplished. Eventually, he turned right off Temple Bar onto Middle Temple Lane, the short street that ran to the Thames. The Temple Church rose on the left, the Middle Temple on the right. Hakluyt had reached his destination. Between the Middle Temple and the river lay an open field, which allowed residents to watch the traffic along the river between Westminster and the old walled city. Stairs at the foot of the lane provided direct access to boats moored there.[21]

Hakluyt's own story of that day began at the moment he entered the lawyer's chamber. Inside he "found lying open upon his boord [table] certeine bookes of Cosmographie, with an universall Mappe." There is no exact modern equivalent of the intellectual pursuit of cosmography as sixteenth-century Europeans practiced it. Its closest modern relative is geography, an ancient science that was only then making its way into the curricula of English colleges. Cosmography, by contrast, also included the study of history in ways that differentiated its practitioners' work from later geographers. The brilliant polymath John Dee in 1570 noted that cosmography included geography along with music, astronomy, and hydrography. A contemporary cosmographer declared (in a book that was quite possibly in the lawyer's room) that this discipline was the most important science known on earth. There was no one "so meane witted, but will confesse her ample use, nor yet so simply learned but must acknowledge her manifold benefites."[22]

The books of cosmography piled in the lawyer's office included much beyond a collection of maps, though maps did usually appear in such works. One of the most famous and widely reprinted works of the sixteenth century was Sebastian Münster's *Cosmographia Universalis,* which had been published repeatedly on the Continent since its appearance in 1544 until Münster's death in 1552 (the year of Hakluyt's birth) and then more frequently afterward. Like other cosmographies, Münster's was the product of a prodigious intelligence. The Latin edition of 1552 (which was sufficiently popular to be reprinted two years later) ran to 1,163 folio pages and contained an astonishing range of material. The frontispiece alone suggests the extraordinary diversity of the contents. Münster offered symbolic representations of Europeans bearing shields, the crests of Roman emperors, larger pictures of four emblematic character types, and a picture of a bucolic scene in which an individual dressed as either a Brazilian Tupinamba (or Tupi) or perhaps a member of an African nation walks, carrying a bow and arrow, toward a naked man resting against a tree. A tusked elephant in the background suggests that the action might be taking place in Africa, though Europeans also knew of Indian elephants by then. In the foreground are three plants Münster identified as gariofili, muscata, and piper. In the background a small sailing ship seems to be heading for a European-style city, apparently dodging the sea monsters that swim along the surface. A baby's cradle swings from a branch over the head of the resting man.[23]

In all likelihood the lawyer knew well the few English works of cosmography in print. Among them was Andrew Borde's *Fyrst Boke of the Introduction of Knowledge,* published in London only six years earlier. Compared to the work of a master cosmographer such as Münster, Borde's book hardly seems worthy. The volume promised to teach "a man to speake parte of all maner of Languages, and to know the usage and fashion of al maner of cou[n]treys." But it did nothing of the kind. Instead it was English propaganda, praising London as the most magnificent city in the world and condemning the non-English, especially the "wylde Iryshe" who lived beyond the boundaries of the English Pale of Settlement. Although much of the book lacks such overt praise or damnation, it also lacks substance, and thus vitiates the promise of cosmography by denying readers access to other cultures. William Cuningham, another English cosmographer, offered a more useful tract filled with information about navigation and a table calculating lunar eclipses from March 1560 to September 1605.[24]

Hakluyt did not mention the frontispiece of the cosmography that he saw on the table, but the images in Münster's book were commonplace. They informed the reader that the hundreds of pages inside contained information about the diversity of the world and its occupants. No subject escaped the notice of a trained cosmographer. Political systems, landscapes, human customs, religious practice, flora, and fauna could all be found there, often with illustrations. Among those illustrations were maps, and any thorough cosmographer would have included the kind of world map that Hakluyt saw that day if, in fact, the map was contained in such a book. The map might have been a single sheet of paper, drawn by hand or printed. Perhaps it was a wall map stitched together from separate sheets because no press could handle such large tasks. It might not even have been printed at all but instead may have been a preliminary sketch of the world that would soon appear in a book of cosmography.

This was probably not Hakluyt's first view of a two-dimensional representation of the world. Since his family came from Hereford, he might have seen the famous *mappa mundi* housed in the cathedral there. That exquisitely painted map depicted the world known to Europeans in the late thirteenth century, the likely time of the map's creation. It conformed to the ancient laws of geography, which placed Jerusalem at the center of the world, surrounded

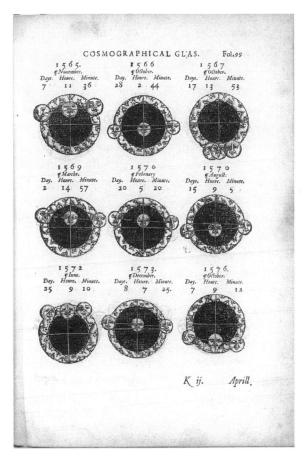

A chart of lunar eclipses from William Cuningham's *The Cosmographicall Glasse . . .*
(London, 1559)
(HUNTINGTON LIBRARY)

on all sides by lands and water in perfect balance. That balance was not coincidental. According to prevailing thought, the same amount of land lay north and south of Jerusalem, and as much territory east as west. These maps are now known as "T-O" maps because the lands form the shape of the letter "T" surrounded by the waters as an "O." Christopher Columbus had T-O maps in mind when he set off on what became his world-changing journey of 1492.[25]

By 1568, the medieval consensus about the world had fractured. Cosmographers and cartographers had to add the western hemisphere to their calculations. As a result, the characteristic T-O shape faded into oblivion. But old myths die hard, even for a wise cosmographer. Münster kept Jerusalem near the center, per its theological significance and historic setting. But he sensed no balance in the continents. Instead North America ("Terra Florida") and South America ("America vel Brasilijins") fill the western edge of Münster's world, though not yet in their modern shape. The Americas have no Pacific coast. Sea monsters, familiar intruders in early maps, troll the waters. The margins of the map contain other sorts of information, including cherubs exhaling to produce wind patterns that had already been identified by sailors. New information existed on the same page as traditional ideas about the world. A posthumous printing of Münster's *Cosmographiae* in 1572 included the same world map printed twenty years earlier, though there had been substantial additions to the text itself.[26]

Hakluyt did not identify the lawyer's map as Münster's, and it is possible that no copy of the map he saw that day has survived. But if its exact identity will never be known, what appeared on that map presumably represented the standard European understanding of the Earth's landmasses and populations. Given the central role of the Temple's occupants in collecting information about the wider world, the lawyer's room invariably contained maps and books that included the western hemisphere. Perhaps the lawyer owned one of the thousand copies of Martin Waldseemüller's wall map of the world from 1507, the first to include the western hemisphere. Maybe he displayed Gerard Mercator's world map of 1538. More likely the lawyer had on hand more recent maps. At least six maps published between 1556 and 1567 in the Netherlands and Italy contained sufficient detail to be a "universal" map. The earliest was Gerard de Jode's re-engraving of a map by Giacomo Gastaldi drawn in 1546 and published in Antwerp in 1555. There are few details for the western hemisphere, but the rest of the world is cluttered with place-names. Over time the details became more abundant, crammed together on later maps by Gastaldi and Paolo Forlani. Two years before Hakluyt's visit, Abraham Ortelius, then thirty-seven years old and selling maps in Antwerp, produced his own version of the world. It lacked the precision of his later, more famous world map that appeared in his atlas in 1570, but it nonetheless suggested his command of current geographical ideas. Perhaps the lawyer had displayed a world map recently made in Venice by Giovanni Francesco Camocio, published in 1567. Though terrestrial globes were already available, Hakluyt never mentioned if one was present in the room.[27]

No map available in Europe in 1568 was particularly accurate about the

Americas. Though information about the western hemisphere had been circulating in letters and print for at least two generations, Europeans remained ignorant about much of this place they called the "New World." The cosmographer Gastaldi (who created one of the maps that might have been in the lawyer's room) included some material about the western hemisphere in his description of the world printed in 1562, but the text was relatively brief compared to his accounts of other parts of the world.[28] The best American map of that age arrived two years later when Ortelius produced his *Theatrum Orbis Terrarum* (roughly translated as "Description of the Lands of the World"). Instead of an encyclopedic cosmography that included maps to demarcate the location of actions described at length in the text in the sixteenth-century sense, Ortelius created what was to become the typical vehicle of the modern scholarly discipline of geography: a series of maps with commentary. If Hakluyt erred on the date of the visit—which is quite possible—this book might have contained the map that he saw.

But even if the lawyer's map lacked the innovative level of detail that Ortelius presented in 1570, the lawyer had become an expert on geography. He used his world map to deliver an impromptu lecture to Hakluyt, who had (by his own admission) no knowledge of the subject. On that point he was not alone; cosmography was not a common subject in English schools.

Hakluyt was fascinated by what he saw. The lawyer sensed his interest and began telling of "the division of the earth into three parts after the olde account." Then he got down to business. He waved his wand to indicate "all the knowen Seas, Gulfs, Bayes, Straights, Capes, Rivers, Empires, Kingdomes, Dukedomes, and Territories of ech part." But this was only the start. He followed that preliminary geographical survey with detailed information about each of these regions. He spoke of "their speciall commodities, & particular wants, which by the benefit of traffike, & entercourse of merchants, are plentifully supplied." He then pointed Hakluyt to a Bible and opened it to Psalm 107. He "directed mee to the 23 & 24 verses," Hakluyt remembered, "where I read, that they which go downe to the sea in ships, and occupy by the great waters, they see the works of the Lord, and his wonders in the deepe."[29]

This was Hakluyt's epiphany, his moment of conversion to his life's cause. Those words from Scripture, combined with what the lawyer had been saying —"things of high and rare delight" to Hakluyt's ears—led him to a decision. The experience "tooke in me so deepe an impression," he wrote years later, "that I constantly resolved, if ever I were preferred to the University, where better time, and more convenient place might be ministred for these studies, I would by Gods assistance prosecute that knowledge and kinde of literature, the doores whereof (after a sort) were so happily opened before me."[30]

With that revelation, Hakluyt departed. He did not describe his walk back to Westminster after that fateful session. He never mentioned whether the streets of the city looked different now that he possessed a surer understanding of London's place in the world and how its enterprising merchants might enrich the realm by trading with distant peoples. He never told if the city smelled differently now that he knew where rare goods originated before they sailed up the Thames in the holds of cargo ships. He never revealed his subsequent conversations with other students at Westminster and whether they were filled with stories of distant lands and faraway places. If his return into the creaky medieval monastery that housed the school inspired memories of England's hallowed history—if the building now seemed a relic or a hoary monument of an insular world—he did not say.

All of it mattered, but none of it was worth comment. He had made his promise to himself. That was enough.

CHAPTER 3

Oxford, c. 1571
Rumors

Hakluyt arrived at Christ Church near the end of 1570. He had been elected as a queen's scholar following his years at Westminster School. For much of the 1570s, he left little obvious impression on the historical record. From 1571 to 1577 Hakluyt was a student, one of the many whose existence made Oxford (and Cambridge) a focal point of English learning. Like countless others, he had arrived in the university town eager to receive the accumulated wisdom of his teachers.

If Hakluyt wrote any letters during these formative years, none have survived the centuries since he first navigated Oxford's crooked streets. Yet there is ample evidence about the community he inhabited. Many of the buildings he walked through survive today. Most of the books that he read can still be found. And chroniclers, heirs to a venerable medieval tradition, provided details about what shaped the lives of English men, women, and children. The writings of the antiquarian William Camden, Oxford's early modern historian Anthony à Wood, and the annalist John Stow, among others, depicted a nation caught in entangling political struggles at home and on the seas. They also told of a society coping with periodic moments of bizarre apparitions and tragedy caused by natural catastrophe. If Hakluyt was in any way representative of his time, he stood in awe of odd celestial sightings, feared the seemingly capricious actions of England's Catholic rivals, and devoured information about serious crimes and monstrous births. Perhaps he also tried to figure out why an inscrutable God had chosen to visit calamities on the English. He also kept an ear out for the many rumors that swirled about in a world where oral communication continued to be at least as potent as the written word.

By the Elizabethan period, Oxford had already gained a vaunted place in the nation's culture. As Camden put it in his *Britannia,* first published in Latin in 1600, Oxford had become, for the English, "our most noble *Athens,* the seat of our English Muses, the Prop and the Pillar, nay the Sun, the Eye, the very Soul, of the Nation." Camden's praise flowed on about this "most celebrated Fountain of Wisdom and Learning, from whence Religion, Letters, and good Manners, are plentifully diffused thro' the whole Kingdom. A delicate and most beautiful City, whether we respect the neatness of structures, or the healthy and pleasant situation." Geography solidified the city's destiny since dense forests prevented "the pestilential south-wind, and on the other, the tempestuous west" while healthy breezes from the east and north purified any "unwholsome vapours" that crept through.[1]

But if Oxford was healthy by Hakluyt's time there, this was a relatively recent event. In previous centuries, even when the city was smaller, Oxford had its problems. As Robert Plot, Oxford's first natural historian, recalled in the late seventeenth century, neither scholars crowded into narrow spaces nor "slovenly Towns-men" who had the unfortunate habit of killing and gutting livestock within the city paid adequate attention to their surroundings. Though various monarchs came to Oxford when they thought it expedient to flee London to escape a plague or some other danger, what they found there often alarmed them. As late as the reign of King Henry VI monarchs tried to prevent the pollution of a city where the locals slaughtered cows in crowded areas and let dung pile high in the street. Even the clear-flowing Isis and Cherwell Rivers that surrounded the city became clouded and muddy, and "malignant vapors" rose whenever the waters ran high. Only Richard Fox, bishop of Winchester and a founder of Christ Church, managed to solve the problem in 1517, when he devised a system for cutting trenches to allow the rivers to flow more freely and thus eradicate the concentration of noxious waste.[2]

At one time Oxford had been surrounded by thick forests, but the city's growth had thinned them there as elsewhere in England. Enormous trees could still be found, of course, such as a famous oak at Magdalen College, but most of the forests near the city had become thinned; by the late seventeenth century the thickest stands of trees were so far from the college town that those who harvested lumber there typically took the wood to London. Camden praised the environs for its "delightful situation," though Plot later believed that what set Oxford apart were its meadows and pastures, better in quality than those found anywhere else.[3]

During Hakluyt's time there, the university itself expanded dramatically, though the city was hardly congested. As recently as the late 1550s approximately 150 students were admitted to Oxford each year. That number had grown to 231 during the 1560s and had reached 413 by Hakluyt's arrival. Within the walls of Christ Church, Hakluyt was surrounded by relics of the college's founding. Under the sponsorship of its first patrons, King Henry VIII and Cardinal Wolsey, architects had designed Christ Church to be magnificent, even by comparison to other colleges in Oxford. The ceiling of its great hall—one hundred and fifteen feet long and forty feet across— soared fifty feet above the ground, dwarfing the men and women who walked through it. Enormous windows allowed the sun to illuminate the building for much of the day, thereby enabling students and visitors to see the college's famous collection of portraits. Less impressive was the college library, which had earlier been part of St. Frideswyde's Priory, a church originally dedicated to St. Lucia. Not quite as tall as the college's main hall, the building was nonetheless imposing, as one early-nineteenth-century engraving suggests.[4]

Few surviving records detail Hakluyt's actions during his first years at Oxford. Extant accounts at Christ Church reveal that he was in residence there by January 8, 1571, and earned his bachelor of arts by late March 1574. He remained at Christ Church until at least Michelmas 1575, and records in the college's archives reveal that he became master of arts there in May 1577. He was licensed as a master of arts on June 27, just weeks before a mystifying disease struck the town and its university. Other local records reveal that he remained in Oxford through 1581.[5]

When Hakluyt entered Christ Church in 1570, as a scholar supported by the Skinners' Company, he began a course of study that concentrated on the classics of Greek and Roman antiquity, supplemented by philosophy, natural science, and mathematics. Encouraged by his cousin the lawyer, Hakluyt also began his serious study of geography during these years. In August 1577, Hakluyt became the third scholar supported with an annuity from the Clothworkers' Company. The appointment suggests that his knowledge of geography and trade already appealed to London merchants interested in long-distance commerce.[6]

Before funding Hakluyt, the Clothworkers had supported John Field, a man who became a radical theologian and launched polemical attacks on the Church of England and the state's support of the Church. Whatever else was known of Hakluyt, he was not likely to repeat Field's assertion that survivals of Catholic ritual in Anglican services constituted abuses "which unlesse they be removed and the truth brought in, not onely Gods justice shal be powred forth, but also Gods church in this realme shall never be builded." Field's subsequent attack on the Book of Common Prayer and the state religion it represented—it was "an unperfecte booke, culled & picked out of that popishe dunghill"—could have only made company members squirm. Hakluyt's training for the ministry would have meant sustained exposure to more orthodox anti-Catholic chroniclers who promoted the Church of England by focusing attacks on Rome and not Canterbury.[7]

Although surviving documents are fragmentary, Hakluyt's education in geography probably took place beyond the halls of Christ Church. The library there possessed little material relating to that discipline; for example, the library quite possibly contained no copy of Ptolemy's *Geographia* until 1583 when it acquired a 1522 imprint. Still, at some point Christ Church did acquire a copy of a 1575 edition of Ortelius's *Theatrum Orbis Terrarum*, and that volume might have arrived while Hakluyt was still there, but as an undergraduate he would not have had permission to read it. More important, in that age in which the spoken word still reigned despite the rise of print, Hakluyt possibly attended the lectures of some of England's leading mathematicians and scientists. Henry Savile, later called "the most learned Englishman in profane literature in the reign of Elizabeth" and "the magasin of all learning," lectured on astronomy, a topic vital for Hakluyt's studies. (Hakluyt also became close friends with Savile's younger brother Thomas, who shared his older sibling's mathematical talents.) The alchemist and professor of divinity Edward Cradocke, another resident of Christ Church, spent time searching for the ever-elusive philosopher's stone (at one point he even published a fifteenth-century manuscript on the subject), and he offered the kinds of ideas that would have appealed to Hakluyt.[8]

In 1577 Hakluyt began what he later called his "intended course." Like other scholars, he learned a number of languages. Those skills came in handy as he began, as he put it, to "read over whatsoever printed or written discoveries and voyages I found extant either in the Greeke, Latine, Italian, Spanish, Portugall, French, or English languages." He integrated the lessons of these accounts into his own public lectures, which were, he recalled, the first that "produced and shewed both the olde imperfectly composed, and the new lately reformed Mappes, Globes, Spheares, and other instruments of this Art for demonstration in the common schooles, to the singular pleasure, and generall contentment of my auditory." Within a decade of his visit to the Middle Temple, he had begun to put into action his earlier resolve.[9]

The documentary record is silent about much of what Hakluyt thought during these years. Not one of his letters is known to survive for the period he was in Oxford. But his years at the college were hardly placid for a young Englishman keen to learn about the larger world. The discipline of geography, as it emerged in that age, required more than study of maps and globes. It also demanded knowledge of who lived in what parts of the earth, the kinds of commodities to be found there, and how goods moved from one nation to another. For Hakluyt, that meant learning about the dramatic events shaping England's role in Europe and the Atlantic basin.

When Hakluyt was finishing his studies at Westminster, London was abuzz with news of the tortures that Englishmen were suffering abroad. In Spain, Camden later wrote, "English marchants and Mariners were drawne into the Inquisition, and condemned to the Gallyes and their goods confiscate[d]." Philip II of Spain harbored hopes that domestic unrest in England would lead to riot and rebellion and the possible restoration of the Catholic Church. To move events along, he ordered that vital goods such as alum, spices, oils, and sugar be banned from export to England. The English responded to this harassment, but not as Philip had intended. "As soone as this was knowne to the Maritime people of England," Camden wrote, "incredible it is with how great alacrity they put to sea, and how largely they carried piracy against the Spaniards." Yet as incipient conflict brewed, the English supported expeditions eastward, into Russia and Persia and with the hope of discovering a quick route to Cathay. But these English travelers could not remain long. "The warres which shortly after grewe hot betweene the Turkes and Persians," Camden concluded, "interrupted this laudable enterprise of the Londoners."[10]

Like other well-informed scholars, Hakluyt gained knowledge of such developments during his time at Oxford, possibly from Camden himself. Though he was likely unaware of rumors swirling in London about rising tensions between the English and Spanish, it would have been impossible to avoid signs of trouble, which had become apparent in Oxford by 1571. A "violent Plague broke out in the University," Wood reported, "as well to the great injury of Learning as to the terror of all, as well of Laicks as Clerks." University officials decided to postpone public lectures and "public and scholastical Exercises in each Faculty." The plague refused to release its grip on the city and disrupted the year's entire academic calendar. To make matters worse, an earthquake rumbled through the town of Kinneston in Hereford on February 17, with dramatic effect. The ground in part of the village sank "after a hideous noyse, and strange crash" so loud "that it was heard by the Neighbours a great wayes off," Camden reported. A mountain "raised up it selfe, as if it had wakened out of a profound sleepe, and forsaking his deepe bed below, mounted up into an higher place, carrying with it the Trees which were rooted thereupon," along with flocks of sheep. The quake gashed the earth, leaving a forty-foot-wide hole that swallowed perhaps twenty acres, which had included a chapel that collapsed. The earthquake was not the only natural disaster that year. The winter of 1570–1571 etched its way into English memories for its terrible floods and storms.[11]

Eleven days after the earthquake roiled his home county, the lawyer wrote from his chambers at the Middle Temple to the queen's close adviser William Cecil, Lord Burleigh. Cecil, then launching what became a meteoric rise within the royal court and the nation, recognized the dangers of the times and feared that he and the queen were the targets of possible assassins. When the pope's order for Elizabeth's excommunication appeared on the door of the bishop of London's palace, Cecil had every reason to believe that England's Catholics might cause trouble. He thus began to pay what one nineteenth-century historian called "a vile band" of private spies to keep him abreast of danger. Living at the Middle Temple, the lawyer presumably knew of these informants, though no evidence survives to suggest that he was in fact one of them.[12]

The lawyer wrote to Cecil after he had interviewed "a young man, a kinsman of myne," who had arrived in England from Grand Malaga shortly before Christmas 1570, just ten months after the queen's excommunication. The lawyer, believing it possible that the visitor "showld understand some secretes," examined him "after his arrivall." He hoped to find out where a growing Spanish army would attack. There were multiple possibilities. They could strike "ageynst the infidelles or ageynst the protestantes in ffrance" or against England, Ireland, or Scotland. The young man believed that the Spanish intended to attack Ireland. The lawyer assured Cecil that this news was "not upon heresay of the common people" but came instead from reliable sources, including a man who was "listening at a lokk hole" when Spanish state secrets were being discussed.[13]

Cecil was just the man for the lawyer to contact. By 1571 he had a reputation as a longstanding foe of the Spanish. "He is a man of mean sort, but very astute, false, lying, and full of artifice," the Spanish diplomat Guerau de Spes had informed Philip II that year. "He is a great heretic, and such a clownish Englishman as to believe that all the Christian princes joined together are not able to injure the sovereign of his country, and he therefore treats their ministers with great arrogance." The lawyer cultivated the relationship further when he told Cecil about an apparent smuggling operation designed to hide revenue from the treasury. That plot featured a man "then young and sclender hipped" climbing up a ladder into a sealed countinghouse to steal and burn the books "that wold undoe them all" if they were discovered. The young man and his accomplice then lit the book on fire but were so inept that they almost burned down a house at the time. Why did the lawyer feel compelled to recount such gossip in detail to Cecil? Perhaps because he believed that any attempt to limit the queen's revenue constituted an intolerable assault on the state itself. This would have explained his desire that the culprit, John Hornaby, be sent to Newgate and "throwen into the dungion" so that the full story could be told.[14] But even such a high-minded motivation had another purpose: in a court in which innuendo circulated with frequency and reputations could rise or fall immediately, the lawyer was trying to solidify his standing as the queen's obedient servant.

During the early 1570s the lawyer was more than a court sycophant; he was also a collector of information, as his domestic spying suggested. But his range of interests, as Hakluyt learned when he visited the Middle Temple, extended far beyond the shores of England. He was keen to know about what could be found across the Atlantic, so he turned his room into something of a clearinghouse for information and, later, as the place where he produced rationales for overseas expansion. Quite possibly much of what he had in his possession has been lost over time. The oldest surviving report dates from early in the decade: an account from the English explorer Henry Hawkes, who had sailed to New Spain and kept a detailed record of what he had seen. On his return, he sent the lawyer a report, written in 1572. At some unknown point, the letter made its way from the Middle Temple into Hakluyt's hands, and he in turn published it in 1589. It was perhaps the first travel account to fall into the family's control that has survived.[15]

Hawkes's report provides an overview of territory stretching from the islands seen by Christopher Columbus to lands traveled a generation later by Francisco Coronado. Though Hawkes claimed to have spent five years among the various residents of New Spain, it seems likely that he derived some of his report from other chroniclers, notably Coronado himself, though it is possible that he did retrace the conquistador's steps. Occasional references to having seen things with his own eyes suggest that at a minimum he traveled extensively in the Caribbean and in the territory in and near Tenochtitlán, modern-day Mexico City, which Hawkes referred to as "Mexico."

Hawkes included information about the people he observed and the lands they occupied. He described how men and women went about nearly naked in the islands but wore more substantial clothing in Mexico City. He told about indigenous architectural practices and even praised the natives' houses, noting that craftsmen had cut the stones well and laid them close together so that "there is some beautie in their wals." He went on at length about the animals he found roaming the land, noting that there were wild hogs, lions, and tigers in the mountains and crocodiles near Tenochtitlán. The climate was conducive to two harvests (probably of maize) each year, though the heat seared any fields that were not irrigated. Fruit grew well across the countryside, and locals could harvest plantains, oranges, and lemons, as well as walnuts and both indigenous grapes and some grapes imported by the Spanish. Imported cattle thrived in America; one colonist had twenty thousand head in his herd and would profit, like all who kept cattle, from the export of tallow and hides to Spain. The industry existed in the islands as well as on the mainland. Spaniards also profited from the production of dyestuffs and sheep, buying and selling locally and exporting their wares to Peru.

Hawkes filled his report with the kinds of news that would have excited anyone eager to learn about the territory and its resources. Gold, silver, and copper could be mined across New Spain. Whoever owned a mine could make a fortune, though the greatest riches were made by miners who owned at least one hundred slaves. But though all sought mineral wealth, New Spain offered such other profitable commodities as salt and cacao. Natural springs boiled so hot that they could cook a quarter of a cow in a half an hour and a sheep even more quickly. Of course, Hawkes also knew that dangers threatened any who traveled through the islands or the mainland. At Vera Cruz children frequently died after birth, and the bite of local voracious mosquitoes caused a man or woman's flesh to swell "as though they had bene bitten with some venemous worme." These insects were more than mere annoyance. They followed all new arrivals, and their bites could prove fatal.

The Tenochtitlán Hawkes found in the postconquest age remained in some ways as it had been for centuries. Although the Spanish conquest had reduced the number of natives in the town and then promoted a substantial growth in the number of colonists and officials, some things had not changed. Earthquakes were frequent, and the city's enemies could hatch plans to flood it. But despite such risks, Tenochtitlán remained vibrant. Americans and Spaniards together flocked to the three fairs held there each week, where they could find "al maner of victuals, as fruits, flesh and fish, bread, hennes and capons, Guinie cocks and hennes, and all other fowle." Hawkes claimed that the city attracted dishonest men and prostitutes, an observation that might have reflected the bias of a traveler who at times emphasized sordid aspects of life abroad but neglected to mention the same phenomena at home. In the city and beyond Hawkes found much to criticize, such as the Spaniards' often harsh treatment of natives, their decision to enslave many of them, and the imposition of a system of forced tributary payments. Though the Spanish ameliorated their brutality through the construction of a legal system in which the natives had some recourse to justice, the invaders nonetheless abused the Americans frequently.

Hawkes was not a trained ethnographer.[16] But his report was still the most in-depth analysis of the indigenous peoples of the western hemisphere at that point by an English observer. When Hawkes complained that Americans were often inebriated from pulque (the fermented juice of local century plants), his readers were probably all too willing to believe that these natives were "given to much beastlines, and void of all goodnes. In their drunkennes they use and commit sodomie, and with their mothers and daughters they have their pleasure and pastimes." But his readers might just as quickly have believed that the Americans possessed much talent, too. Hawkes wrote that the Spanish trained some natives to be fine artisans who worked with gold and copper; others worked as carpenters, masons, tailors, and shoemakers. He noted that many mastered their crafts: as "barbarous people as they are," he observed, they were capable of producing fine art.

Well beyond the fringes of Tenochtitlán, in the parts of New Spain where imperial officials had less authority, Hawkes met "wilde people" who roamed the land wearing little if any clothing, a sign to Europeans of savagery. They were hunters who supplemented their diet with insects and reptiles. Still, despite his disgust, he admitted that many lived until they were one hundred years old. There were also cannibals "that unto this day eate one another." Hawkes claimed they had developed a taste for Europeans. "I have seene the

European printers understood their audience's fascination for cannibalism, so some took advantage and placed graphic images on the title pages. Among the most lurid pictures were those offered with Hans Staden's account, evident here in an early printing of his narrative and thirty-five years later in the edition produced by Theodor de Bry. From Hans

bones of a Spaniard that have bene as cleane burnished, as though it had bene done by men that had no other occupation," he wrote. Such claims might seem outlandish, but they resembled other descriptions of cannibalism in the Americas that had already circulated in Europe, notably in the various (sometimes illustrated) versions of the narrative of the German traveler Hans Staden who had been a Tupinamban captive in the 1550s and returned to tell his tale in often gruesome detail.[17]

Like other Europeans who arrived before him, Hawkes felt compelled to

Staden, *Warhafftige historia vnnd beschreibung einer landtschafft der wilden nacketen grimmigen menschfresser leuthen in der newen welt America* (Frankfurt, 1557[?]), and Theodor de Bry, *Americae Tertia Pars Memorabilê provinciæ Brasiliæ Historiam Continês* (Frankfurt, 1592)

make a record of the natives' spiritual beliefs. He had heard about the "Island of sacrifices," where the residents had told the Spanish that "there are upon it spirits or devils." The fierce winds that strafed the region caused unwary crews to suffer shipwreck, though Hawkes did not note if he believed the spirits downed the unlucky vessels. On the mainland there were witches among the Americans who performed "certeine sacrifices and oblations" for the Devil, though such actions elicited punishment from others. Despite the presence of Spanish missionaries, the locals continued to engage in sacrificial rituals, killing "certaine olde men, and yong children," and believing "in the Sunne and the Moone, saying, that from them they had all things that were needful for them."

Near the end of his report, Hawkes described one of the chief benefits of the Spanish colonization of the western hemisphere. By establishing a claim to territory that stretched from the Atlantic to the Pacific, the Spanish positioned themselves to control the trade to East Asia and the Spice Islands. They thus enriched themselves from cinnamon and gold; one mariner even brought back a pearl the size of a dove's egg. It took enormous effort to sustain the system, but the rewards were obvious. "Many things they bring from thence," he concluded, "most excellent."

When Hawkes's report landed on the lawyer's table in 1572, it must have been the confirmation that he had hoped to receive. It was also just the report to excite a young man who had already promised that he would spend his energies promoting the expansion of the realm.

Hawkes's report arrived at the Middle Temple at a time when many in England were still recovering from the troubles of the previous year. At Oxford, an unknown number of students had spent all their money to flee the town when pestilence arrived, only to discover that they had to beg for sustenance when they returned. The university provided assistance, fearing that the students would otherwise be arrested, mistaken for the "Rogues and sturdy Vagabonds" who also roamed the town (and elsewhere) seeking relief.[18]

The "impressions of misery" that Wood saw in Oxford after the plague of 1571 ebbed over time, but the town and its university never became particularly staid. By 1573, religious dissent had set some of the colleges on a course contrary to the national church, and at least one of the chief dissidents was the canon of Christ Church, something that anyone living there (including Hakluyt) would have known well. By 1574 the acrimony had become so intense that one local troublemaker was jailed and then excommunicated for an act of "abuse, disobedience, and contempt." Accusations and counteraccusations continued to fly in 1575. That October another "sore Plague" broke out at Oxford, prompting a new exodus of scholars from the city. Internecine squabbles seemed to be the order of the day at in the mid-1570s. But many were less high-minded than religious disputes. In 1576, for example, university officials spent time addressing what to them was a serious matter: the public actions and dress of students. Even Wood realized that the dispute was hardly worthy of mention, though he did reassure his readers that the decrees "were made in obedience to the Queen's Proclamation for the reformation" of apparel that had been published that year.[19]

Outside Oxford, other potential threats loomed. The antiquarian Camden might not have known that Hawkes had returned to England and given his report to the lawyer in 1572, but he knew that the year was an auspicious one. "I know not whether it be materiall or no, here to make mention," he wrote, "as all the Historiographers of our time have done, how in the moneth of *November* was seene a strange Starre" over England. It remained fixed in the heavens for sixteen months, though, as the mathematicians John Dee and Thomas Digges had predicted, it began to fade after eight months. But before it slipped back into the darkness, commentators likened it to more significant celestial apparitions. "Theodore Beza ingeniously compared this Starre to that which appeared at the birth of Christ, and at the massacre of the Infants," Camden recalled, and the newly installed King Charles of France boasted of possessing the kinds of powers that Herod had almost sixteen centuries earlier. But five months after the star disappeared, Camden added, Charles died "of a bloodly fluxe, rackt with long and terrible torments."[20]

The miraculous star that hung in the sky too long was one of a series of mysteries that baffled Camden and made their way into the pages of his *Annales*, a detailed account of England from the late 1550s to the late 1580s. Camden had become a well-known antiquarian in the realm, with a network of informants who helped him gather the material for his books. He also traveled in almost identical circles as Hakluyt. Born a year earlier than Hakluyt, Camden arrived in Oxford in 1566 at age fifteen or sixteen. After three years at Broadgates Hall, he moved to Christ Church, where he remained until soon after Hakluyt arrived. In 1571 Camden went to London and began to collect materials for his collections. He was spurred on by Sir Philip Sidney, whom he knew from Christ Church, and Abraham Ortelius, who met with Camden when he visited London in 1577. By then Camden had already begun teaching at Westminster School, where he had arrived in 1575 and of which eighteen years later he became the master. In early May 1586, Camden presented the first copy of his annals to Cecil. The book was an immediate success, appearing in four editions in London by 1594. At some point the social and intellectual worlds of Camden and Hakluyt collided, possibly at Christ Church in 1570 or 1571.[21]

But what would even a reader with the catholic interests of Hakluyt have made of the events that Camden described for 1574? "I know not whether it be expedient to record these triviall things," the annalist warned his readers before he described a series of events that captured his imagination. That year, he wrote, "the pious credulity of certaine Preachers of London was deceived by a young wench, who fained herselfe possessed with a Devill." An enormous whale beached itself on the Isle of Thanet, her head so massive that her eyes were eleven feet apart. The Thames ebbed and flowed "twice in one houre." In November "from the North to the South, fuming Clouds were gathered together in a round," and the next evening "the Skie seemed to burne, the Flames running through all parts of the Horizon, met together in the verticall point of Heaven." Camden must have known that these were the kinds of events readers would recall. After all, he justified his inclusion of such oddities by adding that "the gravest Historians have recorded them in many words."[22]

Few records survive indicating what Hakluyt did from the time he completed his bachelor's work in 1574 until he received his master's degree three years later and began to lecture on geography at Oxford. He may have remained at Christ Church most of the time, though the college's records note that he was away for at least part of 1575. By 1577 he had become an expert in geography and gave lectures using new maps and globes. His pursuit of knowledge led him to the realm's most important ship captains, as well as "the greatest Merchants, and the best Mariners of our nation."[23]

He did not mention it directly in his writings, but Hakluyt might have learned then of current debates about how expeditions across the North Atlantic might benefit the realm. In particular, as Camden recalled, "certaine learned Ingenies of the time, inflamed with an honest desire of discovering the more distant Regions of the Earth, and the secrets of the Ocean," had encouraged investors to support expeditions to "the North parts of *America*," particularly in search of the Northwest Passage. If found, such a passage would "joyne the Riches of the East and Occident together."[24]

Part of the discussion focused on the nature of what mariners would experience as they crossed the ocean. They had listened to the stories told by the English explorer Anthony Jenkinson, reputed to be the greatest expert in the realm about those northern waters, and a Spanish captain named Bernard Le Tor, who had experienced problems when he tried to sail back to Europe from the Spice Islands when "he was cast backe againe by force of waters, comming from the North, violently rushing against his Ship." But those having the debate were convinced that the Northwest Passage must exist and that whoever found it (as the famed Venetian geographer Giovanni Battista Ramusio himself had written a generation earlier) would earn immortality. The publication in London that year of Sir Humphrey Gilbert's *Discourse of a Discoverie for a new Passage to Cataia* no doubt focused investors' attention on that part of the ocean even more intently. As Gilbert had demonstrated, all available evidence indicated that the Northwest Passage existed. If the English found it, the rewards would be immeasurable, both in terms of riches to be made and in ameliorating poverty at home. It was a persuasive little book, which both Hakluyt and the lawyer read. Traces of Gilbert's ideas and language appeared in their later works. Investors also were influenced by Gilbert and believed that such an expedition was needed. Some whose names Camden never recorded hired Martin Frobisher and fitted out three ships for a journey into the North Atlantic in 1576.[25]

The ships left from Harwich, Essex, on June 18. Seven weeks later they landed somewhere near 60 degrees North latitude. There they met some Inuit who had in all likelihood had limited experience dealing with Europeans. Summarizing the first reports that came back, Camden noted that Frobisher had met dark-haired peoples with "broad faces, flat wry noses" who were a "swart and tawny colour" and clothed themselves in scalskin (Camden called them "sea-calves"). The women "were painted about the eyes and the balls of the Cheeke with a deepe azure colour, like the ancient *Britans*." Frobisher wanted to go farther, but even by August the shallows were becoming choked with ice, and so he turned his vessels around and headed for home. He lost five men, whom the English believed were captured by the Inuit.[26]

Frobisher did not accomplish much on his first westward voyage. But he did prove that it was possible for the English to venture forward on such expeditions and to return safely. This was a fact that came to have enormous significance for Hakluyt. When Frobisher set sail again the year after he first returned, Hakluyt was among those who eagerly waited for news about what lay beyond the intellectual and physical horizons of the English world.

CHAPTER 4

Oxford, 1577
The Ice

On May 14, 1577, the twenty-five-year-old Richard Hakluyt joined the faculty at Christ Church. For the next three years he remained in Oxford, probably supporting himself as a tutor at the college, where he spent much of his time reading works of geography.[1] At Christ Church and elsewhere he had access to small collections of books that revealed an entire world beyond the one he could see for himself. These books promised, as their titles often claimed, to tell readers the "truth" about a specific subject, a common rhetorical strategy in an ever-crowded book market. Some of these texts told about Frobisher's exploits in the ice-choked waters of the North Atlantic in the mid-1570s. His journeys signaled the opening of a new era in Elizabeth's reign. Descriptions of foreign places and peoples filled Hakluyt's mind and quite literally captured his dreams. By the end of the decade he realized he could never dislodge those thoughts. For the rest of the century, he tried to turn his obsession with America, nurtured during his student days, into a passion that would consume his nation.

Ever keen to promote the Protestant cause, Hakluyt would have been pleased that a survey in Oxford in 1577 revealed that virtually all Catholics, under pressure from a university still grappling with the legacy of the Protestant Reformation, had left the colleges.[2] With religious discord at least nominally suppressed, the attention of Oxford's residents focused now instead on quotidian affairs. In the summer of 1577, shortly after Hakluyt's installation, an outbreak of a lethal epidemic rapidly killed hundreds in the town. Those deaths signaled the start of a three-year period that propelled Hakluyt from an observer of events to someone who tried to shape his nation's future. These were also years in which Hakluyt and others confronted trauma and disappointment at home while heeding the tales of intrepid sailors who waged a new battle: against the bitter cold of the North Atlantic. Though he never sailed westward on any of the expeditions toward the threatening ice, Hakluyt studied that distant battle closely.

To Anthony à Wood, the greatest early modern expert on the history of Oxford, only one thing worthy of notice took place in Oxford in 1577: the trial of a seditious bookbinder named Rowland Jencks and its deadly aftermath.[3] As Wood told the story, Jencks "in his familiar discourse would not only rail against the Commonwealth but the Religion now established, and sincerely by the generality in the University embraced. He made it also his chief employment, to vilify that Government now setled, profane God's Word, speak evilly of the Ministers, and absent himself from the Church." He kept at such actions for years, "taking glory as 'twere in it," until local officials, "fearing that if he should continue in this his height of wickedness, great scandal would redound to the members thereof," finally decided that he should be sent to London for a trial. During his forced absence, local authorities searched his house looking for "Bulls, Libels and such like things" against the queen and the established faith. Meanwhile, in London those who examined him found him worthy of punishment, so they returned him to Oxford "to be committed to prison, and stand to a trial the next Assizes following, and receive that punishment or doom which the Judge should think equal to his crimes." On July 4, 1577, the assizes met at Oxford. Two days later the judges had rendered their verdict: Jencks, guilty of the charges, was to have his ears chopped off.

Soon after the sentence was passed, Wood wrote, "there arose such an infectious damp or breath among the people, that many there present, to the apprehensions of most men, were then smothered, and others so deeply infected that they lived not many hours after." The dead included Sir Robert Bell, baron of the exchequer, and Sir Nicholas Baram, sergeant at law, each of whom had been dedicated foes of the Catholic Church. The high sheriff Sir Robert Doiley also died, as did his undersheriff, several justices of the peace, and most of the jury. A local physician named George Ethryg noted that six hundred became ill immediately, and one hundred more in nearby towns sickened the next night. By July 18, only twelve days after Jencks's trial ended, a hundred men lay dead; by August 12, the death toll had topped five hundred.[4]

That "infectious damp breath" caused devastating symptoms for the afflicted. "The parties that were taken away by this disease, were troubled with a most vehement pain of the head and stomach," Wood recorded, "vexed with phrenzy, deprived of their understanding, memory, sight, hearing, &c." As the disease progressed, the victims lost their appetite and could not sleep; the pain often drove them from their beds and "like mad men" they ran "about the streets, markets, lanes, and other places." A few even dove into rivers and lakes. Yet while many died, some survived. Local physicians fled the town to save themselves and their families. But their exodus had little obvious impact since none had any clear understanding of the etiology of the epidemic. As Wood put it, "the Physicians were ignorant of the causes, so also of the cures of this disease." Unlike other infectious diseases, which often spread from place to place, this epidemic afflicted only those who were present at the assizes. As a result, no women or children succumbed.

Infectious disease was not rare in Britain or anywhere else in Europe at the time. Epidemics at some point or another raged in every country, many of them caused or encouraged by Europeans' practice of living in confined urban spaces where common vectors—rats, fleas, polluted water, and human and animal waste (including decaying corpses)—spread illness with alarming efficiency. The worst disease was of course plague. Bubonic plague first arrived in Oxford late in 1349, part of the pandemic now known as the Black Death. From its origin in India, plague had spread west with inexorable fury to England and beyond. In Oxford, this "sore Pestilence" was unprecedented. The fortunate fled the city; those who could not escape "were almost totally swept away," according to Wood's account. The colleges closed their doors, and the town lacked enough men to bury the dead. From Oxford, where the pestilence killed as many as sixteen people a day, the disease spread to London. Across Europe perhaps one-third of the population succumbed. From a demographic perspective, the Black Death remains the greatest calamity ever to hit the Continent.[5]

The residents of England, like their counterparts across the Continent, suffered periodic outbursts of plague and other epidemics in the following centuries. Plague appeared in Oxford in 1499, though it apparently did not spread far nor did it cause significant mortality. Another pestilence returned in 1503, and a disease characterized by the sweating it induced, though probably not bubonic plague, raced through Oxford in 1485 and again in 1517 when it killed possibly killed four hundred students. A "sore Pestilence" struck Oxford again in 1507 or 1508, and a disease with similar etiology returned in 1551, though apparently with little loss of life. Plague itself returned in 1571, "to the great injury of Learning as to the terror of all," as Wood put it. That epidemic disrupted the local economy and forced students at the university—which now included Hakluyt himself—to plead for sustenance. Plague struck again in Oxford at the beginning of October 1575, though its fury had passed by early November. Although the infection did not linger long, it was yet another visitation to a city that had by then too long a history of such epidemics.[6]

When the disease hit Oxford that summer of 1577, English physicians had some clues about the nature of infection and possible remedies. Sir Thomas Elyot's *Castle of Health*, originally published in 1539, offered specific advice for times of pestilence. The clue, he argued, was diet. "The bodies most apt to bee infected, are specially sanguine, next cholericke, then flegmatickc, last melancholick," he wrote, "for in them the humor being cold and dry is most unapt to receive putrefaction, having also strait passages by which the venim must passe." To prevent infection and illness, it was necessary to "abstaine from meates inflaming and opening the pores." Potential patients had to avoid heat—from the sun, fire, or in their food. Elyot thus cautioned them to stay clear of "every hot hearbe, & much use of tart things, except Onyons and Cicorie, or Radish with vinegar, for they doe resist against venim." But once pestilence was in the area, even these kinds of cures had only limited potential good. The best way to stay healthy was to flee the area. Herbals and apothecary manuals containing the accumulated lore of medieval Europe suggested treatments for specific symptoms but offered no obvious cure for any illness that had produced such a wide range of symptoms. A medical treatise of 1552 on sweating sickness, a disease "almost peculiar unto us Englishe men, and not common to all men," offered little obvious help. Shortly before the epidemic, English readers could also find the surgeon George Baker's translation of the great Swiss encyclopedist Conrad Gesner's *Newe Jewell of Health*, a vast compendium of cures and recipes for how to make them. Gesner recognized the value of medicines made from the bones of the dead, excrement from children, frogs, silver, and gold, but there is no indication that anyone in Oxford tried any of his recommendations.[7]

Other notions about disease had also circulated among English physicians by 1577. As Thomas Brasbridge wrote in a book published the next year, "sinne is a principal cause of the Pestilence." An epidemic thus represented God's punishment on humans, especially the survivors, "for they that live, feele the smarte of the plague, when as the other, many of them, dye Gods servantes, and for this transitorie life, enjoy that which shall never end." But disease had other unpreventable origins, too. Astronomers warned that odd alignments of planets and stars caused illness, though the God-fearing

Brasbridge refused to give much credence to sets of ideas that seemed "to favour or foster the idolatrie of the Heathen" who prayed to "those celestiall creatures as Gods." Yet Brasbridge, whose work summarized contemporary knowledge, had to admit that plague also came from "corruption of the aire," a phenomenon that had multiple possible causes. In addition to "an evil constellation," such pollution could come from the remnants of a comet, water near houses that stank from the dumping of carrion or dung, "stincking privies," bodies buried too close to the surface, and "common pissing places." Too many people crowded in one room also caused a "corrupt aire" if their habitation was not kept clean or perfumed. Once an infection began, it was difficult to stop since even the clothes of the afflicted could "infect a whole Citie, and the citie may infect the countrie that resorteth unto it." Yet however deadly such an infection could be, Brasbridge also believed that only those "whose bodies are apt to be infected" would become ill. Men and women who ate too much meat or drank too much were particularly susceptible. Though Brasbridge believed that certain herbs could cure an individual who suffered from plague, prayer and repentance proved superior to any other remedy. Even private sins could produce plague, a disease with such horrific symptoms that, as Brasbridge described them, the afflicted wished for a speedy demise instead of lingering in a painful haze between life and death.[8]

But though Brasbridge argued that an individual's moral conduct played a role in his or her susceptibility to infection, not everyone was willing to eschew secular causation in favor of divine punishment. Perhaps the high social standing of some of the afflicted made clerical explanations unappealing for those who struggled to understand the bizarre deaths in Oxford in 1577. Instead of focusing on sin, some observers instead recognized that a "corrupted air" had sprung from the jail chambers where Jencks had been held. "The 4, 5 and 6 dayes of July, was the Assises holden at Oxforde, where were arraigned and condemned one Rowland Jenkes, for his seditious tongue," the chronicler John Stow reported three years later, "at whych time there arose amidst the people such a dampe, that almost all were smothered, very few escaped that were not taken at that instant."[9]

The illness that ripped a hole in the legal and social fabric of Oxford defied any simple diagnosis. For the entire nation, 1577 was less deadly than other years in recent memory, including the disastrous late 1550s, when death rates soared to the highest point in the sixteenth century. Yet there was no denying the force of the illness. Curiously, Jencks himself survived. He had his ears lopped off, as the sentence demanded, but he eventually made his way to Douai in France and became a baker for the College of English Seculars. He lived, as Wood put it, "to be a very old man," dying in 1610—thirty-three years after the illness that his imprisonment had allegedly caused.[10]

If the pestilence of 1577 was to some a punishment from God, then what cruel joke was the deity playing by allowing the seditious Jencks to live? Physicians could derive no logical cause for the suffering, nor could they soon forget the tragedy. In 1584, in a book designed to provide medicinal tips to students attending universities, Thomas Cogan described what had happened at Oxford that deadly summer. The victims were all "infected in a manner at one instant, by reason of a dampe or miste which arose among the people within the Castle yeard and court house, caused as some thought, by a traine and trecherie of one Rowlande Jenkes booke binder of Oxforde, there at that time arrained and condemned." But Cogan, who claimed to have a medical education, believed that the real cause lay elsewhere. In his opinion, the pestilence was "sent onely by the will of God as a scourge for sinne, shewed chieflie in that place, and at that great assemblie, for example of the whole Realme." God, in Cogan's scheme, chose to smite "that famous Universitie" because it was "the fountaine and eye that should give knowledge and light to all Englande."[11]

The events at Oxford in 1577 persisted in the nation's memory. No less an authority than Sir Francis Bacon even turned his attention to the pestilence in the last part of his natural history, *Sylva Sylvarum*, published posthumously in 1627. "The most Pernicious *Infection*, next the *Plague*, is the *Smell* of the *Jayle*," he wrote. "When *Prisoners* have beene Long, and Close, and Nastily kept; Whereof we had, in our time, Experience, twice or thrice; when both the *Judges* that sate upon the *Jayle*, and Numbers of those that attended the Businesse, or were present, *Sickned* upon it, and *Died.*" The natural historian Robert Plot, who described seemingly every facet of Oxford's environment in the late seventeenth century, concurred with Bacon, noting that though some believed that "a *poysonous steam* broke forth from the Earth," there was no evidence of any "ill *fumes* and *exhalations* ascending from the Earth and poysoning the Air." Plot came to the only conclusion that he found plausible: the deaths came from "the smell of the Goal, where the Prisoners had been long, close, and nastily kept." Generations later scholars were still trying to sort out what happened and why. In the end, observers concluded that the disease must have emanated from the jail and was perhaps the same pestilence as the illness that felled many in London at the Old Bailey in May 1750.[12]

For Hakluyt and others the deaths might have provided potent new encouragement for the necessity of English expansion across the Atlantic. In 1577, the very year of the Oxford epidemic, an English-language edition of a medical treatise by a Seville physician named Nicholas Monardes appeared in London. Published under the title *Joyfull Newes out of the newe founde worlde*, Monardes's book proclaimed the wonders to be found in the Americas. He sang the praises of a number of plants that contained curing powers, notably tobacco, a panacea for seemingly every illness ever to afflict the human race. As the translator John Frampton had put it in his dedication, the plants that Monardes described were already arriving in Spain and England and "knowen to bee so precious a remedie for all maner of deseases, and hurtes, that maie happe unto Man, Woman, or Childe." Or, as Monardes himself put it, the "newe Medicines, and newe Remedies" that emanated from the Americas could "cure and make whole many infirmities, whiche if we wee did lacke them, thei were incurable, and without any remedie."[13]

Monardes organized his book by enumeration of plant types, not by symptoms of disease, so a reader seeking the cure to a specific ailment needed to search it with care. But for those who did so, the rewards were obvious. Monardes identified the plant, provided a history of its use, and told how to prepare medicine from it. Though his catalog of plants barely hinted at the diversity of fauna in the western hemisphere, those he identified often had multiple applications. Hence those who knew the symptoms of the epidemic of 1577 might be attracted to a root called Mechoacan, which could "marveilously emptie out the cause of ye large Fevers, and importunate: and all Fevers compounded, and chiefly in the olde Fevers, as Tertians, Quotidians, flematick, and in suche diseases as commonly come of opilations, usyng thereof at the tyme that is needefull." Applied properly, tobacco—arguably the most protean plant that sixteenth-century Europeans found in the Americas—could remedy both severe headache and stomach pain, two of the chief symptoms of the mysterious ailment. Medicines made from sassafras trees growing in Florida could also cure the same problems; balsam and the root carlo sancto also relieved "griefes of the hedde." Bezaar stones from the mountains of Peru had the ability to "extinguishe and kil the malice" of pestilential fevers, as Monardes knew from his own observations since he had offered it to patients on many occasions.[14]

If some clerically minded observers believed that fatal epidemics always signified a manifestation of God's wrath toward a wayward flock, Monardes's book suggested an alternative course, which might have been especially appealing to a reader like Hakluyt.[15] With expansion into the western hemisphere, Europeans might be spared the kinds of horrors that had afflicted their families and communities for so long.

While the dead piled up on the streets of Oxford, Martin Frobisher was busy collecting rocks on frigid islands in the North Atlantic. He had made his first journey into those chilled waters during the summer of 1576, hoping to find the entrance to the fabled Northwest Passage and thus gain access to a quick water route to the Pacific Ocean and the riches of East Asia. Though he had not succeeded, he gathered enough evidence of its possible existence that he decided to mount a second expedition the next year. And so he left Harwich on May 31, 1577, retracing his previous year's voyage through the ocean as if he had cleared a path through a dense forest. He "entred his straites" once again, as the chronicler Stow reported, on another journey "towards *Cataya* by the Northweast Seas." Although once again he failed to find that passage, he nonetheless loaded his ships with "Golde Ore" before departing on August 24, landing at Milford Haven, Wales, on September 20. On May 31, 1578, the one-year anniversary of his previous departure, he led a fleet of fifteen well-appointed ships out of the harbor at Harwich again. But though he sailed during the summer, he encountered what every sailor in the North Atlantic feared: the advance of the winter ice sheet. Ever persistent, Frobisher continued westward. On July 31 he landed at an enormous landmass, which he named Meta Incognita, and again had his men once dig for ore. They departed after one month on shore, arriving in England sometime around October 1.[16]

News of Frobisher's voyages remained limited in 1576 and 1577, but by 1578 Hakluyt, now learned in geography, had access to the bounty of information that began to circulate in books. Among the authors who best understood the importance of Frobisher's journeys was Thomas Churchyard, a man whose writings touched on perhaps every major issue in sixteenth-century England —including the public issues that fascinated Hakluyt. On May 10, 1578, just three weeks before Frobisher set sail on his third expedition, the printer Andrew Maunsell published Churchyard's *A Prayse, and Reporte of Maister Martyne Frobishers Voyage to Meta Incognita* and began to sell it in Paul's Churchyard in London. He dedicated his work to Sir Francis Walsingham, one of the queen's closest advisers, who would later play a decisive role in Hakluyt's career. To Churchyard, Frobisher's return in 1577 elevated him to the level of the greatest mariners of the age—Columbus, Cabot, Magellan— and of the French cosmographer André Thevet, who would also become a close associate of Hakluyt six years later. Frobisher deserved all the praise that could be heaped on him since he had gone to the west with the word of God and met "those that feed like monsters (and rather live like dogges then men)." Churchyard also praised mariners for leading such expeditions, which he hoped would benefit the realm by providing work for idle men who would otherwise give in to base temptation.[17]

Churchyard treated his readers to a long narrative of Frobisher's second journey, giving it the description that a heroic effort deserved. After passing the Orkneys, Frobisher's three ships hugged the Scottish coast before they turned west toward S. Magnus, where the visitors at first terrified the locals but they recovered and soon "entertained them" as well as they could from the meager existence they had extracted from that barren land. They spent the month of June heading farther west, their destination illuminated by a summer sun that hung for hours in those northern skies. By July they approached Freeseland, "where they were troubled with aboundaunce of Ice, and felt extreame colde" in spite of the season. Storms and ice rose up repeatedly, damaging the English ships, but the men persisted and eventually landed on Haulls Island, gathering the ore they "thought necessarie for their purpose."[18]

Once on shore, Frobisher's men set about exploring the land, walking inland four to five miles until mountains blocked their path. On their way back they found "a straunge fish dead, that had been caste from the Sea on the shore, who had a Boane in his head like an *Unicorne.*" This was a fitting present for English royalty, so they hauled the fish aboard to take home with them. They then embarked and landed at a place they named Beares Sound, where the digging for ore seemed especially promising. Within two days they had dug twenty tons and loaded them for the journey back to England. But their good fortune did not last long. Winds from a fierce ocean storm drove the tide into the ships, and ice broke a cable on the *Gabriel,* terrifying the English. Those on the *Michael* cast off to avoid a similar fate, fastening their ship to an ice floe that helped protect them from further damage. But the ice kept coming, relentless in its advance, and so Frobisher and his crews had to search anew for a safe anchorage.[19]

Once the storm passed the ships sailed into Jackman's Sound and then, forced by a tide, into York's Sound. There they had their first encounter with the Inuit who inhabited the region. After sailors on one of Frobisher's ships spotted two tents, some of the men went exploring. The "people had fledde," they realized, but had left behind eight sealskin canoes. More significantly, the mariners found "a Doublet, a Shyrte and a paire of Shues," all of them owned by an Englishman who had been stranded there during the voyage of 1576. The English captain Yorke summoned paper and ink from his ship and left a message "thereby to get some intelligence of the man they presupposed to be alive." The men also left English goods—"Belles, glasses and other toys to embolde[n] the barberous people to use some courtesie"—and then headed back to Jackman's Sound "without any further offence offered to the Infidels." As Churchyard noted, the men remained there to study the area before their departure so that they would better understand "the enemie" in any later confrontation. One of them also sketched the surroundings, which probably became the basis for a watercolor of the scene by the painter John White, who would become famous for his renderings of the English settlement at Roanoke in the mid-1580s.[20]

The first of the crew arrived back in Jackman's Sound on August 1, awaiting orders from Frobisher about how they were to proceed. Each man was eager to avoid causing any insult or injury to the Inuit, a position that reflected their commander's view. "But the Caniballes had sutch suspicion" about their actions that the English sailors soon believed that trouble could not be avoided. Before the English arrived, the Inuit had packed up their hide tents and hid in nearby rocks or canoes "where our menne," Churchyard wrote, "might not easely come unto them." The sailors, fearing the consequences, nonetheless decided to land and continue with their plans. When they did so, the Inuit, so the English claimed, shot at them with bows and arrows and "offered to shewe some defence," a tactic that troubled the invaders who tried to devise "how to bee conquerors in sutch sorte, as might sound to their reputation and Christian credite."[21]

The English divided themselves into two groups, one to seek out the Inuit who fled from them, the other to search for the locals who had hidden themselves in the rocks. In the ensuing skirmish, the Inuit rained arrows on the English, who shot back, though there is no report of any casualties other than one Englishman hit by an arrow. The English gained the upper hand, but rather than surrender, the cornered Inuit "tumbled doune from a high Mountain, into the bottom of the Seas." More came out of the rocks and continued to assault the English, who were busy trying to escape after taking a few of the Inuit captive. The English managed to get their ships out into open water, stowing the human and mineral finds in their ships for the journey back home, thanking God for their "so good happ and fortunate successe."[22]

Having escaped this ordeal, Frobisher ordered the captain of each ship to proceed directly to England. Since he feared that the vessels might be blown away from each other during the journey, he instructed the captains of all of the ships that they should land as soon as possible and not wait for the others. His order reflected his understanding of the cruel winds that barrage the North Atlantic, even during those endless days of summer sunshine. Frobisher, it turned out, was right in his fears: a storm blew up and separated the vessels, ripping the main mast from the deck of one ship and horrifying the men, who feared that leaks opened by the gale could not be plugged. "Yet as all violent thinges doe endure but a season," Churchyard concluded, "so this rage of storme ceased in continuance of tyme," and the ship made it safely to Yarmouth. Shortly after the *Ayde* and the *Gabriel,* each of which had also felt the force of the storm, made their way "gallauntly home to Gods great glorie, and the gladnesse of good people."[23]

Churchyard encouraged the English public to embrace such missions. "The earth was made fore ye childre[n] of men," he declared, "and neither the Spaniard, nor the Frenche, hath a prerogative too dwell alone, as though God appointed them to a greater portio[n] then other Nations." The English were confident that they could dominate the high seas. They certainly could not leave such lands to the Catholics to exploit. At a time of rising unemployment in England, they also did not want to run the risk of the jobless—men who would "cut the throates of the welthy and rich" if they had the chance— causing social tumult when it was possible instead to employ them in more worthwhile activities. "Our Proverbe is, Winne Golde, and weare Gold," Churchyard told them. "The necessitie of millions of men biddes them seeke abroad for some benefite, or lie at home in extreme ruine and beggerie." The solution to domestic trouble and foreign expansion, so obvious to Churchyard, was to follow in Frobisher's wake. "He that lies idlelie at home, and hopes that God will caste kyngdomes in his lappe, maie as well catche at the Cloudes in the ayre, as come by any commoditie of the Earth," he concluded. Real fortune lay to those who seized opportunities.[24]

Authoritative in many ways, Churchyard never claimed to be an eyewitness. But in the mid- to late 1570s, the testimony of individuals who went along on at least one of Frobisher's westward voyages began to circulate. This literature was the stuff observers such as Hakluyt drew from when they composed their narratives of exploration. For Hakluyt, these texts became components of his argument that long-distance travel was crucial for the future of the realm.[25]

Frobisher made his voyages during the age when publishers were trans-forming the intellectual worlds of the English and other Europeans. The reg-ister of the Stationers' Company revealed that at the time accounts about Frobisher's voyages were being printed, readers could learn about monstrous births, spectacular murders, travel to distant lands, celestial phenomena, medi-cine, and witchcraft. Knowledge of such events and ephemera existed earlier, circulated orally and in manuscripts. By Hakluyt's time, such information became embedded in more readily distributable forms, virtually guarantee-ing that more people would gain access to whatever printers deemed news-worthy.[26] Texts like these also appealed to the European market for news about the Americas.

Frobisher's homecoming led to a minor boom in book publishing in London, with each author asserting that he possessed a particular insight. Churchyard's *Prayse, and Reporte* of 1578 was perhaps the most effusive paean to Frobisher, but it was not necessarily the most accurate. Three writers who accompanied Frobisher claimed to offer "true" accounts: Dionyse Settle, whose *A True reporte of the laste voyage into the West and Northwest regions* was published in London in 1577; Thomas Ellis, author of *A True reporte of the third and last voyage into Meta Incognita*, printed in London in 1578; and George Best, who wrote *A True Discourse of the late voyages of discoverie . . . under the conduct of Martin Frobisher*, also printed in London in 1578. The titles reflect each author's desire to present *the* truthful account, a none-too-subtle effort to suggest that the real story had not emerged until each had had his say. These titles were not unusual in this era in which other European authorities claimed to offer "true" accounts of various phenomena, including what the author had seen in a distant place. Though Hakluyt wrote none of these accounts, he would later need to judge among such reports claiming to tell the truth about Frobisher and other explorers.

In an earlier age when the dissemination of information had remained controlled by a small elite, there was little reason to question the reliability of the written word. With the advent of print and the rapid growth in the number of those who became arbiters of knowledge through their use of the press, printers sensed that readers wanted reassurance that the texts they were reading, especially those relating to dramatic events, were reliable. By expanding the amount of information available, printers paradoxically had made some readers question what they found in books. To avert widespread skepticism (or perhaps just to sell more books), some printers took it upon themselves to stamp some books as more authoritative than others. A "true" account was beyond doubt, or so at least those printing these books must have hoped.[27]

Each of the English accounts of Frobisher's journeys offered the kinds of details that were of little use to a national chronicler like Camden or Stow. In Settle's view, the expedition of 1577, which he joined, sought primarily to discover the passage to Cathay. Frobisher believed that a strait could be found along the northern edge of America, "an Island invironed with the sea, wherethrough our Merchaunts might have course and recourse with their merchandize, from these our Northernmost parts of Europe, to those oriental coasts of Asia, in much shorter time, and with greater benefit then any others, to their no little commoditie and profite that doe traffique the same." Settle described the journey itself, including what he saw in the Orkneys, reporting on people who were little known even to others in the realm. The expeditioners sailed past Iceland, a virtually treeless wasteland, and then past Freeseland, where they "met great Islands of yce, of halfe a mile, some more, some lesse in compasse." The details of weather mattered to every sixteenth-century traveler on the seas, so Settle reported the storms and fogs the ships encountered. Time and again, he wrote about the "monstrous and huge" ice that continued to startle the crews. In those frigid seas storms could transform summer into winter, though the endless days reminded the crew that this was in fact the warmest time of the year.[28]

The parts of Settle's account that might have captured readers' attention dealt with the sailor's encounters with native peoples as well as Settle's views of the environment. He told of an encounter between Frobisher's men and Inuit who at first were wary of the English and refused to meet with them. Eager to establish positive relations, Frobisher ordered his men to leave knives and other goods on the ground, and the natives soon came to gather them. But when the English tried to communicate with Inuit and wanted them to stay, the mutual "dumbe signes and mute congratulations" had little effect. Rather than creating a hospitable climate, the English terrified the Inuit, who ran for their bows and arrows and prepared an assault against the more heavily armed visitors. In the skirmish the English captured one Inuk, but a second escaped. As that intercultural contact was going badly on land, the crews on the ships suffered through perhaps the most terrifying night of their lives when a fierce storm blasted each vessel with ice, any shard of which "was so monstrous, that even the leaste of a thousand hade beene of force sufficient, to have shivered oure shippe and barkes into small portions" had not God protected them.[29]

Settle's experience revealed one of the disarming facts of any colonial enterprise: it was normally more dangerous to be on a ship than on land, even land populated by locals who might shower a visitor with arrows on the slightest provocation. Settle recognized the difference. At the time that those on the boats thought they were about to die, some of those on land had managed to find rich mines "in the bowelles of those barren mounteines." When those on shore paddled their rowboats back with their report, the news so cheered the crews that they quickly forgot their recent travails. "Behold the glorie of man," Settle observed, "to night contemning riches, and rather looking for death than otherwise: and to morrowe devising howe to satisfie his greedie appetite with Golde."[30]

Settle's account provided the details that could come only from someone who was on the spot. He marveled at rocks that gleamed with gold, though he reminded his readers of the proverb that "all is not golde that glistereth." He wrote about the fish with the long horn and the fact that some of the crew put spiders into the horn as an experiment (the insects soon died). Settle described a skirmish during which the English shot three Inuit with arrows, and the wounded "leapt off the Rocks into the Sea, and drowned them selves" rather than allow themselves to be taken captive. Settle claimed that the English would have saved the injured. "But they," he concluded, "altogether voyde of humanitie, and ignorant what mercy meaneth, in extremeties looke for no other than death: and perceiving they should fall into our hands, thus miserably by drowning rather desired death, then otherwise to be saved by us." The rest of the Inuit feared for their lives and fled into the mountains, except for two women who could not escape, one because she was elderly, the other because she had a small child. Some of the English figured that the older woman was "eyther a Divell, or a Witche," and so they "plucked off her buskins, to see, if she were cloven footed, and for her ougly hew and deformite, we let her goe." But they took the young woman and the child, and then named the place "Bloudie point" after the deaths of those who fell there. After thirteen days on the island, which Settle believed was "supposed firm with America," the crew departed, but only after they had loaded two hundred tons of ore, which Frobisher believed contained enough gold to pay off the costs of the previous voyage (of 1576) and the present expedition.[31]

Four days later the ships pulled into a sound, where Frobisher hoped to get news of the five men he had lost the previous year. The natives there were nervous, though Settle recognized that they had experience in dealing with other foreign people. "It seemeth they have bene used to this trade or traffique," he noted, "with some other people adjoyning, or not farre distant from their Countrie." Thus when the English left pen, ink, and paper to be sent to the surviving English sailors (they believed that at least three were still there), the Inuit waited for them to leave the area, then picked up the goods. Settle also told about an apparent Inuit plan to capture a few English to trade them for the man, woman, and child then in captivity on the ships.[32]

So far, Settle's account stuck close to the narrative of the voyage. There is little elaboration in the text, though he did at times offer opinions about Inuit motivations, for example, or the foolishness of seeking gold above all else. He also provided a brief ethnography of the Inuit, detailing their physical appearance, material culture, and the fact that he thought they were cannibals: "there is no flesh or fishe, which they finde dead (smell it never so filthily) but they will eate it, as they finde it, without any other dressing. A loathsome spectacle, either to the beholders, or hearers."[33] Unlike Churchyard's work, Settle was not offering praise to Frobisher, at least not directly. He wanted readers for his book, and he believed that they would be attracted to tales of bravery and conflict, scary wintry threats and the intrepid sailors who escaped them. In an age before the existence of the novel, travel accounts stimulated readers' imaginations and helped them to imagine worlds they had never seen. Settle's book had an even greater appeal. By emphasizing the ability of the voyagers to survive the North Atlantic, he suggested to his readers that they, too, could thrive even in harrowing circumstances.

Settle had told a "true" story about what happened. So did Thomas Ellis, who repeated many of the same details. But the books were not identical. A reader of Settle's account might have appreciated the ethnographic specifics and observations about the environment. Readers of Ellis's book, by contrast, found endless details about the weather and the bleakness of the area. When the ships passed Freeseland, the crew stood amazed at its mountains covered with snow, the higher elevations obscured by mist. But it was the ice that left a more vivid impression. They sailed by "great Isles of yce lying on the seas," he wrote, "like mountaines, some small, some bigge, of sundrie kindes of shapes, and such a number of them, that we coulde not come neere the shoare for them." When a gap in the ice did appear, the crew landed, hoping to meet the locals. But the Inuit fled, leaving only two white dogs behind. Frobisher, eager to initiate good relations with them, ordered that nothing be stolen and that the crew should leave behind an assortment of English goods in the hope that they would be able to establish better relations later. But when they left, "there fell such a fogge and hidious mist, that we could not see one another:

whereupon we stroked our drummes and sounded our trumpets, to the ende we might keep together."[34]

The English escaped that moment, but danger always lurked. Though members of the expedition managed to locate a pinnace that Frobisher had ordered sunk in 1577, the ice stalked their every move. A sudden storm threatened to drive Ellis's ship to disaster; the ice had "so environed us, that we could see neither land, nor Sea, as farre as we could kenne." The crew took down the sails and cut cables, enabling the sailors to survive by minimizing the force of the winds that relentlessly pushed the ship into the ice. But though the crew expected to die, Ellis believed that God's intervention saved them from their "dismall and lamentable night." The winds abated in the morning, the mists cleared, and the sailors saw an opening to escape from their frozen tomb. The ships had sustained no real damage, another miracle.[35]

In Ellis's account, the ice played as significant a role as Frobisher or the Inuit. Thus a reader would not have been surprised to find Ellis, now freed from the encircling ice that had threatened to crush the vessels, return to the subject. Soon after their ships had pushed into open water, he wrote, "we came by a marvellous huge mountaine of yce, which surpassed all the rest that ever we sawe: for we judged him to be neere a foure score fadams above water, and we thought him to be a ground for any thing that we could perceve, being there nine fadams deepe, and of compasse about a halfe a mile." Ellis was so impressed by this iceberg and others that he gave his readers an illustration of it from four distinct angles. Despite the harrowing circumstances, the crew pushed onward into the west, encountering yet more storms, including a snowstorm that froze the ship's hatches. Storms would come and go, "the chearefull light of the day" able to chase away "the noysome darkenesse of the night."[36]

The *True reporte* of Ellis offered specific details about the five men Frobisher lost. He wrote that these men possessed all of the internal fortitude and external strength to allow them to survive. Their "valiant minds" could not be compromised by "feare of force, nor the cruell nipping stormes of the raging winter, neither the intermperature of so unhealthsome a Countrie, neither the savageness of the people, neither the sight and shewe of suche and so many straunge Meteores, neither the desire to returne to their native soile, neither regarde of friendes, neither care of possessions and inheritances." Not even "the terrour of dreadfull death itself" could have driven them from their task. They had what it took to live "among a barbarous and uncivill people, Infidels and miscreants." They had not abandoned the effort, he concluded,

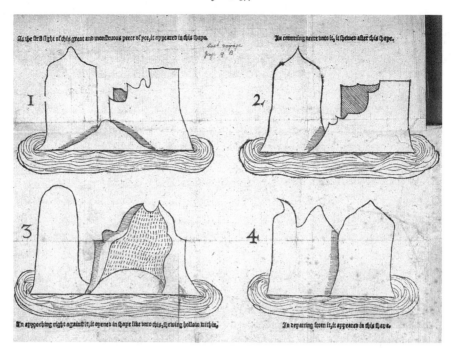

Icebergs had been known to European sailors for generations, but this is a rare sixteenth-century effort to draw one. From Thomas Ellis, *A True reporte of the third and last voyage into Meta incognita . . . by Martine Frobisher* (London, 1578)

(HUNTINGTON LIBRARY)

but instead had been the victims of bad luck. "Fortune," as Ellis put it, had "frowned upon their intentes." Like other observers, he presumed that the Inuit had killed the five men.

But despite their apparent loss, Ellis noted that Frobisher's men nonetheless made overtures to the Inuit. They built a house and left pins, toy soldiers (some on horseback), combs, lace, glasses, and "innumerable other such fansies & toyes: thereby to allure & entice the people to some familiaritie against other yeares." The Inuit might be dangerous foes, but to Frobisher they possessed innate characteristics that made later conversion possible. What better way to lure them toward conversion than showing them the material benefits of English civilization?[37]

George Best's book was the last of the "true" accounts of Frobisher's voyage. His *True discourse* was longer than the others accounts and offered analyses of all three expeditions, even though Best himself had sailed only on the journeys of 1577 and 1578. Though Best's book contained more details than the others, its narrative confirmed the salient facts of the firsthand reports of Settle and Ellis, including the encounter with the horned fish, for which he included a picture of the creature. Echoing the laudatory tone of Churchyard, Best transcended the genre of true reportage. All of the others had praised Frobisher and recognized the drama of the voyages. Best, writing after all three voyages had concluded, used Frobisher's experiences in an argument to stimulate further expeditions. The book was as "true" an account as those of Settle and Ellis, but it had a more pointed argument to make, which may explain why it included additional details.

Best described how later discoverers of new territory should behave and argued that such expeditions needed either government or private financing. He believed that Frobisher's experiences revealed how the English should deal with other peoples, "be they never so barbarous, cruell, and fierce," and how trade could happen without any use of money. His crews' return to England suggested that it was possible to survive in an encounter with the dreaded ice and that it was possible to master the change of seasons and the differing length of days in distant regions. Best warned his readers that Frobisher's voyages revealed the dangers to be faced when confronting people who did not speak the same language, when monstrous beasts and fish lurked in their midst. But such menaces need not discourage further expeditions.[38]

Still, despite Best's encomium, not every English man or woman celebrated Frobisher's achievement. In 1579 the geographer Michael Lok, who believed that English expeditions to find the Northwest Passage were vital for the realm and who would soon provide a crucial map for Hakluyt, left a long and critical report of Frobisher's three voyages. Lok was treasurer of the Company of Cathay, the mercantile firm that had helped to arrange and finance the voyages. In that capacity he served on a committee that examined Frobisher at some point after his third expedition. To Lok's mind and (he claimed) to the others who had questioned the returned captain, Frobisher was "soo arrogaunt and obstinat in his government at Sea" that many refused to be under his command. But that was only Frobisher's first problem. He was

The narwhal as it appeared in George Best's *A True Discourse of the late voyages of discoverie, for the finding of a passage to Cathaya, by the Northwest, under the conduct of Martin Frobisher* (London, 1578)

also indolent, "prodigall and disordered in the Companyes business," a liar whom no one could believe, and "so impudent of his townge as his best frynds are most of all sclandered of hym when he cannott have his waie." If his actions during the three voyages were subject to proper scrutiny, Lok believed that Frobisher would be found "the most unprofitable Servaunt of all" that had worked for the company. The accounts proved Frobisher's recklessness. Advanced funds from the company to fit out his ships and hire his crew, he consistently spent too much, hired more men than the company could afford, squandered resources by being profligate, and mismanaged his crew and the funds he controlled. In all, Lok estimated Frobisher's debt at £10,200, a sum so vast that neither Frobisher nor anyone else was poised to pay it back. The chronicler William Camden also remained skeptical of the northern mariner's efforts, noting the disabling ice, hostile natives, and worthless rocks that the English had hauled back. Rather than a treasure to challenge the Spanish, the ore from Frobisher's journeys was "throwne away to repayre the high-wayes."[39]

Lok and Camden were not Frobisher's only critics. While the company's treasurer chastised Frobisher for his recklessness, Inuit on Baffin Island reviled him for an action that merited little space in the various "true" accounts: the kidnapping of a man, woman, and child, whom Frobisher took to Bristol in 1577. The three died in England, though not before some enterprising artist, possibly John White again, drew each one with care. The man, named Collichang, died from a lung infection, possibly caused by two broken ribs or a previously undiagnosed illness. The woman, Egnock, attended his funeral, at which the physician Edward Dodding (who had performed the autopsy on Collichang) explained to her that the English did not engage in cannibalism. Four days after Collichang's funeral, Egnock was also buried at St. Stephen's Church in Bristol. The child, unnamed, died several weeks later, thereby disappointing the queen, who had wished to meet these newcomers. But the memory of the captives' visit to England survived; engravings of scenes meant to look as if they took place in the North Atlantic but were in fact staged in England appeared in French and German translations of Settle's account.[40]

On Baffin Island the story of the abduction of the three Inuit became embedded in local oral history, its details revealed with precision to a nineteenth-century English whaling captain who landed there and was astonished to discover that the Inuit account of what had happened paralleled English written reports. The local elder Ookijoxy Ninoo's history did more than echo the published accounts from 1577 and 1578. She also revealed what happened to those five sailors who had been captured in 1576. Rather than murdering the visitors, the Inuit had in fact spent the winter with them. When springtime came the English made a new boat for themselves. Eager to sail for England, the men worked at their task before the weather had warmed much, and their hands froze in the bitter chill. But they managed to build their craft, add a mast and sail, and make it into the water beyond the frozen shoreline. The Inuit never saw them again. Poor fortune did take them away, as Frobisher's contemporaries had feared, but it was the ice and the sea, not any native cannibals, that consumed them.[41]

Yet however deceitful Frobisher might have been to those who funded his operations, however dastardly he was to the Inuit, the mariner who appeared to the English public in 1577 and 1578 was a man who repeatedly risked his life in an effort to find the Northwest Passage, mine gold in distant territory, and deduce a way to forge alliances with the Inuit. Few could claim that he succeeded as he had hoped, though maps generated on his voyages and published soon after reinforced the idea that the Northwest Passage did in fact exist and that Frobisher's Strait led into it. But to Hakluyt and others, the failure to reach Cathay was beside the point. Let Lok and those who funded Frobisher worry about the costs. Hakluyt saw that even these disappointing missions served the goals of the realm. When in 1582 he published a list of credible travelers to the western hemisphere, Frobisher's story was critical, so Hakluyt directed readers to the reliable accounts of Dionyse Settle and George Best. And in his *Principall Navigations,* published in 1589, Hakluyt included three narratives testifying to the importance of Frobisher's

These two engravings of Inuit in England, from *La navigation du capitaine Martin For-bisher* (La Rochelle, 1578) and from *Beschreibung der shiffart des haubtmans Martine For-bissher* (Nuremberg, 1580), reveal a number of differences, a reminder of how images, like texts, often changed from one edition to another
(HUNTINGTON LIBRARY)

efforts.[42] As for Frobisher's critics, Hakluyt remained silent. He never mentioned Ellis's account, so it is impossible to know what he thought about it. Michael Lok's report languished in manuscript, a private accounting between a company and an employee who had let them down. Unpublished and hidden among the papers of a company that had ceased to exist, it had no more power to shape the actions of the English than Inuit accounts of the kidnappings. By selectively reproducing the reports of Frobisher's voyages, Hakluyt helped silence the critics of these North American exploits, for no one recognized more than Hakluyt the propagandizing power of a "true" account that reinforced his own beliefs.

On August 13, 1577, just when the disease that had gripped Oxford was in its last lethal stages and eleven days before Frobisher's second expedition left Meta Incognita for its return to England, the court of the Clothworkers' Company met in London and renewed its support of Hakluyt. The continua-

tion of his funds gave Hakluyt the time he needed to dig even deeper into newly printed reports. The company also noted that Hakluyt had begun to study divinity as well as geography.[43]

Six days later, the polymath John Dee sent his *General and Rare Memorials pertayning to the perfect Art of Navigation* to the printer. Dee had been a close ally to Elizabeth even before she acceded to the throne. He had used his skills as an astrologer to choose the most opportune day for her coronation, and she had visited his famed house and library at Mortlake along the banks of the Thames in Surrey. In 1577 he spent three days with her explaining the significance of a comet that raced across the skies. His book on navigation, a forthright argument that the English faced great risks at sea and needed to act to protect their interests, was of keen interest to Hakluyt, and for more than the reason that it supported overseas ventures. In the course of the text Dee referred to contacts he had with "R.H." at the Middle Temple, a reference to Hakluyt's cousin. The close association between the two men and efforts to promote the expansion of the realm had now reached the printed page.[44]

In 1578, after Frobisher had made his first two voyages, Sir Humphrey Gilbert, an ally of the queen, mounted an expedition to the west. He was in

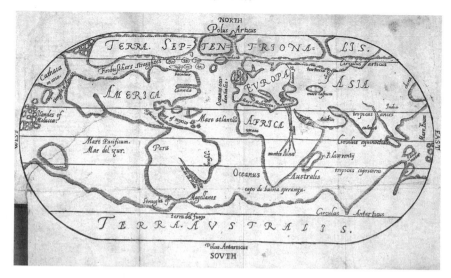

The world and Frobisher's Straights as depicted in George Best's account of Frobisher's mission, *A True Discourse of the late voyages of discoverie . . .*
(HUNTINGTON LIBRARY)

many ways an ideal candidate for such a mission. Besides articulating the most powerful argument to date about why the English should seek the Northwest Passage and colonize territory in North America, Gilbert was also a battle-hardened warrior whose behavior in the Elizabethan conquest of Ireland demonstrated his willingness to use whatever force was available to advance the queen's goals. The fifty-eight-year-old pamphleteer Thomas Churchyard, who had just celebrated Frobisher's achievements, had earlier heaped praise on Gilbert.

Churchyard's enthusiasm for Gilbert's performance knew no bounds. Gilbert had arrived in Ireland in September 1569 with the authority to impose martial law, able to execute a malefactor or rebel "by fire and sworde, or any other kinde of death, accordyng to the quallitie of his or their offences." But he did not immediately set about killing people. Instead, he offered the native Catholics of Ireland the queen's mercy and the ability to keep their lands, goods, and lives if they accepted her rule. Those who refused this offer faced extreme measures, including execution.[45]

Gilbert, in Churchyard's telling, was ruthless. Whenever he attacked, "he killed manne, woman, and child, and spoiled, wasted, and burned by the ground that all he might: leavyng nothyng of the enemies in saffetie, which he could possiblie waste, or consume." His contempt for Catholics who resisted the English Protestants' conquest was legendary. He claimed that even his dogs' ears were too good to listen to the most noble of the rebels. He humiliated Catholics who did accept his rule, forcing them to kneel before him, swear fidelity to the queen, and post a sizable bond they would forfeit if they later resisted. Those who fought against him suffered a worse fate. They were decapitated and their heads laid along the path into Gilbert's tent so that anyone who came to see him needed to "passe through a lane of heddes, which he used ad terrorem, the dedde feelyng nothyng the more paines thereby." The strategy terrorized the locals "when thei saw the heddes of their dedde fathers, brothers, children, kinffolke, and freendes, lye on the ground before their faces, as thei came to speak with the said Collonel." Within six weeks Gilbert had pacified Munster, bringing it, as Churchyard put it, "into an universall peace, and subjection."[46]

In the aftermath of Gilbert's Irish campaign, the queen granted him a patent to a sizable territory along North America's eastern shore. The patent specified that the lands must not be "actually possessed of any Christian prince or people," but the exact location remained vague. Gilbert for his part believed he could claim all of eastern North America north of New Spain, and in 1578 he organized an expedition to his new domain.[47]

Before he embarked, Gilbert met with the lawyer.[48] Hakluyt's cousin instructed Gilbert to establish himself along the coast, which would enable him to be resupplied by English ships and ease the shipment of American goods to Europe. He urged Gilbert to set up his capital in a temperate climate, near fertile fields and with access to ample supplies of fresh water, fish, and game. He then emphasized that the colonists would need to trade with the local population. That meant sustaining cordial relations, which might have come as a shock to a man who previously disdained the indigenous peoples he encountered. He also offered suggestions about the commodities the colonists might produce, such as grapes, olives, cochineal, figs, almonds, lemons, oranges, quinces, potatoes, and sugar cane. Local forests might yield cypress useful for making chests or other trees useful for the turpentine and resin needed to construct ships and houses. The lawyer urged Gilbert to send reports about the soil so that the English could figure out ways to increase their profits. They should not worry if the ground was marshy; long experience at home had taught them that workers could be found to drain swamps. If there were not enough fruit trees nearby, the newcomers would ship them over so the colonists would have ample cider to drink.

The scheme seemed foolproof. The lawyer knew that the English had long experience altering the natural world to meet their needs, so he could not anticipate a landscape in a temperate climate that would be unsuitable. Of course, the fact that the settlement had to be in a moderate climatic zone meant that the newcomers had to steer well south of the waters where Frobisher had been looking for the Northwest Passage. That environment was impossible for any sustained settlement or commerce. But not so coastal lands in regions where the climate, land, and forests resembled those of Europe. It was a perfect plan, with the perfect man to lead a mission, in a situation better than any that could be hoped for.

And yet Gilbert did not even make it to North America in 1578. He had fitted out his ships and sailed off when an enormous storm off the coast of Ireland scattered his fleet. Perhaps he had not quite vanquished the divine forces that protected the Catholic "isle of the saints." Recriminations flew in the aftermath of his monumental failure: officials revoked their earlier permission for his voyage and accused his men of piracy while Gilbert sued William Hawkins, brother of the explorer John Hawkins, who had (so Gilbert claimed) provided an inadequate vessel for the expedition.[49]

By the time Gilbert lost sight of his ships off the Irish coast, Hakluyt was deep into his studies at Christ Church, poring over the newest geographical advances. When the legendary Dutch cartographer Abraham Ortelius came to England in 1577, Hakluyt met him and the two discussed the possible existence of the Northwest Passage. In Hakluyt's opinion, Ortelius came to England only "to prye and looke into the secretes of Frobishers voyadge, for yt was even then when Frobisher was preparinge for his first returne into the Northwest."[50] There seems little doubt that Hakluyt had already gained enormous knowledge about those voyages, and it is likely that he learned about Gilbert's failure of 1578 as well. At the end of the decade, he believed that a new world of opportunity would soon emerge and that he would play a major role in it. And then, in an instant, so much that seemed certain once again became precarious.

On the late afternoon of April 6, 1580, sometime between the hours of five and six, much of England shook. The earthquake that rumbled through the realm caused terror, panic, and wonder. Some believed that such quakes were the result of natural processes; others knew that such calamities struck when God felt it necessary to punish humans. The Church of England responded in characteristic fashion: it issued a pamphlet detailing the order of the services to be performed in the wake of the tumult. Yet though the shaking had been felt across much of the country, the only known fatalities were two young servants attending a church service in London.[51]

Churchyard, who was then sixty years old, was one of the first to offer an account of what happened. On April 8, less than two full days after the unexpected event, Churchyard's pamphlet about the earthquake appeared at the west door of St. Paul's Cathedral in London. It remains the earliest book about the incident that has survived, though Thomas Twyne's compendium of known scientific facts about earthquakes and their causes, which he claimed he wrote on April 13, appeared shortly thereafter.[52] Churchyard's book provides a sense of immediacy so often lacking in retrospective writing (including the writing of history). But more important, the book represents a link between the disparate events of the age. Churchyard chronicled Frobisher's frosty voyages, Gilbert's Irish crusade, and the terrors of April 6. There are no ways to trace the readership that Churchyard's books reached, but printers' willingness to produce his books on these and other subjects suggest that he was a writer whom readers took seriously, or at least one whose works they were willing to purchase. At a time when authors competed to gain the confidence of readers by offering "true" accounts, Churchyard's wide expertise gave him an authority that few could challenge.

According to Churchyard, the quake could be felt across the city and well into the suburbs. Sometime before six o'clock on that Wednesday before Easter, "a wonderful motion and trembling of the earth" shook London, Churchyard reported, "as Churches, Pallaces, houses, and other buildings did so quiver and shake, that such as were then present in the same were tossed too and fro as they stoode, and others, as they sate on seates, driven off their places." Anyone leaning back in a chair might have toppled over. People ran into the street "in great perplexitie," fearing that their houses were about to fall on them. The walls of houses cracked, furniture collapsed, pewter and brass implements wobbled or crashed to the ground. The houses on London Bridge shook. Rivers reportedly rose and fell with the movement of the Earth.[53]

The quake left its mark across the city. Part of the church at Westminster Abbey collapsed, and "the Steeple in the Pallace so shoke, that the bel of the great Clocke sounded therewith, as thoughe it hadde beene stricken with some hammer." The queen was at Whitehall, and she and her court marveled at the strangeness of the sensation. Closer to the Thames, the lawyer and his associates at the Middle Temple also felt the trembling. Sitting at dinner, the

Temple vibrated so violently that the men ran outside "with their knives in their hands, fearing that it woulde fall. [54]

Buildings shook, spires crumbled, bricks fell to the ground. At Christ Church in Newgate Market, Thomas Cobhed was preaching from the pulpit when part of the church roof flew off. The stones hit the shoemaker John Spurling's boy servant Thomas Gray in the head and killed him. Other stones fell on Mabell Everett, another servant, who Churchyard reported was seriously injured "but is not dead." In fact, her injuries were so severe that she died a few days after Churchyard's pamphlet went to press. Others suffered less injury, though there were countless bruises and scrapes. Theatergoers leaped from the stands. Despite the widespread physical damage, the casualties were few.[55]

Churchyard included an unsigned document entitled "A True Reporte of the Earthquake in London." According to that correspondent, men taking a pleasurable stroll on a hill in Morfeeld were thrown to the ground. So were two others perched on a cannon near the Tower of London. Water swayed in its channels, and livestock wandered about as dazed as the humans. Those at the decade-old Royal Exchange, the commercial hub of the city, "wept with feare," their tears a symbol of the anguish felt across London. Everywhere men, women, and children ran into the streets, thanking God for sparing their lives.[56]

In the days and weeks following the disaster, other observers offered their accounts of what had transpired. At the time that it struck, the young humanist Gabriel Harvey was playing cards with two women in Essex. In the midst of the game, "the Earth under us quaked, and the house shaked above," Harvey wrote to the poet Edmund Spenser, his epistolary companion. The rocking was so violent that the two women even stopped their incessant arguing. "Is it not wonderful straunge that the delicate voyces of two so propper fine Gentlewomen, shoulde make such a suddayne terrible Earthquake?" Harvey asked in an attempt to find humor in the terror of the moment. He soon realized that much of England felt the quake.[57]

Harvey looked for scientific causes of the earthquake. So did Thomas Twyne, whose pamphlet, produced within days of the catastrophe, revealed the known laws of all earthquakes. Twyne informed his readers about properties of heat, gasses within the earth, cracks in the surface of the planet where earthquakes were likely, and celestial events (such as eclipses) that had a direct bearing on the geology of the Earth. But in describing this earthquake, Twyne also thought it crucial to tell his readers that the event was not entirely unexpected. He told them he had witnessed an odd apparition in the sky a month earlier—an "exhalative impression in the Aire" that resembled a stringless crossbow. He also noted that at the moment of the quake itself the sun had gone dark even though there was no eclipse. But the people of London and elsewhere paid no heed to such signs, so when it struck they were doing what they normally did: attending church, drinking at a tavern, watching a play. Some, including those riding a horse or sleeping, might not have even realized that an earthquake had occurred. "Some imputed the ratling of wainescots to Rattes and Weesels," he wrote, "the snaking of beddes, tables, and stooles, to Dogges: the quaking of their walles to their neyghbours rushing on the other side." But though some missed the event, the destruction of buildings and the mortal injuries to the two teenaged servants soon made its terror obvious to all.[58]

Yet though he offered readers a scientific analysis of what had occurred, in the end Twyne believed that the ultimate cause was divine, the actions of the "speciall anger of God," though he did not know whether it was a punishment for earlier misdeeds or a "comforte" since the damage was not worse. He urged blasphemers to stop slandering God, adulterers to halt their sinful ways, and murderers to remember "that Abels bloud crieth for vengeaunce." Then he recommended that everyone who read his tract give thanks for the gospel and the queen, attend public prayers, heed the advice of physicians who counseled others on good health, and live with the fear of God. He was not alone in this interpretation. As the dust cleared, religious explanations or recommendations flowed easily. John Stow, already at work on his chronicle of England from the time of Brutus to the present, added details about the quake near the end of his massive volume. The cataclysm could be felt across the land and, he added, "caused such amazedness of the people as was wonderfull for the time, and caused them to make their earnest prayers unto Almightie God."[59]

The earthquake rumbled through Oxford as well. According to Anthony à Wood, the city's residents "being amazed, left their houses and ran in to the open places." Humans were not the only creatures to take notice of the shaking. Birds nesting on rooftops and in the holes in walls all took flight, and cows and oxen "were much affrighted." Wood knew that the quake could be felt well beyond England; Flanders, France and other regions also experienced the tumult, "the sea was so much tossed and troubled, that the Mariners expected sudden destruction." Repeated rumblings in some areas caused greater damage to roofs and foundations of churches and houses alike.[60]

Ministers, always eager to see the sign of God's will in daily events, were quick to recognize the earthquake as a sign. Like Thomas Brasbridge, who believed that plague represented a visitation of divine displeasure that demanded prayer and repentance, clerical responses after the earthquake similarly called for changes in behavior. The Church of England's official response was meant "to avert and turne Gods wrath from us, threatned by the late terrible earthquake." Every parish church was to follow the same service. Each congregant was to read Psalms 30, 46, and 91, and ministers were to lead their flocks through rehearsals of either the first or second book of Joel or the fifty-eighth chapter of the book of Isaiah and, "after that, *Te Deum* or *Benedicte*, with a Chapter of the Newe Testament for the second Lesson." Following the homily, ministers were to instruct parishioners to fast during one meal twice each week and to donate the value of their uneaten meals to the poor, an act that would teach the faithful "that such almes is more acceptable to God, then that which commeth by constraint of Law." [61]

The unsigned pamphlet logically drew on biblical precepts for its order. In the author's mind, the calamity called out for biblically sanctioned responses: repentance, prayer, alms, and fasting. Tales from Scripture provided ample precedent for such a course of action: the prayers of King David in the second book of Samuel to spare his people from plague; similar prayers offered by Nineve and Hester, recounted in the second book of Chronicles, the second book of Kings, and the book of Jonah. Daniel, too, prayed for salvation during his captivity. What did these examples have in common? All seemed to fit the present circumstances in which England's "Godly people" needed to seek forgiveness for their sins. Ministers needed to exhort their followers to pray not only publicly but in their own homes as well.[62]

But if the earthquake was indeed a sign of God's wrath, it was the relative lack of casualties that was most remarkable, a sign that England continued to enjoy divine mercy but that its populace would need to act in a more godly fashion to prevent the "far more terrible punishments" that would likely strike "unlesse we amend our sinfull conversation betymes." One author reminded readers of punishments that God had meted out in biblical times and the warning that always preceded such calamities as Noah's flood (for which God "warned the world a hundred yeare and more"), the murder of Abel (for which God had earlier "called Cayne to repentaunce"), and the captivity of the ancient Israelites (which God did not do until they ignored "all the warnings of his Prophetes, and all the former corrections whych he had used in vaine to reforme them"). A litany of other examples from more contemporary history followed, all intended to demonstrate the author's contention that God never punished without first sending a warning. And, the author reminded, recent events in England—monstrous births, strange comets, bizarre lights in the night sky, perplexing weather—revealed divine displeasure. Even the author's analysis of the earthquake itself suggested that it could not have come from any natural causes (such as wind entering "the bowels of the earth") but instead had to have come from "Gods oncly determinate purpose."[63]

Why had God decided to punish the English? If the causes of the Oxford epidemic of 1577 remained a mystery, there was little doubt about what had prompted the quake of 1580: human sin. The signs were ubiquitous, at least in the mind of the anonymous pamphleteer. Servants had begun to act like masters, and masters were unable to control their servants. "Men have taken up the garish attyre, and nice behavior of Women: and Women transformed from their owne kinde, have gotten up the apparell and stomackes of men." Hatred and a desire for revenge could be found everywhere. An unwillingness to work, combined with overweening pride, prompted some to steal instead of work even though being caught meant a trip to the gallows. Usury had become common and the quality of faithfulness had "fled into exile," leaving the land free for falsehood to run rampant. The worst could be seen on the Sabbath, which English men and women spent "full heathenishly in taverning, tipling, gaming, playing, and beholding of Bear bayting and Stageplayes, to the utter dishonor of God." The time had arrived to eschew the ways of the sinful, to shun a repeat of that "day of Temptation in the wildernesse" when the fates of the ancient Israelites had been sealed by their degrading behavior. The earthquake was, in the end, only a taste of what would come if the nation did not reform and find its proper godly path.[64]

For Hakluyt, who by 1580 had been immersed in the study of Scripture and biblical commentary along with geography, the accounts that followed the earthquake would have symbolized the traditional views of the Church of England and its orthodoxy. From this perspective, such tragedies could be prevented if individuals reformed their ways and through the public expression of faith. In other words, the English did not need to change the course of their lives as long as they lived according to the set of inherited teachings that had always made obeisance to God a central component of everyday life. For

Hakluyt and others who had watched the epidemic of 1577 kill neighbors and friends, these books had the same sense of futility and resignation as the arguments by physicians who blamed infectious disease on sin.

But Hakluyt, who left no record of his thoughts on either the epidemic or the earthquake, acted as if he had drawn a different lesson. In his mind, a godly people who remained insular had given up the opportunity to improve their lives and their collective destiny. He too saw idleness as a problem, as did Gilbert and Churchyard. But in Hakluyt's opinion, which he began to express with ever greater force beginning in 1580, the solution lay not in a general reformation of manners but rather in an aggressive effort to colonize North America. His hero was not an anonymous pamphleteer terrifying audiences with visions of painful death and its horrid aftermath. To Hakluyt, who was only twenty-eight the year the earthquake rumbled through England, the future lay with those willing to expand the realm. Henry Hawkes's report of 1572 had described part of the western hemisphere and suggested the profits to be gained from converting the heathen and gathering the abundant riches of that distant place. Gilbert's *Discourse of a discoverie for a new passage to Cataia*, which had been published in 1576, and the arguments of the lawyer revealed the way to a better future, though neither man had as yet actually sailed across the Atlantic Ocean. Monardes's *Joyfull Newes* suggested that Europeans need not suffer from debilitating epidemics if they could harvest the *materia medica* to be found in the western hemisphere.

But in 1580, it was Frobisher, not Hawkes, Gilbert, Monardes, or the lawyer who had captured the nation's attention. Frobisher was the hero. He and his men had battled the ice and the elements. He had brought back to England ore that seemingly contained gold. He had survived an encounter with cannibals and managed to return a few to Europe. He had begun to bring to England the kinds of riches that the Spanish had already gained in the western hemisphere—"the fruites, the drugges, the pearle, the treasure, the millions of golde and silver," as Richard Willes had put it in 1577 in his translation of the chronicler Peter Martyr's writings.[65]

Frobisher's exploits filled the pages of recently printed books, the medium that Hakluyt realized he must master if he was to live up to his self-appointed task of promoting the realm's interests. Printed books became for Hakluyt a way to inscribe in the minds of English readers and policy makers a path to follow. He knew that a journey by sea, unlike one by land, left few obvious physical traces. There was no upturned dirt where soldiers had trod, no bent leaves of grass or scratches in trees, no stumps to suggest that humans had been in the region and made use of its resources for their own ends. Oceans, unlike lands, do not bear such witness to those who pass over them. Only human knowledge could secure a path through the deep blue. Oral sagas, manuscripts, and printed books all provided information about the location and size of icebergs, the areas where certain fish could be found, the latitudes where ice clung to water for most of the year. These media testified to the human presence on the ocean and the ability to reach a new world and return home again.

If Hakluyt cared about the hundreds who died in Oxford in 1577 or the victims of earthquakes, he never let on. But these events nonetheless shaped his view of the world just as surely as they shaped the perspectives of everyone who lived through them. To a man schooled in the teachings of the Church of England, the misfortunes that struck the realm had a precise meaning. To a student of geography as well as divinity, news that Americans either lacked Christianity or, perhaps worse still, were coming under the thrall of Catholic missionaries, suggested that God was perhaps offering a way to atone for the sins that had brought earlier disasters. By the end of the 1570s, Hakluyt realized that the time had come to marry the twin goals of exploration and evangelization. There was no time to waste lest the sorrows of the 1570s be only a warning for greater divine punishments yet to come.

In the aftermath of the earthquake Hakluyt realized that the likelihood of national success without colonial ventures was the same as the likelihood of catching, as Churchyard had put it, "cloudes in the ayre." The time had come to abandon such lazy fantasies and to do all that he could to create a new England across the sea. As it turned out, the fates that had been cruel to England in the late 1570s were about to smile on Hakluyt.

CHAPTER 5

Oxford, c. 1580
Passages

S ometime between 1577 and 1580 Richard Hakluyt became an ordained priest. He remained at Oxford and in December 1580 joined the Theologi of Christ Church, a group of twenty scholars who planned a life in the ministry. But despite this clerical commitment, Hakluyt's interests, at least as they can be judged from his writings, lay in geography, not theology. What commanded his attention by the end of the decade was the possibility of overseas exploration and settlement. That task might have been a sacred pursuit to some who wanted nothing more than to convert pagans into Protestants or prevent the spread of Catholicism. But Hakluyt also had more secular goals on his mind. Six months before he joined the Theologi he arranged for the Italian linguist John Florio, also living in Oxford, to publish a translation of accounts detailing the French explorer Jacques Cartier's earlier explorations of New France. Hakluyt also began to correspond with the Dutch geographer Gerard Mercator, the first of a series of connections he would make to Continental scholars who shared his interests. Though he still lived in Christ Church, he was beginning to establish himself as a scholar engaged in international debates about the world beyond Europe's borders.[1]

Yet even as his personal horizons expanded, Hakluyt remained little known in England. Even those who knew of his prodigious talents had their minds on more important events. In September 1580, only six months after the earthquake had rocked southern England, Francis Drake came home after a perilous three-year journey at sea. Though he was not the first commander of a circumnavigation of the Earth—an honor that went posthumously to Ferdinand Magellan, whose crew survived after his own death in the Philippines—Drake's return signaled the potential start of a new age. In the future that some English began to imagine, the realm could reap great profits from overseas trade and possible settlement. But despite Drake's heroics, that dream was not yet common among the Elizabethans. Hakluyt saw the potential earlier than most, yet there was no obvious model to be followed. Pursuing his ideas soon brought Hakluyt back to London, to the bustling metropolis where grand schemes might find support.

By the late 1570s, London had become a crowded city. Most of its residents lived in the cramped streets contained within the old medieval walls, extending northward from the Thames in the area spreading eastward from St. Paul's Cathedral. Contemporary maps reveal the astonishing density of settlement, a marked contrast to even the rest of Middlesex. Yet despite the crowding, migrants continued to flow into the city, "so as the other Cities and Townes of the Kingdome were decayed," as the annalist William Camden recorded. Local magistrates feared that not enough food could be found to feed the city's residents or that an "Epidemike infection" would spread quickly from house to house. The queen responded to their concerns by banning new construction "within three thousand paces of the Gates of London." Those who violated the new rule would be imprisoned. The Privy Council also took action. New buildings could rise only on the foundations of earlier buildings, and landlords were to halt their practice of renting every available nook and cranny to immigrants. Despite these actions, London's population swelled, growing from perhaps 85,000 in 1565 to 140,000 by the early seventeenth century. Though no single calamity devastated the population, the city's unhealthy conditions, especially its notoriously dirty water, contributed to horrendous mortality. As one modern historian put it, London, like other cities at the time, had become a "death-trap."[2]

Yet if London could be deadly to the bodies of those who lacked the economic resources to find sufficient sustenance, its intellectual life had no parallel within Elizabeth's realm. It drew toward it people looking for opportunities. Among these seekers were university-trained men who were establishing the discipline of geography and, from its premises, crafting a new vision of the world.

Geography was more than the venerable art and craft of mapmaking. Medieval mapmakers had produced scores of maps depicting the known world, often illustrating them based on travelers' eyewitness reports. Some accounts contained fantastic descriptions of creatures that roamed the edges of the world, and mapmakers, including the anonymous creator of the *mappa mundi* at the Hereford Cathedral, regularly added images of these monsters

John Norden's map of London reveals the density of settlement in the metropolis that rose along the banks of the Thames. From John Norden, *Speculum Britanniae* ([London], 1593) (HUNTINGTON LIBRARY)

to their maps. There was nothing new about these monstrous figures, which had been known in Europe since antiquity, but news about them continued to circulate visually on maps. Travelers' tales continued to circulate as well. By the late sixteenth century, at least three hundred manuscript versions of the account of the fourteenth-century English knight Sir John Mandeville were available in Europe in a variety of languages.[3] Given its popularity, mapmakers logically continued to rely on Mandeville's fabulous descriptions for images to adorn their creations.

But apart from these eye-catching figures, maps began to express a common visual language. By the time Hakluyt was studying geography at Christ Church in the 1570s, mapmakers had begun to follow certain conventions that enabled viewers to understand them quickly. Among the early mapmakers in England, for example, the thirteenth-century monk Matthew Paris depicted the sea on his map as green and used blue and red to demarcate particular places, perhaps to suggest the color of the roof tiles of each house, a visual reflection of a change in architectural practice designed to make villages less prone to catastrophic fires. By the fifteenth century, mapmakers routinely used specific conventions to depict rivers (typically blue on any hand-colored map), roads (normally black), seas or oceans (blue or green), forests (green on colored maps; typically a series of black cross-hatchings on a printed map), and mountains (in most cases a series of inverted "v"s). Cartographers often included miniature drawings of prominent churches or manor houses or drew cattle or sheep in a blank space to denote agriculture. Many of these conventions survive today, though modern mapmakers regrettably eschew the inclusion of buildings or livestock in favor of a more scientific depiction of strata. By the early seventeenth century, these visual clues could be found in a key or legend in a corner of the map, explaining the iconographic language of the map's symbols. In any political context, including Hakluyt's England, the act of making a map was also a form of establishing control; those who determined the location of spatial boundaries on pieces of paper exerted authority over those who looked to a map for knowledge about a particular area. Maps were not isolated pieces of paper or cloth. Each conveyed a specific meaning.[4]

When it came to understanding and describing the physical world they inhabited, the men and women of Hakluyt's England were perched on an intellectual threshold. Before 1558, descriptions of land (specifically real property) tended to be in words, a convention that had existed for centuries and that continued to survive, in moderated form, until at least the eighteenth century. But during the sixteenth century, the English public became adept at reading maps—so adept, in fact, that Shakespeare's characters in *Henry IV, Part 1* could be seen by century's end using a map on stage. In the later sixteenth century, those who owned estates, following a national trend, opted to have their holdings mapped. That shift in mentality reflected growing confidence of wealthy landholders in the measurement of land by skilled surveyors. Like other changes of these times, the shift in practice also reflected the growing influence of print and the wider distribution of guides to surveying, which gave prospective surveyors the information they would need to measure irregular parcels of land (such as valleys). Books such as Valentine Leigh's *The Moste Profitable and commendable Science, of Surveiyng of Landes, Tenementes, and Hereditamentes* suggested that what might have been earlier perceived as an art had now become a legitimate science, thus imbuing it with authority. The growing reliance on the importance of maps could be found in Cecil's desire to have more accurate maps of England and in English support for the mapping of Ireland in the second half of the sixteenth century, one of the more obvious uses of cartography to meet the needs of the state. Technical advances in the creation of maps themselves, especially the transition from woodcuts to copper engraving, made maps more precise. Since copper and other soft metals could be rubbed smooth and re-engraved, the shift also allowed mapmakers to make changes in their maps if demanded by some new information that had filtered into their studios.[5]

For a student during the 1570s, the most exciting development in map-making might have been the publication, between 1574 and 1579, of Christopher Saxton's maps of the counties of England. Though Saxton's creations retained some of the artistry of earlier maps, gone were most of the depictions of individual households and churches, replaced by a more generic representation of the landscape in which a single building served as the representation for a specific place. Hills became small bumps, colored brown, while Saxton depicted stands of trees with a single tree and forests as a cluster of trees. Though the maps were drawn to different scales, each had a scale on it so that the reader could measure distance. Lest a reader not know how to measure distance, Saxton also put in a drawing compass, thereby suggesting to the map user how to get the most precise measurements. Though some of the maps, notably his map of all of England and Wales, featured ships and sea monsters not drawn to scale—the largest fish measured, using Saxton's scale, approximately twenty-five miles long—his rendering of the landscape conformed much more closely to actual distance. Elegant seagoing vessels could be found in the waters off the coast, while smaller rowboats depicted fishermen casting their nets into the sea. Saxton did include specific details, such as a minute rendering of Stonehenge ("The Stonadge"). But the city of Oxford was no more than an unusually large clustering of buildings on the map of Oxfordshire; Saxton made no obvious attempt to draw any of the colleges despite their unique architecture. Ribbons of blue meander through many of the maps, and he covered mountainous regions, like those of north Wales, with brown bumps signifying hills and, on occasion, even larger named mountains. London, the largest collection of buildings on any of the maps, stretched along the Thames for approximately five miles, while a fierce sea monster stood guard at the edge of its bay, facing eastward as if to scare off any who might think of invading the capital by sea.[6]

Hakluyt learned much about maps during his time at Christ Church. He also benefited from his continuing association with the lawyer. During the Elizabethan era, members of the Middle Temple included the most prominent English explorers of the age—including Ralegh, Frobisher, and John Hawkins. The Temple was a training ground for colonial officials well into the seventeenth century. The lawyer remained associated with the Middle Temple from his admission in May 1555 until his death in 1591.[7]

The lawyer was a practical man with a grand ambition: he wanted to spread information about the world to others in England. He hoped that such knowledge would somehow encourage greater English efforts to explore the world beyond Europe and to establish colonies in the western hemisphere. He believed that the best way to convey the necessary knowledge would be visually. He thus wanted to create a map that would show where specific territories were located. Like Hakluyt, the lawyer hoped to promote the interests of the realm. But if the idea of using maps to convey information made sense intellectually, the lawyer had a problem: What, exactly, should this map include? Many Europeans had of course wondered about this problem long before, but the lawyer's problem had less to do with the idea of generating a map than it did with the physical appearance of the map he had in mind.

Sometime in 1567 or 1568, the lawyer wrote to the Dutch cosmographer Abraham Ortelius with suggestions about how to create a new map of the world.[8] He did not want the information contained on this map to be limited to those who wandered through some official residence or office or to be seen only by the bureaucrats who manned various departments of the state. His goal instead was to bring information directly to others like him—to people who would become inspired by this newfound information and would act on it.

What was needed, the lawyer recognized, was a substantial but useable map of the world. As the lawyer told Ortelius, since "men usually live in houses which are neither spacious enough nor light enough within for them to be able to place or spread out conveniently a large world map in them, it will be most gratifying to many to have a map thought out on the following lines: namely that when spread out to its full extent it is quite fit and suitable for a hall or other spacious place of that kind, and also when rolled up at each end on two smooth revolving rods it lies conveniently on a table about three or at most four feet square." To meet these goals, the lawyer proposed that the map be twelve feet long and three to four feet wide, drawn to specific guidelines. Practicality governed his instructions. He thus required Ortelius to "draw north-south meridians for every three feet of the map's breadth, so that when it is rolled up to a size of three or four feet square, at whatever place it is opened all the lines and circles will appear exactly on it, showing the distances of places according to their longitude and latitude." He also wanted Ortelius to include a scale "by which the distances between places may quickly be found by using a circle." The lawyer, who commissioned the work along with the London merchant John Acheley, believed that the map would find an eager audience. "In this way you will perform a most acceptable service to a number of English lawyers, to the students of both Oxford and Cambridge Universities, and to the citizens of London," he informed Ortelius, "and you will produce a map that will sell better in every European city than any other kind." The map would be a boon to students of geography, of course, but it would also be a goad to English merchants or politicians who were otherwise reluctant to get involved in long-distance exploration or commerce.[9]

During the 1580s the lawyer continued to gather information about territories far from England. Yet unlike those who sought to promote Frobisher's achievements, he did not choose to publish any of the reports he received. Instead, he treated the new reports as he had the account he had received about Mexico from Henry Hawkes in the early 1570s: he either kept it to himself or he shared it only with his younger cousin. It was Hakluyt who eventually chose to make such news public, though he did so, as in the case of the Hawkes report, long after the lawyer had received the news at the Middle Temple.

Perhaps the lawyer's discretion encouraged his correspondents to trust him with prized information. That could have explained why Anthony Parkhurst, a veteran of four journeys to Newfoundland in the mid-1570s, wrote to him in November 1578. Parkhurst's report, which the lawyer passed on to Hakluyt, detailed what the English could expect to find on the island. Parkhurst wrote his long letter to the lawyer because he admired how he wielded his "travelling mind and pen" to gain attention from policy makers, a reference to the lawyer's close connections to Elizabeth's court. But though Parkhurst celebrated the lawyer's "labour and travell to bring your good and godly desires to some passe," he feared domestic enemies who would squelch any serious initiatives. The lawyer, Parkhurst knew, wanted to spread Christianity where "princes have not bene so diligent as their calling required." But unenlightened "wicked men" stood poised to halt any initiative even though God had made the lawyer "an instrument to increase the number, and to moove men of power, to redeeme the people of Newfoundland and those parts from out of the captivitie of that spirituall Pharao, the divell."[10]

Parkhurst gave the lawyer the intellectual ammunition he would need to make an argument for English settlements on Newfoundland. He described in depth the cod trade in the waters off its coast, noting that English, Spanish,

Portuguese, and French vessels were already trawling there. Here Parkhurst revealed no secrets. The shallow shoals off Newfoundland had been known to European fishermen for generations, possibly even before 1492. Norse sailors had once plied those waters, and the cod they hauled back to Europe provided the income they needed to maintain their outposts across the North Atlantic. But by the 1570s, the volume of ships in the region had increased dramatically.[11] Parkhurst hinted that he had been to the area as early as 1575; by 1578, the number of English vessels had grown from thirty to fifty a year. That growth reflected the energies of "Westerne men," presumably from the port in Bristol, who were eager to increase their profits. But although Parkhurst celebrated that trade, he feared the fleets of other Europeans. His informants had told him that the Spanish sent perhaps sent perhaps one hundred ships into the area each year, as well as another twenty or thirty vessels from Biskaie, which were on the spot to kill whales for their oil. Ships came from the Portuguese harbors at Aviero and Viana and elsewhere, "from most parts of Spaine," and from all over France and Brittany. The English were there, using Iceland as a base of operations, but not "in such numbers as other nations."

Parkhurst was eager to give the lawyer a positive impression of Newfoundland. He reported that he had planted barley, wheat, oats, rye, peas, herbs, beans, and other foods and that all "have prospered as in England." Newfoundland's forests had fruit and nut trees, as well as pine and fir that reached for the skies and were "big, and sufficient for any ship," a concern to anyone in England who feared the depletion of domestic or nearby supplies for their ships. Cod shared the waters with many other useful fish and shellfish as well as abundant stores of anchovies and squid. Further, despite what some had reported—perhaps he had the chroniclers of Frobisher's voyages in mind—Newfoundland's climate was "not so colde as foolish Mariners doe say, who finde it colde sometimes when plentie of Isles of Ice lie neere the shore." The interior was in fact often "hotter then in England," especially along the southern reaches of the island, which the ice rarely reached. Abundant rivers lured countless edible birds. Various land animals, including elk, deer, bear, rabbits, and foxes, could be found too, providing yet more potential nourishment as well as furs. Newfoundland also had rich stores of mineral wealth and salt, Parkhurst's particular area of expertise. His report included details about specific locales that would be ideal for settlements, but he apologized for not knowing more. Unfortunately, he told the lawyer, he had "bene deceived by the vile Portingals, descending of the Jewes and Judas kinde," who refused to bring him the salt he had arranged to sell in England, leaving him in debt for his voyage. Here was a rare instance in which one of the Hakluyts' professions had any bearing on their promotional activities: Parkhurst hoped that the lawyer's legal expertise would help him with a suit to recoup his losses.

The arrival of the Parkhurst report, which remained unpublished for a decade, signaled the start of a more active promotional phase for both Hakluyts. Again, though the documentary record is slight, during the following year or so each of the cousins made his own argument for the advantages to be gained from overseas development. The lawyer focused on improving woolens for export, which he understood could happen only if the English obtained the dyestuffs they needed from the East and mastered the necessary techniques for using them. As he told Morgan Hubblethorne, who was on his way to Persia to learn about dyestuffs, expanding the woolen trade would create more work for the poor, thereby redressing a persistent social problem. But he also hoped that Hubblethorne would learn all he could about dyeing techniques, both from locals he could encounter and also from "any Dier of China, or of the East partes of the world." He should also hire an expert "in the arte of Turkish carpet making" who could teach the English that craft. The lawyer wanted Hubblethorne to write things down as he went along, so that he could remember it all when he got back or, in a more dire circumstance, that his lessons not be lost if he were killed on the journey.[12]

While the lawyer hoped to import knowledge and talent into England, Hakluyt articulated his first plan for overseas development. In a pamphlet that remained unpublished during his lifetime, he argued that the English could improve their economic and political standing by taking control of the Strait of Magellan, seizing a Brazilian island, and promoting journeys to the East via a Northeast Passage that stretched along the northern edge of Russia and then southward along the eastern shores of Asia.[13] This three-part plan was the only way to thwart the Spanish, who stood poised to control both the East and West Indies, a "peril" to every European nation. He used the knowledge that he had obtained at Oxford to argue that the English could sustain a navy in the Strait of Magellan since that region had everything that they needed, from safe harbors to building supplies and food. The Brazilian island of St. Vincent similarly offered what the English needed. The island and the nearby mainland were able "to victual infinite multitudes of people, as our people report that were there with Drake, who had oxen, hogges, hennes, cirtones, lymons, oranges etc." Readily available supplies of fish, seals, and poultry added to the nutritional horde, and the forests had trees perfect for housing and ships; cattle and goats brought from Europe would "increase mightely in fewe yeres." He also believed that the local Cimarrones, "a people detesting the prowde governance of the Spanyards," could be "easely transported by Drake or others of our nation to the Straights, and there may be planted by hundreds or thowsands, how many as we shal require." Though these natives would work for the English, they would not be kept as slaves, as they had been by the Spanish, but instead would "live subject to the gentle government of the English." They would enjoy such an existence because they had been "made free from the tyrannous Spanyard." The Cimarrones could be transported to the strait to serve the English. Following the logic that Gilbert had articulated four years earlier, Hakluyt also proposed that the English send condemned men and women to the region.

Taking St. Vincent and the strait made sense, as anyone who looked at a map of the world then available would have realized, but the third part of Hakluyt's scheme was more ingenious. He knew that mariners had been searching for a Northeast Passage at the same time as they looked for a water route through North America. But although there was, in fact, a way around the northern shores of Russia, at least in theory—which made the Northeast Passage different than the nonexistent Northwest Passage—there was no effective way to cross those frozen seas in the wooden hulled ships of this era. Hakluyt, whose knowledge of Asia's northern and eastern coasts conformed to that of other geographers, did not realize the impossibility of such a journey, and to him what mattered was what he saw on maps.[14] He recognized that the death of a friendly ruler in Russia could cut off England's cloth trade to that country and to Persia. Sensible policy demanded a solution to such a problem. But Hakluyt had another goal in mind. Locating the Northeast Passage meant finding a way to expand and protect England's cloth trade to the East and to infiltrate the spice trade, "with the interchange of all the commodities of the east and west [partes] of the Worlde."

That same year Hakluyt wrote a memorandum summarizing what was to be gained from seizing the Strait of Magellan. He realized that gaining control of the region would please Don Antonio, the pretender to the Portuguese throne, whom Hakluyt hoped would become England's ally against Spain. The rewards of such an effort were too enormous to ignore. English control of the strait would "depryve the Sp[anish] king of the tresure of the west." It would take trade away from Spain, weaken the Spanish navy, protect English shipping in the West Indies (and open up new markets for cloth exports), and cause domestic deprivation that could lead to rebellion. The

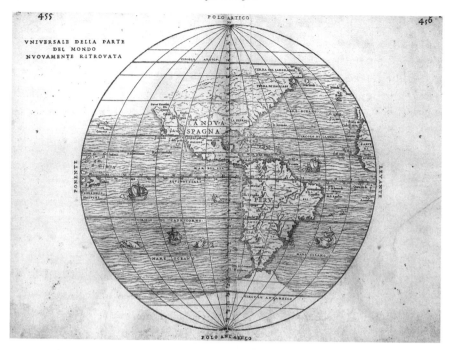

The logic of seizing the Strait of Magellan would have been obvious to anyone looking at contemporary world maps, such as this map in Ramusio's *Navigationi et Viaggi* (Venice, 1556), the book that included the texts of Jacques Cartier's accounts later translated by John Florio at Hakluyt's behest in 1580
(HUNTINGTON LIBRARY)

English would also strike a blow against Rome and the forces of the Catholic Church, as well as for their own safety. Spain, that "prowd nacion," would no longer "be able to annoy us in Ireland as now they doe, or thereafter by the popes instrument to annoy us anywhere."[15]

Hakluyt's Oxford education taught him how to crystallize this argument and promulgate it. Of course, he also benefited from the efforts of his cousin, who continued to give Hakluyt information about England's need for overseas expansion. In these messages, the lawyer consistently emphasized the economic gains of such policies. In his longest early argument, intended for the explorers Arthur Pet and Charles Jackman in 1580, the lawyer gave detailed instructions for a journey via the northeast to a place he called "Cambalu," the Chinese capital where Marco Polo had traveled.[16] The lawyer knew that the English would be traveling among non-Christians, so he suggested that the sailors find an island they could use as a base, far enough from Cambalu so that the Chinese would not feel threatened but close enough to Europe so that in summer vessels could supply the base from England and Norway.

As always, the lawyer wanted travelers to pay attention to where they went. He longed for information about their route, the harbors they saw, the climate, forests, and fish that could support "the offals of our people, as the Portingalles do in Brasill." He hoped that the land would have trees suitable for masts and other naval stores. Because there was little knowledge of these seas in England, he needed to know if any passageways were particularly good for shipping or if an island's residents might become future trade partners; if they didn't already produce goods to trade for English cloth, then perhaps their soil would be suitable for growing something that the English wanted. With that idea in mind, he instructed Pet and Jackman to bring home seeds of any fruit trees or herbs they encountered since such things "comming from another part of the world, and so far off, will delight the fancie of many, for the strangenesse and for that the same may grow and continue the delight long time."

If earlier plans had been based on the assumption that English explorers would find heathens with primitive cultures, the lawyer recognized that in the East they would find advanced civilizations. He thus instructed the mariners to take a variety of finished cloth with them to demonstrate English skill in that area. They were also to haul commodities that the English had obtained elsewhere, including "shooes of Spanish leather," "Venice glasses," and ivory combs. He believed that the Chinese would be especially impressed by English coins, "which is a thing that shall in silence speake to wise men more, then you imagine." He told them to take various other commodities that the English produced and wanted to sell in new markets, including glue, soap, saffron, aquavit, the pelts from black rabbits, thread, garden seeds, metal tools, and bells for hawks' talons.

Naturally, the lawyer sought any maps that the Chinese possessed. Yet though he wanted to obtain information from the East, the lawyer also thought it crucial to share the West's knowledge with local learned elites. "Take with you the mappe of England set out in fayre coleurs, one of the biggest sort I meane, to make shew of your countrey and whence you come," he told them, perhaps in reference to Saxton's map, which had been completed in 1579. "And also the large mappe of London, to make shew of your citie. And let the river be drawne full of shippes of all sorts, to make the

The illustrations from Hans Weigel's costume book might have been what the lawyer had in mind when he told Arthur Pet and Charles Jackman to take along a specific book showing what the peoples of the world, especially of Europe, looked like. The pictures

more shew of your great trade and traffike in trade of merchandize." This suggestion, perhaps a reference to Ralph Agas's map of London, reveals that those who obtained maps could also contribute to them. If a map did not contain images depicting human activity, the reader should draw it on so that the next person looking at it would understand the current situation. Anticipating that Pet and Jackman would meet the Great Chan himself, the lawyer told them to have handy a copy of Ortelius's "booke of mappes." They should do their utmost "to present the same to the great Cam, for it would be to a Prince of marvellous account." The Chinese emperor would also be impressed by recent books providing visual evidence of European dress, flora, and fauna. He probably hoped that Pet and Jackman would take a copy of *Habitus Præcipuorum Popularum*, published in 1577, a volume that included scores of illustrations of the clothes of Europeans in addition to images of denizens of the East, Africa, and Brazil. He also wanted them to borrow a

RVSTICVS IN GALLIA.

CV.
Ein Frantzösischer Bawr.
D Jst ein Frantzösischer Bawr/ Sein fuß sicht im gen Marckt zulauffen/
Ein wilder tropff sicht mechtig sawr. Sein Geuß vnd Käse zuuerkauffen.

included these depictions of a Spanish concubine and a French farmer. From Hans Weigel, *Habitus Præcipuorum Popularum* (Nuremberg, 1577)
(HUNTINGTON LIBRARY)

copy of Henry Lyte's new translation of Rembert Dodoens's herbal, which also appeared in print in 1577.[17]

The lawyer hoped that all of this information would be shared with Chinese merchants and nobles. He wanted Pet and Jackman to take books along on their journey because he believed, presumably from his knowledge of the relatively few works about China that had been published in Europe by then, that such knowledge would be welcomed there.[18] The distance that kept the Chinese from seeing Europe firsthand could be shrunk if they could hold books that contained "those things in a shadow." The lawyer knew that such a sight would "delight them." There was no ambiguity in this message. Like Hakluyt and others, the lawyer recognized the power of books to convey information. Though it might have been difficult for those in the court of the Great Chan to understand the texts that Pet and Jackman produced, no language expertise would be needed to understand the pictures. To his credit, the lawyer believed that this exchange of information via books should proceed in both directions. He thus hoped that mariners would bring back "some old printed booke, to see whether they have had print there, before it was devised in Europe, as some write."

On July 28, 1580, shortly after Pet and Jackman left England for the East, Hakluyt received a letter from Gerard Mercator, the legendary Dutch cartographer, then at Duisburge in Clivia (in modern Germany). Mercator had hoped to get news to England before the two had left for China. He was sure that the "voyage to Cathaio by the East, is doutlesse very easie and short," but warned that other mariners had often given up and returned because they lacked the information necessary to complete their journeys. It was especially difficult to navigate near the north pole, where a captain could sail off in the wrong direction because of variations caused by a compass. If Pet did not know how to recognize the compass's error, Mercator feared he would "be overtaken with the ice in the midst of the enterprise." To Hakluyt and anyone else who had read the terrifying accounts of Frobisher's battles with the ice of the North Atlantic, there was perhaps no greater danger to be imagined. Every year those seas froze hard; the only escape was to seek refuge in a harbor or, better yet, to contact a Chinese ambassador in an icy outpost who might provide assistance. Mercator, who also asked Hakluyt questions about information the English had learned on their voyages, expressed his pleasure at the travel accounts and histories he had read, originally in Ramusio's collection, possibly translated by Hakluyt. He promised to send any other information that Hakluyt wanted, and he hoped that in return he would receive news about the English voyages in search of the passages.[19]

Although Hakluyt's standing as an authority on geography continued to rise, Pet and Jackman fared poorly. The annalist William Camden later wrote that despite the support of London merchants, the two ships never made it to their planned destination. Uncertain tides, dangerous shoals, and a "great store of Ice" forced them to return home.[20] Despite the promise of a sea route to the East so insistently inscribed on existing maps, Hakluyt and others realized again the difficulty of such journeys.

By the time Hakluyt received Mercator's letter, he had embarked on an ambitious program to promote knowledge about North America. He did so by employing an Italian linguist named John Florio to take the third volume of Ramusio's *Navigationi et Viaggi*, which was published in Venice in 1556 and included accounts of journeys to the western hemisphere, and to translate two of Cartier's accounts. Though Florio signed the preface, modern scholars attribute it to Hakluyt. Hakluyt hoped that the book, which the title page declared "Worthy the reading of all Venturers, Trauellers, and Discouerers," would "animate and encourage the Englishe Marchants" by informing them of "the infinite treasures (not hidden to themselves) whiche both the Spaniardes, the Portugales, and the Venetians" had already gained through their journeys to the Americas.[21]

Hakluyt had known about Cartier's journeys since at least the time he first picked up a copy of Ramusio's works, and it is possible that he had seen some of the earlier evidence of the Frenchman's explorations.[22] But he believed that the earlier versions of these accounts, which were published in French or Italian, might not have circulated widely in England, at least not to the "Gentlemen, Merchants, and Pilots" who he hoped would read Florio's translation. He was confident that this book would, like Frobisher's accounts, stimulate the imagination of readers and encourage westward expeditions.

"Here is the Description of a Countrey no lesse fruitful and pleasant in al respects than is *England, Fraunce,* or *Germany,*" he told his readers, "the people, though simple and rude in manners, and destitute of the knowledge of God or any good lawes, yet of nature gentle and tractable, and most apt to receive the Christian Religion, and to subject themselves to some good gouernement." The territory Cartier described contained goods "not inferiour to the Marchandize of *Moscuvy, Danske,* or many other frequented trades." Besides, the journey did not take long, only three weeks from Plymouth, Bristol, or some other port in the west of England to the shores of Newfoundland. These opportunities and others "might suffice," he hoped, "to induce oure Englishemen, not onely to fall to some traffique with the Inhabitants, but also to plant a Colonie in some convenient place, and so to possesse the Country without the gainsaying of any man." That was the argument of Ramusio, "a learned and excellent Cosmographer, & Secretary to the famous state of *Venice,*" and it was so compelling that Hakluyt repeated it here.[23]

Hakluyt used Ramusio's account of Cartier to put forward his first argument for actual colonization in North America. "Why doe not the Princes (saith he) whyche are to deale in these affaires," he began, "sende forth two or three Colonies to inhabite the Countrye, & to reduce this savage natio[n] to some civilitie?" Cartier had told about the fertility of the soil, large populations of birds and animals, and rivers so broad that the French "sayled uppe a hundreth and four score leagues, findying the countrey peopled on both sides in great abundaunce." Colonists could use these inland settlements to search for the Northwest Passage so their ships could "saile to the Country of *Cataya,* and from thence to the Ilands of *Molucke."* If the English should embark on such a plan, it would earn them "immortall praise." To prove his point, he enumerated the achievements of Spanish explorers who had gone by land and sea to the territories and waters northwest of New Spain and discovered, so Ramusio had claimed, the sea that separated America from Cathay (he met ships from Cathay on his journey, thus proving the point), as well as "the Kingdome of the seaven Cities of Civola," territory the Spanish hoped would lead to enormous riches. "Thus much out of *Ramusius,* where you may see this learned mans judgement concerning the planting of Colonies, and inhabiting these countries, which might be a meane, not only to discover the Sea on the backe-side, as he desireth, but also to come unto the knowledge of the Countries adjacent," including Saguenay, which Cartier reported "aboundeth with Golde and other Mettalles."[24]

Simply getting to the Americas and learning what was there was not the way to wealth, Hakluyt cautioned. The accounts of the Spanish in the western hemisphere suggested that success came only from actual settlement. If that was the case, then the English were in an ideal position to profit from colonization. "There is none, that of right may be more bolde in this enterprice than the Englishmen," Hakluyt declared. The Cabots had made it to North America, as various historical chroniclers (including Ramusio) had testified, "so there is no nation that hath so good righte, or is more fit for this purpose, than they are." Fifty to sixty English ships sailed in that direction each year, and they could leave "a sufficient number of men to plant a Colonie in some convenient Haven" where the natural bounty of the area would provide them all they need. The French themselves would have followed this path, but intermittent wars with Spain, domestic insurrection, and the death of the Florentine Johannes Verrazano (who had wanted to persuade the French king to send colonists to Canada) had prevented them.[25]

But though the French failed, the fault lay not in North America itself. Cartier's accounts described an ideal locale for colonization. Along the coastline the climate was temperate, the soil was rich, and the harbors and rivers were ideal for European ships. The presence of a nearby native population also seemed propitious. Europeans could "reduce those poore rude and ignorant people to the true worship and service of God" and teach them how to raise crops and keep livestock like Europeans. Over time, colonists could explore deeper into the interior, perhaps at last discovering the Northwest Passage.[26]

Ramusio saw the value of Cartier's testimony, so he had the texts translated from French into Italian and published in Venice in 1556, even before they were published in France. Hakluyt recognized that "if they were translated into English by the liberalitie of some noble Personage, our Sea-men of *England,* and others, studious of Geographie, shoulde know many worthy secrets, whiche hitherto have beene concealed." Ramusio's books had taught "the best Cosmographers of this age" about Africa and Asia "chiefly by the help of those bookes." Now it was time to use this knowledge to help the English. Yes, Hakluyt knew, "some attempts of oure Countrey-men have not had as yet suche successe as was wished," a reference to the voyages of Frobisher and his men. But their failure stemmed in part from their impatience. Rather than embarking for England in late summer, they should instead have remained in Newfoundland, where they could have found the "farre more temperate clime" that had allowed Cartier and the French to survive a Canadian winter.[27]

By translating and publishing Cartier's reports, Ramusio had stamped them with his own authority. Now Hakluyt was trying to do even more. Take this book and read it for the secrets it contained, he told his readers, and ignore anything that you might have heard from an Englishman who might have actually seen Newfoundland for himself. Trust the book.

Hakluyt knew that the only way to achieve his goals was to tell stories that would convince readers that success could be found in North America. Cartier's Canadian saga was not sufficient in itself. What Hakluyt needed was the story of an English sailor whose feats captured the attention of the realm. For that purpose, nothing could have been better than the story of Francis Drake, who had left England in 1577. When Drake returned alive in 1580, he had sailed through the Strait of Magellan, seen the west coast of North America, and had headed back to Europe via the Moluccas.[28] His was the story Hakluyt needed.

The details of his voyage surfaced only when Drake returned. Whenever success seemed apparent, disaster loomed. On the first leg of the journey they stopped at Canten on the Barbary Coast and then at the island of Maio. High seas made sailing difficult as the ships neared the equator. To make matters worse, Drake was sure that his sailors needed to be bled to preserve their health, a gruesome practice recommended for sailors (and others) at the time. Then the ships lost the wind and listed for three weeks, surrounded by lightning and thunder. They were at sea for fifty-five days before they finally saw Brazil, entering the Río de la Plata on April 26, 1578. Drake had in the meantime abandoned two vessels, though he did transfer the sailors and whatever goods they had on board before doing so. Soon after he ordered the execution of Thomas Doughty, who Drake believed had been seditious. In late August his crew suffered a brutal passage through the Strait of Magellan. After sailing northward and reaching the coast of California, the expedition turned westward, reaching the Moluccas in November 1579. From there they sailed to Java, where Drake found the locals curing themselves from the pox by sunning themselves "to drie up the poysonous and malignant humor." He departed, sailed through the Indian Ocean, around Africa, and returned to England, landing at Plymouth on November 9, 1580.[29]

When Drake returned, the English heaped praise on his actions. To be sure, some questioned his treatment of Doughty. But such criticism was rare. Here was a man who, in the queen's eyes, had achieved a remarkable feat. He had circumnavigated the globe, and unlike Magellan, he had survived. To commemorate his achievement, William Camden reported, Elizabeth ordered that Drake's ship be "drawne from the water, and put aside neere Deptford upon Thames," where it remained for at least a generation. The queen feasted on the ship, consecrating it "with great ceremonie, pompe, and magnificence, eternally to be remembred." She also knighted Drake. So many men and women came to watch the proceedings that the plank leading to the ship broke. Yet even though scores fell, no one was injured or killed. Here was proof, Camden realized, "that the Ship seemed to have beene built in a happy conjunction of the Planets." As the celebrations continued, visitors posted odes to Drake on the ship's sails.[30]

By circling the Earth, Drake demonstrated the ability of the realm's mariners to reach the East by traveling to the West, even through Spanish-controlled waters. Yet unlike Frobisher's journeys, Drake's epic journey did not become the subject of multiple books as soon as he landed. This is in part because his expedition had problems, notably the execution of Doughty. His route angered the Spanish, who felt that the English had trespassed on their territory, especially along the western coasts of North America. And his piracy enraged them further. These dilemmas played to the hands of those who argued that Drake's achievement should be kept a secret, even though it was without question one of the worst-kept secrets of the time. Philip II had known about Drake's raid on Spanish treasuries as early as August 6, 1579, and he continued to receive information about Drake's actions from the Council of the West Indies. A Spanish ambassador relayed his king's hopes that the queen would punish Drake for his thievery and brutality, charging that Drake had chopped the hands off some Spaniards. Though he did not threaten war against the English, he ominously added that wars had begun with less provocation. One contemporary annalist reported that he had "brought home marvelous rich ladeing both of massy gold and silver." After sorting out his marital affairs—his wife, presuming him dead, had begun a romance with another man—Drake left for London, allegedly taking along twenty "horse Load of gold and silver." French readers of the Seigneur de La Popelinière's book of geography of 1582 also would have known about Drake's return and the great pleasure that it brought to the queen. News about Drake was "in everyone's mouth" in Paris by 1584, according to the English ambassador there.[31]

Printers celebrated Drake's achievement. Nicholas Breton squeezed out some forgettable verses in a small book published by March 1581. The Hungarian poet Stephen Parmenius offered praise in one of the two poems that he published during his life.

> Nor can it be in vain that Francis Drake,
> Your noble hero, recently sailed round
> The vast circumference of Earth (a feat
> Denied to man by many centuries),
> To show how father Neptune circumscribes
> The continents, and wanders in between
> To keep two worlds apart.

William Borough drew attention to Drake in 1581 in his treatise on compasses, noting that he was now the most famous navigator in the world. Charles D'Ecluse published a small tract in Latin offering information about the plants that Drake had seen on the circumnavigation. These plants included coconuts and cacao, as well as one (*Drakena radix*) that he named for himself. The queen displayed her pleasure more privately, ordering that Drake keep ten thousand pounds of the bullion he had brought to England. Drake was perhaps the only person to know how much he brought back from his voyage. Almost sixty years later one English writer believed that Drake's mission had repaid investors forty-seven times their initial investment.[32]

English writers continued to offer paeans to Drake for his achievements, but this outpouring of sentiment had little to do with the circumnavigation. Instead, the praise that Drake received after 1586 reflected his stature in his subsequent ventures against the Spanish. Hakluyt himself offered English readers the first substantive account of Drake's circumnavigation in 1589. In 1628 Drake's nephew edited an account and published it "for the honour of the actor, but especially for the stirring up of *heroick spirits, to benefit their Countrie.*"[33]

Hakluyt spent much of the year 1581 preparing his first book, a collection of travel accounts he published under the title *Divers Voyages touching the discoverie of America, and the Ilands adjacent.* By the time he edited those accounts, he had absorbed a basic lesson of the art of navigation. His actions agreed with the ideas put forward six years earlier by William Bourne. "Navigation is this," Bourne wrote, "how to direct his course in the Sea to any place assigned, and to consider in what direction what things may stande with him, & what things may stand against him, having consideration how to preserve the ship in all formes and chaunges of weather that may happen by the way, to bring the ship safe unto the port assigned, and in the shortest time."[34]

Hakluyt laid out his core argument on the title page. *Divers Voyages* showed discoveries "made first of all by our Englishmen, and afterward by the French-men and Britons." The book contained, he promised, "certaine notes of advertisements for observations" that would be necessary for those who planned to go to America. The book also contained two maps "for the plainer understanding of the whole matter." Here was a book that demonstrated that the English had a legitimate claim to own North America and the maps necessary to show any intrepid English man or woman where in the world these territories were located.[35]

Hakluyt next provided two lists to the reader.[36] The first contained the "names of certaine late writers of Geographie, with the yeere wherein they wrote." The second enumerated the "late travaylers, both by sea and by lande, which also for the most part have written of their owne travayles and voyages." These two pages contain more than an enumeration of authorities about travel. They constitute the first real clue to the extent of Hakluyt's knowledge at the time. Appearing when he first entered the public realm, they constitute a kind of memento mori to his mind: a monument, fixed on paper, to the thoughts of a sixteenth-century scholar and activist on the verge of becoming a leading exponent and apologist for English expansion.

The first list began with Abelfada Ismael, "prince of Syria, Persia, and Assyria," who wrote in the year 1300, and concluded with the Englishman Nicholas Chancellor, who had written about Pet and Jackman's recent journey into the Northeast Passage. In between Hakluyt listed those who wrote about geography, including the Milanese chronicler of Columbus, Peter Martyr D'Anghiera, and the Spanish natural historian Gonzalo Fernández de Oviedo y Valdés. He listed Ramusio, who he noted had "gathered may notable things," the German cosmographer Sebastian Münster, the Flemish geographer Gerard Mercator, and three French travelers—Orontius Finæus, André Thevet, and François de Belleforest. He also stocked the list with English writers: the fourteenth-century knight Sir John Mandeville, the early-sixteenth-century cartographer Robert Thorne, the midcentury translator Clement Adams, and contemporary writers such as Sir Humphrey Gilbert, Dionyse Settle, and George Best.

Hakluyt's list of travelers, like his list of writers of geography, was hardly comprehensive. Again, he drew on a variety of Continental authorities, starting with the twelfth-century Spanish Jewish traveler Benjamin of Tudela, and going forward through Marco Polo, the Venetian Zeno brothers, Columbus, Vasco da Gama, Francisco Coronado, and the Frenchmen John Ribault and Thevet. This list emphasized travelers from southern Europe, including four Venetians and seven Portuguese, testifying once again to Ramusio's influence on Hakluyt's understanding of geography. Yet he was also determined to reveal the presence of English predecessors. Of the thirty-six men he listed, seventeen were English (though he acknowledged that Sebastian Cabot was "the sonne of a Venetian"). They included Mandeville, again, as well as the recent travelers Hakluyt either knew personally or whose journeys he had followed with such care: Frobisher, Drake, Gilbert, and Pet and Jackman.

Hakluyt wasted no time in making his argument. He was astonished, he wrote in the epistle dedication to the courtier Sir Philip Sidney, that though America had been discovered ninety years earlier, "after so great conquest and plantings of the Spaniardes and Portingales there," the English had still not yet "set fast footing in such fertill and temperate places, as are left as yet unpossessed of them." Still, all was not lost. In the way that he understood history, "there is a time for all men," and the Portuguese were now "out of date." More significant, "the nakednesse of the Spaniards, and their long hidden secretes are now at length espied, whereby they went about to delude the worlde." He thus hoped "that the time approcheth and nowe is, that we of England may share and part stakes (if wee will our selves) both with the Spaniarde and the Portingale in part of America, and other regions as yet undiscovered." The accounts in this book, he argued, would demonstrate the right that the English had to claim and possess these lands, a task that needed to happen "to advaunce the honour of our Countrie."[37]

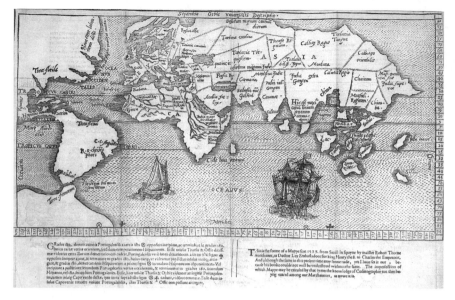

The maps of Robert Thorne and Michael Lok as they appeared in Hakluyt's *Divers Voyages,* the first time he ever printed maps
(HUNTINGTON LIBRARY)

But it was not the pursuit of honor or a prior claim that made the matter so urgent to Hakluyt in 1582. Instead, borrowing language and logic used earlier by Gilbert and by his cousin the lawyer, Hakluyt saw colonization as the necessary cure for the nation's ills. "Ye if wee woulde beholde with the eye of pitie howe al our Prisons are pestered and filled with able men to serve their Countrie," he argued, "which for small roberies are dayly hanged up in great numbers even twentie at a clappe out of one jayle (as was seene at the last assises at Rochester) wee would hasten and further every man to his power the deducting of some Colonies of our superfluous people into those temperate and fertile partes of America, which being within six weekes sayling of England are yet unpossessed by any Christians[,] and seeme to offer themselves unto us, stretching neerer unto her Majesties Dominions, then to any other part of Europe." He added that he had recently met with an older Portuguese cosmographer who had deep knowledge of his nation's discoveries who wondered aloud about the possibility of colonizing the lands north of Florida, which were at the time "unplanted by Christians." The sixty-year-old Portuguese man told the thirty-year-old Hakluyt that "if hee were nowe as young as I . . . hee woulde sel all hee had, being a man of no small wealth

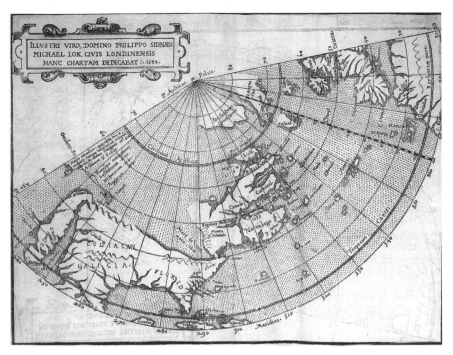

and honour, to furnish a convenient number of ships to sea for the inhabiting of those countries, and reducing those gentile people to christianitie." The history of Brazil suggested that this would be shrewd investment. The first Portuguese colonists who arrived there succeeded; most of them possessed sugar plantations peopled with two to three hundred slaves, with courts and churches nearby "so that eche myll, is as it were a little commonwealth."³⁸

If the economic argument for colonization was insufficient, Hakluyt returned to a theme that had dominated his life for the past three years: the search for the Northwest Passage. He enumerated all the evidence for its existence. In fact, even before the dedication he related a brief account of a journey in 1574 of an unnamed man who had been on an expedition that sailed westward deep into the American continent at 58 degrees North latitude along a channel that headed south and was "without all impediment of ice." Hakluyt made a much more thorough case for the existence of the Northwest Passage in his dedication. He reminded his readers that Sebastian Cabot had told Ramusio that "all the North part of America is divided into Ilandes," which meant that there had to be a water route to the East. John Verrazanus (Johannes Verrazano), who had been three times to the coast of North America, had seen proof of the passage on "an olde excellent mappe," which he gave to King Henry VIII and was now in the possession of Michael Lok and was used by Lok for his map that appeared at the end of *Divers Voyages*. The Spanish natural historian Francisco Gomara had included an account that offered yet more proof. So did the account of Cartier's second expedition—which Hakluyt had arranged for Florio to translate and publish in 1580—which told how the people of Saguenay "doe testifie that upon their coastes Westwarde there is a sea the ende whereof is unknowne unto them." Another account told that the people of Canada claimed that with only one month's sail they could reach a land "were cinnamon and cloves are growing." The native peoples of Florida had told the French traveler Jean Ribault that they could sail to the south sea in less than three weeks. Further, the experiences of travelers whom Hakluyt trusted—Frobisher (who had been "on the hyther side"), Drake (who had sailed "on the backe side of America"), and the Zeni brothers—all suggested the real possibility of the passage. So did the ultimate authority, Gerard Mercator, whose son had shared a private letter detailing (in Latin) the existence of the opening. As Hakluyt rendered the passage, Mercator argued that "there is a straight and short way open into the West even unto Cathay. Into which kingdome, if they take their course aright, they shall gather the most noble merchandise of all the worlde, and shall make the name of Christe to bee knowne unto many idolatrous and Heathen people."[39]

As if all of this evidence were insufficient, Hakluyt added that he had heard a report of a recent law made by King Philip II barring Spanish explorations north of 45 degrees North latitude in America. What could have motivated an expansionist-oriented king, who was famous for his support of long-distance ventures, to promulgate such a measure? Hakluyt, often prone to see malevolent Spanish intent, of course had an answer. First, he claimed that the Spanish did not want to find the Northwest Passage since it would have had little real use to them. Second, the Spanish "have not people enough to possesse and keepe that passage, but rather thereby shoulde open a gappe for other nations to passe that way."[40]

It was easy and logical to chastise the Spanish for their selfishness, but Hakluyt did not reserve his barbs for Iberians alone. Though his text was intended as a paean to English fortitude and ingenuity, he could not resist expressing his disgust with prior failures in North America. The English themselves would in all likelihood have already found the Northwest Passage, he believed, if "in our owne discoveries we had not beene led with a preposterous desire of seeking rather gaine then Gods glorie." The English, this geographer trained as a minister reminded them, had forgotten "that God-linesse is great riches, and that if we first seeke the kingdome of God, al other thinges will be given unto us." The laws of nature themselves made such a statement obvious: "as the light accompanieth the Sunne, and the heate the fire, so lasting riches do wait upon them that are zealous for the advaunce-ment of the kingdome of Christ, and the enlargement of his glorious Gospell: as it is sayde, I will honour them that honour mee." The legacy of failure should have taught a lesson to the English. "I truste that nowe being taught by their manifolde losses our men will take a more godly course, and use some part of their goods to his glorie." If they failed to do so, they would be no better than the avaricious Spaniards and Portuguese who claimed they would convert Americans but in fact sought wealth alone.[41]

Hakluyt argued that the best way to increase the chance for success would be to gain "knowledge in the arte of navigation, & breading of skilfulnesse in the sea men." Philip II, borrowing an idea put forward earlier by King Charles V of Spain, had contemplated hiring "a learned reader of the sayde art of Navigation" and installing him in the Casa de Contracíon (House of Trade) in Seville, where he would, with the support of others, be able to instruct mariners on the lessons to be learned from ancient times to the present. The English, Hakluyt believed, needed to do the same thing. Rather than employ a scholar who would be in residence at a specific location, Hakluyt believed that there should be a fund to support an annual lecture in navigation to be given in London or Ratcliffe. This lecturer would provide vital information in "a matter of great consequence and importance, for the saving of many mens lives and goods, which nowe through grosse ignorance are dayly in great hazerd, to the no small detriment of the whole realme." He had already gotten Drake to pay twenty pounds "to a learned man to furnish him with instruments and maps, that woulde take this thing upon him." Drake was so eager to get the program started that he pleaded with Hakluyt to find someone quickly. Hakluyt obliged, but the man wanted forty pounds each year. Lacking the funds, Hakluyt wrote only that "the matter ceased for that time." Still, if some "noble man" could see his way toward making the final contribution, Hakluyt believed that "the whole realme no doubt might reape no small benefite thereby." Hakluyt concluded by providing some detail about the authors to be found in the volume, singling out Michael Lok, whose map of the Atlantic basin could be found at the end of the book.[42]

Every account in *Divers Voyages* had a political purpose. The texts began with a copy of King Henry VII's letters patent to John Cabot and his three

sons of 1494—"for the discovering of newe and unknowen landes," a document that Hakluyt printed first in Latin and then in English translation.[43]
His decision to translate the document had enormous significance. If Hakluyt
had wished to reach only elite policy makers, including the queen (who was
famous for her linguistic abilities), he could have printed this letter in Latin
alone. Everyone at court would have been able to read it, and many were
sufficiently fluent that they wrote in Latin, too. But Hakluyt had broader
ambitions. Here, as in his hiring of Florio to translate Cartier's narrative in
1580, he acted on the presumption that colonization would occur only if the
English possessed the critical documents in the vernacular. The fact of translation itself was proof of Hakluyt's desired audience.

A note from Sebastian Cabot followed Henry VII's patent. Hakluyt got
the brief account from the chronicler John Stow, another associate whom he
termed "a diligent searcher and preserver of Antiquities," who had taken it
out of "an old Chronicle" by Robert Fabian. Cabot wrote that three or four
ships had left Bristol in early May 1498, sailing westward loaded with English
goods (lace, caps, cloth, "and other trifles"). He gave no details about what the
crew saw when they landed but noted that they did take "three savage men"
captive and brought them to Westminster for the king. They were "clothed in
beastes skinnes, and eate rawe fleshe," Cabot wrote, spoke in a language "that
no man coulde understande," and "in their demeanour like to bruite beastes."
Yet two years later Cabot saw them again at Westminster Palace. Now they
were dressed like Englishmen. Their transformation had been so complete
that he confessed he could not tell them apart from others in court. Seeking
even greater authority for the legitimacy of Cabot's claims, Hakluyt included
a passage from Ramusio supporting the fact of Cabot's journey to the western
hemisphere. Ramusio added that a rebellion by his crew had prevented Cabot
from finding the route to Cathay, though he concluded by noting the potential significance of such an act. "Surely this enterprise woulde bee the most
glorious and of most importance of all other that can be imagined," Ramusio
wrote (in Hakluyt's translation), "to make his name great, & fame immortall
to all ages to come, farre more then can bee done by any of all these great
troubles and warres, which dayly are used in Europe among the miserable
Christian people." This was the affirmation that Hakluyt sought: testimony
from an unbiased observer about the fact of an English landing in North
America in the fifteenth century and a reminder of the great glory to come
from discovery of the Northwest Passage.[44]

The rest of the book essentially followed the same pattern. Hakluyt included texts that provided information about the Americas, often emphasizing the author's Englishness or connections to the realm. Robert Thorne initially sent his "declaration of the Indies" from Seville, where he "dwelt long," to King Henry VIII. Written in 1527, Thorne's book, which exists now only through its publication in *Divers Voyages,* described discoveries he had made with the Portuguese king and included directions to the Moluccas—by a route northward from England, across the Arctic, and then southward to the Spice Islands, a journey that Thorne calculated would be shorter than the longer routes used by the Spanish and Portuguese. Yes, cosmographers had deemed such a route impossible since "the sea is all ice, the cold so much that none can suffer it." But Thorne disagreed with such pessimism: "I judge there is not lande inhabitable, nor Sea innavigable." He claimed that he had inherited from his father an "inclination or desire" to make discoveries. He added that his father and another Bristol merchant had been the original discovers of "the new found la[n]des." But lack of understanding that these lands found earlier were connected to the "west Indies, from whence all the gold commeth," had prevented the English from receiving their due. Thorne looked forward to a return to England, where he would be able to explain his reasoning. Henry VIII must have liked what he read; according to Hakluyt's version, the king sent out two well-stocked ships "having in them divers cunning men, to seeke strange regions." Hakluyt did not tell what they found, but *Divers Voyages* did contain a copy of Thorne's map from 1527 even though it departed in significant ways from the vast majority of maps of the Earth that existed by 1582.[45]

Hakluyt depicted America as a place of opportunity. To further that end, he included works that did not emphasize, or even mention, any English right to North America. He included Nicholas Zeno's thirteenth-century account of a trip along the northern Atlantic, a report that had appeared in one of Ramusio's volumes, not because it was always correct, but because it provided details about what a traveler might find sailing westward from island to island along the Atlantic's northern edge. Jean Ribault's account of the "true and last discoverie of Florida," written in the 1560s, did include a reference to Henry VII's sponsorship of Sebastian Cabot, but that detail was less important than the description of the riches to be found in Florida. As Hakluyt put it in the margins, "Gold, silver, and copper in Florida. Turquesses and aboundance of pearles." And, slightly further down the same page, "Pearles as big as acornes." His other marginal notes drew attention to the fertility of the soil, the way to trade with the natives, and the enticing rivers and havens of the peninsula.[46]

Hakluyt's inclusion of Verrazano's account from 1524 of his discovery of Norumbega served no obviously nationalistic goal. But the account's tale of Americans who rescued a frightened sailor and its speculations about the possibility of converting the indigenes to Christianity served Hakluyt's purpose. In the margin next to the rescue of the young sailor Hakluyt wrote, "Courteous and gentle people." It was also no coincidence that this section ended with ruminations on native religious beliefs, or the lack of them. "We suppose that they have no religion at all, and ye[t] they live at their owne libertie," Verrazano concluded. "And ye[t] all this proceedeth of ignorance, for that they are very easie to bee persuaded: and all that they see us Christians doe in our divine service they did the same with the like imitation as they sawe us to doe it." If Catholics could get such a response, Hakluyt knew his audience would have understood, imagine what could happen when the English arrived.[47]

Divers Voyages was the first publication to appear under Hakluyt's name, and as such it reflected his assessment of that moment of opportunity. But it was not his own work, or at least not entirely. In addition to drawing on the abilities of others, both travelers and their translators, he published ideas that his cousin had promoted earlier. He reprinted the directions that the lawyer had written for the Muscovy Company that had been given in 1580 to Pet and Jackman for their mission to Cathay. He did so since he believed that such notes were "not altogether unfit for some other enterprises of discoverie, hereafter to bee taken in hande." He followed that letter with generic instructions that he claimed had been "framed by a Gentleman heretofore to bee given to one that prepared for a discoverie, and went not." He added that this document was "not unfitt to be committed to print, considering the same may stirre up considerations of these and of such other thinges, not unmeete in such new voyages as may be attempted hereafter."[48]

These instructions appeared at the end of *Divers Voyages* along with a list of "certaine commodities growing in part of America, not presently inhabited by any Christians fro[m] Florida Northward." Hakluyt had derived that list from the authorities in the book and added material that he had found in accounts by Cartier, the French royal cosmographer André Thevet, and George Best, one of Frobisher's chroniclers.[49] Taken together, the two documents left the reader with plans for how to settle an unknown territory and what could be had for the taking in North America. The instructions read now, as they must have then, as if they had come from Hakluyt himself, or perhaps the lawyer. He could not have made his intent clearer. Marco Polo had famously told those who found his account to take his book and read it. Now Hakluyt had determined that readers of his work should take this book on a ship bound for unknown but bounteous lands in North America. If they followed his directions and understood the lessons of the past, they could not fail.

CHAPTER 6

Paris, 1583
The Devouring Sea

Sometime around September 20, 1583, Richard Hakluyt left London bound for Paris. He had a difficult journey across the English Channel. "We came in so high a sea," Hakluyt's traveling companion Sir Edward Stafford wrote from Boulogne on September 29, "that I, my wife and all my folks were so sea-beaten that we were half dead." The party had to stay in Boulogne resting themselves and their horses until they finally felt ready to make the journey to Paris, which they reached on October 7. Hakluyt was then thirty-one years old, entering a European entrepōt more cosmopolitan and far larger than any city in England.[1]

Hakluyt and his supporters knew that Paris had become a meeting place for Europeans who had an interest in the Americas. Thus Sir Francis Walsingham, a favorite of the queen who had commended Hakluyt in March 1583 for his efforts to spread knowledge that facilitated "the discovery of the Westerne partes yet unknown," believed that the young geographer needed to spend time in France. An admirer of *Divers Voyages*, Walsingham urged Hakluyt to continue with his studies in order to "turne not only to your owne good in private, but to the publike benefite of this Realme." Elizabeth herself supported his mission; in December she urged officials at Christ Church to grant him a leave of absence and to approve that leave retroactive to August, the month he had made his plans for France. Walsingham, too, offered assistance, which no doubt reassured Hakluyt, who had complained that the journey to Paris could have damaged his "poor estate."[2]

Hakluyt knew that while he was consorting with Parisians, a group of Englishmen were laying the foundation for a colony in modern-day Canada. He had faith in that westward expedition because it was led by Sir Humphrey

Gilbert, fresh from the killing fields of Ireland. (At least one member of Gilbert's expedition joined after reading Hakluyt's *Divers Voyages,* a book that the courtier and author Sir Philip Sidney termed "a very good trumpet" for the expedition.) Even Gilbert's closest supporters knew him to be a ruthless man, capable of handling any adversity. Gilbert, who once dreamed of acting "cruelly" toward a foe in battle, was hardly alone in his barbarity; a pamphlet published in London in 1581 contained an image of English soldiers marching through Ireland with heads mounted on the ends of their pikes above a poem celebrating the "wonder" of decapitation. Still, his tactics impressed his allies. Any reader of Thomas Churchyard's assessment of him would have believed that a man capable of such acts could surely handle the challenges that he and his crew faced in North America.[3]

But none of Gilbert's talents could save him from the dangers of the sea. On his return to England, his ship disappeared near the Azores. According to the chronicler William Camden, Gilbert, "a man acute and deliberate, esteemed both in Peace and Warre, was by the raging Occan deprived of life, returning from the North parts of America, which we call New-found-Land: whither he a little before, having sold his patrimonie, made a voyage in hope to build there a Colonie." When he had landed, Gilbert had blown a trumpet and thus "proclaimed the Countrey to be under the English regency," an act reaffirming, to Camden at least, the original discovery of this territory by Sebastian Cabot in 1497. But claiming land and starting a colony could not prevent Gilbert's destiny. "He was taught (too late) by the devouring seas," Camden concluded, "teaching others also by his example, that it is a matter of great difficulty, by the expences of a private man to plant a Colony in farre distant Countries."[4] Camden could have added that two of Gilbert's three vessels sank. Only the *Golden Hind,* under the command of Edward Hayes, returned to spread the news of the disaster.

The loss wounded Hakluyt, who had turned down an opportunity to accompany Gilbert, probably because Walsingham or others had already convinced him that the realm needed him in Paris instead. But he had deep knowledge of the mission's plan and in all likelihood knew many who never returned. He also knew that Gilbert's drowning could have catastrophic consequences for future colonization schemes. Hakluyt feared a devastating blow to the English, who were, he hoped, finally on the verge of making a sustained commitment to establishing settlements in North America. He would not yet have known about Gilbert's alleged blasting into the Canadian spring air, but those notes arcing through the trees carried the same expectation of English ownership of North America that Hakluyt had trumpeted more quietly in the pages of *Divers Voyages.*

Strategic matters aside, this doomed venture struck Hakluyt personally, for he also mourned the death of one of Gilbert's associates, a young Hungarian poet named Stephen Parmenius, with whom Hakluyt had shared quarters at Christ Church. Before embarking on the voyage, Parmenius had risen to prominence among the select group of Englishmen who made it their business to sail out into the ocean. He also fell in love with England, and as a result, he, too, wanted to advance the emerging colonial agenda of the realm. Though he knew about the potential risks of any transatlantic venture, he embraced the opportunity to see North America with his own eyes. He revered Gilbert and trusted him with his life. What could Hakluyt have thought when he got the news that on this voyage—*this* voyage, which he had hoped to take— his dear friend had met his fate? How could he ever look out on the waters and see promise instead of calamity? Hakluyt would never again underestimate the power of the sea or the difficulty of crossing the ocean to establish colonies.

At the moment he arrived in Paris, Hakluyt knew much about the sea and its dangers. He was, after all, an avid reader of travelers' accounts. But even those with less obvious connections to oceanic ventures had at least heard about the strength of the waters that bounded their lands. Thousands of Europeans never saw the Atlantic or the Mediterranean, but they would have picked up some ocean lore. After all, many early modern Europeans migrated frequently and traveled long distances in pursuit of military victory or religious rewards, and those who returned from such ventures presumably told of the places they had been. It is almost inconceivable that a European could have grown up without hearing about what lay in or beyond the waters that bounded his or her world. Everyone would have known about local rivers, periodic flooding, and the bounty that nature provided in the way of fish. And many profited from the fact that sailors navigated open waters, bringing news and goods from distant lands to local markets.[5]

In the early modern age, Europeans had ample information about the seas from those who had sailed into them and returned. By the time of Columbus, they had acquired extensive knowledge of wind patterns that made oceanic voyages less dangerous. The printing press had made possible the wide dissemination of travel accounts, including those of Columbus himself, which were first published in Barcelona in 1493 and then translated and printed across the Continent in subsequent decades. In addition, European captains had learned how to arm their vessels with weapons to make them formidable against hostiles. As the eminent French historian Fernand Braudel put it, early modern Europeans had solved "the problem of the Atlantic."[6]

Printers searching for profitable titles discovered a reading public eager to study the natural world, including works that contained material about the seas such as that of the venerable Pliny the Elder. The Swiss bibliophile Conrad Gesner, who had once hoped to create a catalog listing every work published in Hebrew, Greek, and Latin in the century since the emergence of the printing press, offered detailed descriptions of the creatures that stalked the earth and swam in its waters. The fourth volume of his *Historiae Animalium* was devoted to the seas and its creatures and included a section on the monsters lurking in the deep. Readers keen to learn about the secrets of the deep could read the illustrated works of Francisi Boussucti, Guillaume Rondolet, and Sebastian Münster, which appeared in an English-language edition in 1553. The pictures in these works often emphasized the dangerous and the lurid to be found in the seas, in addition to the mundane fish more commonly hauled into ports.[7]

By the time Hakluyt crossed the English Channel, the catalog of the sea had become set in many Europeans' minds, its contents elaborated in the reports of explorers, casual travelers, and naturalists who sailed abroad and came back with reports of their findings. Stories of enormous whales, killer eels, and flying and suicidal fish became part of the lore about the sea through the writings of the Huguenot missionary Jean de Léry and others. Even a reader who never set foot on a ship would have been impressed by the sheer variety and abundance of what existed in the oceans, all of it proof of the diversity and goodness of the divine creation. Explorers bore witness to the extent of marvels contained in the Atlantic basin. But its riches could be harvested only by those who knew how to celebrate its origins and navigate its perils, and printers offered volumes that told of those who never returned from their journeys. Artists depicted oceans populated by monsters eager to snare the unlucky and the unwary. Beasts adorned the edges of manuscripts with elaborations of specific dangers to be found at sea, engraved images for cosmographers such as Münster, and created glistening mosaics for churches. Perhaps the Venetians, whose reliance on the sea was so absolute, got it right: in order to survive, humans had to engage in such rituals as the annual marriage of the sea, thereby demonstrating their weakness in the face of an all-conquering and life-sustaining presence.[8]

Yet this textual and visual heritage of danger did not dissuade Europeans from traveling long distances by boat. During the sixteenth century the Portuguese and the Dutch each commanded vessels from western Europe to the Spice Islands off Southeast Asia. They did so because the spice trade was so profitable and because hauling spices by sea promised better returns on investment than longer and equally dangerous overland missions. It was easier to bring cinnamon, cloves, and pepper to Europe by loading them onto ships than to maintain positive relations with countless intermediaries across southern Asia and the modern Middle East. Seaborne travel had the added advantage of cutting out Venetian merchants, who had for generations used their strategic position between East and West to enrich themselves. If non-Europeans posed a threat, sailors probably knew they could always launch attacks from sea, a strategy that at least on occasion proved remarkably effective, as the Portuguese commander Pedro Cabral discovered in 1500 when he retaliated against the rulers of Calicut for capturing members of his party.[9]

By the time Hakluyt arrived in France he had read countless descriptions of journeys over open water. He may have agreed with Thomas Churchyard, who composed an ode to Gilbert shortly before he embarked on his voyage for the western hemisphere in 1578. Churchyard wrote that sailors lived "at mercie of the Seas" where the "surge and swelling wave" could "swallow up the Shippe" of even the ablest captain.[10] None of what he read about the power and majesty of the sea would have surprised him. As a student of scripture, he knew his Bible's injunctions. "Yonder is the sea, great and wide," declared Psalm 104, "which teems with things innumerable, living things both small and great." Of the foundational myths told and retold in western Europe, two had particular force: Noah's flood, which marked a renewal in the world; and pharaoh's soldiers swallowed by the Red Sea, an event that enabled the chosen people to escape to the promised land. These tales worked because people understood the dangers that seas, storms, and floods posed. As the book of Jeremiah (49:23) put it, "There is sorrow on the sea." It was a lesson Hakluyt would soon take to heart.

The year 1583 opened with danger for Parisians. During January, according to the diarist Pierre de L'Estoile, repeated storms had raised the Seine above its flood stage. In the aftermath, the price of grain rose, thereby increasing the city's problems. Although Parisians were not the only Europeans to suffer from devastations that year—the residents of Seville faced a famine when a "langosta" blighted their crops and a fly called a pulgon destroyed local vines—danger seemed to come to France in all forms. By the end of January news reached Parisians that there had been a terrible riot in Antwerp after the French had tried to take command there. As many as sixteen hundred people had died in battles between local residents and the French, which was a startling blow to national pride.[11] Such challenges were the first of many to face Parisians in the year that Hakluyt arrived.

In the early 1580s, the religious revolts begun by the Reformation had still not subsided. The Elizabethans continued their forced occupation of Ireland long after the first generation of Protestant conquistadors (such as Gilbert) had set their sights on new challenges. In France, Huguenots still suffered for their views. Pierre de L'Estoile paid close attention to the ways that the religious conflict crept into daily life in Paris, keeping track of the king's response to new challenges. L'Estoile followed the king's progress through Paris that year. He condemned Henri III and his minions for a Mardi Gras debauch during which the king's entourage committed "a thousand insolences" until six in the morning of Ash Wednesday. But during Lent the king kept to his religion. He even walked from Paris to Chartres, a distance of approximately sixty miles, while his wife and mother rode there in a coach. L'Estoile missed that detail of the year, but the monarch's religiosity remained of great interest to him. He wrote with clinical detachment about the king's founding of a new religious order, the Penitents, and of Henri's participation in the new confraternity's rituals, which demanded that he don a hood and costume that made him indistinguishable from others. But the new order did not please everyone in Paris; one monk condemned it as a "brotherhood of hypocrites and atheists," while a group of pages at the Louvre mocked the group's attire, prompting the king to have them beaten. By August, worn down by affairs of state, the king created another new religious group, the Hièronimites, and prayed with them daily. Henri must have felt besieged. After he dreamed that wild animals were tearing his body apart, he ordered the execution of his animals at Versailles, a menagerie that included bears and lions.[12]

Sectarian strife was one of many threats in Paris that year. Plague had begun to spread across the French countryside that autumn, prompting processions of penitents to march in the direction opposite to that of Henri III: they trudged barefoot into Paris to Notre Dame. By the end of the year, six groups had come through the city, praying to their God to end the scourge.[13] For Hakluyt, arriving in Paris at a time of plague must have brought back the worst memories from his Westminster days and the epidemic that killed so many in the Oxford colleges in 1577, though there are no surviving letters recording his thoughts about the French epidemic.

On December 13, 1583, according to L'Estoile, Parisians endured an "impetuous windstorm" for two hours. A few days later, a different storm swirled through the city's streets. Rumormongers spread the news that Huguenots were claiming that France would soon fall to Protestants, that Catholic churches would collapse into decrepitude, and that German mercenaries would soon arrive to ensure the Huguenots' success. L'Estoile recognized the rumors for what they were: another attempt to rouse Catholics against Protestants. Though he did not know whether the rumors began with the king himself or with the Huguenots, the diarist dismissed them as "stupid and ridiculous as malicious and seditious."[14] But what would a Protestant visitor to the city have made of this scene of religious conflict?

Hakluyt's surviving writings reveal only glimmers of his thoughts during 1583, so it is necessary to use other sources to reconstruct his world and his views. Because he crossed the channel with the hope of advancing England's maritime dreams, he had presumably read John Dee's *General and Rare Memorials pertaining to the Perfect Arte of Navigation,* a tract published in London in 1577. Dee offered a forthright statement of the need for the English to control the seas around Britain and far into the Atlantic itself. He shared more than the political agenda of the younger Hakluyt. In his treatise, Dee acknowledged an argument made by "R.H.," an "honest gentleman of the Middle Temple," who had worked tirelessly to enhance "the Weale-Publik of England." Dee left the name out of his text, but he was referring to the lawyer. Though Dee instructed his publisher to print only one hundred copies of the book, he undoubtedly offered copies to his close associates and those who helped him. There is also no question that the lawyer would have given Hakluyt information derived from Dee's work before Hakluyt left for Paris, since the book provided essential information about England and its struggle with neighbors who sailed the high seas to rob English ships and fisheries.[15]

Further clues to Hakluyt's thoughts can be found in surviving documents. In addition to his discussions with his cousin and Gilbert, he probably helped prepare Christopher Carleill's pamphlet *A discourse upon the entended Voyage to the hethermoste partes of America,* written in April 1583. Carleill understood that Gilbert's earlier failure laid specific demands on the mission embarking in 1583. Who would have invested in a scheme if he or she believed that Gilbert's luck had run out? He had managed to subdue Catholics in Munster, yet his most significant attempt to conquer the seas had foundered in storms in 1578. But with knowledge about the potential of America circulating more widely in England, as a result in part of Hakluyt's *Divers Voyages,* Carleill argued that the time had come to mount a serious expedition to territory in the western hemisphere that he and other English promoters already believed was claimed by England. In every way Carleill's position echoed Hakluyt's, and the fact that Carleill was Walsingham's stepson made it even more likely that Hakluyt shaped the contents of the pamphlet.[16]

Like Hakluyt, Carleill recognized that the English needed not just to reach North America but to establish colonies there. He had learned all about Jacques Cartier's missions to the West, either directly from Ramusio or perhaps from the English translation of 1580 that Hakluyt had arranged. He had also read about Canada in books written by the French royal cosmographer André Thevet. He despised the teachings of the Catholic Church and feared the spread of Rome's influence. He argued that any "good Christian" would be grieved to discover that "his children and servaunts" who worked with the Spanish, Portuguese, or Italians would need to eschew their Protestant beliefs and absorb a "most wicked doctrine" that they abhorred. He believed that Americans, seduced by European wars, would "little & little, forsake their barbarous, and savage livyng, and grow to suche order and civilitie with us." For four thousand pounds, the English could send one hundred settlers to live among these natives. While they were establishing peaceful ties, the migrants would scout the land for suitable commodities to ship back to England. Carleill knew that Bristol's merchants, who had long been eager supporters of expeditions into the Atlantic, had already pledged one thousand pounds for the mission. The point of his pamphlet was to raise the rest, either in London or from individuals who shared the vision. Investors who contributed to the effort would receive portions of the profits depending on the amount of their initial advance. Surviving documents do not reveal whether Carleill's pamphlet proved crucial for Gilbert to receive the necessary financial backing, but by mid-summer, only a few months after Carleill had offered his arguments to the English public, Gilbert sailed for North America. Soon after, Hakluyt left for Paris, convinced of the rightness of the English, and Protestant, cause.[17]

Hakluyt needed little prodding about the alleged superiority of Protestant views. Either before he embarked or possibly while he was in Paris, he might have received a report confirming what the English believed was the true nature of Catholicism: an English translation of the writings of the Dominican Bartolomé de Las Casas. The book, *The Spanish Colonie, or Briefe Chronicle of the Acts and gestes of the Spaniardes in the West Indies, called the newe World,* by a translator identified on the title page as "M. M. S." and inside as James Aliggrodo, promised readers that they would learn about "many millions of me[n] put to death" in the islands "by all such meanes as barbarousnesse it selfe could imagine or forge upon the anveld of crueltie." Las Casas's scathing denunciation of Spanish actions toward the indigenous peoples of the Caribbean basin had first appeared in print in Seville in 1552, and been reprinted in other languages afterward. Now appearing in English for the first time, it had an enduring influence on the Protestant nation.[18]

The translator believed that the Spanish had killed three times as many people as inhabited all of Christendom. He then summarized the argument of the book, arguing that Las Casas had printed his condemnation of the conquistadors' actions so that the Spanish could recover from "the slaughters and murders of these innocent people, together with the spoiles of townes, provinces, & kingdomes." By printing his commentary, Las Casas, so the translator suggested, might more easily convince the king of the sordid details and thereby help to prevent future tragedies.[19]

After spending the autumn of 1583 in the city, Hakluyt decided to pay a visit to Étienne Bellenger, a French merchant in Rouen with close ties to the Catholic Church. Hakluyt did not make the journey to discuss religion. Instead, he went because he had learned that Bellenger had led an exploratory journey to North America during the winter of 1582–1583. His mission had prominent sponsors, including Charles de Bourbon-Vendôme, who had become archbishop of Rouen in 1550, a post he held (along with the position of cardinal) until his death in 1590. The mission was not Bellenger's first transatlantic experience. According to surviving documents, he had sailed on perhaps two fishing expeditions to Cape Breton (in modern Nova Scotia) earlier, though his principal livelihood apparently derived from his unspecified business on the rue des Augustines.[20]

According to Hakluyt, Bellenger had embarked on January 19, 1583, aboard a fifty-ton bark piloted by a Master Cottee (Michel Costé). He traveled along with a small crew of thirty boys and men. After approximately four weeks at sea, the boat arrived at Cape Breton. The crew then traveled southwest, approximately two hundred leagues (six hundred miles), carefully mapping their journey as they went. Bellenger showed Hakluyt the map they produced. Looking at the evidence, Hakluyt surmised that the French crew had charted "all the Bayes, Harbors, Creekes, Rivers, Sandes, Rockes, Islandes, [and] Flattes," along with estimates of the depth of water, which ranged from fifteen to sixty fathoms (about ninety to 360 feet). His ship entered a body of water that must have been the modern-day Bay of Fundy, a steep channel (now known for the extent of its daily tides) that was so narrow that "a Colverin shott can reach from one side to the other." The crew sailed through the strait, which he estimated was twenty-five leagues (seventy-five miles) long and twenty leagues (sixty miles) wide, to a spot where Bellenger and his associates marked the territory by planting, as Hakluyt wrote, "the Cardinall of Burbons Armes in a mightie highe tree." They then proceeded to do what explorers often did when they arrived at a new place: they bestowed names on landmarks, thereby establishing their claims over distant territory.[21]

Most of Hakluyt's report on his visit to Bellenger consists of the details of what the French found. As ever, such specifics consumed Hakluyt's attention, and he knew that gathering them was crucial if he were to perform the mission that Walsingham had given him. He recorded information about the climate, such as the fact that Bellenger told him that at the latitudes between 42 and 44 degrees the French had found the place "as warme as Bayon, Bordeux, Rochell, and Nantes, varieng a litle as it lieth more to the North or the South." This detail would have been crucial for Hakluyt, whose study of geography suggested that land so far north was not necessarily so warm. Bellenger told Hakluyt that this place seemed ideal for the production of salt. Local forests were even more appealing. Bellenger, Hakluyt wrote, "fownde the Countrey full of good trees to build Shipps withall and namely great plentie of oakes, Cypresses, Pynes, hasels, etc.," as well as abundant herbs.

Gathering information about the local environment was crucial for Hakluyt, and the details he provided in his report were an early indication of the information that would later fill the published volumes Hakluyt hoped would encourage and support English colonization drives. Yet Hakluyt also knew that European sailors who arrived after four weeks at sea needed more than a healthy environment. They also needed to know what the local peoples were like. All Europeans wanted to know if the natives would be friendly or hostile. But Hakluyt sought more precise information: Would the Americans be willing to trade with the newcomers?

When he interviewed Bellenger, Hakluyt got the answer he wanted. Bellenger gave a detailed account of what the local people looked like, noting that they were "of verie good disposition and stature of Bodie." Their hair reached their navels, though they wore bangs in front, and they walked about naked except for "an Apron of some Beastes skynn," which they tied around their midsection with a "long buff [leather] gerdle" tied three times around their bodies using the quills of bird feathers. These girdles had pouches in them that were used to carry, among other things, the tinder necessary to start fires. The natives carried bows and arrows, and Bellenger had brought some back to the cardinal, who would have noticed that the bows were perhaps six feet long and the arrows three feet long, tipped by sharpened bones and affixed to the shafts with leather. Hakluyt included these details in his report to suggest Bellenger's intimate knowledge of the people he encountered, a strategy that Hakluyt knew gave the French merchant's account greater credibility among English readers.

Bellenger warned Hakluyt that not all the natives they encountered were the same. "In divers places," Hakluyt recorded, "they are gentle and tractable. But those about Cape Britton and threescore or fowerscore leagues Westward are more cruell and subtill of norture [nature] than the rest." Bellenger warned Hakluyt that the natives could not be trusted. He did not offer such an opinion casually; two of the men on his journey had been killed by Americans because they had trusted "the salvadges to farr."

Still, despite the danger, Hakluyt filled much of his report with the commodities that Bellenger and his men had received from the Americans in trade. Bellenger did not note exactly where the trade took place, suggesting that the sailors exchanged goods with the natives in various locales. The French offered manufactured goods such as bells, knives, and glass. According to his calculations, Bellenger made a great profit. Among the goods that Bellenger had brought back to Rouen were the skins of elk, deer, seal, marten or sable, beaver (enough to make six hundred hats), otter, and lynx, a hide so precious that he gave twenty to the cardinal, who sponsored the voyage, and others to his friends. He also brought back an unspecified quantity of castoreum, the liquid extracted from the testicles of beaver and celebrated in sixteenth-century Europe for its marvelous healing powers.[22] On his return he sold dried deer flesh in foot-long pieces; dyestuffs to produce a range of colors including scarlet, vermilion, yellow, and blue; quills "red as vermillion"; and rocks that, Bellenger believed, held silver or tin. He added that the fish to be found near Cape Breton were "bigger and better" than those caught off Newfoundland and that there were ample harbors for ships. Still, however friendly the two had become, Bellenger would not reveal all that he knew to Hakluyt. There were, his visitor reported, "Divers other comodities he fownde the secrites whereof he was loath to disclose unto me." Perhaps he would offer Hakluyt other details when he returned from his next voyage, which he was apparently already planning.

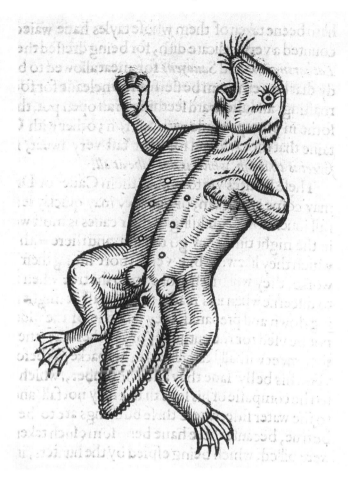

In sixteenth-century Europe castoreum was reputed to have remarkable curative powers but needed to be extracted with care, prompting detailed descriptions and engravings of how to drain the fluid from a male beaver. When Stephen Bellenger spoke of the likelihood of finding abundant supplies in North America, he might have had this image in mind, which had appeared in the second volume of Guilaume Rondolet's *Histoire Entiere Des Poissons* (Lyon, 1558), and was later reprinted in Edward Topsell's *Historie of fourefooted beastes* (London, 1607).

(HUNTINGTON LIBRARY)

Bellenger's entire journey lasted about eighteen weeks. If he left sometime in late January or mid-February, that meant he trawled the waters around Nova Scotia and Cape Breton from about early March to early June and then returned to France by early July, coming home perhaps two to three months before Hakluyt arrived in Paris. When he got home, he drew a map for the cardinal, another sign of the close connections between clerical officials and exploratory ventures that had been evident in Ramusio's Venice as well as in Hakluyt's England. The map does not survive, though Hakluyt did see an early version of it when he paid his visit.

This visit to Bellenger's house and shop made a deep impression on Hakluyt, who drew directly on the Rouen merchant's expedition later in the secret report he prepared for Walsingham and the queen. But in an age when measuring the veracity of any traveler always posed a challenge, Hakluyt told his supporters in England that he had arranged for other Englishmen to hear Bellenger's account. He brought in two ship captains along with an English merchant who lived in Rouen, a sailor, "& other honest men." These men played no role at all in Bellenger's voyage. Yet by listening to Bellenger, Hakluyt realized they could provide independent confirmation at least of the French merchant's account. If asked, they could testify to the teller's bearing, his gestures, perhaps sense if he was exaggerating or, alternatively, holding back. Getting them to listen to Bellenger was not a foolproof way of ensuring that he was telling the truth, Hakluyt knew, but at least he would have been able to measure others' responses to the French traveler.

After the witnesses had gathered to hear Bellenger's report, Hakluyt wrote that a group of English merchants based in Rouen decided to pool resources and contribute to an English expedition that would follow upon the failed Gilbert mission. He offered no specific details about what mission these men intended to support. But since the group included not only those he identified at Bellenger's shop but a number of other merchants and sea captains, too, it is likely that they would have known that Sir George Peckham and Christopher Carleill were each organizing expeditions at the time.

Hakluyt had gotten what he wanted. He had visited a French merchant who had no obvious affinity for a Protestant minister who had already published an account laying out an English claim for ownership of the territory that Bellenger had espied, and he had received a detailed report about a part of the Atlantic coastline that Hakluyt had little information about earlier. He had found in Bellenger a man who was apparently willing to tell at least part of the story to a group of Englishmen, and Bellenger's details were sufficient to prompt them into the actions that Hakluyt had urged. Now the report would go to England. Perhaps there it would provide further support for the overseas ventures that Hakluyt dreamed the English would mount. Perhaps they would achieve the success that had eluded Gilbert.

In the early 1580s, Paris was a thriving publishing center where printers and booksellers found a ready market for tracts on a wide range of subjects. Among them were tetralogical studies by Ambroise Paré and Pierre Boaistuau, along with various books that described parts of the Western Hemisphere—including the first edition of Michel de Montaigne's *Essais* with his speculations on cannibals. So was the newest, and last, book by the cosmographer François de Belleforest. His *Histoire des Prodigeuses*, like Paré's book, told readers about the monsters and oddities inhabiting their world. He even included a chapter on sea monsters, thereby giving recent affirmation (if not quite recent evidence) of the existence of dangerous creatures trolling the seas.[23] Hakluyt never mentioned that he read Belleforest's last book, but since he recommended the French scholar's earlier edition of Münster's cosmography to readers of *Divers Voyages*, it seems likely that he would have had an interest in this account of marvels.

Belleforest died the year that *Histoire des Prodigeuses* and Hakluyt each arrived in Paris, and there is no evidence that this French cataloger of wonder ever met the newly arrived English chaplain. But there is no doubt that Hakluyt met André Thevet, the king's cosmographer. By 1583, Thevet had already had a career that Hakluyt might have wished for himself. Born in Angoulême around 1516, he had received the support of the La Rochefoucaulds, an influential local family who helped him to receive a formal education and to whom Thevet was forever loyal. In the 1540s, Thevet had begun a series of travels that took him through the Continent into the Levant and Africa and, in 1555, to Brazil as *aumonier* (chaplain) to a French expedition led by Nicholas Durand, Chevalier de Villegagnon. Thevet did not enjoy America for long. He became ill in Brazil and returned to France by January 1556, only ten weeks after he had arrived at Guanabara, the site of modern-day Rio de Janeiro. He later asserted that he had sailed as far north as Florida, though some contemporaries dismissed this apparently specious claim.[24]

The first definitive sign that Hakluyt knew of Thevet's scholarship came in the list of geographical authorities in *Divers Voyages*. By then, Thevet was no stranger to readers of travel accounts. He had emerged as a renowned expert in geography in the mid-1550s when he returned to France after his first

Images of the monstrous could be found in works by scholars such as Ambroise Paré, Pierre Boaistuau, and François de Belleforet. These images are from a sixteenth-century English-language edition of Boaistuau's *Histoires Prodigeuses* entitled *Certaine Secrete Wonders of Nature* (London, 1569).
(HUNTINGTON LIBRARY)

trip to the East and published his *Cosmographie de Levant,* which appeared first in Lyon in 1554 and was reprinted in Lyon and Anvers in 1556. In that book he wrote about a journey that began in southern France in June 1549, took him southward through Venice, the Adriatic, and then into the Levant, where he stopped at the legendary cities of Constantinople and Troy. He then continued southwest, back into the Mediterranean, where he crossed directly to Alexandria and then headed east once again, bound for Jerusalem, Antioch, and Tripoli. He set sail again and headed to Rhodes, and from there journeyed back through the Mediterranean until he reached Marseille, probably in 1552. Thevet wanted readers of the *Cosmographie de Levant* to believe that he paid close attention to every place he visited. He provided precise details about various locales and illustrations for direct visual evidence of such

phenomena as lions, tigers, wild horses, and camels; pygmies riding on the back of horned sheep while they shot arrows at birds; an enormous crocodile eager to consume a turbaned man; and hieroglyphics carved onto a stele at Alexandria. His image of the long-lost Colossus of Rhodes revealed the grandeur of that ancient marvel by showing a two-masted sailing ship moving through its legs, with part of one mast grazing his muscular thigh while a flag just missed his penis. Constantinople fascinated Thevet. He provided a brief history of the city as well as descriptions of the janissaries and the Grand Turk, who he claimed was held in the same esteem as the pope to the French.[25]

Later critics recognized that Thevet had in fact borrowed much of what he wrote from others, especially from Pliny's *Natural History* and Coelius Rhodiginus's *Lectionum Antiquarum*, published in Basel in 1542. Perhaps he also derived material from Münster's *Cosmographiae Universalis*. But even Thevet's wholesale borrowing had little obvious impact on the French cosmographer's initial popularity, perhaps because many readers did not recognize the apparent plagiarism. Of course some did realize his tactics. Belleforest accused

Thevet of stealing from his French-language edition of Münster's work, which he had published in 1575, the same year that Thevet published his *Cosmographie Universelle*.[26]

Yet despite such charges, the publication of the *Cosmographie de Levant* put Thevet in an ideal position to spread the word about distant lands. Through that work he recognized the potential audience for travel accounts, evident in the multiple printings of the book so soon after its appearance. He also came to believe, as did Hakluyt, that illustrations within the text could advance his argument, perhaps even become a silent way of attesting to his expertise as an eyewitness. Thevet was not the first to realize that accounts of the world, often including illustrations, could be popular. Münster's Basel publisher Henri Petri had first printed a German-language edition of his *Cosmography* in 1544 and followed it with editions in 1545, 1546, 1548, 1550, 1553, 1556, 1558, 1561, 1564, 1567, 1569, 1572, 1574, 1578, 1588, 1592, and 1598, as well as editions in Latin in 1550, 1552, 1554, 1559, and 1572, and editions in French in 1552, 1555, 1556, 1560, and 1565. Petri also published an Italian version in 1558, and other printers published an English edition in London in 1553, a Czech edition in Prague in 1554, and two separate French versions in Paris in 1575. In such a publishing climate, it was not surprising that after Thevet returned from the western hemisphere he wrote *Les Singularitez de la France antarctique*, printed first in Paris in 1557. That book launched Thevet into the next phase of his remarkable career. Over time, he became aumonier to Catherine de Médicis and then royal cosmographer for Henri II, François II, Charles IX, and Henri III. He also picked up a series of clerical posts and became the overseer of France's most spectacular cabinet of curiosities, the royal collection housed at the palace of Fontainebleau.[27]

Thevet's fame soon stretched well beyond the borders of France. As early as 1561, Giuseppe Horologgi translated Thevet's work and published it in Italian. Seven years later Thomas Hacket published an English-language edition and promised his readers that they would read about "wonderful and strange things" in addition to tales about the "Beastes, Fishes, Foules, and Serpents, Trees, Plants, Mines of Golde and Silver" described by "that excellent learned man Andrew Thevet." According to the book's title page, Thevet's findings would dispel the errors "of the auncient Cosmographers." Like other printers and translators, Hacket was eager to establish Thevet's reputation in England, and so he included (as did others) testimonials to the French cosmographer's character and achievement, including a sonnet.[28]

Those who read Hacket's translation picked up what Thevet's French audience had learned: details about Thevet's trip to the western hemisphere, including descriptions of the Tupinambas and their eating and drinking habits, dreams and visions, style of warfare, marriage and burial ceremonies, ideas about the immortality of the soul, and trading mores. Thevet also included material on notable local birds, such as the toucan, and assorted dangers, including a report on cannibals in the Caribbean and "the island of rats" where rodents ruled. Hacket included Thevet's report on lands he allegedly saw in North America as well, noting that earthquakes, snow, and hail were common on the "Ilande of Canada." Here was the book that readers in England needed if they were to share in the benefits of geographical knowledge then spreading rapidly through Europe. Though Hakluyt did not make specific reference to Hacket's edition, he doubtless knew of it before he embarked for Paris. *Les Singularitez* had at least one other prominent reader in England: Sir Walter Ralegh took a copy along with him on his ill-fated expedition to Guiana in the mid-1590s.[29]

Eight years before Hakluyt arrived in France, Thevet published his masterwork in Paris, a massive two-volume summary of all geographical knowledge entitled *La Cosmographie Universelle*. The scale of the project brought to mind Ramusio's *Navigationi et Viaggi*, a work Hakluyt had long admired. But Thevet's work had a decisive advantage over Ramusio's. Unlike the Venetian geographer, Thevet could make a claim that he had seen at least part of the western hemisphere. Still, like other compilers of accounts, including Hakluyt, Thevet relied on others who had seen territory that he missed, including the writings about Florida left by René de Laudonnière. He also included maps and pictures of specific incidents or places—one of a ship sailing under a star-filled night, another of the Isle of Rats. Other illustrations depicted Tupinambas smoking tobacco, feasting (including ritual vomiting, presumably after consuming an emetic designed to purify the body), curing an ill man, and the capture and grilling over an open flame of local enemies. Thevet's pictures of Florida included the dreaded "succarath," a beast that Hakluyt would learn about in some depth from David Ingram, whose book on his travels in North America had also appeared in 1583. Illustrations for the Canadian text featured images of boar hunting, including one boar (or a similar beast) hunted by a woman. To make sure that he would not be forgotten, Thevet described an island so wondrous that he termed it "a second paradise"—and then renamed it "l'Isle de Thevet."[30]

Yet if Hakluyt was awed by Thevet's accomplishment, he knew that not every reader accepted Thevet's account. Despite the warm reception that his first writings had received, the *Cosmographie Universelle* elicited derision in France. Jean de Léry, who had spent more time in Brazil than Thevet, led the charge. He singled out Thevet's claim about a large city that the royal cosmographer had first labeled "Ville-Henri" on the map he had produced for Henri II in 1558. The error enraged Léry, who knew that the city was a product of Thevet's imagination. When the same place, now labeled "Henri-Ville" appeared on a map in the *Cosmographie Universelle,* Léry wrote that Thevet had ample time "to realize that it was pure nonsense." How did Léry know that Thevet was lying? Because, he told his readers, he had been to the Bay of Guanabara eighteen months after Thevet had left, and no such city could be found there. He admitted that there was a mountain on the spot, but that was all. "But if there is a difference between a mountain and a city," Léry memorably noted, "just as there is between a bell-tower and a cow, then it follows either that Thevet, marking this 'Ville-Henri' or 'Henri-Ville' on his maps, is seeing things, or else that he is deliberately trying to dupe us." Léry, engaged in the kind of literary warfare that was becoming common in the pages of printed books, could not let the matter stop there. He repeatedly attacked Thevet's credibility and even leveled a warning. If the royal cosmographer "finds this refutation of his works on America hard to stomach (seeing that, to defend myself against calumnies, I have razed a city), let him be aware that these are not all the errors I have noticed: as I am witness, if he is not satisfied with the little that I touch upon in this history, I will show him them in detail." Léry understood that the battle he was waging was fought not with drawn swords but with barbed words. The ultimate victor would be determined not by a corpse lying on the ground but instead by the reputation of an author in the minds of a reader. He thus apologized to his readers for going on about Thevet at such length, adding that he "will let the readers judge whether or not I am wrong."[31]

When Hakluyt arrived in Paris, Thevet was preparing to defend himself against what he believed was the slander of Léry. In his *Vrais pourtraits et vies des hommes illustres, grecs, latins, et païens,* a vast compendium of celebratory short biographies published in the city in 1584, he attacked the Huguenot missionary, a literary assault that prompted Léry to abuse Thevet again in the preface to the third edition of his account of Brazil, published in Geneva in 1585.[32] Such disputes had their origins in sectarian strife: the Protestant missionary Léry trying to bring the Reformation to South America while the Catholic Thevet, possessor of multiple sinecures, hoping to spread the teachings of Rome among the Tupinambas.

Although Hakluyt presumably would have sided with a Protestant in such a squabble, he still held Thevet in high regard, at least at first. In *Divers Voyages,* he specified that the *Cosmographie Universelle* was vital reading. More important, Thevet must have become a mentor of sorts to Hakluyt. The French cosmographer was sixty-seven when Hakluyt, in his early thirties, arrived in Paris. Though Hakluyt would later join Léry's critique of Thevet (and Thevet, for his part, would claim that Hakluyt had stolen the text of Laudonière's account from him), during his first stint in Paris the two apparently became such close friends that Thevet told Hakluyt about French plans for exploration. As Hakluyt wrote to Walsingham in January 1584, Thevet, along with the king's furrier Valeron Perosse, had told him that the French planned "to send out certayne ships to inhabite some place for the north part of America, and to carry thither many friers and other religiouse persons, but I think they be not in haste to do it."[33]

There is no way to know why Thevet trusted Hakluyt, not only with such a valuable manuscript but also with the plans of the French nation. In retrospect, such faith in Hakluyt makes no sense, especially given Hakluyt's hostility toward Catholics and his fears that the French, along with the Spanish, were establishing colonies in the western hemisphere so that they could enrich themselves and spread the teachings of Rome to Americans. Hakluyt must have known that in November 1583 "a foul picture of the Queen" was circulating on the streets of Paris, a scurrilous image, according to Stafford, of the monarch on horseback, her "left hand holding the bridle, with her right hand pulling up her clothes."[34] Yet despite the outward hostility between the French and the English, during his remarkable first year in Paris his close alliance with the king's cosmographer must have thrilled Hakluyt. With such a cooperative partner, and with other travelers (such as Bellenger) so willing to tell about their voyages to the West, Hakluyt sat poised to carry out his mission.

Perhaps only two days after Hakluyt left London, Edward Hayes, captain of the *Golden Hind,* pulled the lone surviving ship from Gilbert's voyage into port and reported the sad fate of the other ships on the expedition. He also brought back with him a letter that Parmenius had written to Hakluyt. Because news traveled slowly, knowledge of Hayes's return could not have reached Hakluyt before he embarked. Hence, by the time Hakluyt got the report in Paris, Parmenius was lost, along with the others who were aboard the ship that sank near Newfoundland. Hakluyt, farther from home than he had ever been before, presumably opened Parmenius's testimony at the same time that he heard about his death. It is impossible to know how he took the news.

Born in Buda sometime between 1555 and 1560, Parmenius had come to England during his explorations of Europe. Unlike most residents of territory under Turkish rule, Parmenius's family had become Protestants. Few surviving documents shed light on his early life, though he was listed as a student at the University of Heidelberg in 1579, a stop along what scholars believe was the young poet's journey through the Continent. From there he probably traveled through Italy, though no records survive of his peripatetic mission until he arrived in Oxford, in either late 1581 or early 1582. At that point he met Hakluyt, and the two soon shared lodgings at Christ Church.[35]

Written records offer few added details about the Hungarian poet, but the clues that survive are tantalizing. By 1582 he had become an intimate of Hakluyt and had received the assistance of such notable patrons as Sir Henry Unton, to whom he addressed his brief *Paean*, a published poem, Parmenius wrote, "modelled on Psalm of David 104 and dedicated to the Good Lord and Almighty Saviour in gratitude for a safe journey from Hungary to England." Like other scholars eager to please a patron, Parmenius had the poem printed in London in 1582.[36] By then, Hakluyt had introduced him to Gilbert, who agreed to take Parmenius with him on his journey to the western hemisphere.

Parmenius's association with Gilbert had led to the publication of the Hungarian's *De Navigatione*, a poem whose title (translated into English) declared that it was *An Embarkation Poem for the voyage projected by the celebrated and noble Sir Humphrey Gilbert Golden Knight, to take a colony to the New World.* Printed in London in 1582, *De Navigatione* expressed Parmenius's joyful association with England, his embrace of any Protestant mission to convert the native peoples of the Americas, and his affection for Gilbert and those associated with overseas expeditions. Parmenius wrote that he was "born in the servitude and barbarism of the Turkish empire," though his parents had become "by the grace of God, Christians," and that he had been able to escape the hell that had descended over his native land for the heaven of Protestant universities to the west. Filled with awe at what he had seen in three years of travel, he added that "no situation, no people, no state" had brought such joy to him as Britain: "the delightful friendship of the English has almost dispelled my longing for Buda and the Hungary which I am bound to call my homeland." Because of his newfound fortune, Parmenius felt compelled "to publish some token of my goodwill and respect." He

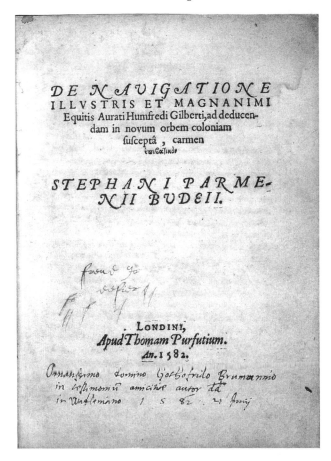

Title page of a surviving copy of Stephen Parmenius's *De navigatione*
(HUNTINGTON LIBRARY).

thanked his "distinguished and learned friend Richard Hakluyt" for introducing him to Gilbert and then hoped that his poem would seem adequate to
Gilbert himself, whom Parmenius had come to revere.[37]

De Navigatione sang the praises of England, of Gilbert, and of the
queen. In it, Parmenius celebrated Gilbert's journey and saw the venture as
a quest "Towards a world our fathers did not know / In seas they scarcely
saw." America was, to him, a tabula rasa, "A land unruled by kings has been
preserved / For you through many centuries." Parmenius thrilled to the
prospect of the Protestant Gilbert leading the English into a land not yet
polluted by "the Moslem wail" or "the scheming hand of Spain." What a

contrast to the Old World, where "African and Asian lands / Are crushed by brutal Moslem regiments," while the dark night of Romish practice had spread, he claimed, over Romania, Greece, and Hungary. Who better to lead the charge than Gilbert, a man whose battlefield tactics were known from Spain to Ireland? Fortunately Elizabeth held "dominion over boundless seas," and hence she could look out her windows toward the Thames, "where she now sees / The sails of Humphrey Gilbert's ship begin / To billow." Parmenius imagined America's voice at the end of the poem crying out for help. "'Please do not ignore / My tears, fair sister,'" the unexplored continent wailed, "'but feel / For me in my misfortune.'" Follow those who had come before, such as Francis Drake, "'Your noble hero,'" and Cabot, who had

> Approached these regions, following the wake
> Of great Columbus: not so near the pole
> That ice abounds, nor parched too much by sun,
> But nicely poised between the harsh extremes
> Of climate, whether heaven's gracious breath,
> The gentle breeze, is what you hanker for,
> Or wealth and produce from the fruitful soil.

For Parmenius, there could be no greater good than joining this heroic fulfillment of England's destiny.[38] For Hakluyt, *De Navigatione* must have seemed like a dream itself. Parmenius had embraced Hakluyt's entire argument, from the need for Protestant expansion to the earlier claims of the Cabots. Though the patriotic excess of his writings mirrored other rhetorical flourishes of the age (including Churchyard's ode to Gilbert), such similarities did not mean that Parmenius only parroted other writers. His poetry, however overwrought, reflected his apparent adulation of England and some of its notable heroes.

Parmenius intended his *Paean* and *De Navigatione* to be read by perhaps five hundred to twelve hundred people, the number of copies of a typical work rolling off any press in the sixteenth century. By contrast, his letter to Hakluyt, written in August 1583, was a private message from beyond the watery grave. Written in Latin when Hakluyt was making his arrangements to join the English ambassador in Paris, Parmenius told his friend about Newfoundland. Like other travelers to North America, Parmenius filled his letter with details about what he had seen, knowing that Hakluyt wanted to gather precise information about every possible site for a colony. He wished Hakluyt to know that though two of the men had drowned, "the rest are in safetie and strong, and for mine own part I was never more healthy." The territory itself was remarkable. Bodies of water teemed with fish—"the hooke is no sooner throwne out but it is eftsoones drawn up with some goodly fish." The land was covered with vines. The soil seemed ideal for agriculture. Strawberries grew in abundance. The weather was so variable that ice could impede a traveler's way as late as May, yet by summer it was hot. On land the air was clear, "but at sea towards the East there is nothing els but perpetuall mists, and in the sea itselfe" there was "no day without raine." Once Gilbert's crew had gathered provisions for their return, they were to return to England, eager to make new discoveries en route.[39]

Parmenius's letter was not the only news that had survived the doomed expedition. Gilbert, too, through the writing of Sir George Peckham, also reached out to Hakluyt, and to England more generally. Before Gilbert left England, he had promised Peckham a tract of land along modern-day Narragansett Bay where Peckham, an English Catholic, could create a refuge for his coreligionists. For his part, Peckham wrote a detailed pamphlet about the colony that Gilbert would create. He described Gilbert's medieval fantasy of becoming a feudal lord presiding over a vast domain where the inhabitants would all have to abide by his rules. Gilbert promised investors direct returns on their investments. Those who invested one hundred pounds would rule over sixteen-thousand-acre parcels that they could people however they chose and hold courts leet and baron, feudal legal institutions that were archaic even by the sixteenth century. All the investors had to do was to pay a token ten shillings annually (in addition to their initial costs) as well as 40 percent of any mineral wealth they found—20 percent to the queen and 20 percent to Gilbert. After three years of occupancy the associates would also have to pay a small fee, a half-penny per cultivated acre, to support the construction of common buildings such as churches and forts. Gilbert's plan, as described by Peckham, also specified the rights and responsibilities of lesser investors. But though finances dominated much of the pamphlet, Peckham also emphasized that freedom to trade in America came with special responsibilities. The migrants had to treat the natives fairly, since Gilbert, like other promoters (including Hakluyt) hoped that his colony would be beneficial to the indigenous peoples. The Americans would learn "the most happy and gladsome tydings of the most glorious Gospel of our Saviour Jesus Christ," Peckham pledged, "whereby they may be brought from falsehood to truth, from darknes to lyght, from the hieway of death, to the path of life, from superstitious idolatry, to sincere christianity, from the devill to Christ, from hell to Heaven."[40]

During the 1580s news about Gilbert's death spread through England. The historian Raphael Holinshed included testimonial from John Hooker in his *Chronicles*, published in London in 1587. Hooker emphasized Gilbert's military success in Munster, noting that he was younger than most men of his rank but nonetheless he had "manie good gifts and excellent virtues" that older men never attained. "For in service upon the enimie he was as valiant and couragious as no man more," Hooker observed, "and so good was his hap to answer the same: for he alwaies for the most part daunted the enimie, and appalled their courage." Gilbert had demonstrated his prowess in an epic battle at Kilkenny, when he and twelve others purportedly defeated an Irish contingent of one thousand men, and when he and his entire of force of five thousand subdued the province of Munster despite the presence of "sundry thousands" of foes. After his military achievements he went to Dublin, where, Hooker reported, his good work led to his knighthood. Soon after his return to England Gilbert married "a yoong gentlewoman, and an inheritrix," and then delved deeply into studies of the nature of government and the art of navigation. In Parliament, in England and in Ireland, he spoke publicly about geography, showing "the great value of knowledge, wisedome, and learning which was in him, and the great zeale he had to the commonwealth of his countrie." No wonder the queen came to support his overseas ventures. But before he succeeded, Hooker added, "he was in a foule storme drowned at the seas. Onelie he of all his brethren had five sons and one daughter, children by their countenances giving a hope of a good towardnesse. And albeit he in person be deceased, yet in their visages, and in the memoriall of his great vertues, and a life well spent, he shall live in fame immortall."[41] A reader could have immediately grasped the meaning of Hooker's praise: Gilbert, undermanned, could conquer the Irish, but he could not conquer the sea.

When Hakluyt published *The Principall Navigations, Voiages and Discoveries of the English Nation* in 1589, he, too, spoke of Gilbert, though not in the reverential tone of Hooker. Hakluyt was more concerned with the expedition than with the knight's purported achievements. He thus included Hayes's report, which bore witness to Gilbert's ship "devoured and swallowed uppe of the Sea." Hayes also wrote about the other victims of the journey. Almost one hundred English men lost their lives on that expedition, Hayes acknowledged, among them "a learned man, an Hungarian, borne in the Citie of

Buda, called thereof Budaeus, who of pietie and zeal to good attemptes, adventured in this action, minding to record in the Latine tongue, the gests and things worthy of remembrance, happening in this discoverie, to the honour of our nation, the same being adorned with the eloquent stile of this Orator, and rare Poet of our time."[42]

As he sat down to complete the *Principall Navigations,* perhaps Hakluyt realized that Parmenius himself accepted the dangers that any vessel faced in the deep blue. "How far the seas extend, how wide / They reach away from land!" he had written in his paean to Unton.

> And they contain
> Both huge and tiny creatures: monsters lurk
> With other savage beasts in some more dark
> And gruesome waters, while a long way off
> The ocean teems with countless living things
> Of minute size.[43]

By 1589, Hakluyt was ready to acknowledge publicly that his beloved friend had become one of the many who died on a transatlantic expedition across those "gruesome waters," another soul lost in the gloaming of the nation's memory. In the future, it would be Hakluyt's burden to keep the colonizing impulse alive despite the ubiquitous threat of the "savage beasts" who dwelled in the devouring sea.

CHAPTER 7

Paris and London, 1584
The Grammar of Colonization

In the beginning of January 1584, Hakluyt was finally ready to go to North America. Still stationed in Paris with the English ambassador, he told Walsingham that it was imperative that the English pursue colonization immediately before the initiative would "waxe colde and fall to the ground." Walsingham had already asked Hakluyt if he could manage the journey. Now, after the deaths of Gilbert and Parmenius, the time had come. "Your honor made a motion heretofore unto me, whether I could be contented to goe myself in the action," Hakluyt wrote back. "I am most willinge to goe now." He was ready to travel, he continued, "in the service of God and my country to employ al my simple observations readings and conference whatsoever."[1]

Hakluyt knew why his service was crucial. The tragedies of 1583 could have ended English interest in the western hemisphere. If the Atlantic could devour Gilbert, then perhaps it remained too formidable for the English. Fishermen sailing out of Bristol or other ports might still command profitable ventures, but those efforts fell far short of actual colonization. By gathering information about overseas expeditions and the legitimacy of English claims to much of North America, Hakluyt's "observations" and "readinges" had given Walsingham and other policy makers (including the queen) the impetus to carry forward with colonization despite the difficulties the English had had so far. The promise that he had made in the lawyer's chambers was perhaps coming true.

In the months after he let Walsingham know about his interest in travel, Hakluyt continued to assemble materials. First in Paris and then in London, he worked on composing what became the longest piece he ever wrote. Unlike *Divers Voyages,* he did not intend to publish this new tract. Instead, he believed that his "Discourse on Western Planting," as the document is now known, should be read by Queen Elizabeth and her closest allies, including Walsingham. On one level an argument for colonization, the "Discourse" also reveals what overseas settlement had come to mean for Hakluyt.

By year's end, Hakluyt had studied a precious manuscript owned by the king of France and had met the queen of England. Henri III had allowed Hakluyt into his library, which he had recently installed in a church in Paris. But Elizabeth gave Hakluyt a greater gift: her attention. It was a remarkable year for him, and not only because of his high-level meetings. The "Discourse" turned out to be more than a recounting of others' experiences. In writing those pages, Hakluyt composed a grammar of colonization. Here was his first effort to craft the language and logic that would guide the English colonization of North America. Though he began it as a secret communiqué, Hakluyt in later years drew from it in his published works. In this sense the "Discourse" was like the blueprint for a building, the crucial but ultimately hidden document needed to construct a new edifice.

In 1584 Pierre L'Estoile continued to chronicle the city of Henri III, a king eager to "continue the reformation that he says he wished to make of all offices." The king began the year with a religious ceremony at the Augustinian convent in Paris and within two weeks had begun to eliminate crooked tax collectors and treasurers. But such official purging of wrongdoers did not interfere with the familiar rounds of festivities and prayer that had punctuated years past. Again the king and his minions paraded through Paris on Mardi Gras. They were, L'Estoile recalled, "mounted and masked, disguised as merchants, priests, lawyers, etc., tearing about with loose rein, knocking down people, or beating them with sticks, especially others who were masked." At St.-Germain they "committed infinite insolences, rioting and disturbing the good people who were there until six o'clock in the morning." Nonetheless, such ribaldry did not mean that the king had abandoned the church. On March 9 he left Paris on a pilgrimage to Notre Dame de Cléry. As was his style, he traveled on foot, along with forty-seven monks, all of them "dressed in the habit of Penitent." On Holy Thursday, twenty days later, he "held his usual procession of Penitents, visiting the churches of Paris all during the night." At the same time about eighty of the Penitents had their own barefoot, music-filled procession.[2]

For Hakluyt, the early months of 1584 held other kinds of promise. He had visited the fur merchant Valeron Perosse, with his extensive inventory of beaver, otter, sable, and other furs purchased from mariners from St.-Malo who had already established a fur trade linking France to Canada. More significant, he continued to gather information for his patrons. By mid-January he had spoken twice to Don Antonio, the pretender to the Portuguese throne, as well as "five or sixe of his best captaynes and pilotes, one of whom was born in Easte India." These men urged Hakluyt to tell the queen that if she supported Don Antonio and agreed to use her navy for their cause, they could combat Philip II of Spain and she could become rich in the process. They already had a base of support in Portugal numbering "about an hundred or sixe score" and had organized a mission from Le Havre to the Guinea coast, where they would gather their followers.[3]

Hakluyt knew that Continental politics would have a direct bearing on any English efforts to colonize North America. The Portuguese pretender interested him precisely because an alliance might strike a blow against Spain's imperial dreams. He was thus open to any meeting that might advance his cause. Through the physician Pierre Pena, an authority on plants (including tobacco), Hakluyt had met a Savoy-born Spaniard named Andreas who had recently traveled from Japan to Paris. Hakluyt did not reveal what he hoped to learn from such an encounter, but he did let Walsingham know that he was seeking "diverse other intelligences tending toward the furtherance of our western planting and discoverie."[4]

Yet while Hakluyt's work proceeded as he had hoped, by January he had to report a potential menace. He had heard from both André Thevet and Valeron Perosse that a French admiral, the duc de Joyeuse, had schemed with the cardinal of Bourbon to "send out certayne ships to inhabite some place for the north part of America, and to carry thither many friers and other religious persons." Hakluyt believed that the plans were not yet well advanced, or at least that the French were not eager to pursue any scheme yet. But even the possibility rankled him, as it must have disturbed Walsingham and the queen.[5]

Over the next few months, while the king cavorted and prayed, Hakluyt gathered information. He was not single-minded in what he did, but everything seemed to draw him back to his core beliefs. In February he met with Bellenger, the traveler from Rouen who had recently returned from North America and offered his assessment of what he had seen. Soon after he met with a Monsieur de Leau from Morlaix, who "tolde me this springe in the presence of divers englishe men at Paris that a man of St. Mallowe this laste yere discovered the sea on the backside of Hochelaga." At approximately the same time he visited the king's library at the Abbey of St.-Martin in Paris, where he saw a French manuscript that described a land of "Cynamon and cloves" that was only a month's journey away. The document specified that Donaconna "the Kinge of Canada" had sailed there himself and brought back the spices that the Indians then named "in their owne language."[6]

Even subjects seemingly far from geography had meaning for Hakluyt. He praised the French intellectual Pierre de la Ramée, or Petrus Ramus, as he was known in his many works, for having funded lectures relating to math "to the great increase of those excellent sciences." Here was an example of what Hakluyt wanted the English to do for themselves, specifically to provide financial support for scholars whose efforts had real-life consequences. For Hakluyt, that of course meant funding lectures relating to navigation. So he reminded Walsingham in April of their earlier discussions and the meetings he had had with Drake and an alderman named Barnes.[7]

Hakluyt did not simply point out the existence of the French system for the improvement of mathematics. Instead, he described how the system worked. Ramus had endowed the initial disputation with a gift worth fifty pounds, leaving "not halfe as much to al the kindred and frendes he had in the world." Ramus, as "one of the most famous clerkes of Europe," chose mathematics for this annual event since in his opinion it was "next after divinitie to be most necessarie for the commonwealth." Hakluyt, who had met with Ramus's executor, Nicholas Bergeron, believed that the English should model a system on Ramus's, down to its most cunning detail. Each three years there would be public contests during which anyone would have three months to argue with the expert. If "certayne indifferent men of lerninge" chosen to be judges preferred the newcomer, he would then take over and hold the position for three years "to read through the course of the mathematikes."[8]

Since his time at Christ Church, Hakluyt had recognized the importance of mathematics as a tool for measuring distance and plotting travels. Now he urged Walsingham to convince the queen "to erect such a lecture in Oxford." But he was not yet finished with his scheme. He also thought that she should establish another lecture in London "for the arte of navigation." She should give fifty pounds to each every year. "In my simple judgement," he wrote, "yt wold be the best hundred pounds that was bestowed this five hundred yeares in England." Lest Walsingham still miss the point, Hakluyt made the link specific. Walsingham must know, Hakluyt added, "how necessarie for the service of warres arithmeticke and geometrie are, and for our our new discoveries and longer voyages by sea the arte of navigation is."[9]

By the time Walsingham received Hakluyt's letter, he would have had long acquaintance with the work of Ramus. Petrus Ramus was the author of a standard Latin grammar (which was translated into English in 1585 but available earlier) and the alleged author of other works, including a commentary on religion in France that had been published in London in 1573. That commentary included a celebratory ode to Ramus by the Westminster schoolmaster Edward Grant, who realized the loss to European letters that Ramus's death had caused. Perhaps Walsingham had even seen the most recent book by Ramus to appear in London: a translation of his definitive work on logic published in 1581.[10]

Still, mathematical debates and Ramus were not really what Hakluyt had in mind when he sat down to write to Walsingham on that early April day. With Paris blooming around him and the scents from flowers and trees inescapable in the city, he continued to gather materials to promote "western discoveries." He hoped that a recently captured Protestant minister and his associates would soon be released by the abbot of St.-Geneva, who had taken him captive. Even the king was on the minister's side, arguing that the Protestants "were not at any communion or sermon" but instead had merely gathered to discuss whether they should leave Paris for a place where they could meet lawfully. Yet despite royal support, French clerics remained hostile to all things Protestant. Hakluyt reported that one of his friends had told him "he herd a frier inveigh very exceeding bitterly against them in a sermon before a great congregation of people." But thoughts about his larger plan were always in mind. "Don Antonio his captaynes of his fleet are not yet departed from Paris," he added, in another reference to the Portuguese pretender and ally of the English, "but look every day to depart."[11]

On April 16, only two weeks after Hakluyt had praised the city for supporting Ramus's scheme, Parisians were stunned when Sieur de Saint-Didier, brother of the cardinal of Norbonne, died in Paris. He was only sixteen or seventeen years old. Two days later, its residents were shocked again when the prominent physician Malmédy, who only four years earlier had helped Parisians cope with plague, slit his own throat at Roussey when he faced staggering debts. These deaths, however tragic, had little direct effect on the English residing in Paris. But the situation soon changed when the English ambassador, Stafford, heard multiple reports that the king's childless brother had died at Château-Thierry. In fact, the duc D'Alençon had not yet died, but his illness was advancing. The queen mother rushed to be by his side, but by the end of May his physicians had given up hope for a recovery. On June 19, he died from a hemorrhage ("un grand flux de sang"). He was thirty-one. Two days later his body, accompanied by four hundred horsemen, arrived in Paris. By then Stafford had received instructions from London that he should pay his condolences to Henri III in a way that would reflect "the great goodwill and inward friendship" between the duke and the queen.[12]

Death was as common an occurrence in Paris as it was in London (or in any other large European city) at the time. Most of the men, women, and children who died succumbed to infectious diseases spread through water contaminated by human and animal waste. Plague struck, too, including a devastating epidemic in 1580.[13] Others wasted away, their lives consumed by the ravages of poverty and malnutrition or taken in the accidents and violence that seemed so commonplace in the squalor of crowded precincts. Hakluyt would never have noticed most of these personal tragedies unless they took place in front of him.

But the death of the king's brother and heir apparent was another matter and immediately invoked intense public interest. The news spread quickly, if unevenly. One of Walsingham's correspondents in Antwerp wrote to him on June 24 confirming the death, perhaps because he feared that the English had not yet heard. Pierre de L'Estoile followed the situation day by day, recording the king's journey on June 24 from the Louvre to the church at St.-Magloire, where his brother lay in an open coffin. It was the Feast of St. John, a time of ritual prayer and celebration. But not in 1584, not for the royal family, and not for the English ambassadorial residence in Paris, where Stafford and his wife ordered their servants to dress in black from head to foot, a fitting tribute to a prince who was a close friend of Queen Elizabeth. The next day the duke's body made its journey from St.-Magloire to Notre Dame. At the Parvis near the Hôtel-Dieu, the king himself was at an open window for much of the day, watching the procession carry his brother's body to its final resting place. Stafford had offered "to perform any honour to the dead body of him that my mistress loved and honoured so much," promising to follow the body along its route if the king wished him to. On Tuesday bearers took the prince's body to St.-Denis, sepulcher of generations of royals, where he was buried on Wednesday.[14]

Soon after the death of the prince, as Hakluyt prepared to leave for London to finish his work, news raced through the streets of Paris of yet another calamity. The Prince of Orange, a cousin to Queen Elizabeth who had in May been urging her to assist peace efforts launched by the duc D'Alençon, had been assassinated in Delft by Balthasar Gérard, an acquaintance of the prince. Immediately the English in Paris and elsewhere on the Continent recognized the gravity of the situation. They wrote frantic reports to their associates in London. George Gilpin, the secretary of the Merchants Adventurers at Middleburg, alerted Walsingham that the Prince of Orange had just finished his dinner "and went from the eating place to his chamber, even entering out of a door to go up the stairs." There he encountered a man from Burgundy, the same man who had told the prince about the death of the French duke. The man acted as if he had more news to convey, perhaps another letter. But rather than produce correspondence, he instead pulled out a pistol and shot the prince "under the breast, whereof he fell down dead in the place and never spake a word, to the wonderful grief of all there present." According to Joachim Ortel, the representative of the States of Holland to England, the shot pierced the prince's heart, killing him before he could speak. News of the killing spread rapidly across the English Channel. Details about the subsequent torture and death of the assassin attracted the attention of observers across Europe, including Englishmen who sent messages with the most recent reports.[15]

The assassination shocked and saddened those who knew and supported the prince. The queen sank into sorrow. Three weeks after the murder, Walsingham confided to Stafford that "no day passed without tears." When the antiquarian William Camden wrote his history of the first part of Elizabeth's reign, he noted that the assassination had triggered in the queen a fear that Philip II, a despot more dangerous than even his father, was poised to "subject all the rest of the Princes of Christendome to his greatnesse, unlesse hee were in time prevented."[16]

In the aftermath of the murder and execution, observers offered riveting, if sometimes conflicting, testimony about what had happened. William Herle, who had one month earlier been sent by Walsingham on a diplomatic mission to the Counts of Emden, investigated the murder for the English court. After sorting out the plot, Herle informed Elizabeth that it originated in the College of Jesus. Jesuits held to a maxim that "they be all Judiths that kill princes, and are therefore stirred up and warranted by the Pope to be canonized for the same, besides temporal advancements if they escape." Jesuits were seething at the imprisonment of William Carter, who had been sent to prison at Tyburn for a book he had printed in England sympathetic to Jesuits. Herle was convinced that members of the Society of Jesus had planned to undermine the queen's realm. Already more than a hundred Jesuits had traveled to England and Scotland, seditiously plotting Elizabeth's downfall.

L'Estoile focused his account on the trial and the assassin's alleged testimony, which included the promise from a Jesuit that "he would be lifted by waiting angels straight to Paradise." L'Estoile described the treatment of Gérard after the trial, adding that no angels had appeared to offer the divine escort that the assassin had been promised.[17]

To observers like Herle and L'Estoile, the assassination confirmed Protestant fears of Rome's intent to govern Europe as it saw fit, eliminating enemies who rose to challenge the power of the Catholic Church. The alliance between Rome and Spain logically worked in the Netherlands, where Protestants resisted capitulation to the Iberian monarchs. As early as 1567 Philip II had wanted to remove the Prince of Orange. In 1580 he announced a reward to anyone who would assassinate him, and his interest never waned. After the murder he rewarded the assassin's family.[18]

Yet if the goal of the assassination was to hasten the fall of the House of Orange and the Dutch people, Gérard, the Society of Jesus, and Philip II had all miscalculated. The "wickedness" of the murder, Walsingham knew by mid-July, had only made the Dutch more eager "to hold out as long as they shall have the means of defence." The time had come for other Protestants to rise to their aid. If they failed to do so, "they shall be forced ere Christmas next to become Spanish."[19]

But the story was not yet over. By the end of the summer a new book had appeared telling Gérard's tale. Hakluyt's boss in Paris, the ambassador Stafford, refused to send it to William Cecil in London, thinking that the book must have already arrived there.[20]

The Paris that Hakluyt knew was not always shrouded in funereal vestments. Though he was in the city when news of tragic deaths arrived, he never wavered from his mission. Walsingham sent him to Paris to find information about the possibilities for overseas expansion, and into the summer months he continued to gather evidence. In all likelihood he was in Paris when Thevet published an enormous book containing entries on esteemed authorities dating from antiquity to the present. Thevet wrote short biographies of earlier writers including Aristotle, Sappho, Thomas Aquinas, Herodotus, Hesiod, Hippocrates, Discorides, and Homer. But he also included prominent figures of his own age, including Cosimo de' Medici, Pietro Bembo, Philippe de Commines, Sebastian Münster, and Johannes Gutenberg—all figures whose works were known to Hakluyt. Perhaps most useful, Thevet published profiles of explorers. Within the pages of the book a reader could find information

In 1584, when Hakluyt had begun his travels between London and Paris, the French royal cosmographer André Thevet published an enormous book with portraits and brief biographies of notables, among them Christopher Columbus and the Incan emperor Atahualpa. From André Thevet, *Vrais Pourtraits des hommes illustres* (Paris, 1584) (HUNTINGTON LIBRARY)

about Columbus, Magellan, Amerigo Vespucci, Hernán Cortés, and Francisco Pizarro, as well as details about a small group of Americans, including the Incan emperor Atahualpa, the Aztec leader Moctezuma, an American native named Quoniambec, whom Thevet claimed he met during his journey to the western hemisphere, and a man named Paraovsti Satovriana, whom Thevet identified as the king of Florida. Each biography was illustrated, with the subject often set in a context associated with his achievement.[21]

Yet if Thevet provided his readers with "true" stories and pictures of famous authorities, a smaller book published in 1584 had a more direct impact on Hakluyt. That year the English minister David Powel put out an edition of Caradoc of Llancarvan's history of Wales. Translated by Humffrey Lloyd into English from the original "Brytish language" in which it had been written two hundred years earlier, the book told Welsh history in ways that were directly relevant to Hakluyt's project.[22]

Dedicated to Sir Philip Sidney, the son-in-law of Hakluyt's patron Walsingham, Powel's book told the history of Wales as it unfolded down to the year 1156. There were no secrets to be found here. As Powel noted, the text had long existed, first in two Welsh abbeys and later in perhaps one hundred manuscript copies, most dating to the fourteenth century. Tragically, Humffrey Lloyd died before he could finish the book and before he could have published other histories, so Powel had the text "committed to the presse." Though reluctant at first, Powell took the job because he agreed that the world needed to know Welsh history. He also wanted to halt the "slanderous" reports of writers who had earlier obscured the achievements of the Welsh people.[23]

According to this history, a murderous family dispute in north Wales had prompted the legendary twelfth-century Welsh prince Madoc to sail deep into the Atlantic in 1170, "leaving the coast of Ireland so far north, that he came to a land unknowen, where he saw manie strange things." This land, so Lloyd wrote, had to have been "part of that countrie of which the Spaniardes affirme themselves to be the first finders since Hannos time." The lessons of cosmography dictated that he found either Florida or New Spain. Hence it was clear that the British had discovered this land long before Columbus or Vespucci. In its aftermath, Madoc organized an even larger expedition.[24]

Lloyd presented proof that Madoc's tale was accurate. He noted that when some Europeans arrived in the western hemisphere, they found people who "honored the crosse[,] whereby it may be gathered that Christians had been there, before the coming of the Spaniards." Powell thought that Madoc and his followers must have landed and eventually lived in Mexico. To prove that point, he noted Hernán Cortés's account of the Spanish invasion included a speech in which "Mutezma [Moctezuma II] king of that countrie," told them that the leaders of the Aztecs were "descended from a strange nation" whose representatives had arrived on their shores from a distant land. More telling were certain linguistic clues. The Aztecs' language included words with British antecedents: "gwrando" for hearken or listen, and "pengwin" for a white head (used to refer to the flightless bird of the same name). "The Iland of Corroeso, the cape of Bryton, the river of Gwyndor, and the white rocke of Pengwyn, which be all Brytish or Welsh words" revealed that "it was that countrie which Madoc and his people inhabited."[25]

This story, affirmed by the survival of scores of manuscripts and a newly printed book, proved that the British were in North America 322 years before the Spanish got there. That was a point that Hakluyt never forgot.

By the time he settled down in London to put his thoughts in writing, Hakluyt had joined a small group of avid readers and travelers who had begun to grasp how the world had changed during the sixteenth century. From Christ Church to Paris, he had searched for information that would enable him to convince English policy makers that the time had come to launch a sustained effort at colonization. As the man behind *Divers Voyages*, he understood how important it was to put into print any evidence that could advance his goals, which he hoped would also become the goals of the English realm. As an advocate for public lectures on mathematics and navigation, he knew that information about the possibility of sailing across the open ocean should not be confined to a small audience but instead made available to a larger public. Colonization could occur only once there was real demand for it in England, and that demand could be created only by circulating ideas in public. Yet when he wrote the "Discourse on Western Planting" Hakluyt violated this core idea. Though the tract did contain personal information, including references to meetings he had had in Paris and things he had seen there, much of it came from material already in print.

In print, but not yet known to many. That was what Hakluyt realized in the summer of 1584. *Divers Voyages* had provided some evidence for a legitimate English claim to North America and information about what could be found there. But in the two years since he published it, he had gathered many more details. Some he had taken from printed books. Some came from personal contacts, such as his association with Thevet and Bellenger. But no one in England had yet compiled such material to make a comprehensive argument for colonization.

The "Discourse" was an extended work of propaganda. Hakluyt divided his material into twenty-one overlapping chapters, each making a related argument about the importance of colonization. He began by demonstrating how "western discoverie" would enlarge the world's number of Protestants, among whom the queen was the most important. No European nation could yet lay a claim to the territory lying north of Florida, in the vast expanse between 30 and 63 degrees North latitude. "Idolaters" dominated those climes, including Americans whom Magellan's pilot Stephen Gomes (Estevan Gomez) had plucked off the shores of Norumbega (modern northern New England) in 1524 who "worshipped the Sonne, the Moone, and the starres, and used other idolatrie." The denizens of Hochelaga (modern Montreal) were no better. They "worshippe a spirite which they call Cudruaigny," who told his followers what kind of weather to expect. But the authorities who bore witness to these heathenish ways, and whose views became fixed in the printed books of Ramusio and Cartier, could convert to Christianity under the proper tutelage. The Apostle Paul in Romans 10 had called for evangelicals to go among such unfortunates. Now that burden fell to "the Kinges and Queenes of England," who had taken upon themselves the "the name of Defendours of the Faithe." To Hakluyt, that title meant more than the obligation to lead the faithful. It also meant making an effort to spread the word and enlarge Christendom itself. Once English colonists learned how to speak to Americans, the newcomers would "by little and little acquainte themselves wth their manner, and so with discrecion and myldenes distill into their purged myndes the swete and lively lignes of the gospell." Of course, these colonists did need protection; even Spaniards toting Bibles had been killed in Florida because they lacked proper security.[26]

Hakluyt knew how to insert scriptural references to make his argument more persuasive, here using Matthew in addition to Paul. But the biblical exegesis he performed needed to be different since Hakluyt was simultaneously promoting reformed religion and attacking Rome. To that end he told his readers of the Portuguese successes in Brazil and the Spanish victories from Mexico to northern South America. Each nation had established an episcopal structure to promote its teaching of the gospel. The Portuguese, who had "erected many Bisshoprickes and Colledges to traine upp the youthe of the Infidells," boasted of their success. So did the Spanish, who in fifty years had constructed more than two hundred churches in the Americas.[27]

Hakluyt dwelled on these clerical successes to make a specific point. "Nowe yf they, in their superstition, by meanes of their planting in those partes, have don so greate thinges in so shorte space," he argued, "what may wee hope for in our true and syncere Relligion" if the English launched their own evangelical program? The Iberians had conflated their religious quest with their insatiable desire for "filthie lucre" and "vaine ostentation." The English, by contrast, needed to enlighten "the soules of millions of those wretched people," and reduce them "from darkenes to lighte, from fals-hoodde to truthe, from dombe Idolls to the lyvinge god, from the depe pitt of hell to the highest heavens." Earlier English efforts to spread their faith had failed, an echo of the frustrations suffered by Paul when he sought conversions in Asia. But the failures of earlier Protestant evangelicals need not mean that the English should abandon the field. Instead, the time had come to try again since "the people of America crye oute unto us their nexte neighboures to comme and helpe them, and bringe unto them the gladd tidinges of the gospell."[28]

Hakluyt then turned from religion to economics. He described how English trades had become "beggerly or daungerous," especially wherever the Spanish had extended their empire, a situation that had forced the English abroad to "flinge their Bibles and prayer Bokes into the sea" and to renounce their beliefs (and their allegiance to the queen). Hakluyt sketched the problems that English sailors and merchants had across Europe and the East. Along the Barbary Coast English ships were seized by the Spanish and those onboard were forced either to renounce their religion or to become victims of the Inquisition. Algerian pirates threatened any English vessel that sailed into Turkish waters, and merchants paid bribes to keep their vessels safe. English trade to France had declined because of levies on imported goods and protectionist efforts to keep better-made English cloth out of the French market, often on the pretext that the English were peddling inferior wares. The English faced challenges like these across Europe. Eighteen years of civil wars had destroyed the markets for imports in Flanders and the Low Countries. The Danish king's ability to confiscate English ships discouraged merchants from sending their wares into Denmark. Russia offered no better prospects. After cultivating officials there to improve trade earlier, the English in 1584 watched jealously as the Russians opened their ports to Dutch merchants without forcing them into the payments that the English had had to make to gain entrée. The death that year of the Russian emperor raised new fears that what trade still existed might be destroyed.[29]

The bleak markets on the Continent should have been enough to motivate any English merchant to seek new targets. But, Hakluyt added, more than economics made the situation dangerous. English merchants and sailors had to swear an oath of loyalty to the Catholic Church if they ventured into the domain controlled by Philip II. After that degrading ceremony, enterprising merchants had to agree to haul goods only to the destinations that Spanish bureaucrats designated. They also had to allow their goods to be searched to make sure that no one was smuggling illegal books. The indignations ended only after the English bribed any local priests who came seeking provisions. Those successful at passing the gatekeepers might have made a profit, but at a terrible cost for those along for the ride, who also had to accept the Catholic Church. "Thus the covetous marchante wilfully sendeth headlonge to hell from day to day the poore subjectes of this Realme," Hakluyt concluded. "The marchant in England commeth here devoutly to the communyon, and sendeth his sonne into Spaine to here masse."[30]

The only logical solution to this intolerable situation was for the English to embrace the offerings of the Americas. Repeating the claim he had made two years earlier in *Divers Voyages,* Hakluyt asserted that the English had a "juste Title" to American territory north of Florida from the discoveries made by Sebastian Cabot under the auspices of King Henry VII, a claim that Ramusio himself supported a generation earlier. He then launched into a long description of the natural treasures of this region. Using the writings of Jean Ribault, Hakluyt recounted the diverse splendors to be found between 30 and 34 degrees North latitude. The English would find everything they wanted in this land of abundant game, dense forests, silkworms "in marvelous nomber," and fertile fields, a place where the meadows were so filled with birds that it was "a plesure not able to be expressed with tongue." Enterprising searchers could find pearls, turquoise, copper, silver, and gold. Florida's sassafras trees, whose virtues had been described in Monardes's *Joyfull Newes out of the newe founde worlde,* could cure any number of deathly afflictions.[31]

Hakluyt intended the "Discourse" to be a private document, but it included much information that had long circulated in print. In addition to the writings of Ramusio and Monardes, he drew extensively from the works of those who traveled to the Americas, the "printed Testimonies of John

Verarsanus and Stephen Gomes," originally written in 1524 and treating territory north of 34 degrees. The testimony about Norumbega, which had
begun to appear in European descriptions of North America before the mid-
sixteenth century, came from Gomes's description, which had been translated
into Italian by Gonsalvo de Oviedo and printed as part of his account of the
West Indies published in Venice in 1534. He then followed with information
drawn from an unnamed French captain from Dieppe, originally published
by Ramusio, who sailed along the coast between 40 and 47 degrees. Again,
Hakluyt used the Italian version of the text to describe the how the natives
lived peaceably near Norumbega, where the land itself offered up an abundance of produce for them. He derived his critique of Spanish imperial
ambition from his reading of Bartolomé de Las Casas's devastating account,
which had been published in English the previous year (and would come to
play a crucial role in English views of Spanish conquest in the Americas).[32]

Hakluyt's use of information he had picked up in conversations and in
reading private manuscripts confirmed Walsingham's belief that Paris was a
city where valuable intelligence could be found. Hence Hakluyt relayed the
information he had gathered from Bellenger, including details of castoreum
and the various pelts the French had obtained. He emphasized that the
profits Bellenger made in North America enticed other French investors,
including the marquis de la Roche, who only that year had taken three
hundred men on a colonizing expedition to the area. But the Atlantic again
proved its abilities to halt such efforts when the three-hundred-ton main ship
wrecked near "Burwage" (Brouage), ending French colonization attempts
that year.[33]

Other contacts were even more useful than Bellenger. Hakluyt provided
details about Hochelaga taken from the account of Jacques Cartier's two
voyages—the information that he had gotten when he examined the manuscript copy in the king's library in Paris. Cartier, like others, extolled the
abundance of nature, listing the trees, birds, animals, and minerals to be
found in North America. He also mentioned a vast freshwater inland sea and
hinted at the existence of the Northwest Passage. Natives informed Cartier
that it was but a one-month journey by water to a land where cloves and
cinnamon could be found.[34]

Much of the information in the document concentrated on the resources
of the Atlantic coast, but Hakluyt was keen, too, to describe "the commodities
of the Inlande." To do so, he once again relied on reports that had appeared in
Ramusio. He thus provided details from Coronado's journey to Cíbola and

parts of Francisco López de Gómara's history of the Indies that described Coronado's travels through the American interior from Cíbola to Quivera. He wrote, too, about Newfoundland, drawing on George Peckham's recently published report of Sir Humphrey Gilbert's journey of 1583, the long letter in Latin that Parmenius had sent him in 1583, and the report of the Portuguese navigator Gaspar Corte Real's journey in 1500 that Ramusio had published. Here Hakluyt's linguistic abilities paid off: the details from Peckham were written in English, from Parmenius in Latin, and Corte Real in Italian. The Portuguese voyage, intended to go to the Spice Islands, ventured far northward, enabling Hakluyt (and other readers of Ramusio) to glean information about what was to be found as far north as 60 degrees North latitude. He then relied on Frobisher's accounts "in freshe memorye" to provide information about the waters and lands between 60 and 63 degrees.[35]

Taken together, these reports from "credible persons" who had seen America north of 30 degrees North latitude provided unassailable proof that everything Europeans wanted could be found in the western hemisphere. The list would have dazzled any reader: gold, silver, emeralds, and pearls; "spices and drugs," including cinnamon, cloves, and musk from beavers; superb silkworms; "infinite multitudes of all kinde of beastes, w[i]th their tallowe and hides dressed and undressed"; dyestuffs to produce many colors for clothes; "millions of all kindes of fowles for foode and fethers"; salt, vines, fruit trees, and naval stores. There were also "excedinge quantitie of all kynde of precious furres," for which Hakluyt himself had become a witness at the workplaces of Valeron Perosse and Matthew Grainer, the royal skinners. Hakluyt could not contain his enthusiasm. "I may well and truly conclude with reason and aucthoritie," he claimed, "that all the commodities of all our olde decayed and daungerous trades in all Europe, Africa, and Asia" could be found for little or no cost in America, but only if the English got there before others who could just as easily take control of this lucrative market.[36]

There were other economic incentives, too, as Hakluyt knew. Following logic first put into print by Gilbert in his *Discourse* of 1576, Hakluyt argued that colonization could address the chronic unemployment and underemployment that plagued English society. Why were there so many pirates and thieves in England and France but not in Spain or Portugal? The answer was obvious. Since the Iberians created American colonies, men who might otherwise commit crimes instead found work either in the new settlements or processing the goods that came back on ships loaded with the natural resources of the western hemisphere. But would-be criminals still remained in the queen's realm. No law had yet halted the mischievous actions of the poor in England. Even the execution of petty thieves did not deter crime.[37]

Hakluyt wedded the dangers posed by vagabonds to opportunities available in North America. It would be better to commit criminals to forced labor in the western hemisphere than to hang them. These miscreants could saw trees for masts and boards. They could watch over the burning of trees and the production of rosin, tar, and turpentine. They could be set to work in mines, drag shallow waterways for pearls, tend to silkworms, or farm. Other Europeans had already shown how such a system could work. The Portuguese had their settlers plant sugarcane in Madeira, thereby transforming the Atlantic island into a profitable plantation. In the Azores the Portuguese had their colonists sow madder and woad, dyestuffs needed for clothing. Little talent or training was needed to extract salt, which was necessary to preserve fish for transport back to Europe. There was also demand for crews on fishing and whaling vessels, and for stonecutters to hew the marble and jet that could be used as ballast on eastward voyages and then used to construct "noble buildings" at home. Men who might prowl the streets of London would be better off building forts, towns, and churches in new English settlements abroad.[38]

Though the colonies would become places to dispose of unwanted people, Hakluyt also recognized that even miscreants could play a crucial role in economic development. They would become consumers as well as producers. He reminded his readers that the native peoples of Canada and Hochelaga had already become eager purchasers of European clothing, especially woolens that helped them cope with their "colde and sharpe" winters. To meet their needs, and the needs of others who would soon join them in North America, people working in the clothing trades in England would find employment. "Cappers, knitters, clothiers, wollmen, carders, spynners, weavers, fullers, sheremen, dyers, drapers, hatters and such like" would find work again, "whereby many decayed townes may be repaired." The growing colonial population would create jobs for others in England—"namely all severall kindes of artificers, husbandmen, seamen, marchauntes, souldiers, capitaines, phisitions, lawyers, devines, Cosmographers, hydrographers, Astonomers, historiographers." Even those who did not customarily work for wages would find employment. According to Hakluyt, "olde folkes, lame persons, women, and younge children" would also be "kepte from idlenes, and be made able by their owne honest and easie labour to finde themselves w[i]thoute surchardginge others." The success that the English had recently had providing clothing to the Dutch was proof that such a system would work. If the queen embraced colonization in North America, the cloth trade westward across the Atlantic would likely soon surpass the trade to the East.[39]

If all of this evidence were still not enough, Hakluyt offered one more startling opinion to demonstrate the urgent necessity of colonization. In the 1580s evidence for England's overpopulation was growing. The able-bodied could not find work, and many turned to crime as their only way to survive. Hakluyt's argument was more subtle than the foolish claim that the "swarm-inge of beggars" meant that "the Realme is too populous." The problem was just the reverse. England was not as strong as it could be because lack of employment had discouraged young men and women from marrying and procreating. But if those same young people came to believe that their economic prospects could be bright, they would no longer abstain. The English needed to become more industrious, something that would only happen once the population grew even larger and embraced the emerging transatlantic economy. More sailors would be needed to travel back and forth across the ocean. Men and women would be needed to people the new settlements. Those who made shoes and cloth in England would need to increase their labor to provide for the colonists. The Spanish had found an enormous market for linens in their American possessions. So could the English if they produced similar goods. The market would be ever expansive, and so, too, the incentive to production that would encourage population growth at home.[40]

After laying out the core economic argument for westward expansion, Hakluyt turned to matters of politics and foreign affairs. Having just come from Paris, with news of the assassination of the Prince of Orange fresh in his mind, Hakluyt was aware that Philip II may have played a direct role in the murder of the queen's cousin. What better time to emphasize that English settlement in America and increased English shipping in the Atlantic would become a weapon to annoy and possibly weaken the Spanish king? By estab-lishing forts north of Florida along the Atlantic coast, the English could use the prevailing winds to their advantage. Hakluyt knew that the clockwise circulation of winds in the area bounded by Cuba, Florida, and the Bahamas meant that ships leaving the West Indies invariably sailed toward the coast of the mainland before heading eastward. Since the Spanish had already become the mortal enemies of Florida's native peoples, the English would find fast allies among the Americans who already delighted in murdering Spaniards whenever they had the chance. Again, Hakluyt's stay in Paris helped him to make this argument since he had managed to read a recently published book by the Sieur de La Popelinière, which offered vivid proof of one bloody encounter. An alliance with "these Savages" would be an ideal way to get back at the Spanish for arming "our Irishe Rebells." The Spanish were terrified of such an alliance, as Hakluyt had heard from the English captain Moffet he had met in Paris the previous winter. Philip's fears could also prevent him from seizing English ships if he believed that "his navye in newfounde lande is no lesse in our danger then ours is in his domynions wheresoever."[41]

Yet if Philip feared the future, the recent decades had been very good to his realm. Hakluyt drew on various authors to demonstrate the power that the treasure fleets had brought the Spanish since the early sixteenth century. With that wealth Charles V had managed to expand Spanish control across Europe, dominating much of France, Italy, Germany, and the Netherlands. He had taken the pope prisoner and sacked the Holy See. In Hakluyt's opinion, this gain had allowed Philip to use his American wealth "to the afflictinge and oppressinge of moste of the greatest estates of Christendomme." It had allowed him to finance schemes to assassinate the Portuguese pretender Don Antonio. Wasn't it also with this wealth that he had "hired at sondry times the sonnes of Beliall to bereve the Prince of Orange of his life"? The list of Philip's depredations was a monument to the staggering insolence of "this Spanishe asse" and the power that he gained from his overseas possessions. With American treasure he had financed rebellion in Ireland and Scotland, aided disaffected English "unnaturall rebelles," supported seminarians in Reims and Rome "to be thornes in the sides of their owne common wealthes," and "suborned by hope of rewarde other moste ungodly persons to lay violent handes upon other Christian princes." As Philips Van Marnix had warned in a recent book published in Dutch, Latin, French, Italian, and English, Catholics with the energy of bees would not desist unless someone stopped them.[42]

But what could the English do to reduce such power? Hakluyt believed that the Spanish empire as it existed could be weakened, perhaps even toppled, if Philip's enemies knew how to attack it. In his mind, the key was in the west. Spain's American possessions lay "farr distante from one another," Hakluyt argued, "and are kepte by great tyrannie, and *quos metuunt oderunt* [hate those whom they fear]. And the people kepte in subjection desire nothinge more then freedome." Philip could be overthrown by a rebellion started in the West Indies, which would disrupt the treasure fleets and open up Spain itself for attack, possibly by Moors. Such actions would lead to a general rebellion in all Spanish territory, where oppressed local people would "cutt the throates of the proude hatefull Spaniardes their governours."[43]

Hakluyt claimed that the Spanish were thin on the ground in the West Indies. They kept control not through force of arms but instead because they had managed to convince the indigenous peoples that they could amass enormous armies if necessary. He suggested that the Americans were hardly alone in falling for such tactics. After all, the ancient Britons had succumbed to the Romans for precisely the same reason: a fear that the newcomers represented only a small fraction of a vast population that could be mustered if needed. English captains with hands on experience in New Spain knew the truth: "the Ilandes there abounde with people and nations that rejecte the proude and bluddy governemente of the Spaniarde, and that doo mortally hate the Spaniarde." Moors hauled by the Spanish to work as slaves in mines had escaped to the interiors of the islands, where they sought any opportunity to harass their former owners. Drake had the connections with the "Symerons" (*cimmarones,* or escaped slaves) to pilfer the Spanish treasure fleet, thereby allowing the English to profit from America's rich mines. Just preventing the wealth from entering Spain would make Philip II "a laughinge stocke for all the worlde," a creature like Aesop's crow, who lost his bright feathers to other birds. "If you touche him in the Indies, you touche the apple of his eye," Hakluyt noted, "for take away his treasure which is *nervus belli,* and which he hath almoste oute of his west Indies, his olde bandes of souldiers will soone be dissolved, his purposes defeated, his power and strengthe diminished, his pride abated, and his tyranie utterly suppressed."[44]

One of Hakluyt's Parisian informants, Custodio Etan (Leitão), the secretary to Don Antonio, confirmed his assessment of Iberian strength abroad. Leitan told him that the Portuguese never stationed many soldiers in their overseas holdings. They controlled Brazil, Guinea, and their possessions in the East Indies with fewer than twelve thousand men in arms, a fact confirmed by an unnamed informant born in Goa. The Portuguese "governed rather by gevinge out of great rumors of power and by secrecie then by any greate force which they had in deede." Ortelius's recent maps revealed the limited extent of Spanish power. Contrary to popular opinion, the Spanish controlled no territory south of the Tropic of Capricorn or north of the Tropic of Cancer. Ortelius's maps bore witness to the paucity of forts north of the equator; Drake's report of Peru revealed the weakness of Spain's southern holdings. Philip II did lay claim to vast territory, Hakluyt knew, but such assertions were the products of delusion. "Somme of his Contries are dis-peopled, somme barren, somme so far asonder also held by Tyranie, that in deede upon the due consideracion of the matter, his mighte and greatenes is not such as *prima facie* yt may seme to be." Were it not for the wealth the Spanish received from the treasure fleets, a French king "of one onely king-domme" would possess the power to force Philip II out of his entire worldly holdings. Once the English realized how weak the Spanish were in New Spain, they would be embarrassed that they once stood in awe of "feble scarr crowes."[45]

And so it went in the "Discourse"—back and forth between ideas that had come from printed books and those from personal observation, insights from interviews combined with the vast storehouse of knowledge that Hakluyt already possessed. The logic of westward expansion was so obvious to him that parts of the discourse consisted of little more than bits of information piled on top of each other. In Paris Hakluyt had acquired a report from an unnamed French captain who either sailed in the Caribbean and along the Atlantic coast of New Spain or gleaned information from others. Hakluyt inserted his insights because he trusted his judgment as the "moste experte and privie to the state and force of the Ilandes, havens, Townes, and fortes" of this extensive region.[46]

Hakluyt the geographer offered up brief accounts of islands and coasts to demonstrate what America was like. But Hakluyt the propagandist for west-ward expansion had additional motives. The information taken from the French captain and unnamed other sources revealed that the Spanish hold on the Americas was precarious. He likened it to the fable of the ass who clothed himself in the skin of a lion to fool others, only to be espied by the fox, who uncovered the deceit. "In like manner wee (upon perill of my life) shall make the Spaniarde ridiculous to all Europe," Hakluyt added, "if with percinge eyes wee see into his contemptible weakenes in the west Indies, and with true stile painte hym out *ad vivium* unto the worlde in his fainte colours." There was no excuse for not trying to take over, especially since the Portuguese bore an unceasing "naturall malice" toward the Spanish.[47]

The "Discourse" was uneven in many ways. Hakluyt emphasized some arguments more than others, and he embellished whenever he could by using arresting images from other writers. He expressed some ideas economically, either because he had little to say on the subject or because he thought the point obvious. Hakluyt knew that voyages to America could be quick because Bellenger had told him so the year before. Just as important, a journey from

England to North America need not pass any dangerous territories where English ships could be raided. There was no danger "of the Cursaries in the levant, nor of the Gallies of Barbarie, nor of the Turke, nor of any state of Italie, neither of the Spaniarde, the frenche, nor the Dane, nor of any other Prince nor Potentate within the sounde in the northe or in the northeaste partes of the worlde." Even storms would not prove disastrous since English ships could often reach the coast of Ireland in the event of trouble. Besides, frequent travel back and forth would also hinder the Spanish, who often relied on the Irish for supplies. Nor would any fear being seized by the Inquisition, forced to throw Protestant Bibles into the sea, or obliged to swear the kinds of "horrible oaths" that the Spanish demanded.[48]

Hakluyt felt no need to dwell on matters that needed little justification. In a brief chapter he argued that westward voyages would increase the queen's revenue, in part through fees levied against ships hauling fish, train oil, and animal skins. Wherever trade existed, money could be made if the English knew how to take advantage of existing opportunities, such as offering Welsh and Irish woolens to Indians inhabiting cold climates. In another chapter he argued that frequent voyages would be a boon to the vibrant English shipping industry as well as a support to the countless people who worked in ancillary trades. Whole towns could be supported by shipping, not only sailors and captains and their families. The industry needed butchers, brewers, rope-makers, smiths, shoemakers, tailors, and others who provided the food and goods needed for a transatlantic voyage. The English would also gain from the knowledge acquired by people who took these "longe voyadges," since their experience would "harden seamen and open unto them the secretes of navigation, the nature of the windes, the currentes and settinge of the Sea, the ebbinge and flowinge of the mayne Ocean, the influence of the sonne, the moone, and of the rest of the celestiall planetts." He returned again to advocating an annual lecture in navigation, noting that the Spanish king Charles V had in fact established such an annual event and required that everyone who commanded a vessel to the West first absorb the expert commentary on the subject. He added that such an arrangement in England might have prevented the deaths of Gilbert and his men, who perished because of the unfortunate advice of those "grosse and insufficient felowes" who had led them into danger.[49]

Hakluyt urged rapid colonization so that the English could maintain control over parts of the Americas. Without a quick commitment, the colonies would fail, a point that Hakluyt knew well from his reading of Ramusio and other descriptions of European efforts to settle in the Americas. He also knew that the French, who had recently returned from Canada (accompanied by two Americans), planned to go back soon. The Dutch would launch colonizing missions, too, if they had the opportunity, an idea Hakluyt learned seven years earlier when Ortelius had paid him a visit "to prye and looke into the secretes of Frobishers voyadge." If the English delayed their efforts, he argued, "the frenche, the Normans, the Brytons, or the duche, or somme other nation will not onely prevente us of the mightie Baye of St. Laurence where they have gotten the starte of us already, thoughe wee had the same revealed to us by bookes published and printed in Englishe before them, but also will deprive us of that goodd lande which nowe wee have discovered." Only fast action could halt the peopling of North America by Catholics who would "inriche themselves under our noses" or even eventually overrun the English. If the English settled in desirable places, such as at the mouths of rivers, they would succeed if they quickly built sawmills to transform trees into boards. Once established, Hakluyt asked, "what noble man, what gentleman, what marchante, what citizen or contryman will not offer of himselfe to contribute and joyne in the action?" No one could resist such a venture that would be profitable to those involved, provide opportunities for the younger brothers of noble families who had few options at home, and supply jobs for the "idle" people who always lurked on the streets of England (and in Hakluyt's mind).[50]

Quick action could also enable the English to find and control the Northwest Passage, something that Hakluyt knew from an informant he cultivated who told him a man from St.-Malo "this laste yere discovered the sea on the backside of Hochelaga." But one need not cross the channel to learn this information. Hakluyt had also seen a map in Michael Lok's possession that revealed the passage, as did the globe in the queen's gallery at Westminster. David Ingram, author of a recent book about his travels, also claimed the existence of this route. Besides, Hakluyt added, Philip II's prohibition against exploration north of 45 degrees North latitude meant that the Spanish knew that the Northwest Passage existed but that they lacked any means to people the region or to defend it from others. The time had come for the English to lay claim to the passage. Even God was on their side, or at least so he told the queen.[51]

Only rarely did Hakluyt feel the need to rehearse extensive arguments. He treated two issues at length that on the surface seem obvious: the deplorable way the Spaniards treated Americans and the legitimacy of the queen's right to North America. On the first point he repeated many of Las Casas's most lurid accusations, echoing the recent English translation presumably known to Walsingham and others in Elizabeth's court. The Spanish had "exercised moste outragious and more then Turkishe cruelties" across the West Indies, an accusation that placed the conquistadors and their ilk in a league populated by the most despised individuals known to western Europeans.[52]

Rather than describe all of the Spaniards' excesses, Hakluyt limited himself to some of the most shocking. He used Las Casas's claim that the Spanish depredations had "dispeopled and made desolate more then tenne Realmes greater than all Spaine comprisinge therein also Arragon and Portingale," a landscape more than a thousand leagues long (the distance greater than from Seville to Jerusalem), which "remaine in a wildernes and utter desolation, having bene before time as well peopled as was possible." How many did the Spanish kill? Las Casas claimed twelve million, a figure Hakluyt increased to fifteen million. The tortures were unspeakable. Spanish soldiers disemboweled men and women. Decapitated whomever they wanted. Ripped babies from the breasts of their mothers and smashed their heads against walls. Roasted local leaders alive. Hanged people with impunity, and chopped off the hands of others. Conquistadors laughed when they tossed young children in rivers and watched them drown, stabbing with their swords any parents who might try to save their offspring. The situation violated every known moral code.[53]

Hakluyt's depiction of the English right to the western hemisphere lacked the moral fervor of his assessment of Spanish atrocities. But as a piece of propaganda it was just as effective. He feared that the queen might listen to those who doubted the realm's claims to the West Indies and to the land on the mainland between Florida and the arctic circle. To convince her that such doubters were wrong, he created a historical argument based on prior discovery, the same strategy he had used in *Divers Voyages*. Here he claimed that the ocean voyages of the Welsh prince Madoc in 1170 meant that the English via their Welsh subjects could lay claim to the West Indies since they had seen them three centuries before Columbus arrived. He also argued that Bartholomew Columbus's earlier dealings with King Henry VII gave the English a right to Christopher Columbus's discoveries. The fact that Christopher had made his voyage with the support of Ferdinand and Isabella was irrelevant to Hakluyt. He sought their assistance only because he grew impatient waiting for his brother to return from England. Besides, Columbus merely discovered the islands of the Caribbean. It was John Cabot who made it to the mainland and thus solidified the English claim to North America. Ramusio supported this argument. So did La Popelinière, who in his recently published book had argued that Cabot made it to Florida first, thereby giving the rights to that place to the English. Even Columbus's supporters Peter Martyr and his son Ferdinand could only claim that the Admiral of the Ocean Sea had encountered the mainland in 1498, two years after Cabot.[54]

Near the end of the "Discourse" Hakluyt felt compelled to dismiss the Bull Inter caetera of May 4, 1493, the document under which Pope Alexander VI had divided the West into Spanish and Portuguese spheres. Hakluyt had no patience for a treatise he felt ill-advised and inappropriate. "It is the Popes manner alwayes to meddle as in this matter, so in other thinges where they have nothinge to doe," he wrote, "and to intrude themselves before they be called." There was ample biblical precedent cautioning against such rash acts. The popes had no powers of prophecy that enabled them to know the will of God, no ability to determine which monarch God favored in a dispute. They did not even possess enough information about the size and extent of the newly discovered territories to make a rational judgment. Why had Alexander VI acted as he did? Because he was himself a Spaniard, Hakluyt argued, who recognized the benefits to accrue to Spain by giving this vast territory to Ferdinand and Isabella. By purchasing the loyalty of the Spanish he also ensured that the Holy See would become rich. But Hakluyt argued at length that the Vatican lacked the power to make such a division of a part of the earth that was larger than Europe and Africa combined. The pope had no biblical authority to perform such an act. Even a Protestant less devout than Elizabeth would have dismissed the bull as yet another symptom of the depravity of the Church of Rome.[55]

Hakluyt ended the "Discourse" with chapters restating the reasons for westward expansion, detailing the provisions needed on transatlantic voyages, and identifying the ideal kinds of individuals who would be necessary from the start to make the colonies as he envisioned them successful. His list of provisions needed for the journey reflected his conversations with mariners who had made long-distance voyages. Even though he had never traveled farther by ship than across the English Channel, he knew the importance of supplies of meat, cheese, spices, vegetables, and alcohol for travelers who could be at sea for six weeks or longer. Barreled provisions would get them across the ocean, perhaps just barely. Once they arrived they would need individuals skilled at providing for all of their needs—cooks, bakers, those who knew how to make and fix nets for fishing, gardeners, hunters, and those skilled in breeding rabbits and ridding fields of pests. They would need seed to plant their first grains and dogs trained to do work that individuals could not do. Greyhounds were ideal for killing deer, bloodhounds for finding deer that were injured in the hunt, and mastiffs for protecting settlements at night from human or beastly intruders. The first settlements would need men who knew how to build forts, use harquebuses and arrows, and produce saltpeter and gunpowder. Shipwrights and makers of oars and sails had to be ready to fix oceangoing vessels and make small boats that settlers would need to trawl inland waterways. And artisans drawn from the chronically underemployed of English cities would have ample work building and tending mills, making pitch and tar, preserving the colors from cochineal needed for dyes, preparing bricks, running lathes, and quarrying for the right stones for tiles. Shoemakers, tanners, "Bottlemakers of London," skinners, barbers, and preachers would need to be on hand to serve the colonists' needs. Surgeons, apothecaries, and physicians would tend to the bodies of any struck by disease or accident. If honey could be found in America, settlers could make mead, a drink popular in Poland, Russia, and north Wales, where it was used as a substitute for wine. Catholics should be barred from voyages since they had predispositions to support the Spanish. Of the Protestants who went, it was best to find "stronge and lusty men" who would be most able to defend the nascent communities. Merchants who had fared poorly, who had been "schooled in the house of adversitie," could make valuable contributions if they were offered the necessary inducements.[56]

Hakluyt, whose life had been lived in libraries and reading books, recognized the importance of books for the voyagers. They needed Bibles, of course, which preachers could use in their daily ministrations, a chore that would reduce the risk of mutiny. But there also needed to be the kinds of books that Hakluyt himself had been devouring: travel accounts. Settlers needed "bookes of the discoveries and conquests of the easte Indies." They also needed "bookes of the discoveries of the west Indies and the conquestes of the same." These tracts were needed "to kepe men occupied from worse cogitations, and to raise their myndes to courage and highe enterprizes and to make them lesse careles for the better shonnynge of common daungers in suche cases arisinge."[57]

That last request became a fitting epitaph for the "Discourse." Hakluyt produced this document because he believed in the power of words, especially the written word. If he could convince a reluctant queen to embrace the colonial mission, then the words of others who had survived travails in the western hemisphere should be sufficient to keep even the most restless young man from breaking the law. Settlers had economic incentive for traveling across the Atlantic. Travel narratives could be a means for making sure that their sights remained fixed on the mission's higher purpose.[58]

The "Discourse" reflected Hakluyt's understanding of England. Twin dangers faced the nation: Catholic Europe and domestic poverty. Henry VII's lack of vision a century earlier had effectively excluded England from the wealth of the Indies. Had the treasure fleets been bound for Bristol instead of Seville, the domestic problems of the English would have disappeared, as Hakluyt believed they had in Spain. But Hakluyt chose not to condemn a century of English inactivity. Instead, he praised those who did manage to sail to the West. They were the worthies of England.

Yet if he did not criticize an earlier royal reluctance to embrace westward voyages, he felt no constraints in his assessment of English society. The problem with England was that its economy did not function properly. Merchants found markets closed to them, and many suffered as a result. There was no stability for artisans and unskilled workers who owned little, and thus no incentive for them to work harder or procreate. As a result, they wandered the countryside or prowled the dark streets of England's cities. In either locale they committed crimes, and for those crimes they were often sentenced to die. That assessment demonstrated some sympathy for the miscreants who awaited the noose: the fault lay, after all, not with an individual man or woman but instead with a damaged and precarious economy.

Hakluyt lived very much within the mental horizons of his day. He believed in the power of words, written or spoken. He saw troubles and engineered solutions from the premise that it was the task, even the burden, of the intellectual elite to diagnose problems and find answers. The opinions that shaped his argument came from merchants, mariners, and explorers. These authorities provided the clues needed to establish settlements abroad. His task was to bring these sources together and to use their insights to craft a plan for planting colonies.

By any measure, the "Discourse" was remarkable. Hakluyt distilled the most up-to-date information about the western hemisphere into one document. He took scattered ideas and gave them a shape. Once he assembled the pieces, the conclusion was inescapable. England had to embrace western expansion. Failure to do so would guarantee ruin at home.

With the completion of the "Discourse," Hakluyt had in some ways reached the height of his intellectual achievements. True, the prose of the document was rough, and many of the ideas had come from Ramusio and others. But to criticize its flaws misses its effect. Never before had Hakluyt or anyone else in England managed to craft a comprehensive rationale for westward expansion. Others could have composed a lesser treatise, including those who actually traveled to America and saw it for themselves. Yet the opportunity came to Hakluyt, who had traveled only a few hundred miles in his life and, before his venture to Paris in 1583, never beyond London and Oxford.

Hakluyt's travels were limited, but the expanse of his imagination was unique. He could have written much—perhaps most—of the "Discourse" without crossing to Paris. He did, after all, compose *Divers Voyages* having journeyed no farther than the two cities that bounded his life before 1583. But his journey to Paris gave Hakluyt credibility that he would otherwise have lacked. Had he stayed home he could not have consulted a Cartier manuscript owned by King Henri III. He could not have seen the storehouse of animal skins kept by the royal furrier Perosse. He could not have interviewed Bellenger. He could not have acquired the unpublished report of the anonymous French captain who provided details about the towns and ports of the Caribbean and the mainland colonies of New Spain. The information that Hakluyt gained in Paris and the people he met there enabled him to add details that would have otherwise been impossible to know.

From Oxford to London to Paris to London. From inchoate notions to a complex piece of propaganda. From words perhaps whispered in confidence to sentences and paragraphs composed on secret pages intended for the queen's eyes. Hakluyt had begun to recover from the traumas of the year that the sea devoured his friends. By doing so, he began to fulfill the promise of his life.

In mid-September, the explorers Philip Amadas and Arthur Barlowe returned to England after a voyage to the coast of modern-day North Carolina. Hakluyt had no time to integrate their views into the "Discourse," which he had by then almost completed. On October 5, Hakluyt presented his work to the queen. On the same day he also presented her an analysis of Aristotle's *Politics,* another document that would not reach a printer. Two days later he left again for Paris, carrying a package from Walsingham to the ambassador. A week later he was back in Paris with Stafford.[59] As he traveled to the European mainland once again in the service of the realm, his thoughts remained fixed in the opposite direction.

CHAPTER 8

Paris and London, 1584 to 1589
Cabinets and Curiosities

S ometime in mid- to late 1580s, Hakluyt visited two cabinets of curiosity
in England. They belonged to men named Richard Garth and Walter
Cope. Garth's cabinet and virtually all information about him have
long since disappeared. Cope, a member of the Elizabethan Society of Antiquaries, also left scant trace in the historical record even though he was a close
friend of the chronicler and surveyor John Stow. But he had frequent visitors
to his house, including a German named Thomas Platter who traveled to
London in 1599 and left a detailed inventory of the things that Cope had
accumulated during his journeys.[1]

When Hakluyt arrived at Cope's house, he was no doubt led, like Platter,
"into an apartment, stuffed with queer foreign objects in every corner." Like
the cabinets kept by many Europeans on the Continent, Cope's contained an
eclectic assortment. There was an "African charm made of teeth," a "handsome cap made out of goosefoots from China," the mummy of a child, paper
made from bark, and a "Madonna made of Indian feathers." From India
Cope had a "chain made of monkey teeth." He had collected instruments,
too, many made of bone, though a forlorn stringed instrument had only a
single string. There were weapons made from wood, stone, leather, and the
bones of fish, and an Indian ax "like a thunder-bolt." Clothing came from
China, Arabia, Java, and India. Saddles "from many strange lands" were
"placed round the top on stands."

Along with the clothing and tools, Cope collected the extraordinary remnants of nature. He had "all kinds of corals and sea-plants in abundance," a
rhinoceros horn and tail, the "twisted horn of a bull seal," a "falcon's head
made of fine feathers," a hairy caterpillar, a "sea mouse (mus marinus)," a
fish he called a "Remora," which could hinder any boat, and another un-

named species that "petrifies and numbs the crews' hands if it so much as touches the oars." He had the tail of a unicorn and the beak of a pelican, "the Egyptian bird that kills its young, and afterwards tears open its breast and bathes them in its own blood, until they have come to life." He also had crowns made from the claws of ungulates, and a "sea-halcyon's nest, sign of a calm sea." Platter learned from Cope that fireflies he had from the mainland of North America were used "instead of lights, since there is often no day there for over a month."[2]

Cope's taste for the marvelous knew no bounds. He managed to acquire bells and baubles from the fool of Henry VIII and the seal of Queen Elizabeth. He also stored the "Turkish Emperor's golden seal" as well as "many holy relics from a Spanish ship which he helped to capture." But more remarkable were the things from nature that defied easy explanation. He somehow obtained a "round horn which had grown on an English woman's forehead," one of the signs of a monster or prophecy that any literate person would have recognized as a mark of God's displeasure. His cabinet also included what Platter described as a "thunder-bolt dug out of a mast which was hit at sea during a storm," which resembled "the Judas stone." He had another stone that was used "against spleen disorders." Human hands somewhere had crafted a marvelous "mirror which both reflects and multiplies objects."[3]

Cope had so much in his cabinet that he had to use every available space for display. Like others, he chose to use the ceiling. Some sixteenth-century collectors, like the Italian Ferrante Imperato, hung the desiccated torsos of crocodiles above the heads of visitors. Cope instead used that space for a "long narrow Indian canoe, with the oars and siding planks, hung from the ceiling of this room." Hakluyt would have already known about such craft and seen a picture of the canoe that Ramusio had included in *Navigationi et Viaggi*. Cope was not the only Elizabethan obsessed with collecting wonders. Near Thames Bridge, Platter visited a house where the owner kept a live camel. Such displays of unusual creatures were known across Europe. Even the Vatican had a menagerie, though by Hakluyt's time it had lost its most celebrated resident, an elephant named Hanno beloved by Pope Leo X.[4]

When Hakluyt went to the cabinets kept by Garth and Cope, he encountered material proof of the splendors that could be found in Europe and well beyond. He may have seen such things in France, perhaps on an even grander scale, since André Thevet was the keeper of the royal family's cabinet at Fontainebleau. By the mid-1580s Hakluyt had the connections that would

Cabinets of curiosity reached their zenith in Italy, but the practices developed there spread across the Continent. This picture is from Ferrante Imperato, *Dell'historia naturale* (Naples: Constantino Vitale, 1599).
(TYP 525.99.461F, DEPARTMENT OF PRINTING AND GRAPHIC ARTS, HOUGHTON LIBRARY, HARVARD COLLEGE LIBRARY).

have enabled him to build his own personal museum. But there is no evidence that he ever chose to do so. Instead, he created a different kind of cabinet—found in the pages of books and accessible to any reader. In 1589 he published that work under the title *The Principall Navigations Voiages and Discoveries of the English nation, made by Sea or over Land, to the most remote and farthest distant Quarters of the earth at any time within the compasse of these 1500 yeeres.* The book included "many beastes, birds, fishes, serpents, plants, fruits, hearbes, roots, apparel, armour, boates, and such other rare curiosities, which wise men take pleasure to reade of, but more contentment to see." Stuffed with curiosities portrayed in words instead of pictures, the book secured Hakluyt's place in the history of England and America. Its publication marked the end of a five-year period when Hakluyt's own life and the lives of the earliest English colonists in North America became intertwined, at least in his mind. Though he did not mention it, Hakluyt invariably wanted the book to have the same effect as visiting an actual cabinet, which was "a singuler delight hav[ing] bene as it were ravished in beholding all the premises gathered together at no small cost, and preserved with no litle diligence."[5]

About six months before Hakluyt had given Queen Elizabeth the "Discourse on Western Planting" in 1584, she had granted Sir Walter Ralegh the rights to "discover search fynde out and view such remote heathen and barbarous landes Countries and territories not actually possessed of any Christian Prince, nor inhabited by Christian people." This was not the first time she had granted one of her subjects the rights to American territory. In fact, Ralegh's patent replaced an earlier grant to his half-brother, the now-drowned Sir Humphrey Gilbert.[6]

Soon after he received the patent, Ralegh arranged for two ships to sail westward into territory he now could claim. Ralegh ordered the captains Arthur Barlowe and Philip Amadas "to discover that land which lieth betweene Norumbega and Florida in the west Indies." They left England on April 27 and returned in September. Like other travelers, Amadas and Barlowe reported on what they had seen in "the Countrey, now called Virginia." But their mission had a more specific purpose. Their "briefe discourse" was intended to provide information to let others "judge how profitable this land is likely to succeede." At home they offered testimony about the fertility of the soil, described the commodities to be found in America, and showed off two Algonquians, named Manteo and Wanchese, whom they had brought back with them. They also brought back their story, which they told to Hakluyt. Five years later he printed an account of this "first voyage made to the coastes of America."[7]

The report contained the kinds of information that was becoming more common in sixteenth-century travel narratives. The unnamed captain who told it to Hakluyt included details about the natural world the travelers observed, dwelling on its luxuriant forests—"I thinke in all the worlde the like aboundance is not to be founde"—and the fact that game could be found "in incredible aboundance." Just as central to such a narrative was the recounting of the initial encounter with the locals, in this case an unnamed man. This American was keen to talk to the English. After "he had spoken of many things not understoode by us, we brought him with his owne good liking, aboord the shippes, and gave him a shirt, a hatte, and some other things, and made him taste of our wine, and our meate, which he liked very well." He soon departed, rowing a small canoe along the shore until he dove in to catch fish. He hauled his fish on the shore, divided his catch into two parts, and indicated that the English were to take one half on one of their vessels and the other half on the other. Then he left.[8]

Over the course of the visit such meetings became commonplace. Only a day after the initial encounter, the brother of a local king named Grangani-meo arrived along with forty to fifty others. Though the natives and new-comers still could not address one another with any real felicity, the two parties dealt amicably with each other. When the English offered presents to Granganimeo, he expressed joy and thanks, prompting the captain to write that the natives' behavior was "as mannerly, and civill, as any of Europe." Soon such ceremonial exchanges began to resemble actual trade, with the English exchanging manufactured goods (such as a tin dish) for local furs. The crew received fifty skins for a copper kettle; the Americans purchased axes, knives, and hatchets, but the English refused to sell them swords. Trade went so well that soon natives and newcomers became friendly. After a couple of bargaining sessions, Granganimeo brought his wife and children onto the ships. He drank the visitors' wine and ate their bread, and the sailors admired his wife, whom the captain described in pleasing terms. She wore pearl earrings "hanging downe to her middle," jewelry so impressive that the crew brought some back for Queen Elizabeth. Soon other Americans also came to trade, bringing the English coral, leather, and dyes. Granganimeo remained a part of the visitors' daily lives, making sure that they had sufficient food (notably venison, rabbit, and fish, along with nuts, fruit, and maize). The soil was so fertile that the English claimed they harvested peas only fourteen days after planting them.[9]

The captain's report contained a wealth of ethnographic detail. The En-glish were impressed that the natives had scavenged the remains of a Euro-pean shipwreck, extracting nails and spikes to make metal tools. As the English traveled into the interior, they noted differences from one group to the next, including tensions that had set one community against another in wars so "cruell, and bloodie" that the territory was "desolate" in some places. They reported that the residents of Sequotan (Secota), unlike the coastal peoples they had met earlier, had no memory of ever encountering anyone or anything from Europe. The English believed that the natives were fascinated with the whiteness of their skin and their ships. The newcomers' weapons mystified them, too, especially the noise of a harquebus being discharged.

Like ancient Romans who carried an icon of Apollo into war, so the residents of Secota hauled an idol with them. At another town the residents provided hospitality, which included cleaning and drying the clothes of the English. Once the English dried off, the sister-in-law of the king led them into the inner room of a house, where she put out a feast of venison, fruit, and roots. "We were entertained with all love, and kindnes," the captain reported. "Wee found the people most gentle, loving, and faithfull, void of all guile, and treason, and such as lived after the manner of the golden age," the report continued. "The earth bringeth foorth all things in aboundaunce, as in the first creation, without toile or labour." In the captain's view, "a more kinde, and loving people, there can not be found in the world." The name of the town was Roanoke, and its appearance in this report was the first information that anyone in England had ever received of it.[10]

Though the English did not always keep careful track of everything they had seen, the America that the Barlowe and Amadas voyage had encountered could not have been more inviting. If Hakluyt (or anyone else) had questions, he could also have turned to Manteo and Wanchese, the two Algonquians who had returned to England with Amadas and Barlowe and had provided supporting testimony.[11] During that fateful summer of 1584, while the twinned deaths of the duc D'Alençon and the Prince of Orange alerted the English to the power of an ascendant Philip II, the journey to Roanoke gave reason for hope. The otherwise blank mental map that Elizabethans had for the middle Atlantic coast of North America began to fill with specific towns and people. The travelers might have painted an exaggerated picture of the paradise across the ocean. But at that moment the return of the two ships to the west coast of England in mid-September signaled a better future.

Hakluyt left no record of his voyage across the English Channel in October 1584. Nor did the ambassador Stafford make any comments about what Hakluyt had on his mind when he arrived back in Paris bearing a package from Walsingham. The only thing that seemed surprising to Stafford was Hakluyt's notion that the English were trying to keep Drake's circumnavigation a secret when in the French capital everyone was already talking about it.[12]

Hakluyt got to Paris on October 15. Four days later the king and queen fled Paris when it was discovered that two or three of the queen's ladies-in-waiting had become afflicted with plague. Though one of Hakluyt's associates joked that there was no need to flee since the court was as lethal as the disease, the royal family's rapid exodus was a sharp reminder that pestilence could invade even the most privileged places. Six weeks later, on December 5, a storm with "impetuous" and "violent" winds blew through the city, knocking down chimneys and steeples, destroying houses, and even uprooting one-hundred-year old oaks. People called this gale "les soufflets de la Ligue"—the breezes of the League, a gesture toward the tumultuous political struggles that continued to inflame passions across the Continent.[13]

Little of import shook Hakluyt's world over the next few months. Paris was a quiet city that winter. L'Estoile filled his journal with the deaths of various Parisians who had ties to the king's court, but little else seemed to matter. Henri III began the year by issuing new rules for the residents of the royal household and arranging for more bodyguards for himself. As always, L'Estoile noted the comings and goings from the court and, like Hakluyt, listened for news.[14]

On February 23, a group of ambassadors came from London. They "arrived in Paris followed by two hundred cavalry, splendidly attired," L'Estoile noted. While they stayed in the city the king himself "paid all their expenses," a sign of his fond feelings for Elizabeth. The ambassadors had come on orders from the queen to convince Henri III to support the Protestants of the Low Countries in their rebellion against Philip II of Spain. At a ceremony at the city's Augustinian church the king accepted a jewel- and pearl-encrusted "necklace of the Order of the Garter" sent as a token of Elizabeth's favor. With great pomp and magnificent ceremony he then offered the Earl of Derby and other representatives of the queen a sumptuous feast.[15]

But as Stafford informed Walsingham, Carnival, "this time of pleasures," prevented the king from having the leisure to act on the English request. In the meantime, the English in Paris and elsewhere waited. As the English captain George Fremyn wrote to Walsingham from Antwerp on the day the queen's ambassadors arrived in Paris, everyone there was eager for the results of the meeting. Stafford, at the ambassador's lodging (presumably with Hakluyt nearby), heard a rumor of a possible plot by the pope and Philip II to assassinate Queen Elizabeth and tried to make sure that his spies kept him informed of the actions of seditious Jesuits and dangerous Scots. The fate of European Protestants seemed to hang in the balance.[16]

By the time Hakluyt offered his next comments on the religious controversies of the age, Henri III had decided not to help the beleaguered Protestants of the Low Countries. That decision was regretted by many in England who continued to see signs of danger emanating from Rome. In Paris, Hakluyt's estimation of the realm's foes got no better. In April 1585 he wrote "that the Spanish ambassadour, the Popes nuncio and the Jesuits" were eager to have their "swarmes of spies" trumpet news of anything in Christendom that benefited Catholics. If they could not find anything truthful to report, they contented themselves by coining "newe rumors and false bruits, w[hi]ch notwithstanding they be most untrue and vague, yet I find by experience that they worke very great and strange affects." But when things did not go their way, these emissaries of Rome sought "a thousand devises and shiftes to suppresse yt," a strategy that failed only when evidence of their shortcomings became well known.[17]

Hakluyt paid attention to these diplomatic machinations because he knew that what happened on the Continent would have a direct impact on any efforts that the English might make to follow up their expedition of 1584. He was thus eager to send Ralegh whatever information he thought would be helpful. He had heard about Sir Francis Drake's preparations for a strike against the Spanish in the West Indies, and he let Walsingham know that nothing could be more disturbing to Philip II and his allies. He also told his patron that rumors had spread through the French court about an English action to take an unnamed island. Such conflicts dominated what Hakluyt called "the business of the tymes."[18] His task was to make sure that they did not interfere with any English colonization of eastern North America.

While Hakluyt worked the rumor mill in Paris, the lawyer was in England. His rooms at the Middle Temple remained, as they had been for several years, a clearinghouse for information about colonization. In 1585 the lawyer wrote two pamphlets to promote overseas settlement. One of them was not published until 1602, and the other remained in manuscript until its eventual publication in the twentieth century. The two pamphlets are in fact so similar that it is possible that the lawyer wrote only one and that the second is a later version changed to fit the purposes of John Brereton, a later promoter of the settlement of Virginia who printed the lawyer's words at the dawn of the seventeenth century. Whether the documents circulated in manuscript remains unknown, so it is possible that the lawyer's words did little for the nascent settlement at Roanoke. Still, the pamphlets reveal the logic that had come to dominate promoters' thinking in the months after Hakluyt had given the "Discourse" to the queen.[19]

Both pamphlets follow the essential logic of the "Discourse." Given the close ties between the cousins, such a similarity is hardly surprising, and it is possible, perhaps likely, that the lawyer helped his younger cousin prepare the document that was to be read by Elizabeth. In the pamphlets the lawyer distilled the lessons of Hakluyt's long and private piece, omitting explanatory material that potential settlers (or those who sponsored them) did not need. There are no long quotations from accepted authorities, nor is there mention of any Continental writers whose works had so obviously shaped Hakluyt's efforts. Neither pamphlet broke new intellectual ground. Though the lawyer never mentioned his sources, a stark contrast to Hakluyt's approach in the "Discourse," it is obvious that the words here were drawn from Hakluyt's piece and so reflect his research in England and France.

The lawyer argued that planting English colonies in North America would enable the English to spread Protestantism, increase the size of the queen's realm, find the Northwest Passage, create jobs for indigent English men and women, harvest the spectacular bounties of American forests and fisheries, expand English exports by creating new markets for woolens, and provide greater security for English ships on the high seas. After he listed thirty-one distinct items (and numbered each so that a reader could follow the argument), he summarized. "The ends of this voyage are these," he wrote.

1. To plant Christian religion.
2. To trafficke.
3. To conquer.

"Or," he added, "to doe all three." The lawyer knew that planting "Christian religion without conquest" would "bee hard. Trafficke easily followeth conquest: conquest is not easie. Trafficke without conquest seemeth possible, and not uneasie. What is to be done, is the question."[20]

None of these ideas was original in 1585. The lawyer raised the specter of Spanish religious tyranny, stressed the possibility of finding work for the underemployed of England, and detailed the abundant natural resources to be found in America. The persuasive power of the pamphlets came from the multitude of details to be found in them, such as the hope that Americans could be taught to tend vines and make olive oil or that "ladies and gentle-women" would become purchasers of boxes made from cedar and sassafras or that colonists would take in native women, boys, and girls to work with English women to make linen, a textile that would find a market in the West Indies and back home.[21]

Although the lawyer was concerned with enhancing "the glory of God by planting of religion among those infidels," and although this act would augment the number of Protestants, he did not encourage the English to mimic the aggressive proselytizing tactics of the Spanish. Instead, he hoped that the natives would embrace English-style Christianity. Still, any attempt by the Americans to repel the newcomers would be suppressed and the English could then "proceed with extremitie, conquer, fortifie, and plant" there, thus bringing "them all in subjection and to civilitie." But this was a last and unlikely resort, not an initial strategy.[22]

During the mid-1580s Hakluyt was a study in motion. He returned to England in early May 1585 and by the end of the month appeared in Bristol. There he showed the dean and chapter of the cathedral the letter he had received from the queen the previous October promising him a position should a vacancy occur. But he did not stay long. By autumn he was back in Paris, renewing his acquaintance with André Thevet. At that point he borrowed from the French cosmographer a manuscript history of Florida written by René de Laudonnière. Back and forth he went again in 1586, to Bristol (where he began to receive his sinecure), Christ Church (where he finally stopped being listed as a student), Paris (where he continued to work for Stafford), and London (where he remained in contact with adventurers and royal advisers). At the end of December 1586, he was back in Paris, paying attention to matters of European statecraft, listening for rumors of alliances succeeding and failing, and arranging for the drawing of a map of the American interior to accompany a recent history of New Mexico. He hoped that the map would help show the English the "rich sylver mines" that could be found in America at the same latitude as Virginia.[23]

While Hakluyt traveled, the lawyer remained in London, acquiring yet more information about America. On September 3, 1585, Rafe Lane wrote to the lawyer from "the new Fort in Virginia." The letter, along with other documents emanating from the nascent English settlement near Roanoke, testified again to the bounty that the English could find across the Atlantic. The soil was fertile, *materia medica* could be harvested in fields and woods, and the climate was salubrious. "If Virginia had but horses and kine in some reasonable proportion, I dare assure my selfe being inhabited with English, no realme in Christendome were comparable to it." France, Italy, Spain, and the East could produce fine wine, oil, flax, rosin, frankincense, pitch, sugar, and currants. But America "do abound with ye growth of them all," though its natives had no use for them. Besides, things could be found there that could not be found in the West or East Indies, though Lane here neglected to mention what they were. The local people were "naturally most curteous, &

very desirous to have clothes, but especially of course cloth rather then silke." The Americans also wanted coarse canvas and goods made of red copper.[24]

Lane's short report is the only extant missive addressed to Hakluyt or the lawyer in the mid-1580s. But other accounts fell into their hands and made them take notice. Actions far away demanded attention, especially when daring raids by the queen's privateers made Hakluyt's dream of an English America come into sharper focus.

As the Hakluyts continued to work in privacy, the attention of their fellow citizens fell on Sir Francis Drake, who had become an instant hero to the English when he returned from the circumnavigation in 1580. "Throughe scorchinge heate, throughe coulde, in stormes, and tempests force, / By ragged rocks, by shelfes, & sandes: this Knighte did keepe his course," wrote Geffrey Whitney in a book of emblems published in Leyden in 1586 for an English audience. Whitney stressed what Drake had experienced at sea as he sailed through "gapinge gulfes" and passed "by monsters of the flood; / By pirates, theeves, and cruell foes, that long'd to spill his blood." Yet God had guided him through every peril, leading him through the Scylla of natural dangers and the Charybdis of human foes. His successes were like Jason's capture of the Golden Fleece, and equally deserving of praise. "You, that live at home, and can not brooke the flood, / Geve praise to them, that passe the waves, to doe their countrie good. / Before which sorte, as chiefe: in tempeste, and in calme, / Sir FRANCIS DRAKE, by due deserte, may weare the goulden palme." Whitney added a picture to make the scene even more memorable: Drake's ship sitting atop the Earth, with two long ropes leading from its prow to the hand of God.[25]

But Drake was not yet done. On September 12, 1585, he led a contingent out of the port at Plymouth and toward yet another appointment with destiny. Among the leaders of the expedition were at least two men who either knew Hakluyt or whose exploits had already captured his attention: Christopher Carleill, another promoter of English colonization in the western hemisphere, and Martin Frobisher. Drake's goal this time was not exploration or discovery. Instead, he embarked with royal permission to liberate English ships that Philip II had ordered seized in Spanish ports.[26]

After accomplishing their initial goal, Drake and his ships followed what had become by then the familiar route across the Atlantic. They stopped first in the Canary Islands, and then sailed westward to the Cape Verde Islands. On the island of Santiago on November 14 they shot off cannon to celebrate

Auxilio diuino.   203

To RICHARD DRAKE *Efquier, in praife of*
Sir FRANCIS DRAKE *Knight.*

A fitting emblem for Sir Francis Drake: his ship guided around the world by a divine hand.
From Geffrey Whitney, *A Choice of Emblemes, and Other Devises* (Leiden, 1586)
(HUNTINGTON LIBRARY)

the anniversary of the queen's coronation. Once they finished those festivities, they pillaged the town, seeking money but finding only food, oil, and wine. Also on Santiago many of those on the expedition visited its famous hospital, where they found the impressive rooms filled with twenty patients suffering from "fowle and fylthie Diseases." That brief journey proved to be a fatal mistake. Soon after the ships departed for the West Indies, pestilence raged aboard every ship. "Until some seven or eight dayes after our comming from S. Iago, there had not died anie one man of sicknesse in all the Fleete," the captain Walter Bigges claimed. But though none appeared sick when they departed, the illness struck with swiftness. It "seized our people with extreme hote burning and continuall ague, whereof some verie fewe escaped with life, and those for the most part not without great alteration and decay of their wittes and strength for a long time after." Bigges noticed that some of the victims had small spots on their bodies, a symptom of plague. By the time the ships stopped at the Caribbean island of Dominica to replenish their supplies, the contagion had run its course. One witness claimed that each vessel lost two or three individuals each day. He could have added that their lifeless bodies were tossed into the sea like so much offal. Drake's recommendation to bleed the victims was useless. When the ships docked in the West Indies, their numbers had been reduced by perhaps five hundred.[27]

Weakened but not defeated, Drake's crews proved more than ready to raid Spanish settlements in the West Indies and New Spain. From Dominica to Hispaniola, then to the mainland communities at Rio de la Hacha, Santa Maria, and Cartagena, from there to Cuba and then a turn northward to St. Augustine, Florida, Drake left a trail of blood through the Caribbean basin. His men spent a month in Hispaniola, systematically burning sections of the city until its residents paid a ransom of gold worth twenty-five thousand crowns. But the raid was costly; more than a hundred of Drake's men died in Cartagena alone, either from wounds in battle or disease exacerbated by Drake's refusal to leave the city until the Spanish had paid him sufficient ransom. "We stayed here six weekes," Bigges wrote, "& the sicknesse with mortality before spoken of, still continuing among us, though not with the same furie as at the first" in the Canaries. Those who survived the *calentour* or *calenture*, "which is the Spanish name of their burning ague," could never again recover their memory or physical strength.[28]

Yet the hardships of the English paled in comparison to those suffered by the Spanish. In Florida, Drake's men forced Philip II's garrison out of St. Augustine, leaving it open for raids from local natives whom Drake had treated well during his stay. The English burned the city to the ground before they left, taking away perhaps 250 slaves whom Drake had hoped to leave at the nascent English settlement at Roanoke. Though the entire venture did not net as much profit as the English had hoped, the costs to the Spanish were high. The effort to rebuild devastated towns diverted funds that the Spanish had planned to use elsewhere, including Philip's ongoing attempt to suppress revolt in the Low Countries.[29]

Drake's ships arrived at Roanoke but found the channel too shallow to land. As a result, the larger vessels anchored two miles offshore and sent smaller boats to the town. Drake soon learned that the colonists were struggling; though he offered assistance, the settlers instead accepted his offer for a return home. A fierce storm drove the vessels apart at sea, and they were not reunited until they landed in England. The travelers bore stories of life in America but left no one behind to maintain the settlement. They also brought back tobacco and introduced it to the English public for its curative powers.[30]

Drake's raid had accomplished both less and more than he and his supporters had hoped. From their privateering, pillaging, and ransoming they managed to bring back a treasure worth sixty thousand pounds, to be divided among the voyagers (one third of the total) and those who provided backing (the remaining funds). But that return came at a cost of approximately 750 lives among the English alone, with infectious disease and violence killing almost a third of the original contingent enlisted for the venture. Still, though the losses were real enough, so were the rewards. They had stolen 240 artillery Spanish pieces made of iron and brass. More important, Drake's ships rescued the Roanoke settlers, possibly saving their lives. Among them was the artist John White, whose paintings of the Carolina Algonquians and their territory provided the best visual information of the western hemisphere produced by any European in the sixteenth century—evidence which Hakluyt (among others) realized was crucial for the promotion of English colonization.[31] By bringing the colonists back, Drake again demonstrated the ability of the English to go to North America and to return, reinforcing the psychological message that a journey westward to a new settlement did not mean a permanent departure from home. Perhaps more important, Drake also proved that the Spanish had little if any authority along the Atlantic coast, even in Florida. Those contemplating a voyage across the ocean might still dread the might of the Iberians on the high seas, but they had little to fear from these foes once they landed in Virginia.

Drake's successes against the Spanish marked a decisive moment for Hakluyt. Before 1586, when news of the privateer's exploits reached home, Hakluyt and the lawyer knew that colonization of North America remained precarious as long as the Spanish dominated much of the Atlantic basin. But Drake proved that the Spanish could not in fact defend the extensive territories they claimed. As the wake from his returning vessels subsided along England's shores, Hakluyt knew that the time had come to press forward. He needed to gather the intelligence necessary for others to take action.

Hakluyt spent the summer of 1586 in England, despite the wishes of

Stafford, who wanted him back in Paris. By the end of the year, he had returned to France. Wherever he went, Hakluyt looked for information to advance his cause. Thevet's loan of Laudonnière's account of Florida came at a perfect moment, and Hakluyt knew exactly what to do: he worked to have it published in French in Paris in early 1586 and the next year in an English translation (which he did himself) in London. When the French edition appeared at the beginning of March, its editor, Martin Basanier, thanked Hakluyt for his efforts. Hakluyt pushed to rescue the text from obscurity because he recognized the contribution it could make to the history and geography of the western hemisphere. Basanier believed that Hakluyt's knowledge of science and fluency in multiple languages set him apart from others and rendered his views all the more persuasive. By November, Basanier had prepared a French edition of Antonio Espejo's history of Mexico. Pleased with their efforts, Hakluyt and Basanier gave a copy of the French edition to Thevet in 1587, possibly before Hakluyt had completed and published the English translation of Laudonnière's account.[32]

Rather than celebrating the occasion of spreading this valuable knowledge, Thevet decided that the two had published the book without his permission, a rare instance of tension in the relationship between Hakluyt and the French cosmographer. Thevet complained that the book constituted plagiarism, and their "sinistres enterprises" (underhanded actions) threatened to weaken the authority he had gained from the publication of his *Singularité de la France Antarctique* printed in 1558 and the *Cosmographie Universelle* of 1575. After committing this "villainy," they then had the gall to think he would be pleased when they gave him a copy of the book. Yet despite his hostility toward the publication of the French-language edition, Thevet offered Hakluyt several manuscripts, including a remarkable illustrated history of Mexico (the Codex Mendoza) that he had recently acquired. That work remained unpublished until after Hakluyt's death, but it had probably come into his possession the same year that Hakluyt translated Laudonnière's account into English.[33]

Hakluyt's translation of Laudonnière's book was part of his campaign to encourage English settlement in eastern North America. The timing was deliberate. Though Hakluyt was eager to spread the news about Florida, he also knew that there had been no reports from the settlement at Roanoke since 1585. That silence could have been interpreted by potential colonists as a sign of failure in America. Hakluyt's burden, then, was to spin Laudonnière's account to provide new inspiration for colonization. There were, the Frenchman had written, two things that induced "travell into farre and remote

When Samuel Purchas offered the first printed version of the manuscript history of Mexico that Hakluyt had obtained from Thevet, he termed it "The History of the Mexican Nation, described in pictures" and noted that it was "the choisest of my Jewels." From Purchas, *Hakluytus Posthumus or Purchas his Pilgrimes* (London, 1625)

regions." The first was "the naturall desire which we have to serch out the commodities to live happely, plentifully, and at ease." Such a life could be had by those who emigrated to start a new life in a better land or by taking advantage of the commodities that sailors brought back from other places. The second impetus for travel was overpopulation at home. But not every part of Europe suffered from that affliction. Cold climates had sent northern Europeans away, "and by this meane hath peopled infinite countries: so that most of the nations of Europe drawe their original from these partes." By contrast, southern regions "because they be too barraine by reason of their insupportable heate which raigneth in them," had no surplus population to spread and were often importers of people. Italy, Spain, and Africa had never suffered from overpopulation and thus had no incentive for emigration. By contrast, France, Norway, Scythia, and Gotland had sent emigrants abroad. But successful colonization did not occur naturally. A nation that depopulated itself by emigration ran the risk of being overrun by local enemies. That was not a random fear but, in fact, what had happened in the Roman Empire. The trick, Laudonnière knew, was to send out enough people to plant a defensible colony yet not so many that the homeland suffered as a result.[34]

The French experience in Florida carried obvious meaning for the English settling Virginia. As Hakluyt informed Ralegh in the dedication of Laudonnière's book, "no historie hetherto set foorth hath more affinitie, resemblance or conformitie with yours of Virginea, then this of Florida." Hakluyt believed it crucial that those working with Ralegh to plant the new colony understand what had befallen the French. They needed "to beware of the grosse negligence in providing sufficiencie of victuals, the securitie, disorders, and mutinies that fell out among the french, with the great inconveniences that thereupon ensued." The French made mistakes in Florida despite the obvious physical advantages that the local environment provided. The English in Virginia needed know what had happened to the south.[35]

Hakluyt knew that Ralegh had multiple reasons for wanting this account to be published at the time. He had already invested in Jacques Le Moyne de Morgues's paintings of Florida scenes when he went there with Laudonnière. Le Moyne, then living in London at Black Friars, was, Hakluyt wrote, "an eye-witnesse of the goodnes & fertilitie of those regions," but his writings about Florida were not included in this book. Le Moyne wanted to publish his account along with his portraits in the near future, but only if Ralegh approved of such a venture. In the meantime, what was to be found in the *Notable Historie* would have to suffice since by 1587 Ralegh was in the midst of another attempt to establish settlements along the Atlantic coast of North America. The report that had come from Stafford about the "safe arrivall of your last colonie in their wished haven" meant that Ralegh was in the strongest position yet to advance his goals in Virginia.[36]

Hakluyt used the dedication of his book on Florida to promote Virginia and the community at Roanoke. The way to wealth in the Americas, as the Spanish and Portuguese had each demonstrated, was to create economies based on the export of both crops and livestock. The Spanish prospered in Hispaniola because the land was ideal for livestock, sugar, and ginger. The Portuguese cleared the forests on Madeira and produced wine and sugar. On the Azores they made woad, and they profited as well in Brazil. What made such ventures succeed? A favorable climate, like the one to be found in Virginia.[37]

Hakluyt here made his most forceful public argument to date for colonizing North America. Ferdinand and Isabella had supported Columbus, he wrote, "before any foot of land of al the West Indies was discovered." Imagine what the English, led by the "most magnificent and gratious" Elizabeth, would be able to do in advancing their goals in the profitable climes of the western hemisphere. Here Hakluyt relied on Antonio Espejo's account of New Mexico, which he had also helped to bring into print in England in April 1587, only a few months earlier. Though Espejo confined his remarks to the region north and west of New Spain, Hakluyt believed that its lessons about pliable Americans were relevant to the peoples of the Atlantic coast. Further, the English had no fear of resistance since they could readily muster enough troops to defeat any Americans who stood in their way. John Davis's recent explorations along the northern coasts of the continent proved that "a great part to bee maine Sea, where before was thought to bee mayne lande." Ortelius's newest projections suggested that the Gulf of California "on the backe part of Virginea" was not as far west as contemporary maps had suggested. All the English needed was an army sufficient to subdue the "naked and unarmed people in Virginea." Even if it took ten thousand to perform the task—a number larger than it took the Portuguese to serve "in all their garrisons of the Assores, Madera, Cape verde, Guinea, Brasill, Mozambique, Melinde, Zocotora, Ormus, Diu, Goa, Mallacca, the Moluccoes, Amacan, and Macao"—they would never be missed in England. Hakluyt here drew again on the secret documents he viewed in Paris that proved that the Portuguese had fewer than ten thousand men in arms across their entire seaborne empire. Once again Hakluyt relied on his contacts in France and the power of the printed word to advance the goals of the realm.[38]

While Hakluyt searched for information and promoted English voyages, a third expedition left England for Roanoke. Ralegh had financed the voyage in the hopes of bringing supplies to the colonists who he believed were still in

America. When the ship departed, no one in England knew that Drake had already picked up the survivors and was bringing them home. The ships never saw each other on their transatlantic crossings. The supply ships reached the coast fourteen or fifteen days after the colonists had left. Led by Sir Richard Grenville, the newcomers searched for the colonists, traveling "up into divers places of the Countrey," as Hakluyt later put it, "to see if he could here any newes of the Colony left there by him the year before." They found the place where the colonists had lived, but now it was deserted. Grenville knew that the time had come to return to England, but he was unwilling to leave the site unoccupied. He chose to leave fifteen men behind, with sufficient provisions to last two years. After establishing this small contingent, Grenville and the rest of his crew departed for England. On the way home he stopped at the Azores, where his men plundered every town they could find.[39]

Though he received no immediate news of the Grenville expedition, Hakluyt remained fixated on the English settlements in North America. By December 1586 he was convinced that the English would succeed best in Virginia "aboute the bay of the Chesepians." The Spanish would not challenge colonization there since even Peter Martyr had admitted that the voyages of Cabot had established the English right to the region. Or at least, as Hakluyt told Ralegh, they would not challenge such a settlement as long as the two nations were at peace.[40] That was a tortured moment for Hakluyt, who wanted Philip II punished for his actions yet wished to keep the Iberians far from Virginia. But though he was desperate for information from across the Atlantic, little came to him in either Paris or London.

Before he left Paris in the spring of 1587 Hakluyt produced his own Latin edition of Peter Martyr's *Decades*. Completed near the end of February, the work reflected no substantial change from earlier editions. His reasons for printing the book were not entirely clear, even to those who knew him. Was there anything beyond the original text in this book, an exasperated Abraham Ortelius asked his son two years later when he noticed an advertisement for the book in the catalog for the Frankfurt Book Fair? "Has he added nothing of his own? And what is the reason for this edition by Hakluyt?"[41]

That Ortelius, a leading scholar of the age with deep knowledge of overseas explorations, could ask such a question reflects the uniqueness and peculiarity of Hakluyt's approach. If Hakluyt wished to promote the English settlement of North America, why should he prepare a new edition of a Spanish work that was already well known to the intellectual elites of Europe?

Peter Martyr's account was once one of the two most comprehensive works offering information about the Americas (the other was the third volume of Ramusio's *Navigationi et Viaggi*). But it was then old and superseded by the stream of books that had come from European printers over the course of the century. Yet the publication of the book still tells much about how Hakluyt understood what he was doing. Ortelius fretted about the advertisement he had seen. If he had seen the book itself, he would have discovered that it was different from earlier editions of the *Decades*. This volume was more compact, and an index directed readers to particular topics. Though Hakluyt omitted the "barbarian vocabulary" that could be found earlier, he did include a map of the Americas with up-to-date information, including details that Peter Martyr never knew.[42] The fact that he had the book published in Paris, instead of London, reveals his close ties to printers on the Continent. Since he published the book in Latin, even though it had already been translated into the vernacular across Europe, his intended audience had to have been other members of the learned elite—many of whom might have already known about the book from earlier printings. It is difficult to imagine much of a market for the tract, at least outside of Spain, where patriotic or filio-pietistic book buyers might have scrambled to get their hands on a fresh copy. But it seems doubtful that Hakluyt was trying to penetrate the literary market of the one European nation he found most dangerous to his country.

But the English had nothing to lose by acknowledging Spanish primacy in much of the West Indies, which takes up most of the *Decades*, or even the southern reaches of the North American mainland. As Hakluyt knew well by 1587, brave English privateers like Sir Francis Drake could use the edge of a sword or a cannon ball to make up for lost time in Spanish America. Circulation of the *Decades* was a comfort to the Spanish only as long as they accepted what the Italian had originally written. If they embraced its arguments, then they recognized the primacy of Cabot's claims to the more northern reaches of North America.[43]

Once again Hakluyt dedicated a book to Ralegh and used the dedication to promote English colonization. He celebrated Peter Martyr's remarkable achievement and his ability to document details about the initial Spanish conquest of "vast regions of the New World," a term he used to remind readers that the Iberians had not discovered all of the Americas. He praised the Milanese historian's "distinguished and skilful pen," which he used to depict "in a most gifted manner the head, neck, breast, arms, in brief the whole body of that tremendous entity America, and clothes it decently in the

Latin dress familiar to scholars." He recognized that Martyr "examines the hidden causes of things, inquires into the hidden effects of nature, and from the innermost shrines of his erudite philosophy he draws comments which he frequently introduces like brilliant ornaments of his style and the fairest of gems." He thought Martyr's abilities superior to those of classical ethnographers such as Cicero, Sallust, and Tacitus. While Martyr praised the Spanish ability to overcome hardships, Hakluyt noted that he "also records their avarice, ambition, butchery, rapine, debauchery, their cruelty towards defenceless and harmless peoples." Hakluyt understood why Martyr included such details: "I am ashamed, he says in one place, to recount these matters, but it is essential to set down the truth." In ancient times Alexander the Great had recognized how fortunate Achilles was to have "a Homer to be the herald of thy praises." Now the Spanish had found theirs, "a man of marvellous genius, excelling by his use of the greatest qualities, mature in judgement, equipped with a cyclopaedic knowledge of almost every field of learning," a man who became "the trumpeter of your labours in the West Indies, and of your spirited and courageous achievements."[44]

Yet as he praised Martyr, Hakluyt sang his own praises. Previous editions of the *Decades* often included only parts of the original text. But Hakluyt, "after conducting the most diligent researches," had managed to publish the entire book "restored, if I am not mistaken, to its original splendour." He corrected the abundant mistakes in a 1530 Spanish edition that contained the only known copy of four of the ten "decades." He added marginal notes, too, "after a careful study of the chronology, the dates and certain other notes very necessary to the student." Hakluyt designed the index for that audience as well. "I have not stopped at this," he added, "but I have inserted a geographical map, containing the chief places mentioned in the work, to serve as a plumb-line, mindful of the true saying, that geography is the eye of history [*Geographiam esse historiæ oculum*]." This editorial intervention made the book more readable to those who did not understand Spanish and Italian, the languages in which much of the literature on the Americas had been written (a reference to Ramusio, among others). Hakluyt hoped that this new addition might inspire "our own island race" through the example of the Spanish. "For he who proclaims the praises of foreigners," Hakluyt added, "rouses his own countrymen, if they be not dolts."[45]

Hakluyt had no doubt that his edition of *De Orbe Novo* would prompt English readers to action. In his desire to provide a comprehensive report, Martyr had recognized the discoveries of Sebastian Cabot, thereby demonstrating the legitimacy of English claims. Although Hakluyt lamented earlier

English failures to colonize North America, he emphasized the central role that Ralegh himself would play in the unfolding drama. No one else had made the commitment to English expansion or had demonstrated unbridled enthusiasm for it. Ralegh's support for the young mathematician Thomas Harriot proved his belief in the importance of navigation. With knowledge to be gleaned from Martyr's book and the work of Harriot and others who promoted navigation, the English would finally venture out into the larger world in a more substantial way. "There yet remain for you new lands, ample realms, unknown peoples," Hakluyt wrote to Ralegh, "they wait yet, I say, to be discovered and subdued, quickly and easily, under the happy auspices of your arms and enterprise, and the sceptre of our most serene Elizabeth, Empress—as even the Spaniard himself admits—of the Ocean." Despite earlier setbacks the "sweet nymph" of Virginia needed to be pursued like any other woman awaiting her husband. Besides, English efforts were sanctioned by the scriptural demand "to recall the savage and the pagan to civility," and the time for that action was now, given the rise of Islam and the threat it posed to Christendom.[46]

Pursue this course, Hakluyt implored Ralegh, and "you will find at length, if not a Homer, yet some Martyr—by whom I mean some happy genius—to rescue your heroic enterprises from the vasty maw of oblivion." In the mean time, Hakluyt promised "to collect in orderly fashion the maritime records of our own countrymen, now lying scattered and neglected, and brushing aside the dust bring them to the light of day in a worthy guise, to the end that posterity, carefully considering the records of their ancestors which they have lacked so long, may know that the benefits they enjoy they owe to their fathers, and may at last be inspired to seize the opportunity offered to them of playing a worthy part." In his mind it was crucial to recall that in ancient times no glory could be greater than conquering "the barbarian" and bringing both "the savage and the pagan to civility." He invoked the classical tragedy of Thyestes —who had been tricked into eating his own murdered children—in an effort to halt internecine battles between Christians that would only lead to "the increase and advantage of the followers of Mahomet."[47]

The map near the front of the book made Hakluyt's idea clear. North of Florida and south of New France, the territory is marked "Virginea 1584." The map also labeled the northwest portion of North America "Nova Albion" and added "Inventa An. 1580 ab Anglis," a reference to Drake's stop there during his circumnavigation. At that moment there were few English men or women in North America, but that dose of reality did not matter to Hakluyt. To him, English claims were beyond dispute.[48]

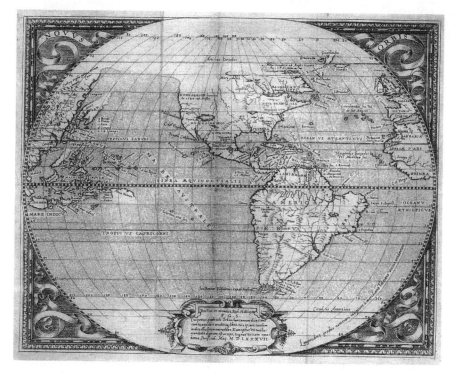

The western hemisphere, as it appeared in the map Hakluyt included in his edition of
Peter Martyr's *De Orbe Novo* in 1587
(HUNTINGTON LIBRARY)

Those few pages written in Latin in Paris during the winter of 1586–1587
encapsulated years of Hakluyt's thought. No glory could be greater than
bringing Christianity to Americans, especially during an age when the forces
of Islam and Rome threatened the course of true religion in the world. What
the English needed was someone to rescue the tales of the island nation, to
bring these stories together, to preserve the fragments of national memory
against the encroachments of time and ignorance. If Ralegh should follow
through on his instincts, he would no doubt dominate such tales. Of course,
he would merit his own Homer or Martyr. Only this time, the scribe would
be named Hakluyt.

While Hakluyt plotted, the queen settled on a more direct course of
action. In late March 1587 she dispatched Drake, fresh from his victorious
romp in the Caribbean basin, to Spain with orders to "take, burne, and pillage

all such Ships as hee could find" on the seas or in ports. That, at least, was how Camden later recorded her orders. Drake sailed through the Strait of Gibraltar, prompting six ships to beat a retreat, and headed directly into the port at Cadiz, where he set fire to every ship he could find, depriving the Spanish of "infinite provision of warlike munitions & victuals."[49]

As Drake struck Cadiz, the Suffolk captain Thomas Cavendish led his three ships into port in England. He had been gone for two years, and news of his achievements would have thrilled the realm's supporters. According to Camden, Cavendish sailed through the Strait of Magellan, burned and pillaged Spanish ports in Chile, Peru, and New Spain, seized Spanish ships off the coast of California, and then continued his journey westward to the Spice Islands. His return to England via the Pacific and Indian Oceans made Cavendish the third person, after Magellan and Drake, to lead a circumnavigation.[50]

Hakluyt was in Paris when these events unfolded, though earlier in the year he had been in England with the Flemish engraver Theodor de Bry. On his visit, possibly arranged by Thomas Harriot, de Bry first saw the paintings of American communities produced by Jacques Le Moyne de Morgues (of Florida) and John White (of Roanoke). At some point after that meeting Hakluyt had departed again for Paris, but he returned to London in January 1588, probably a few weeks before the thickest fog ever to descend on Paris fell upon the French capital. Suffocated birds fell from the skies, and others flew into chimneys they could not see. Hakluyt was back to Paris and its debaucheries by March. Somehow he found time amid other events to marry Douglas Cavendish, who was probably the cousin of the recently returned circumnavigator. He remained close to the lawyer, who named Hakluyt a beneficiary of the will that he wrote in September 1587. Few of Hakluyt's letters for 1588 survive, but among them was a report to Cecil in early April that the Spanish Armada was unlikely to cause any trouble until the beginning of May.[51]

Only weeks after Drake left England, another English expedition set sail for Roanoke. Under the direction of the artist John White, whom Ralegh had named governor of the "Citie of Ralegh in Virginia," the 120-ton flagship *Admirall* and two smaller vessels sailed from Portsmouth on April 26. On board were ninety-one men, seventeen women, and nine boys. Also on board were Manteo and Towaye, who "were in Englande and returned home into Virginia with them."[52]

The ships stopped at small islands and coasted along the edge of Hispaniola before turning northward for the journey to Virginia. On July 22 the vessels anchored at Hatorask (modern Hatteras). From there White led an expedition toward the island of Roanoke and, they hoped, the fifteen men they had left there in 1585. The new governor wanted to interview the men about the region and about the native peoples they met during their stay, though he had already decided that he should lead this contingent northward toward Chesapeake Bay. As the sun set, White led the group onto Roanoke to the spot where the fifteen had been left. "But we found none of them," White reported, "nor any signe, that they had bene there, saving onely we found the bones of one of those fifteene, which the Savages had slaine long before." The next day they found Rafe Lane's camp. The fort he had built had been burned, but the houses remained standing, overgrown with melons and populated now by deer browsing on the fruit. The party returned to the larger group of colonists, "without hope of ever seeing any of the fifteene men living."[53]

While the settlers began to fix the houses at Roanoke and build new dwellings (since there was not yet enough shelter for all of them), one of the newcomers, George Howe, stripped off most of his clothes and took a forked stick into the water to hunt for crabs. He wandered two miles from the others, into an area where a group of local Algonquians were hunting deer. The hunters fired their arrows into Howe, striking him sixteen times. As he lay dying, the hunters came to him and used wooden swords to kill him. They then "beat his head in peeces" and fled to the mainland.[54]

Two days later, as the newcomers still struggled with Howe's murder, twenty-one of the English along with Manteo crossed to the island of Croaton, where Manteo hoped to find his mother and other relatives. The English still wanted to learn what had happened to the missing fifteen men and to "learne the disposition of the people of the Countrey toward us," a reasonable desire, given what had happened to Howe. At first the Algonquians looked as if they were going to attack. But then Manteo cried out to them "in their owne language," which shifted their mood. They embraced their returning kinsman and the English who were with him. Rather than assault the visitors, the Algonquians instead asked that they not take any of their small supply of corn. The English agreed, and the Algonquians then took them home for a feast. They also explained that the fifteen who had been there earlier had been ambushed by thirty residents of Aquascogoc, Dasamongueponke, and Secota. Four had died at the scene. The eleven survivors fled in their small boat, though the natives had no knowledge of where they went.[55]

On hearing what happened, the English plotted revenge. They launched a nighttime raid on Americans they were convinced were those responsible for the deaths. But they made a fatal miscalculation. Rather than gain any measure of revenge, they instead killed a party of Croatons, men and women who had gathered to collect tobacco, corn, and pumpkins that they thought birds and deer would eat if they were not harvested soon. The English halted their assault when one of the native men cried out that they were their allies. When Manteo heard what had happened he was "somewhat aggrieved," yet White noted that "he imputed their harme to their owne follie, saying to them, that if their Weroans had kept their promise in comming to the Governour, at the day appointed, they had not knowen that mischance." The English were so pleased with Manteo's response that they christened him at Roanoke five days later and named him lord of Dasamongueponkc "in reward of his faithfull service."[56]

Five days after Manteo's christening White's daughter, Eleanor Dare, gave birth to a daughter. "Because this was the first Christian borne in Virginia," White wrote, "she was named Virginia." A late summer storm delayed the departure of the ships for England, giving White a few more precious days to spend with his daughter and granddaughter. Two weeks after Virginia Dare's birth, White and the ships left for England. When he arrived home he wrote a report that included the names of the 117 English men, women, and children whom he had left in Virginia.[57]

White knew that he had to get back to Roanoke as soon as possible. He arrived in London on November 20, and after offering his report to Ralegh he set about provisioning a ship with supplies for the planters. He had hoped to leave the following summer and had begun to gather the vessels needed for the expedition, including one under the command of Sir Richard Grenville. But then word spread throughout England that the Spanish had made an alliance with the pope and were preparing to invade England. Grenville received an order barring him from departing. White then scrambled to furnish two pinnaces with supplies, along with fifteen new colonists. They sailed for Roanoke on April 22, 1588.[58]

Soon after leaving port the ships began to encounter other vessels, some friendly and some not. After a devastating battle with a French ship—twenty-three men on White's vessel were killed—the English realized they could not cross the Atlantic. They turned for home.[59]

Late in the fifteenth century the astrologer Regiomontanus foretold that 1588 was to be, as the chronicler William Camden put it, a "*Yeere of Wonder;*" and by the Germane Chronologers to be the *Climacterical yeere of the World*. The rumors of warres, which were before but slender relations, began now daily to be augmented, and were now become, not as before, a variable report, but an assured certainty by the generall voice of all men." Philip II had, by all accounts "prepared a most invincible Navy" under the command of his most skilled captains. The pope himself had long been urging the Spanish king to launch an assault on their common enemies, and now that the Spanish had defeated the Portuguese and seized the East Indies, the time had come to strike. It had become Philip's "duety to enterprize something, which might bee agreeable and pleasing to God," Camden added, noting that nothing would be more pleasing than spreading "the Roman Catholique Religion." The target was England.[60]

Yet despite the extensive preparations, the mission was a disaster for the Iberians. Philip's fleet consisted of 130 ships, Camden recorded, "the greatest and best furnished with men, munition, and all warlike preparations that ever the Ocean did see, and arrogantly named *Invincible*." On May 28 they embarked, bound for glory. By late July, after a series of miscalculations and bad luck, a shift in the wind toward the southwest convinced many of the Spanish to head home. Still their troubles continued. Some of the Spanish ships washed up on the shores of Scotland and Ireland. The Scots imprisoned those who landed. The Spaniards who made it to Ireland were less fortunate. Fearing that these forlorn shipwreck victims would join the always simmering resistance of local Catholics, English commanders ordered two hundred of them decapitated. The rest, fearing for their lives, scrambled back to the beaches and onto their damaged vessels. "Sicke and weake as they were," Camden concluded, "and halfe starved, they re-embarked themselves in their broken vessels, and were for the most part sunke at Sea."[61]

It had been for the English a miraculous year, as the seers had foretold. In Spain, Philip II offered prayers to God, pleased that the carnage had not been worse. In England, Elizabeth ordered clerics in every church to lead a day of prayer and thanksgiving. She rode through the streets of London to St. Paul's to hear a sermon praising God for his divine intervention.[62]

Hakluyt had spent that remarkable year doing what he had been doing since 1583: traveling back and forth between England and France seeking information that could encourage English colonization ventures. He had actually sailed from London to Paris in July 1588, during the fighting. He brought Stafford news about what had happened up to the moment he left, though he could offer no conclusive report. He was in Paris when the fighting ceased. News of the Armada's destruction spread to an incredulous populace by the end of August. There L'Estoile learned that "the great and formidable naval army of Spain," which had aimed to ruin England and might have next set its sights on France, "was miraculously ruined and defeated, and reduced to nothing." L'Estoile knew that the English were taking credit for the victory, though he recognized it was due less to their might than to "a contrary wind" that sank some ships "and threw the remains on such distant coasts that it is still not known what became of it. In this we must recognize the finger of God." None could believe it. The Armada had been "called the Invincible, the Pride of the World, and the Terror of the Isles," a massive fighting force blessed by the pope, who called it his "daughter" and hoped that it would allow the Catholic Church to take control of England. The "God of sea and earth" destroyed this vain gang within three days, vanquishing the "great and proud designs" of the Spanish.[63]

At some point in his rounds, Hakluyt had made a decision to publish a spectacular book, a collection of travel accounts that would show the world how successful the English had been in overseas ventures in the years leading up to the Armada. Even though he and everyone else in Europe remained in the dark about the fate of the settlers at Roanoke, he quite possibly knew more about the history of English expeditions than anyone else in Elizabeth's realm. His efforts to document English travels had already inspired others to perform similar tasks. Robert Parke informed the readers of his translation of Juan González de Mendoza's history of China that he had been set to his task by "the earnest request and encouragement" of Hakluyt, a man whose "manifolde learning and languages" enabled him to be "of singular and deepe insight in all histories of discoverie and partes of Cosmographie." Parke's book, which appeared on January 1, 1589, told readers that Hakluyt already had "in hande a most excellent and ample collection of the sundrie travailes and navigations of our own nation, a matter long intended by him, and serving to the like beneficiall and honorable purpose."[64]

When the *Principall Navigations* appeared ten months after Parke's history, there was little doubt about Hakluyt's prodigious knowledge. Based on extensive mining of existing works that already described specific English travels, Hakluyt also relied on a network of informants who provided details first hand or in manuscripts that had never been published before.[65] This book had a far wider angle than had *Divers Voyages* or the "Discourse on Western Planting." Each of those works established Hakluyt's core argument. The English had supported the ventures of the Cabots in the late fifteenth century, and that assistance gave them the right to the territory that the Venetians had discovered in North America. Those rights descended from Henry VII to Elizabeth and trumped all other claims. In Hakluyt's imagination, the English had a legitimate right to the entire mainland north of Spanish-claimed Florida. That claim extended from the Atlantic to the Pacific and the lands seen by Drake during his circumnavigation. (It was based on that claim that Hakluyt had supported the publication of Antonio Espejo's account of New Mexico.) Like other European promoters of expansion, Hakluyt dismissed any Americans' claims to territory they already inhabited, though he did believe that newcomers had to negotiate for land from the natives.

When he sat down to his task Hakluyt had much more on his mind than laying out an argument for why the English should own North America. He knew that he was creating a work to rival that of Pliny, Martyr, Münster, Thevet, and Ramusio, but with a twist. Each of those authors had set out to record human achievement and their texts (with the possible exception of Martyr's *Decades*) were ecumenical in spirit. Hakluyt was less generous. He had no desire to praise the efforts of someone supported by the Spanish (such as Columbus) or the French (such as Cartier). They were irrelevant for the task he had chosen for himself. His was not to be a massive compendium of knowledge for its own sake. Instead, he set out to transform himself, as he had hinted earlier, into the author of a national epic, the English Homer.

Hakluyt announced that the *Principall Navigations* would include accounts of "the most remote and farthest distant Quarters of the earth at any time within the compasse of these 1500 yeeres." He divided the work into three parts, following Ramusio's strategy. The first part contained "the personall travels of the English" to the East. Readers would find accounts of travels stretching from the modern Middle East and North Africa to India. The second section consisted of accounts to the north, which included territories as diverse as Lapland, Russia, and Persia. The last section related "the English valiant attempts in searching almost all the corners of the vaste and new world of *America*" from 73 degrees North latitude southward to the Strait of Magellan. For good measure he promised to throw in an account of "*the last most renowned English Navigation,* round about the whole Globe of the Earth"—the report of his new in-law Thomas Cavendish. He also included an account of Drake's voyage, the more famous round-the-world English journey, though its provenance remains unclear, a sign of Hakluyt's desire to describe the Pacific even though he could get his hands on far less information for that part of the world than for the Atlantic.[66]

Hakluyt began the book with a dedication to Sir Francis Walsingham. Though the identification of a patron was always to be expected before any work of scholarship, Hakluyt used these pages to tell readers about himself. He wrote about his visit to the lawyer in the Middle Temple and the moment of inspiration for his life's work. He established his expertise for the task by noting that his study at Christ Church included texts in Latin, Italian, Greek, Portuguese, French, Spanish, and English. He boasted about his geographical knowledge and his mastery of new globes and maps. He followed his studies with a period of learning about the larger world from those who had traveled into it—"the chiefest Captaines at Sea, the greatest Merchants, and the best mariners of our nation." He singled out Sir Edward Stafford, who had been his boss for five years, and had taken him across the English Channel to a nation where he "both heard in speech, and read in books other nations miraculously extolled for their discoveries and notable enterprises by sea, but the English of all others for their sluggish security, and continuall neglect of the like attempts especially in so long and happy a time of peace, either ignominiously reported, or exceedingly condemned."[67]

Hakluyt could not abide such aspersions. On his way back to London from Paris the previous winter, he traveled with Stafford's wife, Lady Sheffield, a woman whose "passing good behavior [was] highly esteemed in all the French court." On board that ship he realized he could not stand to hear another "obloquie of our nation." What the English needed was for someone to reply to such heretical claims and gather "the industrious labors, and painefull travels of our countrey men." The task was not easy. Hakluyt called it a "burden" since the reports from "these voyages lay so dispersed, scattered, and hidden in severall hucksters hands." Even after the fact he found it hard to believe that he had been able "to endure the delayes, curiosity, and backwardnesse of many" who provided the original texts he needed to complete his task. The unscrupulous reporters with whom he dealt with made him feel like Pliny, who had complained "of the men of his age: *At nos elaborataijs abscondere atij, supprimere cupimus, & fraudare vitam etiam alienis bonis, &c.* [But we moderns desire to hide and suppress the discoveries worked out by these investigators, and to cheat human life even of the good things that have been won by others]."[68]

Once he had finished harping on his own difficulties, Hakluyt got down to selling his remarkable collection of accounts of "searchers of the remote parts of the world." Men in England had traveled abroad for centuries, but in Elizabeth's age these expeditions had the greatest success. English mariners had traveled to South America, through the Strait of Magellan, and reached Java and Malacca. They had returned home with commodities from China. London became a destination for travelers from the Philippines and Japan. Hakluyt knew that such commercial and diplomatic channels would pave the way for English missionaries to East Asia and the Spice Islands and thus allow "the incomparable treasure of the trueth of Christianity, and of the Gospell," to spread even farther. He promised to reprint the reports of travelers "word for word." If the accounts were in Latin, Spanish, Portuguese, or Italian he would provide a translation "in the next roome," using the metaphor of his book as a mansion with distinct compartments. By linking accounts with specific travelers, Hakluyt (following Ptolemy) claimed that his volume would be more useful than any work of alleged universal cosmography. And, not surprisingly, he thanked those who had helped him, including individuals who had provided firsthand accounts, taken him to visit their cabinets, and the few reliable earlier authorities (Richard Eden, Peter Martyr, and John Bale) whose works contained relevant and trustworthy accounts. A detailed "Table Alphabeticall" at the end provided quick references to individuals, places, and even commodities.[69]

As Hakluyt had promised, the pages of the *Principall Navigations* revealed the words of those who had actually made voyages or, if needed, the words of chroniclers who had either been witnesses or possessed the relevant documents. Because one of his goals was to demonstrate the antiquity of English overseas expeditions, he began with the earliest possible account he could find—the voyage of the empress Helena, mother of Constantine the great, to Jerusalem. That journey took place in the year 337, when Helena, the daughter of the British king Coelus, a remarkable woman skilled in music and languages, decided to go on a pilgrimage to the Holy Land to visit the places where Jesus had trod. She died in Rome at age eighty, possibly returning from her journey to Jerusalem. Her body was taken to Venice, where it was still preserved.[70]

Here, as in many places in the book, Hakluyt provided the Latin original (one of the many accounts he took from Bale) and followed it with his translation. That act might seem obvious in retrospect since Hakluyt was trying to show an English-language audience the antiquity of their talent for long-distance travel. But the mere act of translation testified to Hakluyt's underlying motivation. Had he wanted only to reach scholars, he would have kept the accounts in their original language (as he did two years earlier when he produced a Latin version of Peter Martyr's *Decades*). Hard as it might be to imagine for a book of this size (and cost), his goal by 1589 was to reach a wider audience that included people who lacked his linguistic abilities.

Much of the information in the book testified to Hakluyt's investigative skills and the extent of his contacts. Some of the information had little apparent end. Short accounts of journeys made by the observant friar Richard Canonicus, the poet William the Pilgrim, and the bishop of Salisbury Hubert Walter revealed the fact of journeys to Syria and Palestine in 1190 but offered few details that made these reports particularly notable.[71] Yet if brevity characterized the materials Hakluyt included for the period before 1500, his sixteenth-century materials tended to be more detailed and abundant.

In rare instances only did Hakluyt appear as the author of an account, perhaps playing the role of an after-the-fact amanuensis. For example, he recounted the tale of the Bristol explorer Robert Thorne's voyage in 1527 to the northwest, supplementing it with supporting testimony. Hakluyt inserted the documents because earlier chroniclers had failed to take accurate note of significant discoveries, in this case Thorne's alleged sighting of land known in Hakluyt's time as Meta Incognita, Cape Breton, and Norumbega. His willingness to become the intermediary allowed him to retell a notorious story of an English expedition to Newfoundland in 1536—an expedition made infamous by allegations of cannibalism among the English themselves.[72]

Everything that Hakluyt put in the *Principall Navigations* reflected his belief that the accounts were all true and should be accepted as truth by readers. Everything, that is, except one entry: an account in Latin of the English knight Sir John Mandeville's travels. Unlike many of the authors whose words could be found in the collection, Mandeville was in all likelihood already known to many readers since approximately three hundred manuscript copies of his work already existed in Europe. Still Hakluyt believed that he belonged, reprinting Mandeville's account even though it was the longest entry in *Principall Navigations*. Yet here Hakluyt did something that he did nowhere else: he warned his readers about what they were about to read. After noting that he hoped he had purged the text of the many errors that variant copies contained, he drew his readers' attention to the "monstriferis hominum formis" (men of monstrous shapes) in the account. "Though I do not deny that certain of them were possibly observed by him somewhere," Hakluyt wrote, "yet they are, for the most part, clearly drawn" from the younger Pliny, "and all of these Pliny himself refers to their various authors, loth to put his trust in the majority of them."[73]

A diligent reader following Hakluyt's organization would have started a journey by going south. The intellectual sojourn that began with the brief description of the empress Helena's pilgrimage led to reports from medieval and Renaissance travelers to the Holy Land and Africa (especially Guinea, a frequent target for travelers), details about the payments made by the Turkish sultan and officers in and around his seraglio, a listing of the prices of certain goods (such as pepper and ginger) in Babylon in 1583, a detailed description of the weights, measures, and money used in Babylon, Balsara, Ormuz, Goa, Cochin, and Malacha (Malacca), estimates of shipping charges from Aleppo to Goa, an enumeration of where certain goods could be found, and a schedule of monsoons in and around Goa. Near the end of that section Hakluyt drew the reader's attention back to the danger that often attended voyages through waters controlled by Philip II of Spain. His account of English ships supported by London merchants involved in trade with Turkey anticipated the drama of 1588, again with results pleasing to Hakluyt and other promoters of the realm.[74]

The second section of the *Principall Navigations* followed similar thematic lines. It opened with an excursion of King Arthur to Iceland in 517 and a few other early accounts (including a tenth-century journey by King Edgar with four thousand ships around Britain). Hakluyt included eighteen accounts of expeditions taken between 1553 and 1584. Anyone who knew Hakluyt well would not have been surprised to find various accounts of his correspondent Anthony Jenkinson's trips to Russia or the expedition of Arthur Pet and Charles Jackman to Cathay in 1580, including the instructions that the lawyer had given them. A reader with a particularly good memory would have also recognized that Hakluyt reprinted two parts of his *Divers Voyages* that described the activities of the Bristol merchant Robert Thorne, and that he again relied on Ramusio and Mercator.[75]

In some sense, everything that Hakluyt printed in the first five hundred pages of *Principall Navigations* was an extended prologue for the third part, which included texts dealing with voyages to the West. Prologue, that is, if the book was read (as Hakluyt hoped that it would be) as a way to promote westward expansion. But in Hakluyt's mind, the details about voyages to the South and to the East were crucial to his understanding of the world and his goals for the realm. By leading the reader through the first "rooms," as he called them, he had in fact brought them deep into his own intellectual cabinet of curiosities, a world overflowing with stuff brought into it from distant shores. The time had come for the most spectacular finds, the intellectual equivalents of a desiccated alligator or a canoe from Brazil.

Hakluyt opened the final section with the story of the Welsh prince Madoc's journey in 1170 to "that Westerne countrey," which must have been either New Spain or Florida. This report proved that the British had been to America long before Columbus or Vespucci. He followed with crucial fifteenth-century evidence relating to Columbus's visit to King Henry VII and Sebastian Cabot's voyages, for which he drew on such unimpeachable authorities as Ramusio, Peter Martyr, and Francisco López de Gómara. He then provided the remarkable evidence that he had found in Robert Fabian's unpublished chronicle of life in London. Fabian, who also testified to Cabot's achievement, added details about the "three savages" brought back to England. Originally unintelligible (to the English), clad in "beastes skins" and eaters of "rawe flesh," the three had quickly come to be "apparelled after the maner of Englishmen" and walked the corridors of Westminster Palace without attracting notice.[76]

The vast majority of texts in this third part of *Principall Navigations* owed their existence to Hakluyt's industry and connections. Whenever possible he used trusted printed books, but much vital information had never been printed. Hence he relied on manuscript accounts of the voyages of Sir John Hawkins (who led expeditions to Africa and the West Indies) and his father, William Hawkins (who had led a voyage to Brazil around 1530). The account of Frobisher's first crossing of the frigid waters of the North Atlantic appeared for the first time in print in *Principall Navigations,* supplemented by the published accounts of Dionyse Settle and Thomas Ellis. All of the news Hakluyt had obtained about Roanoke also came from as-yet unpublished reports (including the account provided by John White about the fourth expedition to the settlement) or recently published materials (including White's associate Thomas Harriot's account of Virginia). By including the list of those who "safely arrived in Virginia," Hakluyt gave his readers an image of colonization as a work-in-progress whose ultimate fate, like that of the colonists still waiting in Roanoke but out of the range of communication in 1589, still hung in the balance.[77]

In a physical cabinet of curiosity a visitor would be shown artifacts from journeys abroad and told stories told about them. In the mental cabinet that Hakluyt had constructed, the reader had to imagine what things actually looked like in the material world. For that reason, Hakluyt's inclusion of specific details often supported his goal of promoting colonization. If someone could see what existed on the other side of the Atlantic, then he or she might be more likely to support a venture to acquire it.

One account in the final section of *Principall Navigations* might have caught a careful reader's eye: the story of David Ingram, one of Hakluyt's sources for the "Discourse." Sir Humphrey Gilbert had interrogated Ingram in 1582, and in 1583 he had published *A true discourse of the adventures &c travailes,* his own account of his expedition. No copy of this book has survived, so Hakluyt's choice to include the report in his book is again like a cabinet containing materials that can no longer be found in the world.

Neither the private examination conducted by Gilbert nor Hakluyt's published version of the account provides much information about Ingram's identity. He was, so we learn, a sailor originally from Barking in Essex, back in England for a decade when he reported his story. He was one of approximately 105 men whom Hawkins and Drake decided to leave in Mexico in 1568 after a naval encounter with Spanish ships had so weakened the small English fleet that the commanders did not know if they could return across the Atlantic. Hawkins recalled that the starving men straggled through the Gulf of Mexico; their desperation became so great that the ships docked and the men ate whatever they could find, including "rattes, cattes, mise and dogges," as well as parrots and monkeys. Seeking assistance to patch their ships and gather supplies for the voyage eastward, the English found little solace. Hawkins offered his men a choice: they could leave with him or stay. One hundred men remained, and another hundred chose to go with Hawkins. Though Hawkins eventually made it to Cornwall, the voyage was brutal. Inadequate food led to famine, disease, and death.[78]

Ingram was one of the men who decided to take his chances on land. According to his account, he must have soon departed on his journey, accompanied by Richard Browne and Richard Twide. They began at a place called the Rio de Minas (the "Rio de mynas" according to one contemporary manuscript), though the journey might actually have begun at the Escambia River in Florida. Whatever the starting point, Ingram's general direction was northward, and his pace almost relentless. As Hakluyt related the story, Ingram traveled "by land two thousand miles at the least and never continued in any one place above three or foure days, saving onely at the Citie of Balma, where he stayed six or seven dayes." The account pays virtually no attention to specific details, though Ingram's story of his rescue suggests that he was picked up by a French ship "60 Leagues West from Cape Britton," perhaps somewhere near modern-day Halifax, Nova Scotia. Before they embarked, Ingram and his companions led the French captain to the inland village of Beriniah, where the Europeans offered trifling wares and got furs, silver, and "great redde leaves of trees almost a yard long, & about a foote broade, which he thinketh are good for dying." Once they returned to England, the three men visited Hawkins, who offered them a reward. By the time Ingram told the tale, his companions were dead; he was the only surviving source for his journey and the things that he saw.[79]

Across the hundreds of pages of the *Principall Navigations,* Hakluyt relied on published reports, and he normally indicated where he got them. After introducing a text, he faded into the background, offering readers marginal notes but otherwise following the language and logic of the books he was using. This was not the case with his use of Ingram's account. Instead of reprinting the contents of a book, Hakluyt treated Ingram's report like the testimony of an individual being deposed for a trial. Hakluyt wanted his readers to be aware of the nature of his source. He thus constantly repeated the name of the author: "the aforesaid David Ingram," "the said David Ingram." At one point he referred to him as "the said examinate," reflecting perhaps the fact that he had joined Gilbert in the interrogation in 1582. Given the relative brevity of the text, Hakluyt's editorial strategy distanced him from Ingram's claims even though the inclusion of the text in *Principall Navigations* seemed to indicate Hakluyt's faith in its veracity.

Like many observers, Ingram had a keen interest in nature. He frequently identified the utility of particular plants, animals, birds, and geographic features. Ingram claimed that he and his companions found gold in some rivers and crystal elsewhere. But mineral wealth, though abundant, was only one natural resource awaiting a European harvest. Fertile fields, thick forests, and tempting meadows abounded. Ingram's fascination with plants made him typical of a generation of Elizabethans who purchased herbals. Like others, he often cared more for the economic value of a particular plant than its other features. Thus a description of a palm emphasized not its aesthetic qualities, such as its height or appearance, but its utility: its leaves could produce ropes, the upper branches could be eaten raw, and oil flowing from its roots was an antidote to poisoned arrows. Ingram described American fauna at length, including a description of an unnamed "Beaste bigger then a Beare," which lacked hands and a neck and whose "eyes and mouth were in his breast." The creature was both ugly and cowardly, with the skin of rat "full of silver hairs." At one point he also claimed to have seen the Northwest Passage and to have interviewed locals who told him that "they had seen shippes on that coast, and did draw upon the ground the shape and figure of shippes, and of their sailes and flagges." Hakluyt knew the import of that claim. Ingram's report "proveth the passage of the Northwest, and is agreeable to the experience of Vasques de Coronado, which found a shippe of China or Cataia upon the Northwest of America."[80]

Ingram also described the Americans he met. Such details were crucial, since newcomers needed the assistance of local natives to survive. Though the account occasionally referred to specific groups—such as the residents of a place called "Giricka" who were fascinated by the whiteness of the Europeans' skin—he tended to provide only general comments. In this way, Ingram lacked the instinct for ethnographic detail that could be found in the writings of other sixteenth-century travelers such as the English mathematician (and Roanoke explorer) Harriot, the Huguenot missionary Léry, and the young Dutch adventurer Linschoten. Ingram painted images with broad brush-strokes, noting, for example, that in more southern areas the Americans "go all naked" except for noble men and women who covered their genitals with local plants, while "in the North partes they are clothed with beastes skins, the hayrie side being next to their bodies in winter." He could also be inconsistent. The natives "are so brutish & beastly, that they wil not forbeare the use of their wives in open presence," he informed his readers, but proceeded to add that they were "naturally very courteous, if you do not abuse them, either in their persons or goods." Readers of the account would have learned how to offer tokens of friendship, how messengers conveyed individuals to meetings with local royalty, and how to engage in trade. Ingram provided the names of several towns, though not their exact locations, and he offered a brief assessment of indigenous architecture. He wrote also of the Americans' preparations for war and the weapons that they carried into battle. Cannibals could be found "betweene Norumbega & Bariniah," but the peoples he met were enemies of the flesh-eaters who had doglike teeth. In other words, most of the natives were friendly and could be trusted; those to be feared were distinguished by their appearance and could be avoided.[81]

Such an account would have sent reassuring signals to Elizabethan readers. That the Americans possessed some notion of a hierarchical society, even if Ingram's description of it was less than exact, suggested the potential for converting natives to European, specifically English ways. After all, it would have been harder to teach an anarchic people about the concept of a king or queen; it was much easier to persuade these peoples to replace their own rulers with European monarchs. That the Americans went to battle would not have surprised Europeans, who had always known that war was a part of the world's natural order. The rest of Ingram's details also would have made sense to readers. Like Europeans, the natives possessed houses and did not wander the landscape. In a description of the island society on Curaçao, Ingram noted the cruelty of Spanish overlords and the docility of the Americans, who gave themselves over easily into slavery. That episode convinced Ingram of the potential for exploiting the indigenous peoples: it "argueth the great obedience of those people, and how easily they may be governed when they be once conquered."[82]

Ingram's descriptions of the local peoples, then, mirrored his depiction of the environment. North America was different from England or, for that matter, from anywhere in Europe, but the disparities were less important than the similarities. English men and women could find goods to stay alive in America, and they could harvest natural products for profit. At the same time they could learn the proper rules for trade with the natives. The criteria needed for colonization seemed to be in place. The only type of information still necessary concerned matters relating not to the material world but to the spiritual world: Were the natives susceptible to Christian conversion? Could Christianity thrive on these distant shores?

Hakluyt must have been thrilled that Ingram provided some details about the Americans' religious beliefs. The report claimed that the natives "honor for their God a Devil, which they calle Colluchio, who speaketh unto them sometimes in the likeness of a blacke Dogge, and sometimes in the likenesse of a black Calfe." The color symbolism aside, Ingram's contention that the natives possessed a set of religious beliefs, however barbarous, was an indispensable clue to their possible proselytization, a point that Harriot realized at the same time. True, the Americans' religion needed to be replaced; the English could not tolerate worship of the Sun and Moon or polygamy or devil worship. But he appreciated at least that the natives punished adultery.[83]

At one point Ingram told a revealing story about the potential clash of European and American religions. Ingram and his two associates "went to a poore mans house & there they did see the said Colluchio or Devil, with very great eyes like a blacke Calfe." His companion Brown cried, "There is the Devil," and promptly "blessed himself: In the name of the Father, and of the Sonne, and of the holy Ghost." Twide then "said very vehemently, I defie thee and all they workes." In response to this verbal assault, the devil beat a hasty retreat. "Presently the Colluchio shrancke away in a stealing maner forth of the doores, and was seene no more unto them." Ingram's tale conveyed a significant lesson: he had seen the Americans' devil vanquished with the words of the Bible. By that act he served as witness to the reality of supernatural forces roaming the North American landscape, and he assured readers that Europeans armed with the language of the Christian God could resist demonic overtures. Few observers of Americans could offer more compelling assurance of both the need for Europeans to convert natives and their ability to do so without becoming victims of a devil in the shape of a black calf or dog.[84]

A careful reader of the *Principall Navigations* might have noticed that Hakluyt was not entirely convinced of the veracity of Ingram's report. But its contents were still appealing. Like a collector who cannot ignore an alluring item even if it might be a fake, Hakluyt was seduced by the tale because he knew it would be a treasure in his cabinet, something people would remember and talk about for years. Hakluyt knew that anyone who traveled this far into the book's apartments would be inspired by this heroic tale of godly triumph. Perhaps readers would then summon the courage to risk an ocean journey.

CHAPTER 9

London, 1590 to 1600
Truth and Lies

In the spring of 1590, about five months after the *Principall Navigations* had appeared in print in London, the inhabitants of Roanoke became international celebrities across Europe. Their newfound fame had little to do with the fact that Manteo and Wanchese had recently lived with Sir Walter Ralegh. Instead, their acclaim came from an astonishing publishing event: the decision of the Frankfurt publisher J. Wechel to print four separate versions of the Flemish engraver Theodor de Bry's edition of Thomas Harriot's report on Roanoke. The text of the English version had in fact appeared as a separate small book in 1588, and Hakluyt included these words the next year in his *Principall Navigations.* But what set Wechel's actions apart was his decision to publish editions with illustrations and to do so in English, German, Latin, and French, each with slightly different titles. The Latin title mirrored the English version, but the other versions departed further from the original model. The French edition promised to enlighten readers with a marvelous and strange report, all of it true, about the commodities to be found in Virginia. The German title was even more elaborate: *Wonderful, yet truthful accounts of the situation and customs of the wild ones in Virginia, who recently by the English, around the year 1585 . . . have been discovered.* Perhaps not surprisingly, it was Hakluyt who had the idea that illustrated editions of these books should be published.[1]

It is difficult from a distance of more than four centuries to understand the significance of this moment. Before 1590, Europeans interested in the Americas had ample opportunity to collect books published since 1493 that contained at least some information about the western hemisphere, and about the East, too. Some of those books contained illustrations, and cartographers often embellished their maps with visual evidence about what Americans and their lands looked like. That some Americans had already visited Europe, and had had their images drawn by observers, meant that readers with access to these books would have possessed at least a limited visual vocabulary for the indigenous peoples of the western hemisphere. Readers of cosmographies also had an idea about what Americans looked like. Or, to be more precise, they had ideas about what cosmographers claimed these indigenous peoples did, such as engage in cannibalism or consort with demons.[2]

De Bry's books changed that scenario. Though there had earlier been translations of works from one language into another, no one had yet produced multiple versions of a single text at one time. More important, no printer had offered readers such a sustained group of images about a particular American community. Through the publication of these books, de Bry made the residents of Roanoke representative of all Americans. To make sure that the English understood what they were looking at, Hakluyt translated the original captions (which John White had rendered in Latin) into English.

In 1590, when he offered those translations to de Bry, Hakluyt had in his hands scientific evidence about how at least some Americans lived. Harriot's text was an ideal complement to White's images. But this evidence, made more compelling by the pictures, now caused Hakluyt to reassess his own work. Had he presented an accurate image of the peoples of the western hemisphere before? For Hakluyt this was no minor question. He knew that his books would be read well beyond the oak-paneled walls of the private libraries of English manors or the studies of individuals like his cousin the lawyer. They would be taken on board ships and used as guides by those who trod, ever so warily, onto distant shores. It was that knowledge that had led Hakluyt to do all he could to make sure that the texts he included were accurate. During the 1590s he fretted about separating fact from fiction, a task that would eventually force him to rethink some of the information he had already provided. And he did so during the most personally painful part of his life.

On April 20, 1590, Hakluyt became a rector at Wetheringsett in Suffolk, a small rural parish about ninety miles from London. The patron of the church was Lady Douglas Stafford, Countess of Sheffield (and wife of the ambassador to France), whom Hakluyt had known well in Paris and who had accompanied him on his return to London in 1588. (The countess had even made an impression on the French, notably by assisting the court to modernize the way the king entertained visitors.) Hakluyt eventually acquired a

When not in London, Hakluyt could often be found in Suffolk, where he was rector of the Church of All Saints in Wetheringsett. His son was christened there in 1593, and his first wife, Douglas, was buried there in 1597. The church's exterior is studded with Suffolk flint, a local stone that reflects sunlight
(AUTHOR PHOTO)

manor called Bridge Place in Codenham, about seven miles from Wethering-sett. His book was already being promoted by his associates, including Philip Jones, who prepared an edition of Albertus Meier's pamphlet instructing travelers to record twelve attributes of foreign places—cosmography, astronomy, geography, chorography, topography, husbandry, navigation, the political and ecclesiastical nature of the state, literature, history, and chronicles—while abroad. Jones urged his readers to consult Hakluyt's "rare & excellent worke," which was about to appear to the public.[3] But despite signs of settling into the rural quiet of a county where the night skies were illuminated only by stars, Hakluyt remained focused on the world well beyond the boundaries of rural Suffolk. Perhaps he thought about the four editions of Harriot's account that rolled off the presses at Frankfurt am Main that year.

Unlike previous travel writers, who wove together stories of individual explorers with observations about what regions looked like or could produce, Harriot crafted a systematic overview of the territory around Roanoke. The climate was right for the production of flax, hemp, and the harvesting of the local "grasse Silk"; if the colonists planted mulberry trees, they could tend silkworms and create an industry to rival that of "the Persians, Turkes, Italians and Spaniards." The woods produced *materia medica* in the form of a plant the natives called "wapeih" and sassafras, a tree that Nicholas Monardes had already described in his book, which Harriot noted had recently been published in English. The island where the English docked was also thick with trees that produced the turpentine, pitch, rosin, and tar that seafarers needed. Nearby cedars yielded a precious "sweet wood & fine timber" that was already being used by Europeans for tables, desks, virginals, lutes, and bedsteads. Local grapes could produce wine, though they would need the guiding hand of skilled husbandmen to reach their potential. English dyers would be thrilled to purchase woad and madder, which could be grown in Virginia because it shared a climate similar to the Azores, where these crops flourished. The climate and soil of this newfound land also seemed fit for sugar, oranges, lemons, and quinces that the English hoped to produce to avoid Spanish markets. The forests and fields were also home to an enormous variety of game, including seventeen kinds of fowl. Rocks containing iron had already been assayed eighty to one hundred miles away, and the English believed they might also find copper, silver, and even pearls. One of Harriot's companions traded with the locals for five thousand pearls and then made a beautiful necklace for the queen. Unfortunately, the pearls disappeared when a storm struck during the explorers' return, along with sweet gums that Harriot believed English apothecaries could have used in their medicines.[4]

There was still much to be learned about the American environment, but Harriot believed that crops could be produced at the same latitudes in the western hemisphere as they had been in Europe. Further, Virginia's forests sprouted tall oak, walnut, and towering firs ideal for masts. Fish weirs could be made from willows. The Algonquians used a local sweetwood called Rakiok to make canoes large enough to hold twenty men. Local Indians used maples for their bows. Birdlime could be produced from holly. Ash and beech could be bent for casks and plows.[5]

Harriot paid careful attention to the sources of food in the region. He was enthusiastic about maize, which the Americans used for food and the English, if they added hops, could use for beer. The plant, known as *pagatowr* to the Algonquians, could reach fourteen feet and swayed in the wind over beans (*okindgier*), peas (*wickonzowr*), and pumpkins or gourds (*macocqwer*). Americans' herbs, notably melden (as the Dutch called it) and marigold, had potential for broth and bread. There were also abundant supplies of edible roots, nuts, and fruits, including strawberries that could rival the best of an English garden. Rivers and the ocean itself teemed with fish and shellfish, including sturgeon, herring, trout, crabs, oysters, mussels, scallops, and porpoises. The locals had devised weirs made of reeds to capture some fish, but they were also skilled at spearing fish with sharpened poles "after the maner as Irishmen cast dartes." Large tortoises, some measuring three feet across, could be found on land and in the water. Easily captured, they produced tasty meat and edible eggs.[6]

This bountiful landscape did not sustain itself. Instead, as Harriot recognized, much of it was the result of careful cultivation by local Algonquians. What he described were the results of prevailing agricultural practices, including the tendency of Algonquians to sow herbs and vegetables around their maize stalks. The results were ears of corn with up to two thousand kernels each. Harriot calculated that per acre yields in Roanoke were five times greater than in England. Since the soil could sustain two harvests a year, any individual's needs could be easily fulfilled.[7]

Harriot also described the Algonquians' cultivation of tobacco, that plant that had attracted so much attention in Europe and which Hakluyt knew about from his reading of Monardes's *Joyfull Newes out of the newe found worlde*. The Indians dried the leaves of the plant and beat them into a powder, Harriot wrote, and then they took "the fume or smoke thereof" through a clay pipe. Tobacco purged the body of "superfluous fleame & other grosse humors," opening pores and clogged internal passages and thus preserving "the body from obstructions." As a result of smoking, "their bodies are notably preserved in health, & know not many greevous diseases wherewithall wee in England are oftentimes afflicted." The Algonquians used the plant's sacred power to seek divine intervention. They sprinkled the dried leaves on fires to propitiate their deities, tossed it into the sky "to pacifie their gods" when caught in a storm on the water, dropped tobacco leaves on newly made fishing weirs, and threw it into the air after they escaped danger. They did these things, he wrote, "with strange gestures, stamping, somtime dauncing, clapping of hands, holding up of hands, & staring up into the heavens, uttering therewithal and chattering strange words & noises." The English might have been appalled by such rituals but nonetheless smoked tobacco "after their maner." Once he returned to England, Harriot learned that many men and women at home were already learning of the plant's noble qualities.[8]

Harriot knew that his readers also needed precise information about the Americans themselves. Some people in England would have had an opportunity to meet Manteo and Wanchese, and a few encountered the Inuit Collichang and Egnock and her baby before their untimely deaths. But for most English folk, the indigenous peoples of the Americas remained something of a mystery. The tales about American cannibalism, found in books from Hans Stade, Jean de Léry, and Michel de Montaigne, frightened readers who might be unwilling to risk their lives on a sea crossing only to arrive in a land where the locals consumed uninvited visitors.[9] If the English were to take advantage of the abundant resources of Roanoke, Harriot knew that he had to allay their fearful assumptions about the Americans.

Harriot reassured his readers by emphasizing that the Algonquians would not stop the English from settling the region. They were "not to be feared" but would soon "have cause both to feare and love us, that shall inhabite with them." The Algonquians were of similar size as the English, but they wore deerskin mantles and aprons and little else. Their bows, arrows, and clubs were adequate for hunting or for wars between different groups. Their flat-topped houses made with poles looked like the kinds of structures to be found "in many arbories in our gardens of England." Most of these houses had bark roofs, though some Indians used mats woven of rushes to keep out the elements. A typical house measured between twelve and sixteen yards long (some were as long as twenty-four yards) and tended to be about half as wide as they were long. Harriot reported that towns normally had ten to twelve such houses, though one unnamed community had thirty. Still, he described such villages as "small," which they must have seemed to anyone who had come to Roanoke from London. None of the towns had a particularly formidable defensive perimeter. Though the Americans did occasionally go into battle, the English should not fear them since "running away was their best defence."[10]

Describing what people looked like and how they lived constituted a vital part of any ethnographic report, but Harriot was also keen to tell about the people themselves. They were poorer than the English, or so it seemed to the newcomers, since the natives lacked "skill and judgement in the knowledge and use of our things." The Americans valued "trifles" instead of "thinges of greater value." Although their technology was inferior to that of the English, the Algonquians nonetheless demonstrated such "excellencie of wit" that Harriot believed it would be only a matter of time before the Americans wanted the things that the English possessed. And trade, he knew, would prompt the natives to come to the English, thereby providing an opportunity for them to "be brought to civilitie," and from there to "imbracing of true religion."[11]

That point was crucial for both Harriot and Hakluyt, who were eager to know how to bring natives from the dark night of heathen savagery to the warm daylight of Protestant Christianity. The young mathematician knew that any conversion might be difficult, but not impossible. Since the Algonquians already possessed "some religion," he thought that "although it be farre from the truth, yet beyng a[s] it is, there is hope it may bee the easier and sooner reformed." The Algonquians believed that a supreme god had decided to create the world. He created a number of lesser gods known as *mantoac* to help him, including the Sun, the Moon, and the stars "as pettie goddes and the instruments" of the supreme god. These *mantoacs* began their efforts by creating water and then using it to make "all diversitie of creatures that are visible or invisible." Afterward they created a woman, who, "by the working of one of the goddes, conceived and brought foorth children." Those children were the first to roam the Earth. When Hakluyt retold the story several years later, he added that the natives had no precise idea of how long in the past these events had taken place since they had "no letters nor other such meanes as we to keepe Records of the particularities of times past, but onely tradition from father to sonne."[12]

According to Harriot, the natives believed that the gods had human form and thus created images of them, which they worshiped in a shrine. The natives drew no clear line between the idol and the divine entity itself; at least the "common sort" thought "them to be also gods." Yet, Harriot learned, the gods lived in heaven, where they welcomed the immortal souls of humans to share "perpetuall blisse and happinesse." Not every man or woman was fortunate enough to join the gods there. The Americans told of a place called Popogusso, "a greate pitte or hole" where the unfortunate burned forever. Occasionally the boundaries between Earth and the afterlife were porous. Several years earlier an Algonquian man had returned from the dead to describe heaven, an event so unusual that the Americans felt compelled to report it.[13]

In Harriot's view, such stories of near-death experiences had no theological value. Local political leaders (known as *werowances*) and priests circulated the tales to maintain order. If the people obeyed, their souls could look forward to perpetual bliss. Still, not all did. Harriot reported that the Algonquians punished such "malefactours, as stealers, whoremoongers, and other sorte of wicked doers." Their punishment depended on the "greatnes of the factes" presented against them. For minor crimes the perpetrator was beaten. Werowances or priests ordered executions for those whose transgressions were most severe.[14]

Given its superstitions, idols, and lack of dogma, the natives' religious traditions stood little chance of surviving the arrival of Protestants. That, at least, is what Harriot believed, and Hakluyt would have agreed. Harriot claimed that he had a "special familiarity" with a local priest who had confided to him the Algonquians' beliefs. But he also sensed that the Indians "were not so sure grounded, nor gave such credite to their traditions and stories." Conversations with the English had made them rethink their commitments.[15]

Despite his ability to describe Algonquian culture ethnographically, Harriot could not escape the cultural blinders that virtually all Europeans wore in the western hemisphere. He was convinced that the English possessed superior minds, as their display of scientific apparatus revealed. The newcomers showed off the "Mathematicall instruments, sea compasses," mirrors, books, and clocks that they had brought and claimed that these items "far exceeded their capacities to comprehend the reason and meanes how they should be made and done." The Algonquians thought that the instruments must have been made by gods, not men, "or at the leastwise they had bin given and taught us of the gods." Harriot tried to convince the natives that the English had these marvels because of their special relationship with their own god. Clocks and compasses belonged to the newcomers, a people "whom God so specially loved," and not to the Indians, "a people that were so simple."[16]

As he traveled around the Carolina coastline, Harriot was eager to find natives willing to accept English beliefs. He carried a Bible with him since it contained, as he put it, evidence of "the true doctrine of salvation through Christ, with manie particularities of Miracles and chiefe poyntes of religion." The Americans were "glad to touch it, to embrace it, to kisse it, to hold it to their breasts and heades, and stroke all over their bodie with it," he added, "to shewe their hungrie desire of that knowledge which was spoken of." Consumed with the knowledge that the written word was able to convey messages to an ignorant people, he failed to see that the Algonquians made no separation between the religious ideas of the Protestants and their vessels for transporting those concepts.[17]

Yet as the English reveled in their alleged superiority, Harriot came to realize that such a position was not always beneficial to the newcomers. When disease started to spread among the natives, the Americans so fully accepted English power over natural forces that (as Harriot claimed) they believed any "strange sicknesse, losses, hurtes" or other calamities resulted from offenses to their visitors and the English deity. As that idea lingered, unspecified diseases, probably transported unwittingly by the English, spread among the Americans. "Within a few dayes after our departure from everie such towne," Harriot reported, "the people began to die very fast, and many in short space." As many as sixty might die in a single community, and Harriot reported that in one unfortunate settlement 120 succumbed. But the ailments had no known predecessors and could not be explained. The Algonquians "neither knew what it was, nor how to cure it."[18]

The mystery demanded explanation, and the Americans came to believe the disease and death attributable to the power of the English god. Harriot and the English tried to suggest to the Americans that one way to avoid contagion might be to adopt the English religion and to "bee made partakers of his truth & serve him in righteousnes." They saw another advantage: if the Algonquians believed that the English could decide when illness would strike, the Algonquians would go out of their way to make sure the newcomers had everything they wanted. Nonetheless, no matter what the English said, the Americans would believe that the newcomers controled their god's actions.[19]

The matter was not so easily resolved. If the English did not understand why the Algonquians were dying, the Americans understood all too well that the English were surviving. Harriot thought that "this marvelous accident" had forced some of the Algonquians to adopt the "strange opinion" that they could not tell "whether to think us gods or men." The locals realized that the English had no women among them and that when it came time to help the Algonquians the visitors concentrated their efforts on the men in each settlement. "Some therefore were of opinion that wee were not borne of women," Harriot wrote, "and therefore not mortall, but that wee were men of an old generation many yeeres past then risen againe to immortalitie."[20]

Those who embraced such a view went further than even these speculations. According to one rumor circulating among clusters of houses along the Carolina coast, the English were but the advance wave of what amounted to an invading force keen to kill the natives and seize their lands. According to this native vision, the newcomers would soon be followed by those "they imagined to be in the aire, yet invisible & without bodies" who would "make the people to die in that sort as they did by shooting invisible bullets into them." Local healers announced that the blood the invaders sucked out of wounds "were the strings wherewithal the invisible bullets were tied and cast." Though some Americans offered other explanations for the deaths (perhaps caused by an eclipse the previous year or a comet that trailed across the sky shortly before the newcomers' arrival), the spread of infection caused tension that did not easily disappear.[21]

Harriot recognized that he never saw much of Virginia. He did not have adequate information about the peoples who inhabited the interior or the American climate, though he believed it was similar to that of China, Japan, Persia, Greece, Spain, and Italy. But despite its deficiencies the report conveyed the information that appealed to Hakluyt. He knew from its pages that newcomers could adjust to life in North America. Despite many initial hardships, only four of the 108 men on the journey died there, and three of them were "feeble, weake, and sickly persons" before they made the voyage. Later groups would no doubt bring more cattle with them, in addition to English fruits, herbs, and root crops, all of which would thrive in a place with a salubrious climate and fertile soil. Even the mystery of traveling across the Atlantic was no longer so terrifying. The journey could be made three times a year, Harriot claimed, "with ease and at any season." Under the beneficent leadership of Sir Walter Ralegh, who was eager to grant parcels of land to those who would go there, the prospects for Virginia could not have been better.[22]

The entire report pleased Hakluyt, who did all he could to publicize it after its initial appearance as a small pamphlet in London in 1588. He included the text in the 1589 edition of the *Principall Navigations,* but that was not enough. Knowing that the artist John White had gone with Harriot to Roanoke in 1585, Hakluyt worked with Theodor de Bry to create the illustrated edition of Harriot's *Report.* The result was the series of images that rolled off the printer Wechel's press and provided Europeans with distinct images of what one American population looked like.[23]

Europeans who saw the individuals in Harriot's book would have believed they were savages locked into a primitive culture in which they wore little if any clothing, worshipped idols, and engaged in ritual scarification. But however primitive they seemed, there was no doubt of their potential to be converted. In the visual rendering of the village of Secota (or Secotan), for example, the de Bry engraving reveals an orderly community in which the inhabitants rely on agriculture, supplemented by hunting and fishing, for their sustenance. The main street is straighter than the roads found in most European villages, and the crops are abundant. Local streams overflow with

The town of Secota (or Secotan), as depicted in Thomas Harriot's *A briefe and true report of the new found land of Virginia* (Frankfurt, 1590). Theodor de Bry's engraving of the village of Secota was not accurate; there would have been no need for a straight-edged road through the community, for example, and the native peoples of eastern North America did not practice the monoculture common among the English. But the image nonetheless conveyed a distinct impression of the potential abundance of the region and the ways that its people already demonstrated signs of being civilized.

fish, and though the Americans' worshipped idols, the images of sacred rites revealed a people who were deeply religious.

Unlike many sixteenth-century books, which used illustrations in a slap-dash fashion and often repeated images, the books produced by Wechel used visual images to tell a specific story. The reader encountered Harriot's text

Theodor de Bry's engravings of John White's paintings of Picts, from Thomas Harriot's *A briefe and true report of the new found land of Virginia* (Frankfurt, 1590) (HUNTINGTON LIBRARY)

first, then the engraved version of the illustrations by White of the Carolina Algonquians and their world. At the end the reader had a surprise: a series of images of the Picts, the legendary ancient inhabitants of Britain. The engraved versions lacked the Picts' distinctive blue coloring (which can be found in White's preparatory paintings), but they still conveyed the fundamental brutality of these men and women. Armed, naked, tattooed, and fresh from battle—these pictures were more threatening than any contemporary vision of Americans. But they came with a specific message from Hakluyt: Picts were more savage than Americans but became civilized; with the proper instruction, Americans would as well, and the process would probably take place

even more quickly given the fact that the Algonquians seemed apt to change. The pictures conveyed a lesson perhaps more important than the text. Embedded within these images was a theory of cultural progression. Text and image worked together to advance Hakluyt's agenda.[24]

After the publication of *Principall Navigations*, Hakluyt continued to gather information. He did not tell where he was when his informants contacted him or where he met those who refused or were unable to record their thoughts on paper. Presumably he was in London, at least some of the time. During the 1590s he also spent time in Bristol, an ideal spot for gathering information from those returning from long voyages,[25] and in his parish at Wetheringsett, a place better suited for contemplation than research. But wherever he was, he never stopped collecting. It was as if the monumental *Principall Navigations* was only a first version of the magnum opus he eventually intended to publish.

Like Ramusio and Thevet, Hakluyt knew that he would need to map the world for his readers. After publishing *Principall Navigations* (which included one recent map of the world), Hakluyt wanted yet another new map. He turned, not surprisingly, to Ortelius. Though Ortelius had been skeptical about Hakluyt's publication of the Latin edition of Peter Martyr's *Decades* (published in Paris in 1587), he was less dismissive about the English promoter's efforts to provide accurate information about the Americas. In late August 1590, he wrote to his nephew Jacob Cool from Antwerp, asking him to greet Hakluyt for him and to pass on a message: he would be willing to create a new map of the western hemisphere north of Mexico City if Hakluyt sent him the necessary information.[26]

In the meantime, Hakluyt still collected. Sometimes a new report treated an area that had not been covered the first time around or a reader had information that might be of use. When witnesses came forward, Hakluyt was keen to hear what they had to say, even if it was a report of a journey taken sixty years earlier.[27] Sometimes visitors even brought souvenirs, like the walrus tusk that Alexander Woodson had given him in the early 1590s.

Sitting in his study, fingering a walrus bone or jotting down details from an old man's stories, Hakluyt could have been forgiven if he thought the entire world shared the quiet contemplation he needed to compose his great collections. But those moments of silence disappeared in a moment in early September 1592 when English privateers captured the carrack *Madre de Deus* used by the Portuguese in the East India trade. When the ship arrived at Dartmouth, its treasures included an account that Hakluyt believed was "the most exact" report of Japan and northern China to ever "come to light." It had been printed in Latin in Macao in 1590 and had been, Hakluyt wrote, "inclosed in a case of sweete Cedar wood, and lapped up almost an hundred fold in fine calicut-cloth, as though it had beene some incomparable jewell." The account, like scores of others, ended up in Hakluyt's hands, a testimony to his stature as the preeminent interpreter of such exotica in Elizabethan England.[28]

Upon close examination, Hakluyt found cause for excitement about his "incomparable jewell." The treatise detailed an abundance of gold in China— so much that it could be sold to India, Japan, and Portugal. The Chinese also had rich stores of silver, tin, copper, and lead, in addition to "wonderfull store of pearles" and fantastic supplies of silk. There was so much silk that every year the Chinese sent an entire shipload to Macao. Ships also hauled large quantities of cotton woolens, porcelain, spices, and sugar.[29]

The report, which Hakluyt later attributed to Duarte de Sande, covered eleven folio pages, enumerating details rivaled only by Robert Parke's translation of his *Historie* of China (which Hakluyt had earlier encouraged). Sande told about the country's towns and mentioned the Great Wall, built, as he thought, to "represse and drive backe the Tartars attempting to invade their territories." He described Chinese arts and sciences, including their invention of gunpowder and their printing abilities. He marveled at the longevity of many of those he encountered, which he attributed to the "salubrities of the aire" and the "fruitfulnes of soile" the best in the East (though not as productive as that of Europe). He celebrated the Chinese passion for literature and described the various degrees that scholars received. Not all was praiseworthy, of course. When he published the account Hakluyt added a marginal note alerting readers where to find information about the "idolatrous religion of the king." But while the Chinese had "always lived in great errours and ignorance of the trueth" before Christian missionaries arrived, they nonetheless possessed well-defined religious beliefs. Sande provided details on Confucianism and other groups he labeled "sects." He concluded by mentioning the recent success of establishing a mission there. "These be the first beginnings of Christianity in China," Sande noted, "where, even as in other places of the Christian Common-wealth, the seed is to be sowen with great labour and teares, that acceptable fruits may be reaped with gladnesse."[30]

Hakluyt could have wanted almost nothing more than what Sande had reported. The arrival of the text wrapped in calico and encased in cedar had stirred his imagination as if it were a gift from heaven. But its contents were even more magical: in a healthy climate where great wealth could be found, the natives were receptive to the teachings of Christianity. Hakluyt might have never dreamed that the clerical and scientific parts of his Christ Church years could come together so perfectly.

On June 3, 1593, Richard and Douglas Hakluyt brought their newborn son, Edmond, to the church in Wetheringsett to be christened. Like their contemporaries, they must have wondered if their child would survive the perilous first year of life. In a world where perhaps one in five infants died before their first birthday, these fears would have been realistic. Hakluyt was then about forty years old. The age of his wife, Douglas, remains unknown, though if she was a typical first-time mother she would have been in her late twenties or early thirties by then.[31]

At about the time that Edmond was learning to walk, Hakluyt received a letter from John White, who was then at his home in Newtown, County Cork, near the southwest coast of Ireland. The letter accompanied a report of White's final journey to Virginia, on which he had embarked at the end of February 1590. The effort was mired in disaster. After preparing three ships for an expedition to the West Indies and the North American mainland, White and the others found themselves trapped in port under orders that no ships were to leave. White, who had arranged funding for the vessels through a London merchant, had hoped that Ralegh could use his influence to get an exception to the general orders. But Ralegh did not come through, and so White languished with the three ships loaded with "furnitures and necessaries" destined for Virginia. Then the ships' owners ordered White to travel alone across the ocean, taking only one chest of his goods and depriving him of the passengers he had arranged. Yet since the ships were about to sail (he never explained when the orders to remain in port were lifted), he felt he had no choice but to accompany those who had little regard for the settlers in Virginia and instead rode out into the Atlantic "to seeke after purchase & spoiles." That quest for wealth took months in the West Indies, so long that summer had almost ended by the time White reached the mainland. Then a late summer storm prevented them from going ashore, so White still did not know what had happened to the colonists.[32]

If White's letter gave pause, Hakluyt showed no sign of abandoning his efforts. The publication of Gabriel Harvey's *Pierces Supererogation* in 1593 included a recommendation for readers to discover the accounts of Gilbert, Drake, Frobisher, and Ralegh's Virginia colony in *Principall Navigations,* "a worke of importance." Though he did not always receive news as quickly as he wanted, Hakluyt continued to interview returning mariners, such as Edmund Barker, who had been on a mission to India and Malacca in 1591.[33]

In late 1594 Hakluyt, still at Wetheringsett (and perhaps fending off the almost two-year-old Edmond), responded to a request from Emanuel van Meteren, a Dutch geographer who sought information relating to the Northeast Passage. The Dutchman, acting for others, had asked if Hakluyt could gather all of the needed information about the passage. Hakluyt agreed to help them with his own notes and with suggestions for what books they should purchase; he even agreed to provide a synopsis of works that were not yet in print. To accomplish this task, he had to travel to London and stay there for perhaps a month. He required twenty pounds in compensation, a fee he found trivial compared to the "many thousand pounds" he was confident van Meteren's associates would receive after getting this information. He added that van Meteren should keep this matter a secret, "for that imports me much, and as the Italian says, 'il savio è secreto.'"[34]

As this letter revealed, even from remote Wetheringsett, Hakluyt remained enmeshed in a web of personal and intellectual contacts that stretched across Europe. He knew that he had more information than others and that whatever he charged would be worth it. More to the point, he knew where to get the precious information. He was one of the few masters of this particular game. Van Meteren thought so too. "I believe that there is no man living more eager in searching out the manner of voyages or who can say more about it," he wrote to Jacob Valcke shortly after receiving Hakluyt's offer. "He is," the Dutchman concluded, "the most skilled man in research that I have ever known, and I have known him full twenty years."[35]

By the mid-1590s, the world that Hakluyt knew so well had begun to fracture. The queen's secretary Sir Francis Walsingham, the man responsible for sending Hakluyt to Paris in 1583, died in 1590. He had been remarkably industrious, Camden recalled, a man known for his piety, wisdom, and his ardent adherence to Protestantism, "a curious searcher out of secrets; one that could dive into mens dispositions, and worke them to his owne ends at pleasure." According to Camden, "Papists every where traduced him as a subtle enginere, to screw simple Proselytes within the danger of the law." Yet for all of his talent, his efforts sent him into such debt that he had to be buried at St. Paul's during the evening, "without any Funerall solemnity."[36]

Walsingham's death deprived Hakluyt of his most powerful patron, but his was not the only absence Hakluyt mourned. In 1591 his cousin the lawyer also died, leaving Hakluyt without the man who had set him on his life's journey. Judging from the lawyer's will, written four years earlier, the cousins were perhaps not as close as they might have been. The lawyer left his farm in Eyton to Hakluyt's younger brother Oliver, who was also to receive his "greater saltsellar of sylver." If Oliver could not claim the land, then they were to go to his brother Edmund, and if Edmund could not inherit them then they were to pass to Hakluyt. If none of the three brothers could claim the farm, then the lawyer specified that it should be passed to his sister Winifred. The lawyer also owned more than eight hundred acres divided into "quilletts," or small, detached strips, in Eyton, which he bequeathed to the three Hakluyt brothers and Winifred. He divided his silver among other family members—Oliver, Winifred, and his other sisters Barbara Evissham and Elnor Conesbie—but gave none of it to Hakluyt. Since the will was written while Hakluyt was going back and forth between London and Paris, and before Hakluyt had received his position in Wetheringsett, the lawyer's affections had perhaps turned toward Oliver, who was the executor of the estate and then, like Hakluyt before him, a student at Christ Church.[37]

Hakluyt left no surviving record of his views of his cousin's will. Perhaps he was too busy mourning other losses. The dead included his wife's uncle, the circumnavigator Thomas Cavendish, lost at sea off Brazil in 1591 or 1592; and Martin Frobisher, killed in battle during the English siege of a Spanish fortress in 1594. Frobisher had been shot in the hip during the assault, and though he survived to lead his ships back to Plymouth, he died soon after. Drake and John Hawkins, two of the ablest mariners in England, succumbed to disease on an expedition to the West Indies in 1595–1596.[38]

As the people he knew disappeared from his life, Hakluyt persevered with his task. The times were hardly auspicious. A pernicious drought parched the land in 1591 and 1592, and disease soon followed. "Lamentable is the time present," one observer wrote, noting that God was "hotly incensed agaynste the cyties both of London and Westminster, for he hath sent fourth his worde of displeasure and caused the ayre to be pestilently infected." A "great mortalitie" followed, and many of the inhabitants fled the metropolis. The sufferings had barely faded when plague returned to London in 1594.[39]

Despite his personal losses, Hakluyt remained committed to the promotion of geographical knowledge. Over the winter of 1595, when Emanuel van Meteren was in London, Hakluyt traveled to the city to meet him. He spent a day with van Meteren in January, showing him ancient proof for the existence of the Northeast Passage and telling him of English travelers to the East. Hakluyt also suggested the importance of Ramusio's work, launching van Meteren on a crusade to obtain a copy of *Navigationi e Viaggi*. (He could not find one in London, but he informed his correspondent Jacob Valcke that a copy might be purchased in Paris, Frankfurt, or Cologne.) In February, Hakluyt provided a summary of Cavendish's travels at a cost of eleven pounds for a nine-to-ten-page report. Van Meteren was very conscious of the importance of Hakluyt's efforts and willing to spend what it took to get this information. He knew, too, that he had to abide by Hakluyt's schedule and that the cost of obtaining precious information meant paying Hakluyt enough money to come to London with his own horse (a point he made twice in three letters). Hakluyt, for a fee, apparently shared what he knew. As "the instructor of all the English navigation which has traveled out on discovery," van Meteren knew that this was money well spent. Hakluyt was never content that he had found enough. Fortunately, he had the contacts to gain new accounts, including one who sent him his journal of a voyage to the West Indies and northern South America "to supply a vacant roome amongst your more important discourses.[40] That traveler was Robert Dudley, who had heard reports of Ralegh on a mission to Guiana. The two Englishmen never saw each other, but as Hakluyt soon learned, Ralegh was indeed on his way toward the Orinoco and its mysteries.

Ralegh sailed from Plymouth on February 6, 1595, headed for Guiana. Six weeks later, after making their way along the well-known route through the Canaries, his ships arrived at Trinidad. Wherever he looked in the region he saw signs of the Spanish conquest—names on maps given by the Iberians and native peoples accustomed to dealing with them. Sailing to a nearby island Ralegh spotted a fire along the shoreline, but none of the locals would come to meet the English "for feare of the Spaniards," as he put in his account of the journey that he published the next year. If he missed contact with humans, he nonetheless studied and recorded marvels, such as trees that seemed to sprout oysters from their branches. The sight would have seemed even more bizarre had Ralegh never heard of such a thing, but in fact he had read Thevet's account of America and the writings of Pliny.[41]

Well before he got to the mainland, Ralegh paid attention to the islands. He learned about the ways that the Spanish had mistreated the locals and he spread positive news about the queen, who he promised was a great virgin *cacique* with many more *caciques* under her command; she was also, he assured them, an enemy of the Castilians with a record of liberating those whom the Spaniards oppressed. "I shewed them her majesties picture," Ralegh wrote, "which they so admired and honoured, as it had beene easie to have brought them Idolatrous thereof." Soon islanders called her *Ezrabeta Cassipuna Aquerewana*—"*Elizabeth*, the great princesse or greatest commaunder." That business accomplished, Ralegh began the six-hundred-mile journey to the mainland.[42]

Ralegh's ability to understand Guiana was due less to any innate ethnographic talents he might have possessed than to his reading. He was the kind of explorer Hakluyt spent his life serving: a man who devoured available travel accounts before entering into an unknown territory. For Ralegh, that meant reading Spanish reports. Although other Europeans had known about Guiana before 1595, Ralegh himself found the land still so mysterious, and its rewards so alluring, that he planned to create a secret chart of the region. He begged his patrons not to let it fall into the hands of others, such as the French, who had launched their own excursion to Guiana at the same time.[43]

During his journey Ralegh was eager to learn about the geography of Guiana, as well as the customs of its people and their neighbors. That dual quest led him to interview the oldest local residents he could find, who confided in him about the Amazons who lived nearby. According to Ralegh's account, these informants told him that once a year these women welcomed local kings into their midst, with each woman choosing a partner according to rank for the queens and then by lottery for the others. For one month the women entertained the men. "They feast, daunce, & drinke of their wines in aboundance," Ralegh learned, until the next moon appeared and the men were sent on their way. When infants were born nine months later the boys were abandoned to the care of their fathers, but the daughters they kept and trained to be allies in their wars. The Amazons did not, as legend told, mutilate their right breasts to enable them to fight more easily, but they were nonetheless "very cruell and bloodthirsty, especially to such as offer to invade their territories."[44]

Like other informants Hakluyt trusted, Ralegh paid close attention to the geography of northern South America, specifically the delta of the Orinoco, a wonder that Europeans struggled to understand and then map. But he was more concerned with Spanish efforts to control the region, enslave local natives, and enrich themselves with Guiana's natural wealth, including "gold plates, eagles of gold, and Images of men and divers birds." He described his journey in abundant detail, commenting on the difficulty of passage in some places, the flora and fauna that he observed, and rumors that he heard about Spanish cruelty toward Americans. Ralegh claimed that the English traveled a thousand miles up the Orinoco and its tributaries. The Americans who attended him offered the travelers abundant supplies of food, in addition to parakeets and an armadillo, a creature that Ralegh could liken only to a rhinoceros. He knew from reading Monardes that the horn growing out of the back of the armadillo could be ground into powder and used to cure deafness. In the following days he would see and hear of other marvels, from rich silver mines to monstrous peoples like those described by Mandeville, individuals who "have their eyes in their shoulders, and their mouths in the middle of their breasts, & that a long train of haire groweth backward between their shoulders."[45]

While Ralegh desperately wished to see such marvels with his own eyes, he had to rely on the reports of others whom he trusted. But if he missed the freakish descendants of the ancient monstrous races, what he saw continued to impress him. He urged the English to pay close attention to Guiana. Its riches were too valuable to ignore, and "if the king of Spayne enjoy it, he will become unresistable." Employing the sexual imagery common in his day, Ralegh urged the English to penetrate Guiana, "a Country that hath yet her Maydenhead, never sackt, turned, nor wrought." The land itself had not yet been plundered; its graves were intact and icons still stood in temples. No invading army had yet trod through its jungles, no "Christian prince" had yet gained control of it. With its formidable waters and mountains, it could be defended easily with only two forts, a strategy well within the reach of the English. Taking control of Guiana would be a route to greatness for Elizabeth and her people.[46]

Ralegh's report, accompanied by other eyewitness testimony, transformed the place of Guiana in English minds. The territory, so obviously within Spain's holdings in the western hemisphere, now seemed open for conquest by northern Europeans. The presence of monsters, cannibals, and Amazons did not dismay Ralegh, who bore witness to their existence and believed that the dangers they posed could be overcome. But the English were not the only Europeans to learn about the region. By century's end the entities that Ralegh had described in his text—Amazons, tree-dwellers, armadillos, and monsters—appeared in engravings in Levinus Hulsius's brief book on Guinea, which appeared in Latin and German in 1599. Hulsius had a different agenda than Ralegh. Rather than promoting English adventurers, he instead used Ralegh's book to make an argument about the exotic nature of South America. His efforts complicated European readers' understanding of Americans and their environment, especially when compared to the visual clues earlier provided by de Bry's engravings in Harriot's report. Like other compilers of travel accounts, Hulsius included a map he had created for his book. It included both geographical details and depictions of local phenomena (such as flying fish, cannibals, and warring natives) described by Ralegh and others.[47]

Hakluyt was one of the readers who learned about Guiana from Ralegh. To him, the story contained all of the elements necessary in a travel narrative to instruct those who followed: the abundant resources of the land, the relatively easy passage (with directions about when to sail there), the fact that

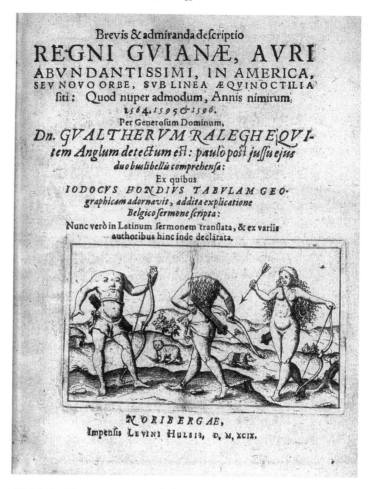

Brevis & admiranda defcriptio
REGNI GVIANÆ, AVRI
ABVNDANTISSIMI, IN AMERICA,
SEV NOVO ORBE, SVB LINEA ÆQVINOCTILIA
fiti: Quod nuper admodum, Annis nimirum,
1564, 1595 & 1596.
Per Generofum Dominum,
*Dn. GVALTHERVM RALEGH EQVI-
tem Anglum detectum eſt: paulo poſt juſſu ejus
duobus libellis comprehenfa:*
Ex quibus
IODOCVS HONDIVS TABVLAM GEO-
*graphicam adornavit, addita explicatione
Belgico fermone fcripta:*
Nunc verò in Latinum fermonem tranflata, & ex variis
authoribus hinc inde declarata.

NORIBERGAE,
Impenfis LEVINI HULSII, D. M. XCIX.

Levinus Hulsius's title page announced the kinds of wonders—including Blemyae with heads on their chests, Amazons, and remarkable American fauna—to be found in Guiana. From Levinus Hulsius, *Brevis & Admirando description regni Guianae* (Nuremberg, 1599) (HUNTINGTON LIBRARY)

neighboring natives—no matter how monstrous—posed no real threat, and the opportunity for profit that the locale afforded to the English. There is no evidence that Hakluyt knew the fine details of Ralegh's story before the adventurer himself published it in London in 1596. But there is no doubt about what happened next: four years later Hakluyt took the entire book and reprinted it, word for word, in his next edited collection. He added marginal notes and supporting documents, also taken from Ralegh. He also reprinted Lawrence Keymis's remarkable table enumerating the "Rivers, Nations, Townes, and Cassiques or Captaines" of Guiana encountered by the English during an expedition of 1596.[48]

Other than the marginal notations to guide the reader through these pages, Hakluyt made no comment about Ralegh's report. Like many of the texts Hakluyt gathered in the 1590s, Ralegh's story about his journey to Guiana testified to the wonders to be found there, highlighted the strategic possibilities for the English, and goaded readers to make similar expeditions into territories that their own countrymen had visited. It was, in that sense, a perfect story for Hakluyt, an embodiment of truth from a trusted eyewitness who put aside personal glory and enrichment for the greater good of the realm. This was the account that Hakluyt would have written himself, had he ever witnessed the magic of the Orinoco.

As his acceptance of Ralegh's report revealed, Hakluyt spent much of the 1590s on his continuing search for new sources. At some point in the middle of the decade he gained entry to the vast London library of Lord Lumley, where he "was permitted to copy out of ancient manuscripts" accounts of the fourteenth-century journeys of John de Plano Carpini and William de Rubruquis. (By the time of his death in 1609 Lumley had acquired a copy of Hakluyt's *Principal Navigations;* by then he also owned copies of works familiar to Hakluyt, including geographical and cosmographical treatises by Ortelius, Münster, Georg Braun, and others.) He also found materials testifying to the reliability of other manuscripts, including an account of trade between English merchants and the Levant, which he swore he "diligently perused and copied out" of ledgers kept by the London mercer Sir William Locke, the London alderman Sir William Bowyer, and others. Sometimes he even took possession of rare artifacts that testified to English travels, such as "a certaine note or letter of remembrance" that demonstrated an English presence in the West Indies as early as 1526.[49]

By the mid-1590s Hakluyt had become an expert in locating ancient manuscripts and gaining permission to copy them. One can imagine him riding his horse around London or into the countryside in search of yet more evidence. Whenever possible, he found written accounts created by those involved in long-distance travels, and he acquired rights to reprint these texts in his own works. He seems to have read everything and encouraged others to publish travel accounts. He listened, too, copying down an account of a journey in the early 1590s to the East Indies told to him by Edmund Barker, an officer on the mission who lived in Ipswich.[50] Such labors remained vital in a world in which crucial information remained unwritten, its survival made more secure when an attentive scribe was nearby.

Those he encouraged knew that Hakluyt's imprimatur mattered. If he pronounced a work accurate, then others would follow his lead. It made a difference to the Cambridge translator John Pory, who translated Leo Africanus at Hakluyt's urging. Such encouragement had specific value in an intellectual community based on obtaining and sustaining financial support in the form of patronage. By demonstrating personal links to the greatest authority on a subject, a scholar could boost his or her own chances of finding assistance.[51] Hakluyt of course understood the ways patronage worked on every possible level, and was himself a master at the game. With patrons who included Lady Sheffield, a cousin of the queen, and Sir Francis Walsingham, Hakluyt knew the importance of establishing and maintaining connections to the powerful. And he must have known that by the late 1590s he, too, had become one of the influential.

By the summer of 1597 Hakluyt's fame had spread throughout the realm. Old mariners were eager to get tell him their yarns before they succumbed to age or the temptations of the ocean. Book publishers were keen to get his approval for their works. Translators wrestled with difficult texts and did research to fill in gaps because Hakluyt thought such labors important. The descendants of merchants and travelers gave Hakluyt documents—possibly their only copies—testifying to their families' importance because they knew that no one else would etch their experiences into the nation's history and thus ensure their posterity. Hakluyt was not of course the only person searching for such records or keen to record recollections. Chroniclers such as Camden and Stow also needed this information. But it was Hakluyt who managed to get more of it into his hands and then to remind his readers that he had done so.

Yet fame was no guarantor of happiness, not in a world where humans could sicken and die quickly. In early August 1597, Douglas Hakluyt passed away. She was buried at the church at Wetheringsett on the eighth day of the month, her death meriting no mention in any of the annals or chronicles of the day. Nor did she figure in anything that Hakluyt himself ever wrote. The keeper of the local church's register was the only person who left any record of her passing.[52] She was in death, as in life, a figure whose existence has left barely a trace on the historical record. But her death, unlike that of the lawyer, Walsingham, Frobisher, and others Hakluyt knew well, left Hakluyt as the sole parent of the four-year-old Edmond.

Less than five months after Douglas's death, Hakluyt was again eager to advance his cause. In January 1598, according to Abraham Hartwell, a translator Hakluyt came to know, Hakluyt arrived at the house of Hugh Castelton, a prelate at Norwich Cathedral. Hartwell was himself on his way to London from Norfolk. During their time together, Hakluyt urged Hartwell to translate the account of Africa written by the Portuguese traveler Duarte (Edwardo or Odoardo to the English) Lopez. Hartwell claimed that Hakluyt was one of his friends who convinced him to take on the translation "to help our English Nation, that they might knowe and understand many things, which are common in other languages, but utterly concealed from this poore Island." Hartwell at first refused the task, believing that he was too infirm "to sit long, that the hourse of my leasure were not many" unless he shirked his regular work. He even said that he had "no great pleasure to learne or informe my selfe of the state of other Nations, because I do not as yet sufficiently know the Estate of mine owne Countrey." He was, in some sense, Hakluyt's opposite: a man who cared little about advancing the interests of the realm even though he had the ability (his knowledge of Portuguese) to do so.[53]

Hakluyt could not understand Hartwell's reluctance, so he pressed him on the issue. Hartwell admitted that Hakluyt was "a curious and a diligent searcher and observer of Forreine adventures and adventurers," and so at Castelton's house he listened to his plea. Hartwell repeated to him what he had told others, but "it would not satisfie him[,] for he sayd it was an answere answerelesse, and it should not serve my turne." Then Hakluyt presented Hartwell with an entity Hartwell described as a "Portingall Pilgrime lately come to him out of the Kingdome of Congo." He was dressed in Italian clothes, and Hakluyt thought that Hartwell should take him away "and make him English." This act would have an immediate reward because the Portuguese pilgrim "could report many pleasant matters that he saw in his pilgrimage, which are in deed uncouth and almost incredible to this part of Europe." Hartwell realized he could not win the argument. "When I saw there was no remedie, I yeelded."[54]

Hartwell took the pilgrim away with him and almost immediately regretted doing so. Within two hours, he later wrote, "I found him nibling at two most honourable Gentlemen of England, whome in plaine tearmes he called Pirates: so that I had much adoo to hold my hands from renting of him into many peeces." He hesitated, and decided that before he killed the pilgrim, he would first read his report. Though the pilgrim spoke a "lewd speech, not altogether ex animo, but rather ex vitio gentis, of the now-inveterate hatred, which the Spanyard and Portingall beare against our Nation," Hartwell nonetheless spared him. He even taught him English, as Hakluyt had implored him to do.[55]

That story, so fantastic as not to be believed, was an allegory Hartwell spun to explain how this account of Congo came into his possession. It was a device intended to get the reader to take the words of the written page as the testimony of a live individual witness, someone to be trusted to tell the truth. Hartwell knew that not all readers would accept the account at face value, especially since the English proverb warned that "a Traveller may lye by authoritie" and the Greek saying that "every Pilgrime is not a Sooth-sayer." The text had its faults, Hartwell warned, but still it was worth reading.[56]

Hartwell had accepted the logic of Hakluyt, the master persuader: the book had become animate, the substitute for a person. In a world where so many of the people Hakluyt loved died, perhaps such a logic was the best way to make sense and preserve at least some order amid the chaos. Perhaps inscribing the living into the pages of a book was one way to escape death's ability to erase a life from memory.

As Hakluyt sat with the growing mountain of paper that he had accumulated testifying to the travels of others, printers and writers bore witness to Hakluyt's chief success: the idea that travel experiences needed to be published so that they could offer instruction to English readers about the world beyond Europe's borders. In England that meant that those who could translate texts from foreign languages, like Hartwell, applied themselves to producing English-language versions of various works that might be of interest to readers. Some of those translators also accepted Hakluyt's notion that the circulation of such accounts would advance the goals of the queen and her realm.

Among those who had learned from Hakluyt was William Phillip. Sometime around 1597 he managed to get into his hands the *Itinerario* of Jan Huygen Van Linschoten, an account published in Dutch in 1596 of one of the most remarkable travelers of the 1590s, who had returned to Zeeland from a three-year journey to Java. When Phillip dedicated his book to his patron Sir James Scudamore in January 1598, he claimed that what Linschoten had to say deserved "no lesse commendation" than the journeys of various English captains. Phillip knew that Hakluyt, "a Gentleman very studious," had rescued accounts of English journeys to the East from possible oblivion; he kept the stories alive so that they could educate others. Now Linschoten's words became, for Phillip, a way "to procure more light and encouragement to such as are desirous to travell those Countries, for the common wealth and commoditie of this Realme and themselves."[57]

John Wolfe, the printer of Phillip's translation, recognized how crucial Linschoten's text was for the English. He did not come to that position on his own. In 1598 he wrote that about a year earlier "a learned Gentleman" had brought him a copy of Linschoten's book, "which he wished might be translated into our Language, because hee thought it would be not onely delightfull, but also very commodious for our *English Nation*." Wolfe did not identify this man, though if it was not Hakluyt himself then it was someone who embraced Hakluyt's mission and logic. Recognizing that the book contained "rare Intelligences" of "Forreyne parts," he then arranged for Phillip to translate it. He also took the unusual step of printing two separate editions of the work. The smaller version contained only the description of Linschoten's voyage; the larger (though not quite as extensive as the *Principall Navigations* of 1589) was a much more extensive work. Each book contained maps, but only the larger included a remarkable series of illustrations, including a portfolio of engravings depicting India, a visual catalog of a distant people almost as thorough as de Bry's version of White's Roanoke pictures. The English-language edition also had a very different title page. Unlike the initial image of the original edition, which featured a sailing ship surrounded by small illustrations of Dutch cities, the edition of 1598 instead featured the image of the king of Cochin (China) among other emblems. The translator Phillip (who was not identified in the text itself) added that it was Hakluyt, "a man that laboureth greatly to advance our *English* Name and Nation," who had recommended that Wolfe publish Linschoten's account. In one marginal note he also sent readers to Hakluyt's writings to find more information about India.[58]

By the end of the century, Hakluyt had become an odd public figure in a realm that was not yet committed to any colonial effort beyond Ireland. He was tireless in his desire to use travel accounts to spur colonial ventures. That desire led him to create what became the greatest achievement of his life: an expanded version of the *Principall Navigations*, which was published in London in three volumes from 1598 to 1600. Readers would have to look no farther for the accumulated experiences of English seafarers.

On October 7, 1598, Hakluyt completed the first volume of the work he now called *The Principal Navigations, Voiages, Traffiques and Discoveries of the English Nation, made by Sea or over-land, to the remote and farthest*

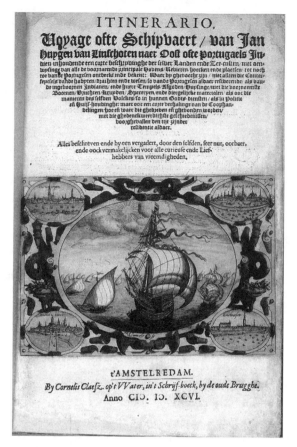

The title pages of the first edition of Jan Huygen Van Linschoten's work, *Itinerario, Voyage ofte Schipvaert* (Amsterdam, 1596), and the English-language edition brought to press at least in part through Hakluyt's energies, *John Huighen Van Linschoten, his Discours of Voyages into ye East & West Indies* (London, [1598]), hint at the different agendas of

distant quarters of the Earth, at any time within the compasse of these 1500 yeeres. It had been only fourteen months since he laid Douglas to rest in Wethering- sett. Edmond was approaching his sixth birthday.

On the title page Hakluyt announced that the work contained accounts of "woorthy Discoveries" that the English hade made in their northern and northeastern voyages. He promised his readers testimony about ancient trades, historic voyages, and even the defeat of the Spanish Armada in 1588. Hakluyt dedicated the book to Sir Charles Howard, the lord high admiral of England and, perhaps more important, the brother of Hakluyt's patroness

printers in Amsterdam and London, specifically with the inclusion and exclusion of images of Dutch cities. A portrait of Linschoten appeared in an edition published in 1599. (HUNTINGTON LIBRARY)

Lady Sheffield. Never one to shy away from explaining how much effort such volumes demanded, Hakluyt told how he devoted himself to his continued study of "the sweet studie of the history of Cosmographie." After extraordinary effort and the "wearying out of my weake body," he wrote, "at length I have collected three several Volumes of the English Navigations." He promised to bring "to light many very rare and worthy monuments, which long have lien miserably scattered in mustie corners, & retchlessly hidden in mistie darkenesse, and were very like for the greatest part to have been buried in perpetuall oblivion."[59]

Still, despite his sacrifices, Hakluyt knew he could not achieve his goals on his own. Passage across the sea was always difficult and dangerous. Or deadly, as Hakluyt knew when he wrote that "so few" of those who ventured outward regularly "grow to gray heires." What the English needed to do was to educate seafarers about what they might face. Hakluyt returned again to his belief that the English needed to fund annual lectures on navigation. He reported that King Charles V of Spain had established just such a lecture, as well as the position of pilot major, to reduce the number of wrecks between the Iberian peninsula and the West Indies. Hakluyt himself had received the written works of three of the Spanish men who offered lectures on "the Art of Navigation." But the English had not yet reached the same level of commitment despite the earlier efforts of Henry VIII and Edward VI. At least one of Hakluyt's readers saw the obvious benefit of such a lecture. When Edmund Wright dedicated his *Haven-Finding Art* to Howard on August 23, 1599, he referred to Hakluyt's plea and stressed the continuing need for such a lecture.[60]

Hakluyt wanted readers of *Principal Navigations* to know the sacrifices he had made, the years of toil, "so much traveile and cost, to bring Antiquities smothered and buried in darke silence to light." He struggled to "preserve certaine memorable exploits of late yeeres by our English nation atchieved, from the greedy and devouring jawes of oblivion." He wanted to use the techniques of "Geographie and Chronologie (which I may call the Sunne and the Moone, the right eye and left of all history)" to bring together records of "ancient and late Navigations by Sea, our voyages by land, and traffiques of merchandise by both." The task took a toll; he complained about "restlesse nights" and pains produced by the heat and cold he endured while he gathered accounts. He had traveled to "many famous libraries" in his effort to read "ancient and moderne writers" who could provide insight, and he had studied and recorded "old records, patents, privileges, letters, &c.," which he "redeemed from obscuritie and perishing." But this research was expensive to conduct, and while doing it Hakluyt complained that he missed opportunities for profit that would have otherwise come his way. Still, his commitment to the realm made it all worthwhile since "this Common weale wherein I live and breath, hath made all difficulties seeme easie, all paines and industrie pleasant, and all expenses of light value and moment unto me."[61]

Having rescued crucial stories from oblivion, Hakluyt now interpreted their central meaning for his readers. Posterity needed to know about the achievements of English navigators and explorers such as Richard Chancellor, Hugh Willoughby, Arthur Pet, and Charles Jackman. Although the

English had not yet done as well as European nations that already had colonies, the voyages led by these men were more valuable since they sailed into unknown territory. The English had no knowledge of what they would find on their voyages to the Northeast, no shining example to light their way. These mariners lacked "cleare lights and inducements, or if they had any inkling at all, it was as misty as they found the Northren seas, and so obscure and ambiguous, that it was meet rather to deterre them, then to give them encouragement."[62]

Some might have found the uncertainty paralyzing, but the English persisted despite the risks. In the North Atlantic English sailors faced fierce winds and waves. Navigating the known coasts of Scandinavia was dangerous enough, but even that trial paled in comparison to what the mariners encountered farther north when they sailed "unto what drifts of snow and mountaines of yce even in June, July, and August, unto what hideous overfals, uncertain currents, darke mistes and fogs, and divers other fearefull inconveniences." Such information had been available to English readers since the mid-1570s, but the *Principal Navigations* offered more since some of its pages contained stories told directly to Hakluyt.[63]

Farther south, the journey across posed less acute problems, as the experience of the Spanish and Portuguese demonstrated. Though many Iberian vessels never made it to their intended destinations, many did succeed. By getting across, they could satisfy "their fame-thirsty and gold-thirsty mindes with that reputation and wealth, which made all perils and misadventures seeme tolerable unto them." They were helped by not having to face human enemies at sea and by having mid-Atlantic islands to support their ventures. The Spaniards also benefited from their African trade, which they used for tusks, grain, silver, gold, and slaves.[64]

Stressing the advantages the Spanish had made readers realize how much harder the English efforts were, and hence how much more remarkable their achievements, a point Hakluyt emphasized by telling the tales of heroic English explorers. Among them was Chancellor, whose travels took him a thousand miles into Russia to Moscow and who wrote an account of what he saw there. Hakluyt believed this account to be authentic, and he thanked Lord Lumley for letting him into his library to copy it down. Others, too, traveled deep into the East, navigating Russian rivers, crossing the "unknown and dangerous Caspian sea," risking their goods and their lives every time they stepped on a boat.[65]

Hakluyt whetted his readers' appetites by distilling some of the volume's crucial reports. He told them that his research in ancient sources had proved that fifteen hundred years earlier London was famous for its "multitude of merchants and concourse of people." He gave a brief metaphorical synopsis of a long poem that contained an overview of the commodities to be found in different regions and for maintaining trade. As in his other writings, he was careful to thank those who had helped him or had provided a service to the nation through their own industry. He wrote at length of the treasures in Lord Lumley's library, precious manuscripts about the Tartars that Mercator and Ortelius had sought but never found. Hakluyt sensed that his readers might not believe some of the extravagant claims made in this account that dealt with "their hords and mooveable Townes," "their fond superstitions, their bestiall lives, their vicious maners, their slavish subjection to their own superiours, and their disdainfull and brutish inhumanitie unto strangers." But he vouched for their authenticity and their rarity. No one else had found them earlier—another sign of Hakluyt's industry and ability—and printing them preserved records that might otherwise disappear. He also trumpeted his information about Iceland and the North Atlantic, which he believed served as a correction to the work of notable scholars (including Münster) whose works contained "manifold errors." And he included accounts of the defeat of the Armada.[66]

Hakluyt had always been a scholar willing to praise the work of others. In 1598, some of them paid him back with a series of effusive Greek, Latin, and Italian epigrams before the main text of this new 619-page book. A poem composed in Homeric Greek congratulated Hakluyt who, "wandering on the salt-sea, has visited very many peoples," and thus became "worthy of praise for those remaining at home." The geographer Richard Mulcaster offered elegiac Latin couplets dwelling on England, "fertile mother of great things." Stories of England's overseas ventures had been documented earlier, but, Mulcaster added, "The glory belongs to Hakluyt alone, with his very rich feather [quill] / to have shown his daring deeds to his fellow citizens." The "fatherland" owed much to Hakluyt, he continued,

> Since for what reason does our Britain boast itself more
> than because, in addition to everything else, it becomes powerful
>   through its fleet?
> Which [fleet], before hidden in shadows, he frees so that now
> each may know how noble is the work of the fleet.
> If we use it like Daedalus, we shall rise to the heights,
> but if like Icarus, the sea has something to swallow.

Other verses offered by Mulcaster, Marc Antony Pigafeta, and Camden continued the theme: "But what, Hakluyt, does this world owe you for showing these things?" Camden rhetorically asked. "Your praise, believe me, will be no less than the world."[67]

At this moment of his great professional accomplishment, Hakluyt almost disappeared from the documentary record. For the year following the publication of the first volume of the revised *Principal Navigations,* barely a trace of him can be found. Other than Edmund Wright's late endorsement in August 1599 of Hakluyt's call for an annual lecture in navigation, his only other known appearance was at a meeting of directors of the East India Company in mid-October 1599.[68]

Eight days after he met with the directors of the East India Company, Hakluyt dedicated the second volume of the *Principal Navigations* to Sir Robert Cecil. Though the volume contained accounts of English voyages to Africa, India, and China, Hakluyt offered his views on the colonization of North America, almost as if he could not wait for the publication of the third volume. He particularly praised Virginia, a region that even the Spanish admitted was a "better and richer countrey then Mexico and Nueva Spania it selfe." Learned authorities including the Venetian Ramusio and the Frenchman La Popilinière acknowledged that the territory stretching from Florida north to 67 degrees North latitude was by right of discovery in the possession of the English. Even Spanish writers and their allies, notably Peter Martyr and the geographer Francisco López de Gómara, admitted that this land belonged to the English. So did a "secret mappe" produced in Mexico for the King of Spain, then in the possession of Thomas Harriot, and "intercepted letters" that had come into Hakluyt's possession.[69]

But all of these arguments were meaningless if the English did not have individuals somewhere on that land to maintain the claim. That was the crucial importance of establishing colonies. No one in England knew if any of the Roanoke settlers had survived, but Hakluyt felt he had to employ his authority to redirect colonization efforts away from the troubles in Ireland and the elusive potential of the Orinoco and toward the proven heaven of Virginia. The time had come for the queen to send over one to two thousand people, "and such others as upon mine owne knowledge will most willingly at their owne charges become Adventurers in good numbers with their bodies and goods." Together those colonists would expand the queen's territory, enrich the realm, and "reduce many Pagans to the faith of Christ." If the

English pursued this opportunity, its gentry might finally realize the time had come to abandon "those soft unprofitable pleasures wherein they now too much consume their time and patrimonie," and to apply themselves instead to the more obviously lucrative and likely effort. Even the French could sense the opportunity, as Hakluyt knew when he recalled how Parisian leaders responded to Hakluyt's publication of the accounts of Florida by Laudonnière, Ribault, and Dominique de Gourgues in 1587. Hakluyt believed that the French remained in the dark about the opportunities that existed in the Americas. Had this knowledge circulated earlier, the French would have had "very ample and manifold occasions of good and honest employment abroad in that large and fruitfull Continent of the West Indies." But their moment had passed, and the English should not similarly allow opportunity to slip away.[70]

This was vintage Hakluyt. He was too impatient to wait for the publication of the travel accounts relating to English expeditions to the Americas even though he was already preparing them for publication. He was eager to demonstrate his superior knowledge and his ability to know things—the contents of a secret map or mysterious correspondence—that others did not know because they did not spend all of their waking hours gathering documents and building a case. He remained an optimist who believed, or at least claimed, that there could still be at least one English survivor of the painful expeditions to Roanoke fifteen years earlier. But he was also enough of a realist to know that whoever survived in the woods would not last forever and that the English claim would weaken if he or she perished. And he remained committed, as he had been for almost two decades, to pushing the English toward what he believed was the only logical course of action if they were serious about their stated commercial, political, and religious goals. If the French could recognize a lost opportunity, how could the English fail to do so themselves? The only thing odd about Hakluyt's argument was its appearance in a book that had no obvious connection to the Americas, other than its description of mid-Atlantic islands where English voyagers could stop on their journeys to the West.[71]

On November 23, 1599, almost exactly one month after he signed his dedication to the second volume of *Principal Navigations*, Cecil heard that Hakluyt would get the next vacant chaplaincy at London's Hospital of the Savoy. Six months later, the Privy Council (with Cecil as its secretary) wrote to the archbishop of Canterbury recommending Hakluyt for an expected vacancy at Great All Hallows on Thames Street. Hakluyt had "taken great paynes in his callinge," they wrote, having served under Stafford in France "in a dangerous tyme" and had also spent time and labor "in matter of navigacion and dyscoveryes, a labor of great desert and use." The council let the archbishop know that Hakluyt was someone they might want to employ in the future, and since he would be needed to serve the queen it would be best if he could "be provided of some competent livinge to reside in these partes." Though Hakluyt never got the position, the fact of the promise (along with the position he did receive in London) testified that he had become a master not only of precise details of long-distance journeys he never took but also of the arcane ways of privilege and promotion at the highest levels of the English government. Hakluyt knew that Cecil had made the appointment for one position and the promise of another possible. So, following his by-then familiar path, he once again thanked Cecil publicly, this time when he signed the dedication of the last volume of the *Principal Navigations* on September 1, 1600.[72]

By any conceivable logic, Hakluyt should have used the opening pages of the final volume of the trilogy to lay out his argument for the English colonization of North America. After all, nothing of substance had happened since his plea of October 1599. If there were any survivors of Roanoke wandering around Virginia—a distinct possibility according to one leading modern historian—no one in England was able to mount an expedition to find them. But this time the dedication was shorter than any reader could have expected, as if Hakluyt had no need to make any more arguments about the need for colonization.[73]

Instead, Hakluyt made obvious the marvel of the western hemisphere and its novelty to Europeans. This last collection, which ran to an astonishing 868 pages, described America known, he wrote, "by the chiefest authors *The new world*." It was "new" Hakluyt declared because it had only recently been discovered by the Genoese sailor Columbus. (Hakluyt neglected to mention that the Spanish had sponsored Columbus's journey, though he did reprint the offer that Bartholomew Columbus had made to King Henry VII.) "And *world*," he added, "in respect of the huge extension thereof, which to this day is not thoroughly discovered, neither within the Inland nor on the coast, especially toward the North and Northwest."[74]

By this point Hakluyt had gathered more materials relating to the Americas than any European before him. He had so much that he invented a new way of presenting his information. In the first two volumes, he had used "the methode of time onely" to organize his findings, with the result that readers could be taken to various parts of the world according to a chronological framework (of European discovery) rather than viewing the materials relating to one area in a certain section. Here Hakluyt changed course, following what he called "the double order of time and place." He also decided to use non-English travels to provide information about places the English had not yet explored in depth, such as Florida, Canada, the Gulf of California, and New Mexico, the largest of fifteen provinces that Hakluyt located "on the backside of *Florida* and *Virginia.*" He also published documents stolen from Spanish ships seized by the English in the West Indies. He printed them to annoy the Iberians who continued to be hostile toward the English. There was another reason Hakluyt used such materials, which he admitted: in places which English travelers had not yet described—"where our owne mens experience is defective"—he supplemented his text "with the best and chiefest relations of strangers."[75]

The breadth of material in this third volume was extraordinary by any measure. Hakluyt greatly increased the materials relating to the West Indies, boasting that there was "no chiefe river, no port, no towne, no citie, no province of any reckoning in the *West Indies,* that hath not here some good description thereof, aswell for the inland as the feast [sic] coast." He concluded the volume with materials drawn from the Casa de Contracíon in Seville and information extracted by the Spanish pilot majors and lecturers on navigation, a bitter reminder that England's foes had managed to arrange such events already.[76]

Despite the vast mass of information that he was about to unleash on what he hoped was an eager audience, Hakluyt was disappointed that he could not provide information on the kinds of diseases travelers might encounter and how to battle them. He had in fact planned to include a book on tropical medicine by George Wateson. "But being carefull to do nothing herein rashly," he decided to have the text checked by his friend Gilbert, that authority on finding a secure haven, who deemed the work "very defective and unperfect." Gilbert was an expert in physics and mathematics, not medicine, but in that learned world of Elizabethan England where expertise in one field often blended into another, Hakluyt trusted that Gilbert would either write his own study on tropical medicine or confer with physicians in the College of Physicians who would. Hakluyt also hoped to find information "for the cure of diseases incident unto men employed in cold regions," which would be of special benefit to any English men or women who chose to sail to the Northwest, where he found "divers worshipfull citizens at this present much inclined."[77]

At the end of his dedication, Hakluyt made a rare personal revelation, unlike any that he had written publicly before—and unlike any comment that survives in his unpublished letters and writings. Over the past three years, as it turned out, Hakluyt had feared that his "profession of divinitie, the care of my family, and other occasions" might divert him from completing his work. As a result, he nurtured his "very honest, industrious, and learned friend" John Pory in the study of "Cosmographie and forren histories." Pory had already translated Leo Africanus at Hakluyt's urging. Now he stood poised to use his talents to benefit the entire realm.[78]

Those were not of course three normal years for Hakluyt. Douglas had died almost exactly three years earlier. Edmond was now soon to turn seven, and Hakluyt knew that he had to continue to make a living. He remained dependent on would-be patrons (like Charles Howard) and those who came through with clerical positions (notably Lady Stafford and Cecil). At one point in 1600, Hakluyt claimed that had he had more time he would have polished his "rude lineaments" of his "Westerne Atlantis or America" before he presented the printed work to Cecil. But the same shortage of time—or his fear of the creeping powers of forgetting—propelled him to complete his greatest work then.[79] He was forty-eight and had spent more than half his entire life trying to fulfill the promise he made in his cousin's study.

When Hakluyt presented his three large volumes to his patrons and his reading public, he believed that everything in these pages was accurate. His reluctant decision to use Spanish authorities on parts of the world the English had not yet described suggests how serious he was about providing a complete picture of the Americas. It was hard enough to swallow the fact that Spaniards knew more about parts of the western hemisphere than the English. The only way to justify their inclusion would be if they passed the unspoken text of credibility that Hakluyt applied to everything in the *Principal Navigations*.

The completed trilogy was a work of monumental proportions. The section on voyages to the north, which had twenty-two accounts in 1589, now included thirty-nine. Hakluyt added more accounts to his other parts as well; the second volume (on travels to the South and Southeast) swelled from thirty-eight to sixty-four reports, and the volume on the West from thirty-three descriptions and forty-four accompanying documents to almost two hundred accounts and supporting documents.

Yet despite the growth, Hakluyt did not keep all of the texts he had printed in 1589. Instead, he excised perhaps the most famous travel account that he had earlier included: the Latin version of Mandeville's travels. He never explained why he dropped this text. He could have written that Mandeville's story had long been available in hundreds of manuscripts and in printed editions. Perhaps he grew wary of Mandeville's excesses, which he alluded to in his warning when he printed the text earlier. But such skepticism hardly justified omitting the English knight's tale from his account. After all, Hakluyt did include Ralegh's account of his journey to Guiana, a journey in which Ralegh claimed to have picked up firsthand information about cannibals and Amazons and heard stories about *blemyae* whose faces could be found on their chests.[80] The antiquity of the text was also not a factor since Hakluyt included such ancient authorities as King Arthur and the Welsh prince Madoc.

But Mandeville's was not the only text dropped from the second edition. More significant was Hakluyt's decision to omit the account left by David Ingram, the sailor from Barking in Essex who had survived a shipwreck to tell of America's marvels. Ingram's account was in many ways an ideal report for Hakluyt. After all, here was a purported eyewitness whose story had fit Hakluyt's promotional agenda only a decade earlier. Ingram's claims about the bounties of America, the mores of the natives, and the descriptions of Indian communities were skimpy, as any reader would have realized. Yet even the most astounding aspect of Ingram's account—his claim that he had walked from Mexico to Nova Scotia—was not altogether unbelievable; Ramusio, after all, had included the account of Álvar Núñez Cabeza de Vaca and the stunning overland march of the survivors of the expedition led by Pánfilo de Narváez from Florida to Mexico from 1527 to 1536.[81] Though Spanish and Italian readers who had access to Cabeza de Vaca's thorough account would have logically rejected Ingram's more superficial treatment of his experiences (and could more reasonably suspect that Ingram tended to embellish what he saw or perhaps even fabricate his evidence), English readers who had had less access to printed books in Spanish or Italian might have been more willing to give Ingram the benefit of the doubt, especially since he was English himself.

So why did Hakluyt drop Ingram from his collection of trustworthy accounts? The documentary record provides scant clues. Perhaps Ingram's report was less convincing than the account of Job Hortop, another sailor on that ill-fated Hawkins mission, who had published his report in London in 1591. Unlike Ingram, who trolled the mainland as a freeman, Hartop spent the years after he went ashore in longtime service as a captive of the Spanish, a fate in every way less desirable than Ingram's. Hakluyt showed his faith in Hortop in the most obvious way: he included the account in his revised collection. A better clue to Hakluyt's views comes from Samuel Purchas, who in the mid-1610s acquired many of Hakluyt's manuscripts. Purchas, the self-appointed literary heir of Hakluyt, provided a note on Ingram in *Purchas his Pilgrimage,* a work that appeared in three editions (of 1613, 1614, and 1617). "David Ingram reported many strange things which he saith he saw in these parts," Purchas wrote in 1613, "Elephants, Horses, and beasts twice as bigge as Horses, their hinder parts resembling grey-hounds; bulles with eares like hounds; beasts bigger than beares, without head or neck, but having their eyes and mouths in their breasts." Ingram, according to Purchas, also described "an other beast, *Corberus* he calls him *Colluchio,* which is (saith he) the devill in the likenes of a dog, & somtimes of a calfe; with many other matters wherein he must pardon me, if I be not too prodigall of my faith." Purchas went on to point out that Ingram had described how the natives punished adultery, but he omitted the rest of Ingram's ethnography. He concluded by noting that "they that list [desire] to beleeve, may consult with the Author." The following year, when he printed the second edition of his travel accounts, Purchas added brief notes about Ingram's companions, noting that Hakluyt had already chronicled their fates.[82]

Purchas, then, did not believe Ingram's account.[83] Since the first two editions of his work were published while Hakluyt was alive, and since he was either in the process of acquiring Hakluyt's papers or they had already come into his possession, it seems likely that Purchas's voice here was a substitute for Hakluyt's. Hakluyt had brought his own story together with that of Ingram in 1589; in 1600 he sundered them. Ingram became an odd relic from an age of wonderful discovery, someone who told an improbable tale that Hakluyt could not trust.

In the end, as he sat contemplating the colossal task of preparing the expanded edition of the *Principal Navigations,* Hakluyt had to decide if he should include Ingram's account with its soothing recital of the traveler's ability to vanquish the savages' devil with the Bible or whether he should omit it and let other texts teach that lesson. To maintain his reputation and to advance his lifelong quest to promote expansion of the realm, all of his selected accounts had to be trustworthy. The reader had to have faith, like Hakluyt, that the written word corresponded to the unseen reality. Perhaps Hakluyt had read Michel de Montaigne's essay on cannibals, first published in 1580, in which the French essayist had warned that clever travelers often dissembled and so it was better to trust simpler viewers. (Hakluyt's old associate John Florio published the first English translation of Montaigne's essays in 1603.)[84] There could be no greater disservice to the cause of overseas expansion, no greater damage to the reputation of the Crown, than to send misguided colonizers into an unpredictable situation. As the English made their forays into North America in the early seventeenth century, the reassuring but dubious story of Ingram was not just incredible. It was dangerous.

By the mid-1590s, the cause of expansion could be served only by the truth about a new world as Elizabethans such as Hakluyt understood it. Victory over the Armada in 1588 gave the English the chance to gain territory in the western hemisphere. The publication of the illustrated edition of Harriot's account in 1590, with its anthropological approach, assured readers that cultural evolution would transform America's natives into proper English men and women. Colonization could succeed if English readers obtained a comprehensive history of English journeys across the continents along with a justification of discovery and accurate information about America's peoples and resources. With such evidence in hand, English men and women would recognize the benefits of colonization. Surely, Hakluyt believed, some would then decide at last to leave the known world behind and embark on a colonizing voyage.

That idea motivated Hakluyt throughout the most trying period of his life, the decade in which he lost his early patrons, his cousin, and his wife and in which he had to learn to become the only parent for his son. The stakes were high, and they were personal. To propel the English toward colonization had practical advantages for a cleric who believed that applying his skills to organizing travel accounts would please those who controlled pastoral appointments and sinecures in the national church. Perhaps it was that reward that kept him going as he sat at tables groaning under the collective weight of the printed books and unpublished manuscripts piling ever higher in the 1590s.

Hakluyt collected and copied, but he also used his prodigious skills to craft arguments that would advance his goals. If he sensed falsity on the part of an authority, there was no reason to include that person's words in what became a priceless portable library of knowledge. In Hakluyt's calculus of truth, Ingram did not pass the test. Of course, excising a tale did not mean that it faded away. Mandeville's account continued to be printed and circulated long after Hakluyt's death.

By the end of the century, Hakluyt was all too conscious of the passage of time. Reminders were everywhere. London's residents had been walking past the hulk of Drake's *Golden Hind,* where it was grounded in 1580. Over twenty years even that marvelous vessel had suffered from the elements. When the Swiss traveler Thomas Platter saw it in early October 1599, he surmised that it had been "very large and stoutly built of some hundred tons, quite fitted for so long and perilous a voyage." But it was already becoming a shadow, a monument "rotten with age and now decaying." It still fascinated, like a religious icon. Platter himself broke off one piece to take back with him to Basel, a pilgrim wandering home with what would have been to propagandists such as Hakluyt a piece of the true cross.[85] Hakluyt never wrote about the wreck of the *Golden Hind,* the ship that had skirted so many dangers on its memorable expedition. Perhaps he knew that books stored away in libraries lasted longer, especially those that preserved the treasures of a nation.

CHAPTER 10

London, 1609
Virginia Richly Valued

On January 23, 1609, John Chamberlain, an inveterate letter writer who spent his time gathering news at St. Paul's, informed Dudley Carleton (who would become ambassador to Venice the next year) that a pinnace from an East Indian expedition had arrived at Dartmouth carrying one hundred tons of cloves. Another ship had also arrived there from Virginia "with some petty commodities and hope of more, as divers sorts of woode for wainscot and other uses, sope ashes, some pitch and tarre, certain unknowne kindes of herbs for dieng" that might turn out to be cochineal.[1]

By year's end the arrival and departure of long-distance voyages had become notable spectacles. The royal family went to the docks to feast and present a gold medal to Sir Thomas Smythe, the governor of the East India Company, while they all watched the departure of another great ship. Ralegh, whose estate had been confiscated earlier in the year, rose triumphant again with the return of a ship from Guiana "richly laden they say with gold ore"— news that prompted the diplomat Sir Thomas Roe to organize a return to South America "to seeke his fortune." Such overseas successes raised hopes, and perhaps helped Londoners such as Chamberlain forget for a time that they lived in a city periodically ravaged by disease, such as a sickness (possibly smallpox) that had afflicted the capital in the spring, killing thirty-three people in one week in March.[2]

Hakluyt was, of course, more attuned to events abroad than most of the city's residents, and he invariably paid attention to ships arriving from both the western hemisphere and the East Indies. He had been thinking about Virginia for two decades by then, ever since Thomas Harriot and John White had returned from Roanoke. He knew well the difficulties of establishing English settlements abroad. The lost colonists at Roanoke, the drownings of

Parmenius and Gilbert, and the tribulations of Ralegh in Guiana tempered the enthusiasm that anyone would have for such a journey. So it must have been a moment of some satisfaction to hear of a ship from America docking in London. The vessel from the East Indies would have been less surprising, since Hakluyt had believed for close to a decade that voyages to the Spice Islands could be profitable.

By the time the Virginia Company was being launched, Hakluyt had become the preeminent English authority on the Americas, celebrated in poetry as well as prose. He had attained that status not because he had actually seen Virginia or the West Indies or anywhere farther than France. But the authority of his writings in this age when the printed book rose to prominence placed him in a category by himself. He was the expert. Those who planned travels read his books before they went. Some took his books with them, presumably packing them into the holds of ships. Perhaps some had them in hand when they first spotted land after weeks at sea. Even wily explorers whose success depended on their quick response to the unexpected recognized the crucial role that Hakluyt played in the circulation of information. They came back with stories to tell but with no obvious means of telling them. He stayed in England, always imploring them to publish their stories even when he had to translate the texts himself. By embracing the potential of the printing press, Hakluyt spread information about these voyages far and quickly.[3]

And yet, at the peak of his celebrity, Hakluyt turned from almost everything he had worked so tirelessly to create. He continued to help others chronicle voyages, but his own efforts diminished. Instead he took up new challenges, turning his attention from the Atlantic to the Pacific. He passed on the opportunity to go to Virginia, though in 1609 he did print his translation from Portuguese of an account of Hernando de Soto's travels in eastern North America. But his interests had already changed. Several years after Jamestown's founding he gave away or sold his unpublished manuscripts to another minister, Samuel Purchas. Hakluyt's self-appointed task was over. His mission was complete. If the English were to succeed in the colonization of North America, others would need to make good on the promise of his writings.

On January 29, 1601, only a few months after the publication of the third volume of the *Principal Navigations*, Hakluyt appeared before the managers of the East India Company in London. The "historiographer of the viages of the East Indies," the company's notes recorded, read to the assembled "out of his notes & bookes divers instruccions for provisions of jewelles." They asked him to write down what he told them, especially about the most logical places in the East Indies where "trade is to be had" so that this information could benefit the English merchants who would pursue economic opportunities there. Perhaps they had in mind what one contemporary poet had reminded his readers: "Pearles low-priced in *India* are precious in *England.*"[4]

The subject of Hakluyt's remarks was not "jewels" in the sense of precious minerals. What he had in mind—what he recognized was perhaps ultimately most profitable—was spices. Throughout the course of the sixteenth century the English had played almost no role in the spice trade that had brought astonishing wealth to European merchants. Those who became rich were the ones who fitted out vessels for the arduous voyages around Africa and India to the Spice Islands. The English ignored that commerce at their peril. Spices had first come to Europe with returning crusaders centuries earlier. The trade had helped to make Venice rich in an age when Ramusio's city was the launching place for overland journeys from Europe to the East. Now the coffers of Portuguese merchants had grown fat from the business, while Portuguese sailors took advantage of their superior knowledge of wind patterns, sailing routes, navigational techniques, and ports that could provision their ships on voyages lasting many months. Europeans had long since fallen in love with what one modern scholar has called the "tastes of paradise." The time had come for the English to become involved. That, at least, was the thinking of the managers of the East India Company, which had been founded in 1600 with the precise idea that the English could thrive in the commerce. But there were risks, too, both from locals and from European rivals. The Portuguese were the first notable threat, though they themselves were hardly invincible. Within a generation of the company's founding some of its men were tortured and killed by the Dutch on the Indonesian island of Ambon.[5]

Hakluyt had much to offer the managers of the East India Company. In the *Principal Navigations* he had already published accounts of travels to the region, and he gathered additional manuscripts that eventually found their way into Purchas's hands. Among his reports was the tale of Edmund Barker, told directly to Hakluyt, about the journey of the tall ships *Penelope, Marchant Royall,* and *Edward Bonaventure* to the Spice Islands in 1591. The narrative contained more than an account of what happened on the journey. Barker also recounted in some detail the seizure of the *Captain of Malacca,* which had departed from Goa on its way to the islands. The English took control of the vessel and its cargo, though the captain and crew escaped in the dark of the night. Still, what mattered most was the ship's cargo, for it provided clues to what the English needed for a thriving East Indies trade. The ship carried clothing ranging from red knit caps made of "Spanish wool" to shoes, silks, and worsted stockings. It also held cargo from Venice, including glass and what Barker called "papers full of false and counterfeit stones (which an Italian brought from Venice to deceive the rude Indians withal), abundance of playing cardes, two or three packs of French paper." The English found no silver, though the crew did consume large quantities of Canary wine, arrack, and raisin wine.[6]

Henry May, who sailed on the same expedition, wrote that in early February 1592 the English departed from Pulo Pinaom on a voyage to Malacca. Soon after the ships left they captured an eighty-ton ship from Pegu with fifty men aboard and a pinnace about one-half its size following behind. Both of the ships were carrying pepper. A short time later the English seized two Portuguese vessels also bound for Malacca. They were burdened with calicoes and *pintados* (another colored cloth) along with victuals for those in Malacca. He learned that ships from St. Thomas and Goa, along with other ports, often brought wine or food to Malacca "because that victuals there are very scarce." Food was not lacking in the East Indies, of course. As the English discovered when they anchored at Nicubar (Nicobar) northwest of Sumatra, local Muslims rowed out to the ships in canoes burdened with "hennes, cocos, plantans, and other fruits." Eventually they brought silver, too, which the English obtained by selling them cloth from Calicut in exchange. May was quick to point out that the silver was not from local sources but instead was recovered treasure from two recently sunk Portuguese ships. Those ships had been bound for China but never made it, yet the English profited from the disaster. As the ships headed for home they stopped at Ceylon, where there "groweth great store of excellent cinamom, and the best diamonds in the world"—an odd claim given the fact that though the spice could be found there the minerals could not.[7]

By publishing these recent accounts, Hakluyt solidified his status as a leading expert on English travel to the East. But while he was a master of the printed word he was also its servant. It was no surprise that when the East India Company requested a hearing, he hauled several books along on his visit on January 29, 1601. Those he chose were substantial—Ramusio's influential *Navigationi et Viaggi*, the English-language edition of Linschoten's

Itinerario, and the just recently completed version of his own *Principal Navigations.* It would have been almost impossible for one person to have carried all these books at once, which meant that Hakluyt had some assistant bearing the load or that a committee from the company met him somewhere else. (No record survives of the location of the meeting.)[8] Wherever it took place, these books were as much the star of the show as Hakluyt himself. The anonymous company member who took notes on the occasion often included the precise references, or at least the author and title if the page numbers could not be recorded.

Hakluyt began by talking about pepper, the most popular spice of the age. The Portuguese had imported most of their pepper to Lisbon from Malabar, and they had seven cities there under their control serving as staging points. Pepper also came from the area near Calicut, but the Portuguese had been unable to sustain friendly relations with the locals there and so the trade was unpredictable. Yet there were other islands and provinces where pepper could also be grown. From Linschoten (among others) Hakluyt had learned that there were ten locations on Sumatra ideal for pepper production. The spice grew in Java, too, and in Malacca, Siam, and nearby locales. No less an authority than Sir Francis Drake testified to the long peppers he had seen on the island of Baratene, a fact he had described in the account reprinted in *Principal Navigations.* Here the chronicler of the meeting caught the precise citation so that those in attendance could check the original context.

Other spices grew in more limited territory. Cinnamon mostly came from Ceylon, Malabar, the island of Nicubar, and Java. (Ceylon might have been especially attractive to the members of the company since Hakluyt told them it was governed by a "mortall enemy" of the Portuguese.) Cloves primarily could be found in the Moluccas, where the Portuguese kept two forts (on Tidore and Ambon). Nutmeg and mace came from Banda and nearby islands, and Drake (as Hakluyt had noted in his book) found nutmeg, pepper, and spices on Baratave (Batavia?). Nutmeg could also be found on Sunda and Java, as Linschoten had written. Camphor, which was "much used in medicines and is one of the richest wares of India," came from Borneo, Chinchen in China, Sumatra, and Java. Anil grew on Cambaya, but those with resources could purchase it in Bantam, the principal city of Java.

Hakluyt provided an extended list of the available spices and their origins. He told the company members where they could find amber, musk, civet, benjamin, frankincense, myrrh, snakewood (used to make cures for poisons and illnesses), and lignum aloes. Rhubarb grew in northern China. Merchants still hauled it through Usbeke to Ormus and then to Java and Sumatra. But there was no need to go to the Spice Islands to get it. "The best is brought for the most parte over land to Venice," Hakluyt instructed them, advising them to read the preface to the second volume of Ramusio's *Navigationi et Viaggi*. As always, Linschoten was the most reliable guide, giving readers details about the importance of the root of China, which could be used "against the French poxe," as well as about such diverse plants as opium, tamarindi, and galanga.

Hakluyt's testimony before the East India Company tells much about his status in Elizabethan London. Rather than rely on firsthand accounts from travelers, the company members instead placed their trust in a man whose claim to expertise rested on his meticulous presentation of other travelers' accounts. He, by turns, then supported his own claims by referring the company to specific citations in books that he knew well. He referred to his own *Principal Navigations* three times. Three times he cited the second volume of Ramusio's work, then available only in Italian-language editions. He drew on Juan González de Mendoza's *History of China*, a work he had earlier helped usher into print in an English-language edition, on six occasions. The work he cited most frequently was Linschoten's *Itinerario*, which had been published, again with Hakluyt's support, in London in 1598. Hakluyt referred to Linschoten twenty-one times in his report. This pattern of citation indicates that Hakluyt obviously placed great trust in Linschoten's account, which is not surprising given the nature of that marvelous book and the young Dutchman's encyclopedic knowledge of the peoples and plants of the East. In all likelihood, Hakluyt showed the company members the detailed pictures in Linschoten's book.

At some point, probably soon after that meeting, Hakluyt returned to the managers of the East India Company. This time he responded to their concern that the queen would not support their ventures if they planned to do business in territory claimed by other Europeans. The anonymous scribe who left the record of the meeting noted that its intent was to prove "in whate partes of the same Indies the Spanish King hath Sovereigntie and in what other partes he hath no coller to barr other Christian Princes &c from trade." Hakluyt addressed the problem in two ways. First, he identified the places where the Spanish maintained a presence. Second, he named the regions which were "wholly out of ye Domynion" of the Portuguese and Spanish "in the easte Southeaste and Northeaste partes of ye world." The first list enumerated the twenty-six "Counteries, Ilandes, Citties, Townes, places,

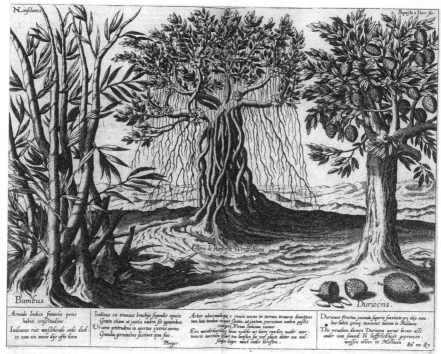

Linschoten's descriptions of the East, which had a deep influence on Hakluyt, included depictions of Indian flora. These pictures and others could be found in the English-language edition encouraged by Hakluyt, but also in the original Dutch edition of 1596 and a Latin edition of 1599, thereby suggesting the large number of Europeans who might have studied them. All three versions used the identical plates, with captions in both Latin and Dutch. The English-language printer needed to alter the numbers in the lower right corner so that the pictures would be inserted in the proper place in that edition. From *Linschoten, his Discours of Voyages into ye Easte & West Indies* (London, 1598) (HUNTINGTON LIBRARY)

Castles, fortresses as thei are actualie at this present, possessed or Comaunders of" from the Cape of Buona Speranza on the African coast to the Moluccas. According to this reckoning, the Spanish had claimed the right to trade in such prominent locales as Hormuz, Goa, Macao, Ambon, Malacca, and Manila. But neither of the Iberian powers had a viable presence in such places as Madagascar, Siam, China, Sumatra, Java, New Guinea, Japan, and Korea. How did Hakluyt make his case? Again, he relied on printed books, including authorities he had known for years such as Gonsalo Fernández de

Oviedo y Valdés, López de Gómara, Duarte Sande, and the Portuguese writer Antonio Galvano. He cited the documents recovered with the English interception of the *Madre de Dios* in 1592 as well as the narratives relating to the circumnavigations of Drake and Cavendish. Not surprisingly, he referred those listening to him to Linschoten's "notable worke" based on seven years' experience in the East Indies and the "excellente Cosmographer" Ramusio.[9]

Hakluyt's approach revealed his faith in the information contained in printed books, or at least in his faith in his understanding of what others had seen abroad. That's why he had the books with him when he spoke, and why he provided exact citations for bits of information. He asked the company's managers to believe him even though he was not an eyewitness but, instead, offered a new kind of expertise: the knowledge of someone who knew the original manuscripts, had pored over the various editions of travel accounts, and whose own authority manifested itself in print.

When Hakluyt spoke to the East India Company in its formative years, he synthesized certain information about spices to be found in the East. He also provided the nascent company with the ideological justifications it would need to raise funds to pay for its missions abroad, which began in earnest only a few years after Hakluyt's presentation. In the years that followed, the company sponsored missions to the East Indies to find these precious commodities. Hakluyt stayed home.

By the time Hakluyt addressed the East India Company, he had become a celebrity in the circles of those who dreamed of establishing colonies or reaping great profits from distant climes. One measure of his stature can be found in the ways that other authors invoked his name. The chronicler John Stow listed Hakluyt as one of his authorities for the 1601 edition of his *Annales*. That same year, only weeks after the third volume of *Principal Navigations* appeared, the translator John Pory thanked Hakluyt for persuading him to translate Leo Africanus's history of Africa. Hakluyt responded with praise for Pory's book, which Pory's printer managed to get into the text and thus stamp it with the ultimate imprimatur: "I do hold and affirm it to be the very best, the most particular, and methodicall, that ever was written, or at least that hath come to light, concerning the countries, peoples, and affairs of Africa."[10]

Pory's translation had an enormous influence on English perceptions of Africa. Four years after its appearance Ben Jonson relied on its contents in his *Masque of Blackness*, which he wrote to be performed at Whitehall in early

January 1606. Jonson's contemporary William Shakespeare drew on Pory's *Africa* for both *Othello* and *Anthony and Cleopatra*. The playwright John Webster's *White Devil* of 1612 relied so closely on Pory that one modern observer has claimed it as almost a case of plagiarism. Sir Walter Ralegh found material in Pory's work for his own global history, which appeared in 1614.[11]

In essence, then, Pory did the hard work of translating the text (which Hakluyt had earlier seen in Ramusio's edition, the first major work to popularize the account) because he trusted that it was the best available work about Africa.[12] Those who then drew on Pory's account had not only the text itself; they also had Hakluyt's words of approval that this was a worthwhile translation of the most important work on the subject. In an age when English contacts with Africa and Africans were rapidly expanding but before the full-scale English rush into the slave trade, this intellectual pedigree made the book unusually important.

But if Pory saw the value of Hakluyt's opinion stamped into his book as crucial, other writers and travelers were just as happy to read the master's own books or, in the case of the East India Company committee, to hear him read from them himself. Thomas Harriot, who it could be argued knew more about eastern North America than Hakluyt since he had seen it himself, believed the book so important that he recommended it be carried along on an expedition to Virginia in 1602. The "Booke of Voyages," as he termed the *Principal Navigations,* was the only book that he thought vital. It was as crucial on board as fifty dozen knives, five dozen hatchets, twenty iron shovels, clothes for the sailors, compasses, saws, powder, and shot. Three years later the eminent antiquarian William Camden produced his paean to Britain itself, "the most flourishing and excellent, most renow[n]ed and famous Isle of the whole world." In it he noted that the "Discoveries of the learned and industrious M. Rich. Hakluit" made him the ultimate authority on English travelers abroad.[13]

While others came to see the *Principal Navigations* as the fundamental text for a new era of overseas exploration, Hakluyt remained busy. But his interests began to diverge from his earlier focus on promoting English colonization of eastern North America. Or perhaps it would be more accurate to note that in the 1590s, as he wrestled with the mountain of information that came into his hands from English travelers, his interests became more catholic. The *Principal Navigations* included much of interest for anyone in England who dreamed of creating colonies across the Atlantic. Yet Hakluyt realized that much of the story of travel and what could be learned from travelers' experiences remained untold.

That realization came to him during the time he was organizing his materials, an activity that proved so time-consuming that Hakluyt had little energy left for other pursuits. In particular, he could not follow the advice of his associate Walter Cope, whose cabinet of curiosities he had visited in London and which had proved so important to him that he singled Cope out in *Principal Navigations*. Cope had told Hakluyt that the accounts in the book were useful but that the volumes lacked a short summary that, as Hakluyt recounted the suggestion, "would prove most acceptable to the world, especially to men of great action and employment." Hakluyt knew that he could not pull off that task at the same time that he prepared the *Principal Navigations* for the press, noting that he could "not conveniently alter my course." But he recognized the importance of the suggestion and searched for a way to provide a short treatise that would draw out the crucial themes of his masterpiece.[14]

Yet rather than write an account that he was so obviously well suited to produce, Hakluyt chose instead to prepare an English-language edition of Antonio Galvano's *Discoveries of the World*, a global history slanted to emphasize the significance of long-distance commerce, especially the spice trade. Fearing that some of his readers might be skeptical about his choice of such a text, Hakluyt wrote in the dedication in late October 1601 that Galvano was a man who exuded "pietie towards God, equitie towards men, fidelity to his Prince, love to his countrey, skill in sea causes, experience in Histories, liberalitie towards his nation, vigilance, valour, wisdom and diligence." He was even willing to serve his country by becoming governor of the distant Portuguese colony on Maluco (Malacca?) for six or seven years, a testimony to his dedication to the greater cause of his nation. He was, in short, the perfect person to write such an account, with the slight problem that he was not English. Still, what he had to say was important for the English, and the edition of his work was thus worth the effort. The appearance of the book in 1601 along with the comments he made in his dedication meant that Hakluyt had to have turned to the project soon after delivering the text of *Principal Navigations* to his London printers.

Galvano's book was relatively brief, especially compared to the heft of Hakluyt's recent creation. Hakluyt's summary of the book's contents reveals that it was hardly a standard history of the world. Instead, it began with "the first Discoverours of the world since the time of the flood" and then proceeded immediately to "what waies from age to age the spicerie, drugs, and riches of the East were conveied into The West." Hakluyt reported that Galvano focused on the various empires that arose and how they were governed, how the Gothic invasion of the Roman Empire had halted the profitable commerce to the East, how Muslims grew in power "with their overrunning of Afrike and Spaine," and then the eventual restoration of trade to the East Indies, first by Muslims and then by Venetians, Genoese, and Florentines.[15]

At that point this history of the world became more nakedly Portuguese in its focus. The shift can be found in Galvano's treatment of the Portuguese king John I's seizure of Ceuta in Barbary in 1415. King John's third son was Don Henry, whose mother, Philippa, was the sister of King Henry IV of England, and he came to play a decisive role in this history since he "was the first beginner of all the Portugall discoveries" and kept at that task until he died forty-three years after he began. It was Don Henry, better known as Prince Henry the Navigator, who encouraged Portuguese kings to be patient in their efforts to reestablish the spice trade. He knew it was difficult to make the arduous journey around the Cape of Buona Speranza on the southern edge of Africa but only by following that route could the Portuguese bring "the Spicerie into Europe" and thus become "the chiefe Lords of the riches of the Orient."[16]

Hakluyt recognized that this Portuguese achievement had immediate results elsewhere in Europe, notably in Spain. By emulating the followers of Prince Henry, the Spanish ventured into the Antilles and West Indies, "the infancies of both which most important enterprises" in Hakluyt's estimation. Over time, with Portuguese and Spanish sailors venturing ever farther, Europeans came to learn about the wider world with its many "Islands, rivers, baies and harbours, of many rich provinces, kingdoms, and countries." These nations then set about the task of organizing long-distance trade. To do so, they erected "castles in sundry convenient Islands and places" and began to draw trade to those entrepōts. The best way to understand their success was simple. "Take a sea card or a mappe of the world," Hakluyt suggested to Robert Cecil, to whom he had dedicated the book, and follow it around the coast of Africa toward the Spice Islands, being sure to have in view all of the islands from the Azores and Madeira in the west to the Moluccas, Philippines, and Japan in the east. Galvano's book, Hakluyt argued, made that imaginative journey make sense by revealing the names of "the first discoverours, conquerors and planters in every place," as well as "the natures and commodities of the soyles, together with the forces, qualities, and conditions of the inhabitants." The same kind of information could be found about the West as about the East.[17]

Hakluyt's comments reflected his longtime appreciation for Galvano's book. He had, it turned out, been in possession of an English translation since 1589. But during the 1590s he recognized that what he possessed was a defective product that in too many places reflected the original translator's imperfect understanding of Portuguese, poor command of English, and ignorance of the places described in the text. Hakluyt wanted to do his own translation from a Portuguese original. But though he had written to contacts in Lisbon for a copy he had not found one. It was one of the few times that he acknowledged that he did not get what he wanted. As a result, Hakluyt tried to reconstruct Galvano's book by consulting the authorities used by the Portuguese author himself. This was no easy task. "It cost me more travaile to search out the grounds thereof," Hakluyt complained, "and to annexe the marginall quotations unto the worke, then the translation of many such bookes would have put me unto." He hoped that by adding quotations from original texts he would inspire readers who had leisure to seek out "the pure fountains, out of which those waters which are drawne are for the most part sweete and holsome."[18]

Yet whatever potential the book contained, it was less than perfect for Hakluyt because it contained few references to the English. (Hakluyt estimated that the nation was mentioned only four times.) But the absence of the English should not be taken as a commentary that the volume lacked worth or reflected Portuguese aversion to the English state. Instead, as Hakluyt pointed out, Galvano concluded his account in 1555, a point at which there had been "little extant of our mens travailes." Further, the English still did not possess the kind of record of the Portuguese and the Spanish since they had not yet "come to ripenes, and have been made for the most part to places first discovered by others." When the English did perfect the art of overseas exploration and trade "and become more profitable to the adventurers," the time would come when Hakluyt or another writer "endued with an honest zeale of the honour of or countrey" could integrate these efforts into such a volume.[19]

The book that Hakluyt published and attributed to Galvano presumably reflected the manuscript that came into his hands. But given the quality of the original that he received and the extensive annotations that Hakluyt added to the margins, it is difficult to see this product as anything other than Hakluyt's own. Only a writer committed to the idea of overseas exploration would have understood the history of the world as the history of exploration writ large. Hakluyt's history was a narrative of successive discoveries and their implications. The first section treated the "ancient" discoveries, which began with the creation of the Earth and continued to the European discovery of the Canary Islands near the end of the fourteenth century. Hakluyt confirmed or amended the text with frequent references to unquestionable authorities, notably Pliny. The lengthier section on the "late" discoveries picked up the story from the first Portuguese conquest on the Barbary Coast in 1415 and continued until 1553, the year that an English merchant vessel sailed in search of the Northeast Passage and, according to Hakluyt's note, managed to arrive in Moscow by sea. Within that long section Hakluyt inserted another break at 1492, which signaled the rise of the Spanish as the most important explorers of the sixteenth century. Virtually the entire text on these "late" discoveries dwelled on the efforts of the Portuguese in the East and the Spanish in the Americas, two subjects that obsessed Hakluyt. Lest any reader doubt the reliability of Hakluyt's reconstructed text, he provided references to authorities he trusted—the historian João de Barros on the Portuguese voyages and Ramusio, López de Gómara, and Peter Martyr on the Spanish in the Americas.[20]

Hakluyt's marginal notes drew attention to aspects of the narrative that seemed worthy of notice. He pointed out a section on mermaids and the snorting fishes of the Americas. He included the papal indulgence of 1441 that granted "everlasting pardon, and al other things demanded of him, unto those which should die" in the explorations. That statement was sure to attract the notice of English readers, who were too young to have remembered the first fires of Reformation in their land (including the dissolution of its monasteries) but might have remembered the pope's excommunication of Queen Elizabeth in 1570. Hakluyt also slipped in a notice of the first shipment of African slaves to Portugal in 1443. Not surprisingly, the marginal notes directed readers to the few places where English explorers appeared in the text, such as the alleged discovery of Madeira by Machim (also known as Robert Machin), who claimed to have built a chapel to his lost love on this newfound land, and Ralph Fitch's account bearing witness to the fact that the native men of Malacca attached bells to their penises (a phenomenon also witnessed by Fitch in Pegu, also mentioned in the text).[21]

Soon after Hakluyt arranged for the publication of his version of Galvano's text, a translator and promoter of commerce named William Walker produced an English-language version of a pamphlet that described a recent Dutch expedition to the East Indies. Entitled *The Journall, or Dayly Register, . . . of the voyage, accomplished by eight shippes of Amsterdam,* the short book was essentially a plea for English interest in the region. "The benefit is most apparent," he noted in the dedication to his patron Sir Thomas Smythe, the sheriff of London, "if we do but consider either the necessitie of the enterprise, or the gaine depending thereon." Establishing commerce with the East was "more then necessary, both the restraint of traffique in the King of *Spaines* dominions, and also the under-rate of the Hollanders spices, in regarde of those brought out of the Indies by the way of *Turkie.*" The benefits of such a venture were obvious: profits to be made from the sale of "divers naturall commodities, which otherwise would lye dead"; useful employment of England's tall ships; growth in English captains' knowledge about the seas; increase in revenue flowing through the royal treasury; "and the enriching of all the Adventurers." If the English did not intervene, fleets from Portugal, Holland, and Zeeland would monopolize the business.[22]

Yet however obvious the need for such a pamphlet, Walker's inspiration was not his own. Like John Pory before him, his efforts sprang from the suggestion of Hakluyt. All of the reasons for expanding English trade to the East had been "seconded by the perswasion of M. Richard Hacluyt," Walker added, "a man for his matchless industrie in collecting the *English Voyages,* most incomparably wel deserving of this state."[23]

In this age the printing of travel accounts had come to be seen, as Walker demonstrated, as an act of patriotism. But the production of such works could be complicated, and even counterproductive. Walker believed that the Dutch opened operations in the East because they had learned about its resources from the narratives of Francis Drake, Thomas Cavendish, James Lancaster, Ralph Fitch, and Thomas Stephans (Stevens)—all of them English masters whose accounts had been published, as Walker noted, in the second and third volumes of *Principal Navigations.* The *Journall,* which combined a day-to-day accounting of the expedition along with ethnographic commentary, gave the English added intellectual stimulus for voyages to the East Indies. It even included a parallel listing of words in English and "Malish" (Malay?), "which language is used throughout the East Indies, as French is in our Countrie, wherewith a man may travell over all the Land." He added that Portuguese was another useful language in the East Indies, since "there are many Interpreters which speake Portugall."[24]

In the years that followed, Walker's patron Sir Thomas Smythe went on his own eastward mission, though his destination was Russia, not the Spice Islands. Soon after he became treasurer of the Virginia Company, a position he held until he resigned under pressure with allegations that he had acted improperly while overseeing the struggling colony's finances. Yet as the impact of the *Journal* began to fade, words in Malay would eventually command Hakluyt's attention.[25]

Hakluyt spent much of his time in the early years of the century in London. He was present at the meetings of the Westminster Abbey chapter every few months from May 1602 to May 1616. In early May 1602 he became a prebendary at Westminster. Nineteen months later he became an archdeacon, a position he held until 1605. Among other duties he managed the church's real estate holdings and the appointment of a bell ringer, and he understood the necessity of keeping an inventory of Westminster's moveable property. He was also there when the church dismissed students because of the plague in July 1603 and at the meeting in early December when the school ordered the return of students only "if the sickness increase not."[26]

On March 30, 1604, Hakluyt married a widow named Frances Smithe. If he ever wrote about her, those letters have long since disappeared. She is as much a shadow in the historical record as Hakluyt's first wife, Douglas, someone whose existence remains only in the sparse vital records that mark a birth, a marriage, or a death. His son, Edmond, had turned eleven about three months earlier, but Hakluyt did not mention him in any surviving documents either. Nor did he describe events that later chroniclers recalled, such as an unusual period of lightning in late December 1601, or an earthquake that rocked London on Christmas that year, or the queen ordering jailed prisoners to the oars of galleys intended to drive the Spanish from the coast of Kent, or the bonfires that sprung up in London in January 1602 to celebrate an English military victory in Ireland, or that a man who bore false witness had one ear chopped off near Westminster and the other in Chancery Lane in May 1602, or even the disemboweling and quartering of a Catholic priest in mid-February 1603 for the crime of remaining in England despite a statute of exile. Nor did he write about the devastating plague of 1603, which killed more than twenty-five thousand Londoners at a time when the city had about 140,000 residents.[27] Hakluyt would have known of all of these things, but he never commented on them.

While he attended to his clerical career and family life, others traveled once again to the mid-Atlantic coast of North America. One of those travelers was a captain based in Weymouth named Samuel Mace, whom Harriot had instructed to take along a copy of *Principal Navigations*. Mace and his shipmates went to America at the request of Ralegh with the specific goal of finding any survivors from the Roanoke journeys of the mid-1580s. They failed in that pursuit, though they did bring back "Sassafras, Radix Chinæ or the China root, Benjamin, Cassia lignea, & a rinde of a tree more strong than any spice as yet knowen, with divers other commodities" that might become important in the future. John Brereton, who publicized Mace's findings, offered his assessment of the region after his journey there in the summer of 1602. He, too, emphasized the many natural resources to be harvested and provided a positive picture of the people he met.[28]

Brereton's brief pamphlet included a narrative of his journey, a note on the commodities to be found in the region, and a small treatise by Edward Hayes, an associate of Hakluyt's who had provided the account of Sir Humphrey Gilbert's ill-fated expedition of 1583. Almost two decades after the disaster that had killed Stephen Parmenius, Hayes argued that this northern part of Virginia (modern New England) was the ideal locale for a colony since it provided a staging ground for voyages from Britain to East Asia through the as-yet undiscovered Northwest Passage. The commodities to be found in America, including naval stores, pearls, furs, and precious metals in addition to the trees, animals, and plants enumerated by Brereton, would draw trade from other parts of Europe. "These commodities," he declared, "are of great use and estimation in all the South and Westerne countreys of Europe[,] namely Italie, France and Spaine." Sailors from those nations had already been traveling to Newfoundland to get what they needed; in the future, they would redirect their ships toward the English settlement "and trade with us, when once we have planted people in those parts." Even the Portuguese and Spanish would be drawn to the English for trade. Through such exchange the English would also be able to sell much of the cloth produced within the realm.[29]

Hayes drew extensively on the rhetoric of Hakluyt, noting the possible emigration of ten thousand men, women, and children who could work in America. According to his report, the natives held no animus against the English, and even if they did, they lacked the kinds of sharp tools or weapons to inflict much damage on any immigrant settlement. Besides, the English had no "intent to provoke, but to cherish and win them unto Christianitie by faire meanes." The Americans might not all be trustworthy, but they posed no obvious risk. Like other travelers, Hayes also thought the English would be able to master the American interior quickly and that they would discover a new trade route that would allow them to go back and forth to China in under five months, laden with "Spices, Drugges, Muske, Pearle, Stones, Gold, Silver, Silks, [and] Clothes of gold" that would make the journey profitable.[30]

By the time Brereton's book appeared in London, Hakluyt was back at work seeking English investment in North America. This time he held a number of meetings with merchants in Bristol, long the primary English western port, where Hakluyt was prebendary of Holy Trinity Church. He then traveled back to London to see Ralegh, whose "most ample Patent" (to use Purchas's term) from Elizabeth included that region. Anyone who planned to go there needed his permission. Robert Saltern, who had been to Virginia a year earlier with Bartholomew Gosnold, went with Hakluyt to obtain permission to explore lands that the queen had granted to her favorite. Ralegh gave them the right to go there, and the merchants then outfitted two ships for the journey. Before embarking, local suppliers loaded the storage bins with "slight Merchandizes thought fit to trade with the people of that Countrey," the commander Martin Pring later wrote, "as Hats of divers colours, greene, blue and yellow, apparel of coarse Kersie and Canvasse readie made, Stockings and Shooes, Sawes, Pick-axes, Spades and Shovels, Axes, Hatchets, Hookes, Knives, Sizzers, Hammers, Nailes, Chissels, Fish-hookes, Bels, Beades, Bugles, Looking-glasses, Thimbles, Pinnes, Needles, Threed, and such like."[31]

Pring's chronicle of the voyage provided his readers with details that Hakluyt had always sought. He described the local landscape, mentioned the fertility of the soil and its suitability for English crops, and added information about the physical appearance of the Americans and the clothes that they wore. Like Thomas Harriot almost two decades earlier, Pring took note of the crops that the Indians tended. The colonists were so impressed with the Americans' birch-bark canoes held together by woven twigs that they took one back to Bristol with them. It was seventeen feet long and four feet across, and it could carry nine standing men. Yet it weighed only sixty pounds, "a thing almost incredible in regard of the largenesse and capacitie thereof." His report also offered the by-then familiar description of luxuriant forests, enormous game populations, and vast stocks of fish on the coast, including endless schools of cod. Local supplies of sassafras could be harvested as a cure for French pox, plague, and other illnesses.[32]

Hakluyt did not publish the account, though it bore his mark. But Hakluyt, again, did not see these things for himself. While the ships explored the American coast, Hakluyt was at Westminster Abbey on May 23, attending the chapter meeting.

At the end of January 1603, Queen Elizabeth grew tired of London's incessant rain and commotion and decided to leave her lodgings in Westminster to enjoy the peace and quiet of her manor at Richmond in Surrey. She had always been in excellent health, which the antiquarian Camden had attributed to the fact that she abstained from wine and consumed a "most temperate dyet." But over those late winter months she began to change. She ordered her courtiers to cut off the ring she had worn since she rose to the throne years earlier "as it were in marriage to her Kingdome at her inauguration." Over time the ring had "so growne into the flesh, that it could not be drawne off." Having it removed signaled a change, "as if it portended that that marriage with her Kingdome contracted by the Ring, would be dissolved."[33]

In early March, still at Richmond, Elizabeth fell ill. A "heavy dulnesse, with a frowardnesse familiar to old age, began to lay hold on her," Camden recalled. Her gums swelled and returned to normal, and then she began to lose her appetite. Camden later reported that she "gave her selfe over wholly to melancholly, and seemed to bee perplexed with some speciall feeling of sorrow." She lingered for three weeks. According to John Chamberlain, a friend of one of her physicians, she refused any medicine and believed that if she lay down she would never rise again. "Here was some whispering that her braine was somwhat distempered," Chamberlain wrote a few weeks later, "but there was no such matter, only she held an obstinate silence for the most part." Her attendants finally got her into bed on March 21, but she did not last long. Elizabeth died three days later at the age of seventy. She had reigned for forty-four years and five months. Her courtiers took her body first to Whitehall, where it lay "wrapt up in seareclothes and other preservatives." On April 28, the funeral procession bore her body to Westminster Abbey for burial. The antiquarian Edmund Howes, who prepared a new edition of John Stow's *Annales,* took note of the fact that she died on a Thursday, the same day of the week on which King Henry VIII, King Edward, and Queen Mary had also perished.[34]

As soon as news of her death reached London, Elizabeth's advisers and the peers of the realm met and quickly announced her passing to the nation. By late morning they traveled from Whitehall to the walls of the gated City, "where their coming was seriously expected of all," as Howes recalled. The

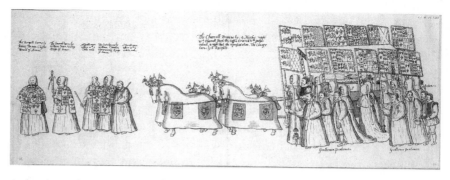

A sketch attributed to William Camden depicted the ornate parade of the queen's body as well as Lord Cecil and Sir Walter Ralegh, among others. From *The Funeral Procession of Queen Elizabeth* (London, 1791?).

lord mayor and the city's aldermen met the councilors at Ludgate and escorted them to the high cross in Cheapside. Once there, they proclaimed that James VI of Scotland was now to be King James I of England. Chamberlain claimed that they also announced the king's accession at Whitehall, Temple Bar, "and other places," a reminder that in this city (as elsewhere) news traveled most expeditiously through public oration. James's ancestry made him the only likely candidate, though rumors flew that others might be next on the throne. Cecil read the proclamation "most distinctly, and audibly," and the men he was with immediately dispatched messengers to Scotland to alert the new monarch. On hearing the news James arranged the affairs of his Scots court and began the journey to London, arriving on May 7. When he reached the capital only the elderly had any memory of the time when there had last been a man on the throne.[35]

Elizabeth's funeral procession, witnessed by thousands and purportedly sketched by Camden, snaked far through London's streets. Representatives from seemingly every group in the city marched in a line that stretched for blocks. The queen's bier, almost obscured by the flags of the realm's many dukedoms and principalities, was drawn by two magnificently bedecked horses. The pen-and-ink sketch of the cortege depicted the queen's principal adviser Cecil and her favorite Ralegh walking alone. They were among the few individuals in the city to do so; most of the others in the procession clustered together in rank. But not Cecil, who walked several yards in front of the bier carrying her body, nor Ralegh, who could be found near the end.[36]

The queen's subjects leaned out their windows to get a glimpse as the palanquin crept by. "There was such a generall sighing, groning, and weeping, as the like hath not beene seene or knowne in the memory of man," Howes concluded, "neither doeth any history mention any people, time, or state, to make like lamentation for the death of their soveraigne." Soon the English erected a fitting testimonial within Westminster, a "magnificent memorial" in the words of one Swiss visitor who described it, to a "PRINCIPI INCOM-PARABILI" (an incomparable ruler), as one of her monuments in the church attested.[37]

News of the queen's death spread quickly through the realm. On April 10, as they waited in Milford Haven for the winds to pick up for their journey to America, Martin Pring's crew heard of her passing.[38]

Presumably, Hakluyt was either in the procession or waiting for the funeral train to wend its way into the abbey. It is possible that he had not actually spoken to her for almost twenty years, since that day when he returned from France to present the "Discourse on Western Planting." But his contacts to the court had been continuous since then, especially with Ralegh, whose patents to North American lands and eagerness for information about explorations kept him in close touch with Hakluyt. The patronage that Hakluyt received from Cecil, evident most recently in the dedication of Galvano's *History of Discoveries,* suggests that Hakluyt's ties to the court remained in place.

Elizabeth's death signaled a change in the domestic policies and foreign relations of England, though on that early spring day when her earthly remains edged toward her crypt no one in London could have known exactly what the accession of James would mean for her realm. All that was known for sure was that the reign of the Tudors, which had begun in 1485, had now ended.

At some point after the queen's death, Hakluyt sat down and scrawled notes about the East Indies. He sought to identify the places where England's foes had established themselves across the region. The Portuguese maintained a post on Ormus, an "island fortified" in the Persian Gulf. At places Hakluyt identified as "Dyall, Damain et Banam" the Portuguese also kept forts, which they needed to "defend themselves from the force and assaults of the people of that country" where they "have not any command of the country at all" and could not stop others from trading there. The Portuguese held positions in Goa and Cochin, too, but they needed those forts to protect them from the locals and could not prevent other Europeans from arriving and plying their wares. The Portuguese fort on Malacca was in even worse shape; its residents had "been surprised by the people of the country," hardly a sign that they could control trade there. In the Moluccas the Portuguese kept another ineffective fort at Fedora. The residents "of the country," Hakluyt noted, "are as ready, and more desirous, to entertaine trade with any other than the Portugalls." He then listed places across the Indies where the Portuguese had even less of a presence: Sumatra, Java, most of the Moluccas, "Zelon," "Bengalu," Pegu, "Mogar et Narsinga," Siam, and the "whole Empire of Chyna, and many other great kingdoms" in which "the portugalls either dare not trade, or trading in them doe it by tolleration."[39]

Hakluyt's notes recommended a commercial treaty between King James and the king of Spain, whose subjects then included the Portuguese. He thought that either should be able to establish posts in areas where neither had dominion and where local kings were "willing to entertayne all merchants w[hi]ch resort to their dominions for trade." After all, the Spanish had no greater claim to the East Indies than the English did to Russia, a place where merchants conducted business. Hakluyt and his merchant allies thus sought permission to trade in places already known to Europeans and in places not yet discovered, and they also hoped to be able to replenish their supplies at Spanish posts. In a nod to the new politics of the Stuart court, which would soon lead to Ralegh's imprisonment and eventual execution, Hakluyt asked that the Spanish forts of the East Indies be as open to the English as English ports had become "fre and open to the merchants and people of the king of Spayne."[40]

In the months that followed Hakluyt's interest in Portuguese expeditions grew. Ralegh gave him a special navigational map called a rutter, written in Portuguese in 1543, which he hoped Hakluyt would publish. For reasons unknown, Hakluyt never did. But he did continue his pursuit of information about Portuguese expeditions. On March 18, 1604, he met with a Portuguese pilot named Simon Fernandez in London. Fernandez had recently returned from Lima, and he told Hakluyt about a Portuguese expedition to the Philippines during which the Europeans found silver in the Solomon Islands. He also met with Luis de Tribaldo, whom he referred to as "a Gentleman of qualitie" who lived with the Spanish ambassador in the English capital. In July 1605 Tribaldo, who was then in Valladolid, Spain, sent Hakluyt an extended report on Juan de Oñate's expedition in New Mexico. The report, written by Andrés Garsia (Garcia) Céspedes, detailed tensions between the

Spanish and the Americans, including a bloody assault on Acoma and the subsequent efforts to expand their territory in the region. Tribaldo also informed Hakluyt about Spanish explorations along the coast of California and told him that Céspedes had read all of the new reports and prepared a book about them, "an excellent Volume" in Tribaldo's opinion. But Céspedes had not received permission to publish the work since Spanish authorities "will not have all these things particularly to come to light." If Hakluyt thought about the difference between the ability to print travel accounts in Spain and England, he did not mention it.[41]

Hakluyt's *Principal Navigations* saw more of the world than the man who assembled the collection. Copies of it became a fixture on board ships bound for distant parts. Thomas Smythe, an advocate of free trade between nations, twice referred to Hakluyt's work in his own book, once when he looked out "over the famous River of Volga" and again when he noted that Sir Jerome Horsey's writings about the Russian emperor had already been reported by Hakluyt. The geographer Robert Stafforde sent readers of his treatise on the kingdoms of the Earth to Hakluyt (and Harriot) if they wanted to learn more about Virginia, a subject of possibly great interest when the book was published in 1607.[42]

Yet not everyone who read the *Principal Navigations* believed that it contained such important truths. Nor did the English at the dawn of the seventeenth century necessarily believe that establishing colonies in North America was always a good thing. In early Stuart England, some wondered openly about the dangers the western hemisphere posed. That was one idea embedded in the new king's *Counterblaste to Tobacco*, his first publication as protector of the English realm. James used the pamphlet, printed in 1604, to counter the widely held idea that tobacco was a panacea. Part of his critique focused on the important role the weed played among Americans, notably in their heathen rites. Other Europeans also questioned the desirability of tobacco because of its close association with devilish practice.[43]

The king opposed this particular American product; others went much farther in their efforts to distance the English from overseas enterprises. In 1605 the playwrights George Chapman, Ben Jonson, and John Marston wrote *Eastward Hoe*, which was produced by the Children of Her Majesty's Revels at Black-Friars. Rather than following Hakluyt's argument about the potential good to be had from establishing English settlements in North America, *Eastward Hoe* satirized such enterprises. "I tell thee, Golde is more plentifull [in Virginia] than copper is with us," one character declares, "and for as much redde Copper as I can bring, Ile have thrice the waight in Golde." Rumor had it that colonists had so much gold they made chamber pots out of them and forged golden chains for their prisoners. The playwrights scoffed at the idea of America as a newfound paradise with a temperate climate and ample food; colonists "shall live freely there, without Sargeants, or Courtiers, or Lawyers, or Intelligencers." In this new world, "You may be an Alderman there, and never be Scavinger; you may be any other officer, and never be a Slave." Yet as the plot unfolded so did the schemes of those who thought that going to America would solve their problems.[44]

More alarming to any promoter of colonization would have been the work of Joseph Hall, who eventually became bishop of Norwich. By the late 1590s, when he was only in his mid-twenties, Hall had turned against the idea of travel and exploration (though he would later travel to the Netherlands and France, eventually seeking medical help in The Hague in 1617 for what he later called "a miserable distemper of the body.") He began to publish satirical works by the turn of the century and apparently began work on a more extended attack on the idea of travel, titling it *Mundus Alter et Idem—Another World and Yet the Same,* as one later translator put it. Published in 1605, it cast colonies as dystopias to be avoided at all costs. Hall did not launch a direct attack on Hakluyt in these pages, though there is no doubt that the literature being satirized included collections of travel accounts.[45]

In appearance and structure, *Mundus Alter et Idem* resembled many travel accounts being produced by printers in England and on the Continent. The first Latin edition was printed in Frankfurt, the English editions, presumably translated by Joseph Healey, in London in 1609 and again in 1613 or 1614. Like other travel accounts, it included a series of maps, including a world map that situated this newly described territory in relation to known places.[46]

Hall's elaborate descriptions of such locales as Tenter-Belly with its provinces of Eat-allia (also known as Gluttonia) and Drink-allia are pure farce, drawing strength from resemblances to medieval and contemporary travel accounts by such authorities as Mandeville, Peter Martyr, and Ralegh. In Eat-allia the residents were, in the words of the translation, "generally of an unmeasurable groseness." The only men worthy of a proper greeting were obese—"all cheeks to the belly, and all belly to the knees"—and the women resembled them. In Drink-allia they worshiped Bacchus in a ritual that involved (among other things) filling a goblet attached to a statue of the god with wine and watching it go in pipes to his mouth and penis so that it "makes a pretty

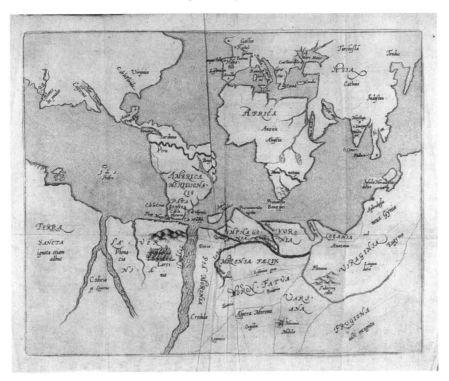

The fictional continent at the bottom of the world, as it appeared in one edition of Joseph Hall's *Mundus Alter et Idem* (Frankfurt, 1607)

shew as hee both pissed wine and spewed it, all in one moment." Shee-landt— which had provinces called Scoldonna, Cockatrixia, and Shrewesbourg, and a principal city of Gossipinga—was a land dominated by women, with its details borrowed directly from tales of Amazons. On the nearby Ile Hermophradite, where the typical resident had male and female characteristics and names such as "*Mary Philip, Peter-alice, Jane-andrew,* and *George-audry,*" any human who had only one sex was a marvel, with the locals "shewing them as prodigies & monsters, as wee doe those that are borne double-headed, or other such deformed birthes." The people of the land known as Fooliana walked around "in painted feathers, as the *Indians* doe; for seeing that these light things kept the little birds warme enough, why (say they) should we desire now being farre more able to beare out the cold then those poore and tender creatures are?" Men and women there were faithful to their spouses, at least until a man saw a fairer woman. Women, too, changed partners, apparently in response to their mates' declining virility: "Assure your selves that shee taketh the first dislike, if her husbands Cocke-shippe bee, any way declining." In Shrewesbourg, any woman who was "gentlier than ordinarie" toward her husband was to be indicted for "high treason against the state." If the evidence of her neighbors was sufficient for a conviction, she had to exchange clothing with her husband, have her head shaved, and spend a day in a public pillory where others would pelt her with rotten eggs and dirt. When she returned home she was to beat her husband and then bring "a cudgel into the Court, all died with the fresh bloud of her husbands broken pate."[47]

Despite the ferocity of such satire, neither Hall nor any others who publicly questioned the benefits of colonization won the day. As Hakluyt and his associates knew well, the English in fact seemed ready to try again to establish an American outpost.

On April 10, 1606, Hakluyt's name along with those of seven named and an unknown number of unnamed others appeared on a list of recipients of a patent to North American lands stretching from 34 to 45 degrees North latitude and from the Atlantic Ocean to a point one hundred miles inland. This territory was to become the base for two colonies, one composed of gentlemen and investors from London, and the other with similar groups from Bristol, Exeter, and Plymouth. The patent allowed them "to make habitacion plantacion and to deduce a Colonie of sondrie of our people into that parte of America commonly called Virginia and other parts and territories in America either appertaining unto us or which are not nowe actuallie possessed by anie Christian Prince or people." The patent explicitly protected the lands of other Europeans in North America, as long as they maintained actual possession there. Hakluyt had long believed that the English had a right to this territory by right of earlier discoveries. The chance for success have would have appeared just as good to others, who believed that Britain was, as the geographer Robert Stafforde put it in 1607, the "rich Diamond set in the ring of the world, nurce of the most valiant, wise, and victorious men."[48]

Despite his reservations about tobacco, James saw value in Virginia. Following Hakluyt's logic, the Virginia Company's patent specified that the English should spread "Christian religion to suche people as yet live in darkenesse and miserable ignorance of the true knowledge and worshippe of god." The king hoped that such efforts would eventually "bring the infidels and sal-

vages lyving in those partes to humane civilitie and to a settled and quiet
governmente." The assumption, always embedded in documents that en-
dorsed European colonial schemes in the Americas, was that the native peoples of the Atlantic coastal region lacked not only an understanding of Christianity but also the domestic and political practices that logically followed
adoption of what the English believed was the one true faith. Such a view
might have come as something of a surprise to readers of Harriot's work or
even the *Principal Navigations,* who would have already learned that these
Americans possessed religious beliefs, a settled economy, and their own working governments. But to acknowledge the Americans' customs and practices
as legitimate would undermine English claims to the territory. Better to
assume that they needed Christianity to live properly.[49]

The patent itself detailed what the colonists would possess and how they
were to govern themselves. Each group of colonists would own "all the landes
woodes soyle Groundes havens portes Ryvers Mynes Myneralls Marshes
waters Fyshinges Commodities and hereditaments" from the place they first
settled extending fifty miles inland. A council would govern each colony
according to rules approved in England, though it would be subordinate to a
group of thirteen men called the Council of Virginia, which remained in
England. Local councils had the authority to order exploratory mining for
gold, copper, and silver, with the understanding that if these minerals were
found the colonists would owe one-fifth of their haul to the king. The colonists also had the authority to coin their own money to facilitate trade among
themselves and with Americans.[50]

The patent guaranteed the colonists what they needed to survive. They
had the right to transport as many of the king's subjects "as shall willinglie
accompanie them or anie of them in the saide voyages and plantacions." They
could defend themselves with arms and had the right to expel anyone who
lacked a legitimate claim to being there. The colonists could also engage in
piracy, though they had to pay a small percentage of their profits to the king.
To ensure the colonies' initial success, the king allowed them to export weapons from England or Ireland for seven years without paying any custom or
duty on what they obtained.[51]

The patent of April, along with a detailed set of instructions issued seven
months later for how the colony was to be organized, laid out the structure of
governance. It also emphasized that everyone who went there would retain
the rights of those in England. The same legal status would apply to anyone born in the colonies, too, who would "enjoy all liberties Franchises and

Immunities" as someone born within any English dominion. As the king's subjects, those who lived in the colonies could not trade to non-English without the proper license; those who ignored this statute would forfeit their goods to the king. Anyone who robbed any other English would be pursued "with hostility" along with any accomplices. But those who abided by the laws of the colony and the realm would hold their lands in free and common socage only (not in capite) like the residents of the manor of East Greenwich in Kent.[52]

After the company had received the patent and its instructions for organizing its government, the council drew up detailed guidelines for what the first colonists should do when they landed in Virginia. The surviving document bears no names, but given the fact that Hakluyt was a member of the council, the instructions invariably reflected either his direct intervention as the author or at least a close knowledge of the ideas he had promulgated in *Principal Navigations* and elsewhere. Either way, the document reflects Hakluyt's ideas about how Virginia stood the best chance to succeed.[53]

The instructions outlined what the first settlers were to do. They were not to establish their settlement along the ocean, because doing so would make them vulnerable to enemy attack. This is what the history of the French and Spanish in Florida had taught, something that Hakluyt knew well from his intimacy with continental reports. Instead, the colonists were to find a river navigable for a sailing ship of fifty tons perhaps one hundred miles from the coast. The planners hoped that this river would bend away from the coast toward the northwest "for that way you shall soonest find the other sea."

Some of the advice seems obvious. Once they arrived at their destination, for example, the English were to "make election of the strongest, most wholesome and fertile place." They needed a location that could sustain the nascent community because frequent moves would ruin much of their food and put a severe drain on the limited supply of labor. But not everyone should live there. Instead, the settlers should build a storehouse near the mouth of the river. Its residents needed to have a small boat so they could sail quickly up the river if enemies approached. The early warning would protect the main settlement, where the residents could line the banks of the river and shoot at any intruders who dared venture upstream.

The council took nothing for granted. Its instructions specified how many men (there is no mention of women or children) should perform certain tasks. Of the 120 men who the council believed would travel as far as the main settlement, forty had to set to work immediately to build the public buildings, notably the storehouse for the company's food. Another thirty should begin to prepare the land for crops and planting the first season's seed. Ten others should stand watch lest any danger approach. The last group of forty should go on a two-month exploration of the interior. If the explorers spotted any high lands, twenty of them should take pickaxes and start poking the earth in search of minerals. The other twenty should go back to the banks of the river and begin to erect boughs that could guide later arrivals. The explorers should have a rowboat (known as a wherry) with them, "such as is used here in the Thames," which they could use to send back to the main camp for provisions.

As the explorers began to grasp the lay of the land, they needed to determine the course of local rivers. In particular, they had to find out if rivers flowing to the ocean began in the mountains or, better still, started in a lake, which would naturally feed a river that ran "toward the East Indian Sea." The council suggested that the explorers hire a local guide to help them, though they should be sure that the English had compasses with them in case the Americans deserted them in the woods. Also, the council urged the settlers never to let one of the Americans carry the English weapons, "for if they run from you with your shott, which they only fear," they would turn on the hapless Englishmen and kill them with arrows. The council knew that their greatest advantage over the locals was the lethal force and startling noise of their guns. To maintain that advantage would take psychology. The Americans must never learn that guns could miss their mark. It was thus crucial that whenever a native was nearby only the most accurate marksmen take a shot, for if the Americans saw the English miss they would become emboldened and assault them.

This fear of Americans ran through the entire set of instructions. Colonists had to make sure that no natives lived between them and the coast, for example, for if the Americans ever grew "discontented with your habitation" they would "guide and assist any nation that shall come to invade you." The settlers needed to establish trade with the locals as soon as possible in case their crops failed and they needed to turn to indigenous farmers for food. Most important, the colonists needed to hide any deaths in their ranks from the natives. "Do not advertise the killing of any of your men, that the country people may know it," the council warned, for "if they perceive that they are but common men, and that with the loss of many of theirs they diminish any part of yours, they will make many adventures upon you."

Such warnings fit English knowledge of Americans derived from travel accounts, primarily reports found easily (if not exclusively) in *Principal Navigations*. But the council members also used their understanding of medical practice to guide the migrants. The colonists were to avoid settling on a "low or moist place, because it will prove unhealthful." But how were people so new to the territory to determine where they could live? They needed to pay close attention to the bodies of their new neighbors. "You shall judge of the good air by the people," the council observed, "for some part of that coast where the lands are low, have their people blear eyed, and with swollen bellies and legs; but if the naturals be strong and clean made, it is a true sign of a wholesome soil."

Nothing seemed beyond the range of the council's instructions. Every detail, however minor, called for clarification. The pinnace that carried the men to their upstream settlement needed to be pulled out of the water and under the fort, and the men had to "take her sails and anchors ashore" lest "some ill-dispositioned persons slip away with her." The woods surrounding the new town should not be too thickly forested since it would be difficult enough for the newcomers to clear twenty acres a year and those trees could provide ideal cover for hostile natives. The settlers had to build their houses "even and by a line, that your street may have a good breadth." Houses needed to be erected in a square surrounding the central marketplace with "every street's end opening into it." Such a strategy would enhance the settlers' ability to defend themselves since gunmen could be mustered quickly in any direction. The council even warned the settlers not to let the mariners who were going to return to England engage in trade with the locals. If they did so, they "will debase the estimation of exchange, and hinder the trade for ever after."

The set of instructions reflected Hakluyt's information about the Americas and his attention to detail. But the tone of the document suggests that some on the council did not agree with everything that Hakluyt had been writing about for more than two decades. With the notable exception of the secrecy surrounding his "Discourse on Western Planting," he had always been an advocate for the free dissemination of information about new territories, even when his efforts to publish documents in French or German stood to benefit few in England. Someone on the council felt otherwise. The settlers needed to send a "perfect relation" back to England to report how the initial plantation had proceeded. But the newcomers were forbidden to send their own letters back home. Only the president and Council of Virginia had the authority to correspond with anyone in England lest a disgruntled colonist "write any letter of anything that may discourage others."

On November 21, 1606, the king granted Hakluyt permission to join the mission. He did so because Hakluyt was already part of the group of adventurers who had received permission "to lead a colony of a number of our subjects to those parts of America" known as Virginia "and other territories of America which either already belong to us or are not actually already possessed by any Christian prince or people." Hakluyt's presence (along with that of another minister named Robert Hunt) was necessary since the Americans needed religious instruction. To make the deal irresistible, the king even granted Hakluyt and Hunt the permission to receive clerical funds if they established a church in Virginia. Their English sinecures would remain secure for five years.[54]

Everything was in place for Hakluyt to go at last to Virginia. His books had been providing guidance for English mariners for years. He had urged the English to colonize the Atlantic coast of North America, and they were now willing to do so. The plans that the council devised for how to create settlements that could survive—and thus avoid repeating the disaster of Roanoke—reflected his views, if not (in the final instructions to the first settlers) his approach to sharing information. The information that the English had been gathering since the visit of Bartholomew Columbus to Henry VII more than a century earlier, now made public through Hakluyt's extraordinary talents and energies, had finally encouraged an English monarch to take a direct hand in overseas colonization. Even Hakluyt's family's wellbeing was secure if they chose to remain behind and he suffered the fate of his friend Parmenius or the intrepid Gilbert. He had even been celebrated by the poet Michael Drayton, who ended his "Ode to the Virginia Voyage," first published that year, singing Hakluyt's praises.[55]

But when the Virginia Company's crew and colonists made the final preparations on their vessels to catch the morning's tide on the Thames on December 20, 1606, Hakluyt was not on board. A month after the king had urged him to travel with them, he was at home. Rather than see for himself what America looked like and whether his ideas for settling there would work, Hakluyt remained close enough to Westminster to be a witness at such official church acts as leasing a rectory to another prebendary. Hakluyt's signature on these documents proves only that he remained in London. He never explained why he made that decision.[56]

News about the new colony in Virginia appeared in London in late 1608 when an unknown author published a poorly edited version of a letter that Captain John Smith had written. The letter detailed Smith's actions from the time he sailed from London in December 1606 until the beginning of June 1608. Apparently read by members of the council, the text soon made its way to an author identified only as "I.H." That man, probably a hack named John Healey, took the letter and offered it to the public as *A True Relation of such occurrences and accidents of noate as hath hapned in Virginia since the first planting of that Collony.* The first version of the book lacked an author, though the printer later produced a copy in which Smith was identified. Yet however awkwardly produced and edited, the *True Relation* offered London's residents, Hakluyt included, the first news about life in the new colony.[57]

The small book hardly painted a positive picture of the settlement. According to Smith, storms tossed the ships at sea and lengthened their crossing of the Atlantic. They arrived on April 26, four months after they left, and almost immediately ran into problems with the natives they met near the coast. But after the initial discomfort, Smith acknowledged that the colonists began to have better dealings with the Americans. In early May Smith traveled with others, including Captain Christopher Newport, to explore the region. The natives treated them well, "daunsing and feasting us with strawberries, Mulberies, Bread, Fish, and other their Countrie provisions whereof we had plenty." In exchange the colonists offered pins, bells, beads, needles, and glass objects. Though the English felt confident enough to erect a cross, a typical gesture of Europeans arriving in the Americas, early optimism soon faded. One native group attacked the immigrants' fort, killing an English boy. In the weeks that followed sickness stalked the colonists who remained behind after Newport left for England on June 22. As Smith saw it, "God (being angrie with us) plagued us with such famin and sicknes, that the living were scarce able to bury the dead." The leaders fell ill along with the others. Smith survived, but Bartholomew Gosnold died after lingering for three weeks.[58]

The *True Relation* contained sufficient desperate news about the colony that it is hard to imagine that the Virginia Company sanctioned its publication. By September 10, forty-six settlers had died. The mortality did not surprise Smith, who described his men as ill, unhappy, and so sunk in despair that "they would rather starve and rot with idleness, then be perswaded to do anything for their owne reliefe without constraint." He could not have known that his colleagues were dying in large part because the settlers had followed their written instructions. They sailed up a broad river searching for a protected spot where they could defend themselves. When they arrived in April that location, which they called James Fort, was on the banks of a briskly flowing river swollen by winter run off and spring rains. But the river became shallow in the summer, and salt from the Chesapeake moved upstream when the spring runs subsided. The colonists who relied on the river for their drinking water fell victim to typhoid fever and dysentery.[59]

Still, despite the hardships, Smith's pamphlet also revealed that the surviving colonists had begun to learn how to manage in their new environment. He frequently mentioned trading with locals for food, thus suggesting that it would be possible for others to plant and await their own crops. The land's bounty was obvious: "More plenty of swannes, cranes, geese, duckes, and mallards and divers sorts of fowles none would desire." The land was fertile, fish were abundant in local streams, and "a better seat for a towne cannot be desired." Smith followed the company's instructions when he explored the woods. He carried a compass and even speculated that one river ran so fast that he supposed "it might issue from some lake or some broad ford, for it could not be far to the head."[60]

The emotional center of the narrative, which would have drawn the attention of anyone in London in 1608, was the story of Smith's brief captivity and release by Powhatan, the *werowance* of a confederacy of perhaps thirty indigenous groups clustered near the Chesapeake Bay. Though the *True Relation* mentioned occasional disputes with locals, which led to at least two deaths and serious threats of violence by both colonists and Americans, for the most part Smith's account provided the kinds of details that Hakluyt always looked for in a narrative: specific resources to be found in particular areas, the customs (including religious beliefs) of the local population, and some sense of whether the region would be suitable for English settlers. The details about Smith's captivity thus provided a romantic story that would capture a reader's imagination and observations about the natives' society and Virginia's environment that could spur further migrations.

As Smith told the story, he was treated exceptionally well during the time he spent with Powhatan. In that sense he was lucky; he escaped the fate of John Robinson, whose body had twenty or thirty arrows in it when Smith saw his corpse. Fearing that his captivity might be taken as a hostile sign by the English, Smith received permission from Powhatan to send a letter back to the main camp to let the others know that he "was well, least they should revenge my death." The Powhatans kept Smith well fed during his captivity, and he often described their settlements in an admiring tone. The headman told him about the region, including "the Countreys beyond the Falles" that were of such special interest to the English, who sought the passage to the Pacific Ocean. He also warned Smith about a dangerous people nearby called

Pocoughtronack, "a fierce nation that did eate men." While he remained with the Powhatans, Smith also took the opportunity to tell them about his world. This sharing of information on both parts revealed to readers in England that the indigenous peoples of Virginia possessed the intellectual capacities to engage in high-level conversation. The *True Relation* did not cast Americans as incapable of civilization or culture.[61]

Soon after Smith's return from his captivity an English ship arrived to supply the colonists. Within a week, an accidental fire burned much of the fort along with most of the settlers' clothing and food. As the plight of the English worsened, Powhatan sent them food. Smith acknowledged how well he in particular got along with Americans and described the sense of trust earned from mutual respect. By the time that Smith embarked, those alliances had become secured: the English offered to help the Powhatans defeat their enemies, and the headman reciprocated: "with a lowd oration he proclaimed me A werowances of Powhaton," Smith wrote, "and that all his subjects should so esteeme us, and no man account us strangers nor Paspahegans, but Powhatans, and that the Corne, women and Country, should be to us as to his owne people." The English accepted the offer "with the best Languages and signes of thankes I could expresse," and the Indians under Powhatan's charge treated the English well. When problems arose and the colonists felt compelled to detain a few of the locals, Powhatan sent his daughter to Smith to negotiate their release. She was, Smith wrote, "a child of tenne yeares old, which not only for feature, countenance, & proportion, much exceedeth any of the rest of his people, but for wit, and spirit, the only Nonpariel of of his Country." It was the first time that the English learned of the Powhatan named "Pocahuntas." When Smith embarked for his return home, he believed that the English settlement seemed secure and at peace with the Powhatans. He imagined that the newcomers would succeed in Virginia.[62]

There can be little doubt that this text fell immediately from the print shop into Hakluyt's hands, though he never mentioned it. Hakluyt would have been appalled at the slipshod production of the small book, a reflection less of Smith's original letter than the individuals who edited it and prepared it for the press. It lacks the professionalism that characterized Hakluyt's works and those he helped shepherd through production. Yet its argument and its core message must have pleased him. Unlike the instructions from the council the previous year, Smith's report contained news both positive and negative, an approach to the dissemination of information that Hakluyt em-

braced. He would not have been surprised at the death toll suffered by those
first settlers at James Fort, nor would he have been shocked to hear that some
of the broad rivers flowing into the ocean might possibly lead to the Pacific.
Most important, Hakluyt would have seen enormous promise in a report of
English settlers coexisting with Americans. The natives' rituals and their
ignorance of Christianity needed to be overcome, of course. But Hakluyt had
long believed that such success was imminent if the English acted, as Smith
did, reasonably.

Smith's report appeared in print while English colonists were still living
along the James River. The quick circulation of the account reveals a substantial change in the way that the English thought about the possibility of
establishing a settlement in North America. A delay of three years separated
the initial English arrival in Roanoke and the first publication of Harriot's
report. Now the waiting time had been reduced to months. The swift dissemination of a largely positive report played directly into the hands of the
Virginia Company and its investors, including Hakluyt, who knew that the
colony's success depended on encouraging other English men, women, and
children to cross the Atlantic.

As the English settlers on the James tried to survive that first killing
season, the *Principal Navigations* made yet another journey. On July 30, 1607,
William Keeling, sailing on English ship the *Dragon* to the East Indies,
began to think about Sierra Leone. "I having formerly read well of the place,
sent for the Booke, and shewed it my Master, who as my self, took good liking
to the place."[63]

Hakluyt himself stayed in London and remained active. As in the past, he
translated travel accounts and persuaded others to translate them into English. With Hakluyt's (and others') encouragement, a scholar named William
Phillip sat down with the substantial work of the Dutch writer Gerrit de
Veer, who had written about Dutch travels to the Northeast. In 1609, that
book appeared in London with the title *The True and perfect Description of
three Voyages, so strange and woonderfull, that the like hath never been heard
of before.*[64]

Phillip, like Hakluyt before him, recognized the significance of these
efforts to get to East Asia via a northern sea route. There had been, he knew,
many attempts "to find a passage by those poorest parts to the richest; by
those barbarous, to the most civile; those unpeopled, to the most popular; those Desarts, to the most fertile Countries of the World." While the

accounts that followed presented the efforts of the Dutch, Phillip recognized their direct value for the English. Here was information from those who had gone before. The Dutch were, he claimed, the first to have made it as far north as 81 degrees North latitude, though they could not stay there. Instead, they "wintered in 76, where they had no Inhabitants, but Foxes, Beares, and Deare, to keepe them company." Phillip also thought that knowledge of those frozen wastes would make the English recognize their need for godly support. This was exactly the lesson that Hakluyt wanted taught. The English must learn how to get to other parts of the world for trade and possible settlement but must always appreciate the divine favor they already enjoyed.[65]

In late September 1608 Hakluyt became steward of Westminster Abbey. It was a difficult time at Westminster, as Hakluyt knew when he signed off on a report in early December that noted anticipated expenses for the church "by reason of the dearth of all thinges," a situation sufficiently dire that some of its principal officers should skip some meals there to save money. In the spring of 1609 he offered the Virginia Company his translation of a book entitled (in the English version) *Virginia richly valued, By the description of the maine land of Florida, her next neighbour.* The book was based on the explorations of Hernando de Soto and the six hundred men he led on a thousand-mile journey through the North American interior. The book was written, not by Soto, who died during the expedition, but instead by someone Hakluyt identified as "a Portugall gentleman of *Elvas,* employed in all the action." Hakluyt dedicated the book to the council of the Virginia Company. This was no mere supplication to a patron seeking support but a response to the efforts of Smith and his colleagues on that far shore. Hakluyt introduced an English-reading audience to a text that was of obvious relevance for the renewed effort to establish an English settlement in Virginia. Though the book was "small in shew," as he put it, it was "great in substance" and yielded "much light to our enterprise now on foot." The text provided details about "the present and future commodities of our countrie," as well as "the qualities and conditions of the Inhabitants" and "what course is best to be taken with them."[66]

Hakluyt's comments began with an enumeration of the commodities to be found in Virginia. Repeating the strategy he used with the managers of the East India Company, Hakluyt referred his audience to existing reports and books, such as the narrative of Álvar Núñes Cabeza da Vaca, "who first traveled through a great part of the Inland of Florida, next adjoining upon our Virginia." According to the Spanish castaway, Florida "was the richest countrie of the world." The residents there wore cotton clothing and had gold, silver, "and stones of great value." Cabeza da Vaca claimed there were "rich mines of gold" in Yupaha and that the copper axes used in Cutifachiqui had gold mixed into them. Hakluyt then referred to the writings of Antonio de Herrera, "the last Chronicler of the West Indies," who told of the gold and silver imported into Santa Helena. Hakluyt estimated that those mines were located at 35½ degrees North latitude. Soto's narrative also spoke of valuable mines at Chisca, a finding confirmed by the *cacique* of Costa. Three other reports confirmed Chisca's riches, and those accounts, too, could be found in the book.[67]

But there was no reason the council had to accept such foreign authorities. Instead, as Hakluyt told them, they might just as easily accept the report that Thomas Harriot had only recently delivered to them at the house of the Earl of Exeter. Harriot, who had seen the American mid-Atlantic coast with his own eyes, had informed the council that natives had often told him that "to the Southwest of our old fort in Virginia" there existed "a great melting of red mettall, reporting the manner of working the same." "Besides," Hakluyt added, "our owne Indians have lately revealed either this or another rich mine of copper or gold in a towne called Ritanoe, neere certaine mountains lying West of Roanoac."[68]

Gold and copper were not the only precious things to be found near Virginia. Soto's report also spoke of an abundance of pearls, and Hakluyt believed that cotton wool and "Turkie stones" also merited attention. So did American flora, especially numerous mulberry trees to support a silkworm industry and cochineal. Hakluyt was especially enthusiastic about the buffaloes that Soto's crew spotted frequently. The hair of these beasts was "like a soft wooll, betweene the course and fine wooll of sheepe," and Americans used it for shoes, boots, and shields; besides, the beasts could be yoked for an English plow. Hakluyt reminded the council that the accounts of Coronado and Espejo, which he had published in *Principal Navigations*, suggested that the animals could be found across the wide swathe of America north of 33 degrees North latitude. As Hakluyt concluded his latest words about North America's commodities, he added that there were two references in the text to the possibility of finding a water route to the Pacific.[69]

In the last part of his comments Hakluyt turned his attention to America's indigenous peoples. He noted that the text revealed, as had other reports that had come across the Atlantic, that the Americans were talented public speakers. The Gentleman of Elvas believed that every native who had come to speak to Soto "delivered their message or speech in so good order, that no

Oratour could utter the same more eloquently." Yet despite their rhetorical strengths, the Americans "are not overmuch to be trusted: for they be the greatest traitors of the world," as the details in the narrative proved. "They are great liars and dissemblers" who could "be also as unconstant as a wethercock." Yet Hakluyt knew that the English could not ignore their new neighbors. They should be treated "gently, while gentle courses may be found to serve." But if such a strategy failed, "then we shall not want hammerours and rough masons enow, I meane our olde soldiours trained up in the Netherlands, to square and prepare them to our Preachers hands."[70]

In the end, Hakluyt urged the council to provide the necessary guidance for those going abroad. If they did so, he was sure that "the painfull Preachers shall be reverenced and cherished, the valiant and forward soldiour respected, the diligent rewarded, the coward emboldened, the weake and sick relieved, the mutinous suppressed, the reputation of the Christians among the Salvages preserved, our most holy faith exalted, all Paganisme and Idolatrie by little and little utterly extinguished."[71]

With that remark, Hakluyt launched the English council members into the Portuguese book. It was expert commentary on a Spanish expedition, with details matching information culled from other sources, including Ramusio, about the indigenous peoples of the Americas and the resources of the land they inhabited. Five weeks later Hakluyt's name appeared in the second charter of the Virginia Company as an owner of two shares of the company's stock, later valued at twenty-one pounds.[72] He never wrote about America again.

CHAPTER 11

Wetheringsett and London, 1614
The Malayan Dialogues

In 1614, Samuel Purchas published the second edition of his collection of travel narratives. Unlike Hakluyt, Purchas tended to rewrite the accounts that came into his possession, weaving them into a narrative that reflected his clerical bearing. He had published the first edition only the year before. But that volume had sold so quickly that he feared a "second impression" would appear before he could add the new material he had gathered, particularly pertaining to Europe. He considered the possibility of simply producing new pages, but they were so numerous that "it would have seemed a loose bundle of shreds and ragges: which being thus sowed together in fit places, make the Pilgrimes weedes more handsome." Purchas, never immodest, also claimed that he had enriched the work by studying many authorities he had not used in the first edition. His efforts took a toll. The changes could not have been made "without my great cost and paines," he claimed, "which might rather merit Elogies then Apologies."[1]

Purchas could not have produced either of his books on his own. He was indebted, as he had written a year earlier, "to seven hundred Authors, of one or other kind, in I know not how many hundreds of their Treatises, Epistles, Relations and Histories, of divers subjects and Languages." The effort had been time-consuming, especially for a man who lacked "that Academicke leisure," and the "benefits of greater Libraries, or conference with men more skilful," and was already busy, as he mentioned, tending the needs of his family and his flock. Still, he was a man "addicted to the studie of Historie" who finally decided "to turne the pleasures of my studies into studious paines, that others might againe, by delightfull studie, turne my paines into their pleasure."[2]

Like many travelers and scholars, Purchas relied on Hakluyt. He acknowledged him as the man who brought together the accounts of Parkhurst,

Peckham, Parmenius, and others that offered information about northeastern North America and "bestowed" them on the world. In 1614, as his collection swelled, Purchas praised the published books of both Ramusio and Hakluyt. But he also thanked Hakluyt for providing actual guidance for his "many written Treatises" of voyages and discoveries. Hakluyt had been, Purchas wrote, "as Admirall, holding out the light unto me in these Seas, & as diligent a guide by land." He did not mention a more important fact: Hakluyt was in the process of giving or selling Purchas his papers, including translations of manuscript travel accounts that Hakluyt had gathered after the publication of *Principal Navigations* but had not published.[3]

By then, it had been five years since Hakluyt had printed anything related to North America. Instead, he concentrated his energies in other directions. Two years earlier Hakluyt and his son, Edmond, had come into possession of a manor called Bridge Place in Coddenham, approximately eight miles south of Wetheringsett along the road that ran to Ipswich, the county's most important city and its connection (via the Orwell River) to the sea. The church in Wetheringsett looked much as it had since 1500, with nineteen crosses (sixteen of them along its arches) as well as a picture of the Trinity. (Those sacred images did not last much beyond Hakluyt's time; they were destroyed by order of a rampaging iconoclast named William Dowsing in the summer of 1643.) The manor was still evident on a survey made by the agricultural improver Joseph Hodskinson almost two centuries later. The church at Wetheringsett stands still, and the Suffolk flint embedded in its exterior walls continues to catch the sun as it must have in Hakluyt's day.[4]

Coddenham had had human occupants since the Neolithic age and was probably the site of a Roman villa, at least judging from the remains dug from its soils. A road constructed when the Romans occupied Britain ran directly from the region toward London. Traveling along a similar road, Hakluyt might have noticed the startling diversity of birds living in the area. More than 250 species could be found in Suffolk over the course of a year, drawn to the county's varied landscapes. There were fewer mammals then, but Hakluyt, like many another resident of rural Suffolk, would have seen his share of bats, shrews, hedgehogs, foxes, martens, badgers, rabbits, and all variety of rats and other rodents. Perhaps he even caught sight of the occasional otter that periodically swam up the county's rivers. Various kinds of deer might have still roamed Suffolk's fields and forests in the early seventeenth century.[5]

Hakluyt had ample time to gaze across the Suffolk landscape during his travels back and forth to London, where he continued to be active at Westminster. As he moved through those gentle rolling hills that separated his house on Tuttle Street in the Westminster suburbs of the crowded capital from his rural retreat, Hakluyt's mind might have been thousands of miles away. Perhaps he dreamed about what was going on in Jamestown and wondered if his stock in the Virginia Company would be profitable. More likely his mind drifted toward the East and the nascent commerce conducted by the East India Company. It was for that merchant operation, not the Virginia Company, that Hakluyt undertook his last major intellectual feat, the production of a book of dialogues in English and Malay that he hoped would promote commerce in the Spice Islands.

Two years after he completed that work, Hakluyt died. By then he had apparently arranged to transfer his unpublished manuscripts to Purchas, including documents he had translated but for some reason never published. If thoughts of America flickered through his mind in his last days, he might have feared for the troubled English colony's survival but knew that he done much to promote its settlement. Besides, in 1616 any reasonable observer would have believed that the realm's real profits lay in the Spice Islands, not along the muddy banks of the James.

In 1608 the Dutch legal scholar Hugo Grotius published a treatise entitled *Mare Liberum* (*The Free Sea*). Hakluyt acquired a copy of the book and produced a translation, possibly as early as 1609 (the year he shepherded *Virginia Richly Valued* through production). Unlike the work of the Gentleman of Elvas or any of the other travel accounts that Hakluyt had typically spent his time translating or cajoling others to translate, Grotius's book did not provide new information about shipping routes or commodities to be found in exotic locations. Instead, the jurist intended to lay out a justification for freedom of commerce on the high seas.

Grotius sought to legitimize Dutch trade in the face of Portuguese claims of a commercial monopoly between Europe and the East Indies. The law of nations, as Grotius understood it, dictated that (in the words of Hakluyt's translation) "any man may saile freely to whomsoever." The Portuguese possessed no monopoly over trade between Europe and the Spice Islands because of any right that came to them from the discovery of the route or "by title of war." Nor could the Portuguese claim they had an exclusive right to the seas. The law of nations dictated that "traffic is free with all." Not war or peace or truce could interfere with the right of the Dutch to sail to the Indies. Grotius's dedication of the work to "the Princes & free States of the Christian

World" put this competition into a larger context, noting that it had always been the rich and powerful who believed that laws existed to suit their own purposes. That specious proposition had "in all ages" been disputed by "some wise and religious men (not of servile condition) who would pluck this persuasion out of the minds of simple men, and convince the others, being defenders thereof, of impudence."[6]

Grotius wrote his treatise, as Hakluyt knew, with the specific goal of promoting Dutch trade to the East. Yet the very same arguments that made sense for the Dutch also fit the logic of the English East India Company, which quite possibly had urged Hakluyt to make the translation. "By the law of nations navigation is free for any to whomsoever," Hakluyt's translation stated at the start of the first chapter. Since God had put desirable commodities in different places, trade was natural. Even nature itself supported such an argument. "That ocean wherewith God hath compassed the Earth is navigable on every side round about," he argued. Did not the "extraordinary blasts of wind, not always blowing from the same quarter, and sometimes from every quarter . . . sufficiently signify that nature hath granted a passage from all nations unto all?" Seneca had thought this "the greatest benefit of Nature, that even by the wind she hath mingled nations scattered in regard of place and hath so divided all her goods into Countries, that mortal men must needs traffic among themselves."[7]

Grotius spent much of his time attacking the arguments made by the Portuguese for a monopoly over trade between Europe and the Spice Islands. The Dutch jurist systematically destroyed each pillar sustaining this position. The Portuguese could not claim a monopoly of trading rights with the islanders because the Europeans were visitors there, not conquerors. "When they pay tribute and obtain liberty of trade of the princes" of the islands, the Portuguese "testify sufficiently that they are not lords but arrive there as foreigners, for they do not so much dwell there but by entreaty." In addition to lacking title to these already peopled and governed lands, the Portuguese also had no exclusive rights granted to them from the Bull of Donation, which had divided up much of the world between the Portuguese and the Spanish in 1493. Such an argument was specious because the pope was "not a civil or temporal lord of the whole world." Instead, his authority extended over Christendom but not "over infidels seeing they appertain not unto the Church." That the Portuguese were "wholly bent to lucre" and not engaged in a grand missionary project further undermined their legitimacy. Their actions in the islands, like those by the Spanish in the Americas, actually undermined any evangelical intent. In the Spice Islands, "no miracles, no signs and tokens, are to be heard of, no examples of a religious life which might vehemently persuade others to the same faith, but many scandals, many wicked deeds, many impieties."[8]

Grotius relied on a range of ancient authorities to destroy the argument that any nation could own the seas. Although someone could lay a claim to a part of the shoreline or a river valley, no such claim could be extended to the sea itself, both because nature "commandeth it should be common" and because the ocean "cannot easily be built upon." Humans could impose limits on other humans about where they could fish along the shore, for example, but "the rents which are set down for fishing upon the seacoast are reckoned in the number of royalties, and bind not the thing, that is, the sea or fishing, but the persons." A ruler could place limits on the fishing rights of individuals under his or her control but could not impose the same limitations on others: "the right of fishing everywhere ought to be free to foreigners, that servitude be not imposed on the sea, which cannot serve." Unlike Roman lawyers who had made arguments relating to inland seas, Grotius referred to the entire ocean, "which antiquity calleth unmeasurable and infinite." Passage through the vast seas did not confer rights of discovery analogous to those that followed setting foot on previously unknown lands, the kind of argument that Christopher Columbus made (though Grotius did not mention it) after making landfall in the Caribbean in 1492. "If they call this possession," Grotius commented, "that they sailed before others and after a sort opened a way, what can be more ridiculous?" Besides, "ancient testimonies" demonstrated that the Portuguese were hardly the first to sail into the deep seas; "Moors, Aethiopians, Arabians, Persians, and Indians" had all preceded them. The Portuguese could not be said to possess the ocean since "in that huge coast of shore [they] have nothing except a few garrisons which they may call theirs." Besides, ownership implies that others' use diminishes the alleged owner's property, yet the Portuguese "could not forbid navigation, whereby the sea loseth nothing."[9]

Back and forth the argument went, shredding Portuguese claims because they flowed from flawed premises. Just as the pope lacked the authority to divide lands beyond the fringes of Christendom, so "he is not lord of the sea." His division of the seas between the Spanish and Portuguese needed to be understood for what it was: an effort not to divide ownership of something that the pope could not control but instead a desire to minimize "strife between the Castilians and the Portugals." Even though Grotius admitted that the Portuguese had in fact been the first Europeans to sail around Africa in the late fifteenth century, in the intervening decades the Spanish, French, and English had all made inroads toward the East, thereby making the Portuguese claims all the more specious because they were unenforceable. Drawing on the work of Plato, Aristotle, and Cicero (among others), Grotius also emphasized the essential "liberty of trading," which was "agreeable to the primary law of nations" and could not be halted by an outside party. Even the pope could not make an exception here "unless he be temporal lord of the whole world (which wise men deny)." Instead, "no authority of the Pope is of force against the perpetual law of nature and nations whence this liberty took beginning, which shall continue forever."[10]

Grotius's argument made obvious sense to Hakluyt, who had in his own works often referred to venerable authorities whenever they supported his view that the English should engage in trade with distant peoples. Though Grotius referred specifically to the Dutch, Hakluyt could easily extend his argument to the English. "The Hollanders cause is so much the more just because their profit in this behalf is joined with the benefit of all mankind which the Portugals go about to overthrow," Grotius argued. Making an analogy to the condemnation of someone who engrossed corn, Grotius believed that an effort to exercise complete control over trade with any other place was equally unacceptable.[11]

Although not everyone in England (or in other areas) agreed with the arguments of the *Mare Liberum*, its constituent parts made it a likely text for Hakluyt.[12] Grotius's text arrived when the English East India Company was making a sustained effort to establish links to the Spice Islands. Yet unlike his other translations, Hakluyt apparently kept this one private. In this sense, the text was similar to the "Discourse on Western Planting," his only other major manuscript (besides the analysis of Artistotle) not intended for immediate publication.

Hakluyt in all likelihood translated that text from Latin into English in London, possibly in the same rooms where he had worked on the writings from the Gentleman of Elvas. If so, it took no great leap of the imagination for him to realize the central importance of the text to his new role as a prime shaper of the East India Company's policies toward the Spice Islands. The English possessed no right of discovery in the East, as they could claim they did in parts of the West. Nor at that point had the English made much investment in their East Indian operations, even though the profits to be gleaned from the spice trade, as Hakluyt had told the council of the East India Company, were enormous.

Yet it was perhaps not a coincidence that Hakluyt kept his translation of Grotius's work private. After all, though the book provided justification for English shipping in channels that had been mapped and long controlled by the Portuguese, it also suggested that the English right to North America could be disputed. Hakluyt had long believed that the English could claim mainland North America north of the ill-defined northern boundary of La Florida by right of discovery made by the Cabots, Gilbert, and others. Grotius's tract did not eradicate those claims specifically, but it undermined English desires to maintain a monopoly of trade between England and North America. Though Grotius admitted that distant lands could be claimed, such claims were legitimate only if the lands remained settled—a condition that still did not apply for the English in North America—and if the newcomers had the permission of the local population.[13]

There was of course no way for Hakluyt to keep these ideas for himself. After all, Grotius had written his text in Latin, and Dutch printers were already well skilled at marketing their wares widely. All Hakluyt could do was to hope that his translation would help the supporters of the East India Company without raising threats to English settlements on the James.

While Hakluyt sat with Grotius in one hand and quill in the other, his countrymen three thousand miles across the Atlantic must have wondered why they had booked passage to Virginia. One of them, a man identified as William White, sent a report back to England describing a purported sacrifice of indigenous children. When John Smith had demanded an explanation, the Powhatans had explained that they needed to placate their "Divell," who would otherwise deprive them of game. White also described the ritual torture and execution of an English settler named George Casson. He was "stripped naked and bound to two stakes," White reported, "with his backe against a great fire: then did they rippe him and burne his bowels, and dried his flesh to the bones, which they kept above ground in a by-roome." Powhatan then ambushed thirty of the others, including Captain John Ratcliffe. The report, hardly the kind of document the company's council wanted to circulate, appeared in Purchas's collection in 1614, perhaps one of the documents that Hakluyt had passed on to him.[14]

The best-known report from those early years was written by George

Percy, the Earl of Northumberland's youngest brother. Though Percy's report was not printed until 1625, his account of Virginia was in fact written sometime before 1612 and was one of the texts that Hakluyt had acquired and passed on to Purchas. Percy provided a detailed account of the voyage from London to Virginia and paid close attention to the Powhatans and their rites. Though he praised the environment, he sent back a necrology that alarmed all who read the report. On August 6, 1607, only months after the settlers arrived, John Asbie died of the "bloudie Flixe. The ninth day died George Flowre of the swelling. The tenth day died William Bruster [Brewster] Genteleman, of a wound given by the Savages." The list went on and on. Three others died on August 14, two more on the fifteenth, another on the sixteenth, and still another on the seventeenth. On August 18 two more succumbed, another the next day, and on August 22, Bartholomew Gosnold, a member of the local council, perished. The horror continued. Five more men died between August 24 and August 28, and two more died during the first week of September.[15]

What had happened to them on the banks of the James River? "Our men were destroyed with cruell diseases as Swellings, Flixes, Burning Fevers, and by warres, and some departed suddenly, but for the most part they died of meere famine," Percy reported. "There were never *Englishmen* left in a forreigne Countrey in such miserie as wee were in this new discovered *Virginia.*" The men were unable to house or feed themselves adequately. "Our drinke [was] cold water taken out of the River," Percy memorably wrote, "which was at a floud verie salt, at a low tide full of slime and filth, which was the destruction of many of our men. Thus we lived for the space of five moneths in this miserable distresse, not having five able men to man our Bulwarkes upon any occasion." Percy believed that divine forces had prevented the natives from attacking when the English were so weak, "our men night and day groaning in every corner of the Fort most pittifull to heare." At times three or four of the afflicted died in a single night, "in the morning their bodies trailed out of their Cabines like Dogges to be buried."[16]

Eventually the Jamestown settlement became more stable, at least in the sense that the community gradually expanded and escaped the fate of the English settlers at Roanoke two decades earlier. Each year after 1607 English ships left London or other port cities carrying men and boys, and lesser numbers of women and girls, who agreed to exchange a few years' labor for the chance to start a new life in Virginia. Yet by the time of Hakluyt's death, the troubles that Percy had described had only partially disappeared. Typhoid, dysentery, and salt poisoning continued to ravage the bodies of the newcomers, and relations with the Powhatans at times degenerated into hostility. Despite the paeans to the regional environment and claims of the land's great potential, the colonists could barely keep their economy going during those first ten years. The Virginia Company for its part circulated propaganda acknowledging that some of the English had been forced to salt down and eat the corpses of their neighbors or spouses but suggesting that things in general were improving.[17]

Despite such hopes, English investors remained wary. John Chamberlain, who believed in 1609 that the colony could be a valuable source of naval stores and dyestuffs, became doubtful about the venture. By 1612 he thought that the settlement would collapse because of the "extreem beastly ydleness" of the settlers, who "will rather die and starve then be brought to any labor or industrie to maintain themselves." In August 1613 he bitterly reported that many who had signed up as subscribers "were not so redy to go to theyre purses as they were to the paper," forcing the company to pursue charges in the Court of Chancery against those derelict in their payments.[18]

Paying attention from London, Hakluyt could have reasonably guessed that any hope for England's future lay in the East Indies, not on the death-stalked shores of Chesapeake Bay. That was no place to continue his work or bring a family.

In 1611, eighteen-year old Edmond Hakluyt arrived at Trinity College in Cambridge. He had been, like his father, a queen's scholar at Westminster. The next year Hakluyt turned sixty. Perhaps it was crossing that threshold, or perhaps it was Edmond's departure for Cambridge, that prompted Hakluyt to write his will. That document provides the most precise evidence that the life he had led promoting English expansion had in fact made him quite comfortable, if not wealthy.[19]

Hakluyt identified himself on August 20, 1612, as a "person of Wethering-sett," suggesting that he lived there and only traveled to other locales, notably London, for his work. Not surprisingly, he bequeathed his recently acquired manor to Edmond. But Bridge Place was not the only rural property Hakluyt had acquired. He also left Edmond his lands in Leominster Oare presently demised (leased) by Hakluyt's brother Oliver "for sixtene nobles a yeare." In addition, Edmond was to receive his "tenements lying in the north west end of Tuttell-streete" in Westminster, near the White Hart Inn. This was presumably where Hakluyt spent his time when in London since he specified in his will that Edmond could have that property only if he paid off a debt of three hundred pounds to a Fleet Street resident named Thomas Peters, who would provide the funds to Hakluyt's widow, Frances. But if Frances paid off the three hundred pounds, then she would receive the Tuttell Street house. In either event, Frances was to have the silver, jewels, and furniture of whatever residence she was living in when Hakluyt died. Hakluyt remembered his other relatives, including John Davyes, the son of his cousin Dorothy Patrickson, who was to receive five pounds, a gift reflecting the fact that Davyes had counseled Hakluyt on his purchases of his manor at Coddenham and his Tuttell Street property. In addition to such personal ties, Hakluyt also left property to the poor of Wetheringsett and the nearby community of Brockford and to the college at Westminster, which had been such a nurturing locale for his studies. Everything else he left to Edmond, who was also the executor of his father's estate.

Missing from this last inventory of Hakluyt's was any mention of the books or manuscripts that had come into his possession over the previous generation. The materials for which he was best known were no longer in his grasp, at least not to the extent that he felt compelled to mention them in his will. Perhaps he did not list them because he had already passed them on to Purchas. Or maybe the intellectual treasures contained in those vast piles of paper were commodities of incalculable worth. He certainly still had books in his possession, and one of them demanded close attention.

When Hakluyt had spoken to the East India Company in late January 1601, he urged them to get a "trusty interpretour in the Easterne Arabian tongue, for by using the Portugal tonge, you are in greate danger of being betrayed." For evidence he pointed out the sorry example of the Dutch, who were betrayed "7 tymes in their first voyage." In the years since he had kept a close eye on the development of trade between Europe and the East. A correspondent named Josias Logan had written two letters to Hakluyt informing him about trade in central Asia. More important, Logan wrote that Samoyeds had provided information about a network of rivers that could be followed and might run to China. The discovery of the Northeast Passage, these letters suggested, was imminent.[20]

Getting to the East Indies via that passage would have been a godsend to the English. But once they arrived there they needed to know how to speak to those who controlled the most important commodities, particularly spices. What the English needed was a book that would help them to learn how to speak the indigenous language of the islands. Fortunately, the Dutch had already produced such a work: Gothard Arthus's series of dialogues in Latin and Malay. At its meeting in late January 1614, the court of the East India Company noted that Hakluyt had prepared an English-language version of Arthus's book. "A book of dialogues, heretofore translated into Latin by the Hollanders," they reported in their minutes, "and printed with the Malacca tongue, Mr. Hakluyt having now turned the Latin into English, and supposed very fit for the factors to learn, ordered to be printed before the departure of the ships."[21]

The book appeared in 1614, though not with Hakluyt's name on the cover. Instead, *Dialogues in the English and Malaiane Languages* was sold as the work of Arthus translated into English by a merchant named Augustine Spalding. But the situation is not that clear. Spalding himself, like the East India Company's representatives at its January meeting, knew where the true credit belonged. Spalding dedicated the book to Sir Thomas Smythe (Smith), whom he identified as the governor of four companies (East India, Muscovy, Northwest Passage, and Sommer Islands) as well as the treasurer of the Virginia Company. Spalding thanked Smythe for funding a lecture on navigation at his own expense "for the better instruction of our Mariners in that most needfull art." He also praised Smythe's organization of England's East India ships, his employment of "skilfull Mathematicians and Geographers in the South and North parts of the World," as well as his support for the publication of "these Dialogues of the languages of the Isle of *Madagascar* and of the *Malaian* tongues, presented unto you by Master *Richard Hackluyt*, a singular furtherer of all new discoveries and honest trades, to be set forth in our English tongue." This work would have particular appeal to the company's agents residing in all the Spice Islands.[22]

The book printed a series of dialogues in two columns, with English on the left and Malay on the right. These dialogues did not resemble the lists of words that could be found in some collections of travel accounts (like the word list in John Florio's translation of Cartier's narrative that Hakluyt had arranged in 1580). Instead, they were meant to be practical phrases for predictable scenarios.

The first dialogue set the tone for the book. It provided the language needed for "the coming of a certaine ship" and the initial meeting between those on board and a local king. In the dialogue, a character named David and another named Abraham have met with anticipation. "Whence come you so earlie?" David asked Abraham. "Out of the market place," Abraham replied. "What newes?" David prompted him. "Have you heard nothing of the comming of any ship?" "I heard the thundering of Ordnance," Abraham answered, "which is a signe of ships comming." David proceeded to tell Abraham that the ship carried food (rice, raisons, and almonds) as well as various kinds of clothing. Such commodities would be welcomed there, both of them knew.[23]

By providing the words for the kinds of goods that English ships would be hauling to the East Indies, the *Dialogues* allowed those on board to prepare themselves for their arrival. The text also provided lessons in what the sailors should expect when they disembarked. The first dialogue continued with a description of the approach of an elephant wearing red cloth, led by musicians pounding on drums and blaring trumpets. The man on the elephant carried a letter from the local king welcoming the new ship. In response, the ship's captain provisioned young men to carry presents to the king. "Doth he present them in stead of a tribute for his goods," Abraham asked, "or is hee compelled to pay more in stead of custome?" "No," David answered, "seven for an hundred are paid in stead of custome." When he received the presents, the king then entertained the visitors. "They eate and drink," David told his companion, "and al kind of delicates and fruites are set before them, they play, dance, and al manner of pleasures are exercised, they sound the Trumpets, Cornets and other Pipes, and strike up with Drummes." The king then gave the captain a sample of the local cloth. "Is this the manner of this Countrie?" Abraham wondered. Yes, David responded, "this is the manner with this King, and hath bin also with others."[24]

The dialogue then took the reader into the king's court, offering yet more details about what would happen when the locals met the new arrivals. At one point the king summoned an unnamed woman, asking her if all was "ready for the receiving, and well intertaining of strange guests." She assured him that they were. The women had stretched a cloth of blue silk "garnished with gold" across the room over the heads of those below and had draped more silk around the pillars. Over the place for the king they had draped a cloth of red velvet "leafed with gold, and for the strange guests, that greene velvet cloath intermingled with the Rhinoceros and Tigers of gold." The entertainment was also ready. The women chosen to dance had green and red silken clothing, gold necklaces, wore "tablets" on their breasts "garnished with precious stones, gold rings on their fingers glittering with Carbuncles and Diamondes, and have put golden bracelets upon their armes and leggs." The king was pleased by the arrangements. "It is well," he told the woman, "see that al things be so prepared, that I bee not disgraced."[25]

When the ship captain appeared at the court, the king learned that the visitor already knew Malay from his previous time there. The words of one of the king's attendants were exactly what any foreigner would want to hear: "*Iia taeu dirinia bassa Maleyo*" ("Hee himselfe understandeth the Malaian language very well"). The captain brought a promise from the English monarch to provide any ships the local king might need for his own defense. The Malay king was pleased. He promised to compensate the English king, and then the celebrations began in earnest. "Give unto the Captaine that hee may eate of the fruites," the king declared, "cause the Musick to be exercised, and let there be dauncing, strike up the lesser Drummes, play on the Flutes, and let the Drumster performe his dutie well." Bring out the feast, he continued, and give the captain "some of the rosted capon, and of the boyled henne, with the broth, and let him taste the fishes taken in our water." Send the mariner drink, too, but tell him that the Malay king had taken medicine that day and so had to avoid alcohol. The king brushed aside the captain's thanks and told his servants to bring him new clothes, "to wit, a red coate, a taffatie girdle edged with gold, a yellow garment shining with intermingled gold, a girdle having Arabian letters wrought in gold, and a dagger with a golden pummell garnished with precious stones, the haft whereof is made of black Corall." In the end, after the king had ordered that a buffalo be slaughtered to feed sailors who had little fresh food on their journey, an elephant took the captain and the others back to their ships along with a supply of oranges and pomegranates.[26]

The dialogues that followed tended to focus on more practical situations. The second dealt with a discussion that might follow when a ship docked after a long voyage about the ship's origin and how many men died at sea. Those who studied it also learned how to say that they had come to the Indies to purchase pepper, nutmeg, and cloves and that they carried valuable goods to trade with those who had what they needed—"gold, silver, cloathes, Corall beades, yron, lead, blacke and white, and other merchandizes of all sorts, as looking-glasses, knives, sizzars [scissors], combes, spectacles, Jewes harpes pipes, glasse, and whatsoever may be imagined." They also learned one of the most important phrases: "*Daúlat Túankoe*"—"God preserve and defend the King." The next dialogue was even more practical, containing the language needed to barter with the locals. "This is too much, I will not buy so deare," one line read. "How much therefore will you pay?" ran the response. "I will pay you three and a halfe." This kind of haggling over prices continued until the exasperated local finally replied, *"Datan issocki bet á bry morra ken inan"*— "Returne againe tomorrow, and I will sell you all things at a reasonable price." A later dialogue continued this same theme, anticipating an impatient shop-keeper sending one haggling visitor away. "Surely no man shall gaine any thing by you," the frustrated merchant finally replied. "If all men were of that niggardly disposition, I should certainly be compelled to shut up my shop, for I should not gaine thy maintenance."[27]

Each dialogue conveyed information that might be useful in exploring strange landscapes. One provided the language needed for someone who was lost in the woods and contained the crucial warning: *"Carna adda miskil malam berialan ken herrimon"*—"You cannot travel by night, without danger, by reason of the Tygers." Another taught the vocabulary needed for those who purchased on credit and now owed shopkeepers for their purchases, and the next provided the phrases necessary to ask directions. One detailed the rituals associated with weighing pepper, a transaction of fundamental impor-tance for any European in the East Indies. For those engaged in the trade, it would be necessary to learn, for example, how to call out, "Ho, Weigher, make ready to weigh, I will note the weights, but see yt I receive good waight." The longest dialogue contained the words needed to carry on a con-versation at a feast, surely a common feature of island life, given the time needed to prepare for such an event. The twelfth dialogue recounted the phrases used in preparing a ship for a long voyage and how to survive such a journey, even in calm seas. "This calme is a forerunner of misfortune, tem-pest, and shipwracke," one said. "Take an oar," his companion responded, "and row with it." That same dialogue also contained crucial advice for any who traveled on such an expedition: "Hee that will goe to Sea, must be obedient to the governours of the shippe, as well as the sicke patient to the Physitian." One of the brief dialogues at the end of the book claimed to pro-vide phrases in the "Madagascar language," presumably to be used when ships resupplied their provisions on the long journey toward the Spice Islands.[28]

Taken together, the *Dialogues* provided more than a grammar of a lan-guage that the English (like the Dutch) believed was universally intelligible in the Spice Islands. By learning Malay, those who read and memorized the book differentiated themselves from the Portuguese whom, these Protestants hoped, had so alienated the locals that the East Indians were desperate to establish trade ties with other Europeans. But the dialogues were a kind of travel narrative, too. They alerted anyone going east that the people there were hard bargainers and that it was crucial to stand up to them to get the best price. It was important to anticipate the marvels of the East, such as elephants that might transport them to a visit with a king or man-eating tigers roaming the jungle at night. And it was just as important for travelers to know about the protocols of trade, from the feasts common in the region to how to negotiate with the man who weighed the pepper. Travelers had to know how to please those in authority, on their ships (the captains), on the docks (those who had fresh food for starved crews), and in the courts of Muslim royalty; properly submissive foreigners would be rewarded.

In some sense, the *Dialogues* might have seemed a strange final work for Hakluyt's famed energies. After all, many people could translate Latin into English. But to dismiss the book as a vocabulary list would be to miss what led Hakluyt to its pages. The *Dialogues* brought together much that had engaged him since he first crossed the green lawns of Christ Church more than forty years earlier. Lurking in those pages was an ethnography of a useful place and its non-English speaking natives composed in a pointedly instructive way. Enumerating the commodities of a distant place, as Harriot did for Roanoke, was useful. But how much better would it be if those who sailed for weeks to get to a place with such treasures learned how to speak to the indigenous people at the same time that they learned of these resources? How better to teach about the rituals of feasting and treating and bargaining than to put the reader into the text and force him to wrestle with an unfamiliar language? What better way to accentuate the differences between home and away than to describe how pepper was weighed and then make the reader haggle with the man who measured it?

There was no drama of any interest in the *Dialogues*, certainly nothing that could compare to the clever plays of Shakespeare or the staged magnificence of Ben Jonson's masques. But its lessons would enable readers to become more effective travelers and more respected emissaries of England. The text had enticements, too. Who could resist the chance to ride on the back of an elephant and wear silk robes garnished with gold? This book would surely lure adventurous men to take passage to the East Indies, the region that had occupied so much of Hakluyt's time since the turn of the century.

While Hakluyt's attention was presumably focused on the *Dialogues* and its reception, he continued to receive reports about European explorations abroad, including English journeys to the Americas. Among them were multiple accounts of Henry Hudson's ventures in search of the Northwest

Passage, including an abstract from his journal covering his fatal journey, which began in April 1610 and ended in mutiny in June 1611, when Hudson, his son, and seven others loyal to him were set adrift in small boat. They were never seen again, according to the eyewitness report by Abacuk Pricket, which also passed through Hakluyt's hands. Hakluyt received news from explorers such as Robert Fotherby, whose report of 1615 into northern waters was among the last travel accounts to reach his eyes and yet another reminder of the difficulty of sailing through waters perpetually "hindred with Ice." Hakluyt also obtained reports from the intrepid explorer William Baffin. These accounts described a journey to Greenland in 1613 and included details about whaling (and the dangers it could pose, for one of the crew was killed during a hunt) as well as repeated comments about the weather and the position of the Sun during an arctic summer. Another report by Baffin told of his fourth voyage in search of the Northwest Passage in 1615, an account characterized in part by the detailed effort to establish the longitude of places far from England.[29]

Given the central role that Hakluyt had played in English expeditions to the mid-Atlantic coast of mainland North America, it is not surprising that explorers sent accounts describing expeditions to the territory the English still called "Virginia." They included a letter that Bartholomew Gosnold had written to his father in 1602 noting that the region had "as healthfull a Climate as can be," a statement based on his assessment of the stature, well-being, and age of the Americans they encountered. Not all reports contained such optimistic views. Hakluyt had also received George Percy's account of early Jamestown, including his listing of the colonists who succumbed to disease, and a riveting account of the shipwreck of Sir Thomas Gates near Bermuda in July 1610. The latest report he received came from Samuel Argall, who told how he had captured Pocahontas and ransomed her in exchange for English colonists held by Powhatan.[30]

Yet though Hakluyt received these reports and passed them onto Samuel Purchas, he promoted English mercantile efforts without specific mention of Virginia or any other American destination. He pushed Ralph Handson to translate Bartholomew Pitiscus's *Trigonometry: Or The Doctrine of Triangles* because he realized that mastering this technique had direct relevance for overseas trade. The second part of that book applied the science of trigo-nometry directly to "questions of navigation, performed arithmetically by the doctrine of Triangles, without Globe, Sphære, or Mappe." No wonder that Hakluyt employed his "earnest perswasion" on Handson to translate it and

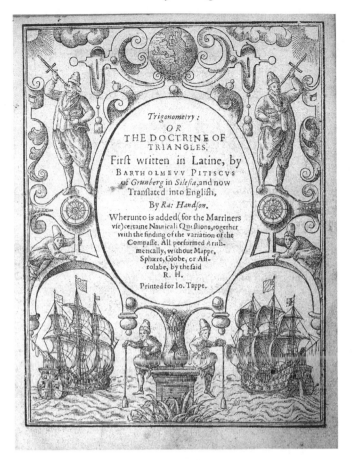

Title page from Bartholomew Pitiscus, *Trigonometry: Or The Doctrine of Triangles*, trans. Ra[lph] Handson (London, [1614]), one of the last books Hakluyt promoted (HUNTINGTON LIBRARY)

that Handson agreed to do so in part because Hakluyt had, as he put it, "deserved well of our Nation."[31]

Hakluyt remained fascinated by the East, and those who sailed there took what he had to say seriously. When the East India Company commissioned John Saris to command their eighth voyage on April 4, 1611, they instructed him to take certain books along: the religious works of William Perkins, John Foxe's *Book of Martyrs*, and "Mr Hakluit's Voyadgs to recreate their spirits w'th variety of historie." Saris's relationship with Hakluyt went further still. The captain sent him a map of China he had obtained in 1612. Saris had orig-

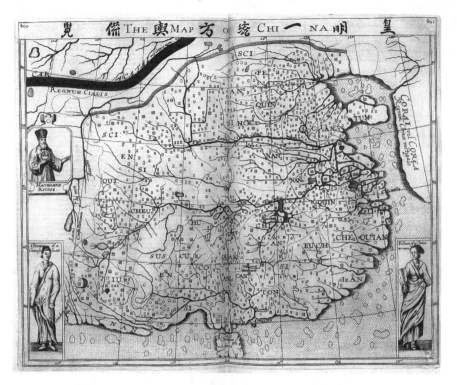

This map was one of many things that Hakluyt offered to Purchas, who printed it in
Hakluytus Posthumus or Purchas his Pilgrimes (London, 1625)
(HUNTINGTON LIBRARY)

inally hoped to present the map to Prince Henry, but he died in 1612, so he
turned to Hakluyt. The map ended in Purchas's hands, and he included it in
his book in 1625. Even before he published it, Purchas had referred to Hakluyt
in 1614 as his "greatest Benefactor." By the time Purchas printed his major
work and included the materials that Hakluyt had passed on to him, the largest
number of these unprinted texts dealt with the East. They included a remarkably detailed account of the English in Java from early 1602 until late 1605,
when the newcomers managed to establish trade despite widespread illness
and occasional "perfidious treacheries of the Javans." Not surprisingly, given
his work for the East India Company, Hakluyt received reports of many of the
journeys they financed, including a long account of the twelfth (and last)
journey sponsored by the company, which returned to England in July 1614.[32]

In early December 1614 Hakluyt became the treasurer of Westminster

Abbey. His signature in the record books from that month to the end of November the following year reveal that he was either living in London then or traveled frequently from Wetheringsett to the capital. Those signatures constitute the last evidence of Hakluyt's life.[33]

By 1615 Hakluyt's fame had spread around the world. He had been involved in the production of twenty-six books, most published in English. Most of those books were published in London, but Hakluyt also had books printed in Paris (in French and Latin), Madrid (in Spanish), and Frankfurt (in Latin, French, and German). At home his name had become linked with the explorers whose accounts he printed, as William Warner demonstrated in 1612 when he praised the efforts of Gilbert, Frobisher, Candish (Cavendish), Drake, and others and sent his readers to Hakluyt's collection. English explorers routinely hauled his books on their voyages. Some were more enthusiastic still: they inserted him into the landscapes they explored. The trend had started in 1608 with Henry Hudson, who, according to Purchas, provided a history of "the Northerne Discoveries of Seas, Coasts, and Countries." Hudson had set sail on the *Hopewell* "to discover the Pole," but his journal suggested "that hee came to the height of 81 degrees, where he gave Names to certayne places, upon the Continent of Greenland formerly discovered, which continue to this day, namely, Whale Bay, and Hackuit Headland." On June 17, 1611, three years after Hudson's journey, an English captain named William Gourdon and Josias Logan, the English factor at Pechora who had written to Hakluyt about trade with the Samoyeds, were navigating between ice floes near the Cape of Callinos. They discovered a river, "which we called *Hakluyts* River, where wee did see certayne *Samoieds,* with their Deere," but the natives fled instead of trading with the newcomers.[34]

In 1615, Robert Fotherby, on a voyage "for Discoverie of Seas, Lands, and Ilands, to the Northwards" spotted Hakluyt's Headland when he guided his twenty-ton pinnace the *Richard of London* from Fair Haven, where he had landed to repair ice damage to the ship. Fotherby never got closer than six leagues to the promontory because even in summer ice prevented easy crossing of those seas. As he explored the coast of Greenland, trying to escape the enclosing fog and the dangerous shards of icebergs, Fotherby came upon an island that no European had seen before. He called it Thomas Smiths Island (modern-day day Jan Mayen). Jutting from it was "a Mountayne of wonderfull height and bignesse, all covered with Snow, which I called *Mount Hakluyt,*" Fotherby reported. The land near the eight-thousand-foot-high mountain (now known as Beerenberg) was rock-strewn and barren, supporting moss instead of grass. A year later William Baffin, on yet another voyage of discovery for the Northwest Passage, explored the frigid waters that would later bear his name. While there he identified an island that the English called "Hakluits Ile" at 78 degrees North latitude.[35]

For a man who never traveled far, Hakluyt's name on promontories in these frozen outposts was one of the more unlikely developments of his life. After all, English explorers, like other Europeans, tended to name places after themselves (such as Baffin Bay) or their patrons (Virginia, James Fort, Sir Thomas Smiths Island). That these mariners labeled these lands after Hakluyt was but one testimony to his achievement. In the early seventeenth century, several cartographers identified Hakluyt's Isle on the northern edges of their maps. That speck of land in the northern reaches of Baffin Bay is one of the closest to the north pole on a map of the northern hemisphere in the Mercator-Hondius atlas of 1636. The name is literally squeezed into the top of three other surviving maps, a label on the northernmost point they identified. These were quite likely the most inhospitable places in the world, at least of those known to Europeans before the nineteenth-century explorations of Antarctica. Two hundred years later, when another British expedition went to Baffin Bay searching again for the Northwest Passage, Hakluyt's Island remained on the map as those English ships, like many before, made the perilous journey through the towering and jagged walls of ice.[36]

In 1616 the Virginia Company needed an infusion of cash to keep its colonization efforts alive. The request was hardly novel; a lack of funds and supplies had plagued the venture for years, a fact well known to those in London paying attention to the ships returning from Jamestown.[37] To raise funds the company's council issued an eight-page pamphlet. The *Briefe Declaration of the present state of things in Virginia* did not ignore the problems that had beset the colony, though unlike Percy's account it did not dwell on them, either. To do so might dissuade potential investors.

The council members knew that Jamestown had a poor reputation. The initial high hopes embedded in the patent of 1607 had led the company to send "Men and Ships, Cattle, and all kinde of provisions, with Governours and Captaines for peace and war" across the Atlantic. "No earthly meanes seemed then wanting for the speedy reducing of that barbarous Nation, and savage people, to a quiet Christian Common-wealth." But the reality was crueler than anyone could have anticipated. Despite careful preparations, "many disasters on Sea and Land, too long to be here recited," had defeated

Guillaume de Lisle's map of North America, c. 1700, with inset showing Hakluyt's Isle (marked "I. d. Hakluyt") on the northern reaches of Baffin Bay
(HUNTINGTON LIBRARY)

the initial efforts so "there onely remained a poore remnant of those Men and Women, Cattle and provisions, that escaped the danger and which are now remaining there to rayse and build up that intended Colonie." The experience had been so dispiriting that the initial gentleman investors, who had received reports of the settlement's struggles, abandoned hope for the colony and refused to send further support.[38]

But the council had not abandoned hope. Under the continuing administration of the treasurer, Sir Thomas Smythe, they maintained their belief that Virginia could prosper. Despite what others might have heard, the council claimed that those who remained along the James had in fact begun to prosper. "They sow and reape their Corne in sufficient proportion, without want or impeachment," they argued, "their Kine multiply already to some hundreds, their Swine to many thousands, their Goates and Poultry in great numbers, every man hath house and ground to his owne use, and now being able to maintaine themselves with food, they are also prepared and ready, once having the meanes, to set upon the Minerals, whereof there are many sorts." In addition to this search for precious metals, the colonists had also begun "to make the Land profitable to themselves and th' Adventurers."[39]

Seven years earlier the company had promised to pay a dividend to every-one who invested in Virginia. The time for that payment had now passed, the council noted. But that should not cause others to ignore the new plea. In-stead, present circumstances indicated that the prospects were much brighter. "We are now by the Natives liking and consent, in actuall possession of a great part of the Country," the company declared, though it had to admit that much of the rest of the initial patent was forest, much of it not yet surveyed. Still, the time had come to apportion the land that the colonists had cleared. Each person who had "already adventured his mony or person" would receive fifty acres for every share worth twelve pounds, ten shillings. Once the settlers had cleared more land, the council was confident that each share would bring at least two hundred additional acres. To ensure that such future profits came to those willing to risk body or cash, the company sought new subscriptions at the same rate of twelve pounds, ten shillings, per share, to be paid within a month of the time that the investors had signed their name in a book to be kept at Smythe's house. This financing would entitle the investors to lands on either side of the James near the existing settlements. Each would be treated as an equal partner even though the initial investors had "endured the most difficult part" of the venture.[40]

The circulation of the pamphlet in London perhaps helped keep the venture afloat, though skeptics remained. John Chamberlain, perhaps won-dering why he had invested in Virginia, listened intently when he heard that Sir Thomas Dale had returned to London in June 1616 in the company of ten to twelve Powhatans. Among them was Pocahontas, who was then married to John Rolfe. "I heare not of any other riches or matter of worth, but only some quantitie of sassafras, tobacco, pitch, and clap-board, things of no great value unles there were more plenty and neerer hand," Chamberlain complained. "All I can learne of yt is that the countrie is goode to live in, yf yt were stored with people, and might in time become commodious, but there is no present profit to be expected."[41]

The pamphlet might well have been the last thing that Hakluyt ever read about Virginia. He held on to his two shares but purchased no more.[42]

On November 23, 1616, four and a half months after Baffin had named that island after him, Hakluyt died. Three days later the clerics of Westminster Abbey buried the long-serving prebend inside the walls of their sacred enclosure. Then they forgot where they put him. He had walked in that ancient temple in his youth, learned from its schoolmasters, and returned as an adult to help guide the institution through the death of one monarch and the accession of another. In later years Hakluyt's fame stretched farther than ever, though within England his passing merited little notice. Neither his death nor that of William Shakespeare, who had died exactly six months earlier, seemed worthy of mention to Edmund Howes when he put out his revised edition of Stow's chronicle in 1631.

Yet over time Hakluyt's reputation (like Shakespeare's) increased. One generation after another of English observers sang his praises. In the mid-nineteenth century, when the British Empire reigned over much of the world, one group of Victorians obsessed with geography and the spirit of discovery formed a new learned society and named it after him. To this day it continues Hakluyt's legacy by publishing scholarly editions relating to voyages and travels—the same materials Hakluyt himself had organized for printers. Hakluyt would no doubt have relished the fact that the society has translated and published works written in languages that he knew (such as French, Italian, Spanish, Latin, and Portuguese) and others he never studied (such as Persian, Arabic, and Chinese).[43]

But it would be wrong to assume that this later hero worship reflected the predominance and popularity of Hakluyt's views when he died. A possible anticolonial backlash remained a threat. Joseph Hall's critical work continued to circulate. Another edition of his *Mundus Alter et Idem* was printed in Leipzig in 1613, and in 1617 he produced an anti-Hakluyt screed warning his fellow citizens of the dangers of long-distance travel, even though he himself had been to the Netherlands in 1605 and France in 1616. If readers in 1605 could dismiss the first edition of *Mundus Alter et Idem* as a work of satire, it was harder to ignore the new polemic, entitled *Quo Vadis? A Just Censure of Travell.* In this pamphlet Hall argued that God had endowed Britain with what it needed to thrive. "God hath given us a world of our owne, wherein there is nothing wanting to earthly contentment," he argued. "Heere growes that wealth, which yee go but to spend abroad; Heere is that sweet peace which the rest of the world admires and envies: Heere is that gracious and well-tempered government, which no nation under heaven may dare once offer to parallel: Here all liberall Arts raigne and triumph: And for pleasure, either our earth, or our sea yeelds us all those dainties, which their native Regions enjoy but single." The proof of divine favor was ubiquitous: "Heere

Heaven stands open, which to many other parts is barred on the out-side with ignorance of mis-beleefe."[44]

Hall recognized that at times travel made sense, especially since discoveries had opened new opportunities at home. Those engaged in such trade served the nation's interests. "Either *Indies* may be searched for those treasures, which God hath laid up in them for their far-distant owners." He also recognized that the state needed to be informed about other nations, thereby endorsing travel on official or diplomatic business.[45]

But travel for travel's sake, especially by the young (who he correctly believed tended to be those who traveled most often), was to be condemned. Hall directed particular venom toward Catholic missionaries, accusing them of using demonic forces to advance their agenda. "If the power of falsified reason prevaile not," he declared, "these desperate factors of *Rome* (as I have been informed) have learned out of their acquaintance in the Court of the Prince of darknesse, to imploy stronger aid." They relied on "Magicall delusions and devilish incantations" to strengthen their hand. Better to stay home among the true believers enjoying the Almighty's grace. God had made "this Iland as it were an abridgement of his whole earth," in which "all the maine and materiall commodities of the greater world" could be found. In such circumstances, travel promised little. "Enjoy therefore (happy Countrimen) enjoy freely God and your selves; enrich your selves with your owne mines, improve those blessed opportunities which God hath given you, to your mutuall advantage; and care not to be like any but your selves." Hall, at least, remained committed to the argument he put forth here; a generation later he included *Quo Vadis?* in a volume of his collected works.[46]

In linking long-distance travel to Catholic evangelicals and restless youth, Hall in his own way challenged the future of the English settlement on the shores of the Chesapeake. The timing could not have been worse. After all, at Hakluyt's death the future of Virginia remained much in doubt. The struggling outpost at Jamestown survived only because the English kept sending men, women, and children there. Those migrants kept the settlement viable despite the diseases that continued to kill many of the newcomers.

In 1616, the economic prospects of Virginia were not bright. Though colonists there had figured out how to produce tobacco, a debate raged in England about the nature and benefits of the plant. Immigrants since Smith had recognized its use by natives, news that might have pleased some in Europe who believed in the plant's phenomenal curative powers. The physician Edmund Gardiner, who relied on "the learned *Hackluit*" among other authorities, described tobacco's myriad benefits in 1610, praising in particular the product of Trinidad. Four years later William Barclay, another physician, offered a defense of tobacco as a medicinal. He informed the readers of his pamphlet that he had used it himself as had a French man in Nantes who lived to be 120 years old. Still, despite its virtues, Barclay recognized that some "English abusers" used it purely for pleasure. Though other medical writers had also recognized the benefits of tobacco when consumed orally or applied as a poultice, Barclay believed that smoking also brought tobacco's virtues directly to the brain, which it fortified. A year later an author identified only as "C. T." similarly hailed tobacco's virtues. He warned off young people by reporting that they should avoid smoking since tobacco made them "tender and not able to endure the aire," ruined their teeth, and prompted them to drink alcohol. But for everyone else tobacco had such obvious benefits that the English needed to learn how to produce it themselves. Sales had reached two hundred thousand pounds each year in England and Ireland. To prevent the abuse of a plant with such widespread healing powers that even a poisoned dog could recover if it was given tobacco, the English needed to learn how and where to plant it, how to tend the crop, when to pick it, and the processes of drying that were so crucial for producing a healthful product.[47]

But in 1616 not everyone in England believed that cultivating the crop was the best idea. The poet Joshua Sylvester, for one, picking up the anti-tobacco theme earlier propounded by King James I himself, assaulted the tobacconists of England for selling a plant that he believed had catastrophic physical, psychological, and spiritual effects, including stunting growth, dimming the intellect, destroying memory, and promoting antisocial behavior—no coincidence that smoking was popular among "Theeves, Unthrifts, Ruffians, Robbers, Roarers, Drab-Bibbers, Blasphemers, Shiftters Sharkers Stabbers." Tobacco was also so addictive that it impoverished its users. That Americans used it was no recommendation: "For, what to Them is Meat and Med'cinable, Is turn'd to Us a Plague intollerable." If using tobacco was good, Sylvester reasoned, then why was it "that lewdeth loosest, basest, foolishest, The most unthrifty, most intemperate, Most vicious, most debaucht, most desperate, Pursue it most?" The obsession with the weed, he concluded, offended Christendom. That same year John Deacon published a lengthier diatribe against tobacco, seeing it as a symbol of the vices embraced by the English through contact with anyone not English. The realm suffered from other problems, too, of course, but "the filthie Tobacco fume (thou maist plainly perceive) is now adaies become the Trojan horse-bellie of those other hidden mischiefes, and the onely Metropolitane of all those monstrous disorders." He even linked its consumption and those who sold it to the Gunpowder Plot of 1605, a final proof that the plant brought together those committed to the overthrow of England. As Deacon put it, "Thou maist now very plainly perceive by that which is spoken, what a pestilent crew of pernicious persons all those our disordered *Tobacconists* were (for the present) to the publike good of our State." Anyone who read such accounts might have wondered if tobacco's future was as ephemeral as its use, "no sooner in the mouth" as one playwright put it in 1601 (in a script reprinted in 1616) "but out at the nose."[48]

Tobacco's opponents seemed to outnumber those who rose to its defense. Barnabe Rich, a veteran soldier who often wrote about military matters, launched an attack on tobacco in 1614, estimating that there were seven thousand tobacconists in and near London who together took in £319,375 per year, an astonishing drain on the economy. In Rich's hierarchy of sin, the places to purchase and smoke tobacco ranked lower than alehouses (which he admitted he had visited) and higher than brothels. Two years later he expanded his attack. Countering any suggestions (such as that by "C. T.") that domestic production should be encouraged to ease the economic hardship of the commerce, Rich argued that the excessive cost was one of the chief problems with tobacco since it "maketh a rich man a poore man, a poore man a starke beggar, a wise man a foole, an old man to dote, and a yong man to admire his owne ignorance." Despite its occasional benefits, tobacco was to Rich "an engine of the Divels own devising" that prompted otherwise healthy individuals to engage in objectionable behavior, sicken, and even die.[49]

Yet despite such attacks, the colonists in Virginia came to believe that tobacco was an ideal way to generate the funds the settlement needed. John Rolfe, who would later marry Powhatan's daughter Pocahontas had begun to plant West Indian tobacco seeds near Jamestown in 1612. The result was a crop that the colonists liked and believed would become profitable if it was exported to England. That calculation saved the colony but not the Virginia Company, which collapsed in 1624. By then the colonists and the Powhatans had engaged in bloody warfare, an ominous foretelling of later strife between Natives and Anglo-American colonists in North America. Even before the worst of the violence began in 1622, Edmond Hakluyt decided he had had enough of this enterprise. On June 13, 1621, he sold his two inherited shares in the Company.[50]

Four years after the Hakluyt family severed its formal ties to the colony in Virginia, Purchas produced a vast collection of travel accounts which he entitled *Hakluytus Posthumus, or Purchas his Pilgrimes.* The book promised a

"History of the World, in Sea voyages, & lande-Travells, by Englishmen & others[,] wherein Gods Wonders in Nature & Providence, The Actes, Artes, Varieties & Vanities of Men, wth a world of the Worlds Rarities, are by a world of Eywitness Authors, Related to the World." He crowded the title page with images ranging from the tomb of Queen Elizabeth to two maps of the world, as well as his own portrait, and a promise that the book included accounts "left written by Mr. Hakluyt at his death More since added, His also perused & perfected."

Yet while Purchas acknowledged Hakluyt's help—and counted on the reputation of Hakluyt to help promote the collection—his acknowledgment was less than effusive. When he published the third edition of his work in 1617, he had paid less homage to Hakluyt. He listed him among the 1200 worthies in the "Catalogue of Authors" that he had consulted, repeated his earlier praise for gathering together works about Newfoundland, and often mentioned Hakluyt's books in marginal notes as the source of some of the information in his volume. By 1625, he had grown even more distant. "As for Master Hakluyts many yeeres Collections, and what stocke I received from him in written Papers," Purchas wrote, the reader would find a number of references in the "Table of Authours." Purchas told how he would "thus farre honour" Hakluyt: "though it be but Materials, and that many Bookes have not one Chapter in that kind, yet that stocke encouraged me to use my endevours in and for the rest. I was therein a Labourer also, both to get them (not without hard conditions) and to forme and frame those Materials to their due place and order in this Ædifice, the whole Artifice (such as it is) being mine owne." Sensing the hostile reception that such arrogance might elicit, Purchas went on the defensive: "Traduce mee not, nor let any impute to boasting what I have said of my sole working."[51]

Purchas was no mere hack, though his reputation has never been the equal of Hakluyt's. Still, when he looked at the materials he had assembled from travelers, he offered an important clarification to the English understanding of the "New World." "[W]e begin at *China*," he wrote, "which the Ancients knew not, and take all the East and North parts of *Asia* from the *Caspian* Sea, the *Arctoan* Regions, all *America* and *Terra Australis*, comprehending all in that *New Title*." He had such confidence in his abilities that he informed readers in the listing of authors where he needed to fix Hakluyt's work. Hakluyt had published the narrative of Sir Francis Drake's circumnavigation, but Purchas offered it again "now reviewed and corrected." The account of the third circumnavigation led by Candish (Cavendish) had also

Unlike Hakluyt, for whom there are no known surviving images, Samuel Purchas placed himself on the title page of his most significant collection, *Hakluytus Posthumus, or Purchas his Pilgrimes* (London, 1625)—the collection inspired by Hakluyt's work
(HUNTINGTON LIBRARY)

been published by Hakluyt, yet appeared here "now corrected and abbreviated." He prefaced his version of Antonio de Herrera's 1601 account of the West Indies with the acerbic comment that he had "found this Worke translated in M. *Hakluyts* Papers; but I can scarsly call it *English*, it had so much of the *Spanish* garbe." Purchas explained that he had studied the original Spanish version along with a defective Latin translation, an effort that led him to make his own new translation—necessitated, he wrote, for "correcting and illustrating the phrase and sense; being before very rude, obscure and in very many places utterly sencelesse."[52]

Yet if Purchas wanted to distance himself from Hakluyt and thus demonstrate that it was his own extraordinary efforts that had produced the book, he bore witness to how much time Hakluyt had spent gathering accounts of English voyages to the East during the last years of his life. Hakluyt had never published these works, so there was no need for Purchas to tell his readers that he was offering better versions of them. Instead, he merely denoted their origin with the letter "H" in the table of authors. These works dominated the third book (out of five) in Purchas's collection, from an account of Benjamin Wood's 1596 journey to the East Indies to the detailed narrative that Nicholas Dounton provided of Sir Henry Middleton's expedition that embarked on July 11, 1611.[53]

Before the turn of the century, Hakluyt had gathered materials together with the explicit goal of publishing them in order to advance what he believed were matters of vital national interest. His only major unpublished works were the "Discourse on Western Planting," which had been commissioned as a secret treatise, and his analysis of Aristotle's *Politics*. Yet after the publication of the final volume of *Principal Navigations,* Hakluyt receded into the background, at least as the author of well-known works. He continued to collect travel reports relating to America and other locales and passed many of them on to Purchas. He translated the Gentleman of Elvas's account of Soto's travels and proved instrumental in the publication of the Malayan dialogues. He also gathered texts together that shed light on English experiences in south and east Asia, a region of the world that Hakluyt believed was open to any European who wanted to trade there, a point he made in his unpublished translation of Grotius's *Mare Liberum.* What Purchas got from Hakluyt was more than enough for a volume on English travels to the East Indies. But Hakluyt never committed it to print. Instead, for unknown reasons, he left those precious manuscripts in the hands of a man who later took credit for the work.

In 1617 Richard Harvey had a copy of the 1587 edition of Peter Martyr's *De Orbo Novo* in his hands. Like many other early modern readers, he wrote in his book. In this case, the message was not a commentary on the text but instead a simpler expression: "R^d. Hackluyt is deade, 1616. 1617."

How much more fitting could it have been? The man who had made a promise to himself early in his life had fulfilled it but he died before anyone could have known if England's colony in America would survive. Hakluyt himself was cautious about investment in the Virginia Company. He never

Richard Harvey's inscription in a 1587 edition of Peter Martyr's *De Orbe Novo*
(BRITISH LIBRARY)

became a colonist or one of the famed adventurers of England. For reasons he
never explained, he turned down every opportunity to sail across the Atlantic.
Instead he poured his energies into collecting, reading, and telling stories,
taking advantage of the opportunities afforded by the revolution in print to
disseminate his works to a wide audience. In his last years he had more
interest in the East Indies than in the Atlantic world. Martyr's account had
been among Hakluyt's most important acquisitions, as he knew when he
arranged for it to be published. Harvey seized the exact volume in his hands
and with his inscription informed future readers that the man responsible for
shaping the English vision of the world was no more. Hakluyt lived on only in
the musty pages of his collected travel accounts.

A Note on Method and Sources

Richard Hakluyt is an elusive quarry. The year of his birth can be inferred from later documents, but not with absolute precision. There are no known surviving portraits of him, even though he lived among a group for whom portraits were frequent if not common; even Samuel Purchas had his picture printed on the title page of his last work in 1625. Hakluyt rarely mentioned either of his wives or his son, Edmond, directly. None of his kin left memoirs of his existence, not even as minimal as the family genealogy of the Ramusio clan that can be found in the Biblioteca Marciana in Venice. Other than minimal clerical notations that reveal his continued service in Westminster and Wetheringsett, there are no elaborate records of that part of his career. The library at Christ Church owns his published works, and several of its students (including Charles Dodgson [Lewis Carroll]) have given commencement orations about him. But Hakluyt's library is not there or in any other known locale, so it is impossible to do the kind of detailed study of him as a reader (and writer of marginalia) that is possible for scholars whose papers and books survive. He was famous enough to be buried in Poet's Corner in Westminster Abbey, but not famous enough to merit a plaque telling of his bones being laid there. In this sense his unmarked presence within a well-known church mirrors Ramusio's experience; the Venetian lies near the shores of the Adriatic in an unknown location in Madonna dell'Orto, with its brilliant paintings by Jacopo Tintoretto but no marker to the city's greatest geographer. Hakluyt's wife Douglas is buried at the church in Wetheringsett. But though the church still stands, it is locked most days and Douglas's grave cannot be found. Rain and wind have taken a toll on the stones in that cemetery lying on two sides of the small church, obscuring the memory of virtually everyone who filled its pews in Hakluyt's age.

Yet even though Hakluyt's physical remains have not been found, he is always lurking, ready to peek out from the pages of a work of history. One measure of his contribution to modern knowledge can be found in the number of times words from his works have been used to provide precise definitions for certain terms; *The Oxford English Dictionary* employed him almost sixteen hundred times in its references. More important, by printing accounts (and passing unpublished manuscripts to Purchas) Hakluyt helped to ensure the survival of scores of travel accounts. Fortunately, sprinkled among those accounts he provided glimpses of himself. The vast majority of letters that bear his name appear in the pages of the two editions of the *Principal Navigations*. It comes as no surprise that these volumes have provided every scholar of Hakluyt, and many scholars of his age, with abundant material—at least enough to understand his opinions.

Despite the efforts of many scholars, no trove of unknown manuscripts has ever been found, or at least not yet. This means that Hakluyt needs to be extracted from known works, mostly printed books. We need to follow the slight clues he and those he knew left behind. This means paying attention to the physical edifices in which his thoughts and actions appeared. For Hakluyt, this means close attention to the books he wrote or edited, as well as those of others he encouraged. It means remembering, too, that virtually all we know about him comes from documents that he selected. If we are getting only glimpses of him through those texts, it is because he wanted it that way. Everything that we know about him must be viewed through this self-conscious screen. One early biographer noted that he kept "constant intelligence with the most noted Seamen at *Wapping* near *London*" and from them "and many small Pamphlets and Letters, that were published and went from hand to hand in his time" he was able to create the *Principal Navigations*.[1] But other than the references he included in his books these contacts remain largely unknown.

Most scholars who have written about Hakluyt have focused on his ideas. This approach makes sense because his books contain expressions of his thoughts and imaginative research can reveal the sources of his inspirations. But these modern works tend to pay little attention to the world he lived in— not simply the intellectual world where his ideas jostled with others' but the real world where Hakluyt lived as a student, cleric, cousin, husband, father, author, client, assistant to an ambassador, and a gatherer of stories.

In this book I have tried to fill in some of the gaps by recreating aspects of the world he inhabited. By traveling to Paris, Oxford, London, Wetheringsett, and Codenham, I have tried to get some understanding of the physical world he saw, a process that is easier in rural Suffolk with its seemingly timeless settlements and fields than in either of the metropolises where he worked. I have relied extensively on contemporary chroniclers, especially William Camden (an acquaintance of Hakluyt's) and John Stow, whose writings circulated during Hakluyt's life, as well as individuals who inhabited places where Hakluyt lived when he was there (notably the Parisian diarist Pierre L'Estoile and the London letter-writer John Chamberlain). I have also tried to gain access to his world through visual clues, specifically images that Hakluyt himself would have likely seen. Hakluyt was not someone who used many illustrations in his own books, though in *Divers Voyages* and in the *Principal Navigations* he did include a few maps. But it was a visual representation of the world lying on his cousin's desk that got him started, and the cosmographies that he consulted might well have contained illustrations since such mid-sixteenth-century works tended to have engravings in them. Further, Hakluyt played a role in the circulation of images in books that he steered into print, notably the English-language edition of Jan Huygen van Linschoten's *Discourse* and Thomas Harriot's *Briefe and true report of the newfound land of Virginia*. In bringing Linschoten to English readers and the engravings of Roanoke to much of Europe, Hakluyt helped to preserve crucial images and cultures from the sixteenth century. These pictures can be as valuable as the texts for understanding Hakluyt's world and especially Europeans' understanding of peoples and places beyond their boundaries.

Had Hakluyt done nothing besides gather materials together and arrange for their publication he would have made an important mark on his era and been remembered today. At a minimum, the two editions of the *Principal Navigations* constituted major collections of travel writings and thus provide direct access to a vital part of the early modern world. But of course Hakluyt also formulated plans for the expansion of the English realm. In the process, he created a language to justify overseas expeditions and colonization. Later that language became part of the foundation for the British Empire, an entity that did not exist during Hakluyt's lifetime. Though scholars continue to debate the origins of the empire and what it meant—and even how assiduously the English sought to create it in the sixteenth and seventeenth centuries—references to Hakluyt are ubiquitous.

Hakluyt was a creature of the age of print. Although modern scholars have made forceful arguments about the central importance of manuscripts, orality, and visual artifacts as modes of communication in the sixteenth century (and well beyond), there can be little doubt that Hakluyt recognized the power of the press and the force of the printed word. That recognition can be found in the fact that he published his most important works. Only three of his major efforts—the "Discourse on Western Planting," which was intended as a secret document for the queen, his analysis of Aristotle's *Politics*, and his English translation of Hugo Grotius's *Mare Liberum*—remained apart from public view. Though he did not publish all the travel accounts that he acquired, the fact that he passed many to Samuel Purchas suggests that he had no intention to keep them private, only that he either lost interest in another major editing project or had better ways to spend his time. (Purchas, apparently, had almost nothing else to do, given the sheer volume of the four editions of his travel collections, which appeared in 1613, 1614, 1617, and 1625.) The fact that there is only one known manuscript copy of the "Discourse" (in the New York Public Library), his translation of the *Mare Liberum* (in the Library of the Middle Temple), and only two copies of his analysis of Aristotle's *Politics* (in the British Library) suggests that Hakluyt did not participate in the culture of manuscript circulation common in his era. Other inhabitants of his world were not so quick to embrace the printing press, as scholars have demonstrated. Newsletters and musical compositions, among other written works, often circulated widely in manuscript. So did travel accounts. More than three hundred manuscripts of Sir John Mandeville's fantastic tales are extant, and many of them date from the era after the creation of the printing press. Manuscript accounts of Mandeville circulated in multiple languages, another startling contrast to Hakluyt's major works.

Yet although the culture of print was by definition an engagement with the public, its mechanics continued to pivot on a series of private acts. Hakluyt lived in an age when writers, unless they happened to be members of elite families, needed to rely on patrons to support their work. Within this world of letters and intimate relations, Hakluyt was seemingly always able to find support. The world of patronage was simultaneously private and public— private in the acts of supplication by the putative author, and public in the acknowledgments those authors included in their dedications. These pages at the front of books reveal the kinds of connections that existed in the world of the literate. Debts other than the financial kind could be reckoned here, such as the assistance that Hakluyt provided to writers and translators such as John Pory and Augustine Spalding, who acknowledged what they owed him in books that bore their names. Thus the prefatory matter in such printed books becomes a tool to understand his influence and a way to trace, however imperfectly, his network of relations. Hakluyt's intellectual labors also helped him gain clerical sinecures, which gave him the time to continue his research. His declining productivity after 1600 suggests perhaps that his position at Westminster Abbey was more demanding than his earlier assignments, or that he had lost his enthusiasm for the Virginia venture, or that he had become more interested in the Spice Islands, or maybe—as he suggested in the dedication of the second volume of his revised *Principal Navigations* in 1599—that he believed the time had come to focus on things other than travel accounts. The fragmentary records of the first years of the East India Company make it impossible to know if he was more than an occasional adviser to the operation, though his interest in translating the Malayan dialogues into English reveals at least sustained interest in the company's affairs.

Hakluyt had perhaps more faith in the power of print than many of his contemporaries. There was no reason to gather travel accounts and publish them unless he believed that the information contained in these reports would not otherwise circulate as he hoped. Only rarely did his books include previously printed material. There were exceptions, of course, notably in his decision to arrange the four language translation of Thomas Harriot's *Briefe and true report* in 1590 even though that account had been printed in 1588 and again in 1589 by Hakluyt himself. But in general his volumes suggest that he was an active collector eager to spread stories not yet well known or to keep before the public accounts that needed to be examined in the context of other travels. Ralegh's account of Guiana, for example, had been printed relatively recently when Hakluyt included it in the third volume of the revised *Principal Navigations*. Yet in Hakluyt's work the explorer's tale took on a new significance precisely because it was, to use Hakluyt's metaphor, but one of the many "rooms" in the house that represented English travel abroad. Hakluyt's authority confirmed legitimacy on accounts that might otherwise be dismissed as marginal, fraudulent, or useful only for the bizarre exotica they contained. Given that Ralegh's book had been used by Levinus Hulsius exactly in that way the year before it appeared in the *Principal Navigations*, its inclusion by Hakluyt in its totality (and without the awe-inspiring engravings) lent it a gravitas it might otherwise have lacked. Further, inclusion in *Principal Navigations* meant that the best-informed scholar of travel in Elizabethan England had faith in the veracity of a report. Hakluyt's decision to excise the accounts of Sir John Mandeville and David Ingram suggests the power of exclusion, too: the incredible could not be tolerated lest they have an undue influence on the credulous.

Yet for all of his efforts to further English expansion in the western hemisphere, at the dawn of the new century Hakluyt apparently decided to use his prodigious energies in other ways. Surviving records reveal that he became an adviser to the English East India Company during its formative years, and that the company's managers saw great value in his efforts. It was presumably this turn toward the East that fueled Hakluyt's decision to work on two translations that bore directly on the possibilities of English participation in the spice trade—his unpublished translation of Grotius's *Mare Liberum* (a book already available in Latin and hence to the community of European scholars) and his work on the *Malaian Dialogues*. Neither work had direct bearing on the struggling English efforts to maintain settlements in Virginia or anywhere else in the western hemisphere. Though he did offer the account of the Gentleman of Elvas in an effort to sustain enthusiasm for the Virginia Company's efforts, it seems likely that his interests had shifted away. Perhaps he felt that the publication of the revised *Principal Navigations* was the best he could offer and that other issues had become more pressing. He would not have been alone had he thought that the English would have better success in the East Indies than in the Americas. As John Chamberlain's letters reveal, anyone paying attention to events in London in the first two decades of the seventeenth century would have logically concluded that valuable commodities might someday be extracted from Virginia, but real wealth was already appearing on the city's docks every time a vessel weighed down with spices made its approach up the Thames.

Yet if the documentary record suggests a shift in his interest toward the Spice Islands, it is crucial to recall that throughout his adult life Hakluyt had an interest in territory well beyond the western hemisphere. Although Hakluyt's ideas shaped English attitudes toward the Americas, he always wanted to participate in a larger intellectual world that did not end at the English Channel. His first serious intellectual effort—at least the first made clear in the surviving record—was his engagement with the third volume of Ramusio's collection. From the time that he worked with the linguist John Florio to publish that volume in 1580 until the publication of the *Malaian Dialogues* in 1614, he sustained ties to Continental sources and scholars. Here it is possible that his relationship with his cousin was especially crucial, since the lawyer's surviving papers reveal ties to one prominent European cartographer (Abraham Ortelius) and to issues of the European and Old World economies (such as details about Persian carpets and Chinese dying techniques). From the moment of his intellectual awakening in the lawyer's chamber at the Middle Temple, then, Hakluyt knew that his fate as a scholar would be tied into a larger scientific community more concerned (in many instances) with promoting knowledge than with pushing the agenda of a particular state.

Wherever possible I have tried to make these connections explicit so that Hakluyt can be understood not only as a planner of expansion but also as a participant in a pan-European discussion about the nature of the world beyond Europe's borders. Hakluyt did not necessarily prefer this world of scholarship to his work on behalf of English interests, but his ongoing interest in the growth of knowledge in the Americas explains at least in part his determination to publish Continental authorities. Many works appeared not in the pages of *Principal Navigations* but as individual imprints, including the books by Jacques Cartier and Marc Lescarbot on New France (1580 and 1609), Antonio de Espejo and Peter Martyr on New Spain (1586 and 1587), René Laudonnière on Florida (1587), Juan González de Mendoza on China (1588), Duarte Lopez on the Congo (1597), Leo Africanus on Africa (1600), and, most notable of all, the four-language edition of Thomas Harriot's report. If Hakluyt was a promoter of or an apologist for an English empire, his decision to publish these works suggests at least that he wanted his fellow citizens to understand the specific contribution that England could make in a world more thoroughly understood and explored by others. But even then his decision to publish works in Latin, French, German, and Spanish must be part of any assessment of his political role.

This book began with Hakluyt sitting in his study holding a walrus tusk in his hand, a memento of a "new" world still taking shape in the minds of Europeans. By the time he owned that tusk he had made his promise and launched himself on an intellectual journey that made him a reigning European authority on much of the world, at least to people in England who continually sought his advice or told him their stories. He left no record of holding something specific near the end of his life, though one can imagine him in possession of a precious library filled with books and manuscripts, perhaps even a horde of souvenirs sent to him by his correspondents who had seen distant lands. Maybe he sat there puzzling over Malayan phrases and wondering how his effort to promote the English colonization of North America had led him on his own journey. Perhaps as he lay dying his mind wondered back to the words of Ortelius, which had appeared in a book that

Hakluyt had urged toward the press: "And when the time commeth, that we make an ende of our travels, and personall view of forren parts, it will bee a singular pleasure unto us, whensoever we are so disposed to recognize, and recount those things which we have seene, quietlie & in our chambers, without any trouble of journie, or toile of body."[2]

Hakluyt never saw the western hemisphere or the Spice Islands. As a result, he was not a reliable eyewitness to the stories he told. But set in his time, he becomes a witness with much to tell about how late-sixteenth- and early-seventeenth-century Europeans came to understand their encounters with Americans and others.

Sources

There is no single collection of Hakluyt's papers. Most of what he wrote with his own hand has disappeared over the almost four centuries since his death. Fortunately, the formal expression of his thoughts can be found in the books that he wrote and edited, and his major works have all been reprinted at least once in the past century. This note indicates the major sources for his life and ideas, but should be supplemented with the extraordinary bibliographic work done by David Beers Quinn and the forthcoming work of Anthony Payne.

The most important works for understanding Hakluyt are his own, starting with *Divers Voyages touching upon America* (London, 1582; facsimile reprint, ed., David B. Quinn with the title *Richard Hakluyt, Editor* [Amsterdam, 1967]); *The Principall Navigations, Voiages, and Discoveries of the English Nation* (London, 1589; facsimile ed. 2 vols., ed. David B. Quinn and Alison M. Quinn, Cambridge, 1965); and *The Principal Navigations, Voyages, Traffiques and Discoveries of the English Nation* (3 vols., London, 1598–1600; 10 vols., Glasgow, 1903–1905 [rpt. 12 vols., New York, 1969]). The document known as "The Discourse on Western Planting" was first published in *Documentary History of the State of Maine*, vol. 2 (Cambridge, Mass., 1877). All scholars should now employ the brilliant edition by David Beers Quinn and Alison M. Quinn, Hakluyt Society, Extra Ser., 45 (London, 1993), which contains facing manuscript and typescript pages as well as a superb index. Hakluyt's translation of Grotius's *Mare Liberum* is now available in an excellent edition by David Armitage: Hugo Grotius, *The Free Sea*, trans. Richard Hakluyt (Indianapolis, 2004). Most of the primary writings of Hakluyt and his older cousin can be found in E. G. R. Taylor, ed., *The Original Writings and Correspondence of the Two Richard Hakluyts*, Hakluyt Society, 2nd Ser., 86–87

(London, 1935); this collection includes the "Discourse on Western Planting," which has been the most frequently cited by scholars. The most important guide to Hakluyt's writings is David B. Quinn, ed., *The Hakluyt Handbook*, 2 vols., Hakluyt Society, 2nd Ser., 144–145 (London, 1974). Quinn and Alison M. Quinn's "A Hakluyt Chronology" (1:263–331) provides the most comprehensive outline of Hakluyt's life. For other documents relating to Hakluyt not included in Taylor's edition, see Emanuel van Meteren's correspondence in Gerrit de Veer, *Reizen van Willem Barents, Jacob van Heemskerck, Jan Cornelisz: Rijp en anderen, naar het noorden (1594–1597)*, 2 vols. (*'s-Gravenhage*, 1917), 2:201–208; D. B. Quinn, "The Voyage of Étienne Bellenger to the Maritimes in 1583: A New Document," *Canadian Historical Review* 43 (1962): 339–342 (reprinted in Quinn's *Explorers and Colonies: America, 1500–1625* [London, 1990], 285–399), and Heidi Brayman Hackel and Peter C. Mancall, "Richard Hakluyt the Younger's Notes for the East India Company in 1601: A Transcription of Huntington Library Manuscript EL 2360," *Huntington Library Quarterly* 67 (2004): 423–436. Those interested in Purchas should begin with Loren E. Pennington, ed., *The Purchas Handbook: Studies of the Life, Times and Writings of Samuel Purchas, 1577–1626*, Hakluyt Society, 2nd Ser., 185–186 (London, 1997).

Hakluyt has attracted biographers since the seventeenth century. See, for example, the following early modern biographical treatments: Thomas Fuller's account, originally written in 1662, in *The History of the Worthies of England*, 3 vols. (London, 1840), 2:78; Anthony à Wood, "Richard Hakluyt" in *Athenae Oxonienses: An exact history of all the Writers and Bishops who have had their education in the most ancient and famous University of Oxford*, 2 vols. (London, 1691), 1:349; and William Oldys, "Hakluyt," in *Biographica Britannica: Or, The Lives of the Most Eminent Persons who have Flourished in Great Britain and Ireland*, vol. 4 (London, 1757), 2461–2474. Later studies include James A. Froude, "England's Forgotten Worthies" (1853), in his often reprinted collection *Short Studies on Great Subjects*, which included his seemingly immortal line that Hakluyt had written "the Prose Epic of the modern English nation."

Many scholars have wrestled with Hakluyt's writings, and those who have attempted biographies have relied primarily on them. The best of these works is George B. Parks, *Richard Hakluyt and the English Voyages* (New York, 1926; 2nd ed., New York, 1961). Other efforts (in chronological order) include Walter Alexander Raleigh, "Richard Hakluyt," in *The English Voyages of the Sixteenth Century* (Glasgow, 1910), 119–147; W. P. M. Kennedy, "Richard

Hakluyt: The Spirit of Our Race," *Canadian Magazine* 66 (1916): 491–495; "The Tercentenary of Richard Hakluyt," *Geographical Journal* 48 (1916); Foster Watson's contribution to the English Pioneers of Progress: Empire Builders series, *Richard Hakluyt* (London, 1924); James A. Williamson, "Richard Hakluyt," in Edward Lynam, ed., *Richard Hakluyt and His Successors,* Hakluyt Society, 2nd Ser., 93 (London, 1946), 9–46; E. G. R. Taylor, "Richard Hakluyt," *Geographical Journal* 109 (1947): 165–174; J. Hamard, "Richard Hakluyt, Historien," *Les Langues Modernes* 52(1948): 249–257; a book designed for young readers by Frank Knight, *They Told Mr. Hakluyt* (London, 1964); and the introductions to editions of Hakluyt's writings, including Jack Beeching, ed., *Voyages and Discoveries* (London, 1972; rpt. Harmondsworth, 1985), and Irwin R. Blacker, ed., *Hakluyt's Voyages: The Principal Navigations, Voyages, Traffiques & Discoveries of the English Nation* (New York, 1965). There have also been many studies of specific aspects of Hakluyt's writing and career. The best starting point is Quinn's *Hakluyt Handbook,* which contains articles on many aspects of his work. Among the best of recent critical studies are a series of articles by David B. Quinn conveniently reprinted in his *Explorers and Colonies: America, 1500–1625* (London, 1990); a chapter devoted to travel writing in Richard Helgerson, *Forms of Nationhood: The Elizabethan Writing of England* (Chicago, 1992), 149–191; a chapter on Hakluyt and Purchas in David Armitage, *The Ideological Origins of the British Empire* (Cambridge, 2000), 61–99; Mary C. Fuller, "'Ravenous Strangers': The Argument of Nationalism in Two Narratives from Hakluyt's Principal Navigations," *Studies in Travel Writing* 6 (2002): 1–28; and David Harris Sacks, "Discourses of Western Planting: Richard Hakluyt and the Making of the Atlantic World," in Peter C. Mancall, ed., *The Atlantic World and Virginia* (Chapel Hill, N.C., 2007). See also (in chronological order): J. G. Kohl, *Descriptive Catalog of Those Maps, Charts and Surveys Relating to America Which Are Mentioned in Vol. III of Hakluyt's Great Work* (Washington, D.C., 1857); Foster Watson, "Hakluyt and Mulcaster," *Geographical Journal* 69 (1917): 48–53; Alfred A. Cave, "Richard Hakluyt's Savages: The Influence of Sixteenth-Century Travel Narratives on English Indian Policy in North America," *International Social Science Review* 60 (1985): 3–24; Emily C. Bartels, "Imperialist Beginnings: Richard Hakluyt and the Construction of Africa," *Criticism* 34 (1992): 517–538; Pamela Neville-Sington, "'A very good trumpet': Richard Hakluyt and the Politics of Overseas Expansion," in Cedric C. Brown and Arthur F. Marotti, eds., *Texts and Cultural Change in Early Modern England* (London, 1997), 66–79; Anthony Payne, *Richard Hakluyt and His*

Books (London, 1997); Payne, "'Strange, remote, and farre distant countreys': The Travel Books of Richard Hakluyt," in Robin Myers and Michael Harris, eds., *Journeys through The Market: Travels, Travellers, and the Book Trade* (New Castle, Del., 1999), 1–37; and William H. Sherman, "Bringing the World to England: The Politics of Translation in the Age of Hakluyt," *Transactions of the Royal Historical Society* 14 (2004): 199–207.

The institutions that provided support to Hakluyt during his education are all well documented. On the Middle Temple, see Charles Henry Hopwood, ed., *Middle Temple Records,* 3 vols. (London, 1904); Sir Lynden L. Macassey, *The Middle Temple's Contribution to the National Life* (London, [1930]); and George Godwin, *The Middle Temple: The Society and Fellowship* (London, 1954). For the companies that supported him, see John J. Lambert, ed., *Records of the Skinners of London* (London, 1933); Tom Girton, "Mr. Hakluyt, Scholar at Oxford," *Geographical Journal* 119 (1953): 208–212; Thomas Girton, *The Golden Ram: A History of the Clothworkers' Company, 1528–1958* ([London], 1958); G. D. Ramsay, "Clothworkers, Merchants Adventurers and Richard Hakluyt," *English Historical Review* 92 (1977): 504–521; and C. S. Knighton, ed., *Acts of the Dean and Chapter of Westminster, 1543–1609,* 2 vols. (Woodbridge, Suffolk, 1999).

Hakluyt, of course, did not act in isolation. In addition to the general debt he owed to his English predecessors, such as Richard Eden (*The decades of the newe worlde or west India* [London, 1555]) and Richard Willes (*The history of travayle in the West and East Indies* [London, 1577]), Hakluyt owed an enormous intellectual debt to two individuals: Giovannia Battista (Giambattista) Ramusio and his cousin the lawyer. There is far too little scholarship on the lawyer; even the recently completed *Oxford Dictionary of National Biography* did not include an entry about him. The best information remains Taylor's edition of the two Hakluyts' *Writings and Correspondence.* Ramusio, by contrast, has generated important scholarship. The most obvious place to start would be with the introductions to the modern edition of his trilogy: Marica Milanesi, ed., *Navigationi e Viaggi,* 6 vols. (Turin, 1978–1988); see also Antonio del Piero, "Della vita e degli studi di Gio. Battista Ramusio," *Nuovo Archivo Veneto,* n.s., 4 (1902): 5–112. A chronicle of Ramusio's family, "Cronaca delle Familigla Ramusio" can be found in the Biblioteca Marciano in Venice (CI VII Cod. xxxccv (=8839)). The pioneering work on him in English was by George B. Parks, whose efforts made clear the deep intellectual connection that Hakluyt made with Ramusio; see his "Ramusio's Literary History," *Studies in Philology* 52 (1955), 127–148 and *Contents and Sources of*

Ramusio's Navigationi (New York, 1955). Those interested in Ramusio's actions beyond his work on *Navigationi et Viaggi* will find much of value in his correspondence with Pietro Bembo; see Ernesto Travi, ed., *Pietro Bembo lettere*, 3 vols. (Bologna, 1987–1992). Works which I found particularly useful in understanding Ramusio's Venice include (in chronological order): Felix Gilbert, "Biondo, Sabellico, and the Beginnings of Venetian Official Historiography," in J. G. Rowe and W. H. Stockdale, eds., *Florilegum Historiale: Essays Presented to Wallace K. Ferguson* (Toronto, 1971); J. R. Hale, ed., *Renaissance Venice* (London, 1973); Frederic C. Lane, *Venice: A Maritime Republic* (Baltimore, 1973); Edward Muir, *Civic Ritual in Renaissance Venice* (Princeton, N.J., 1981); Patricia F. Brown, "The Self-Definition of the Venetian Republic," in Anthony Molho, Kurt Raaflaub, and Julia Emlen, eds., *City States in Classical Antiquity and Medieval Italy* (Ann Arbor, Mich., 1991); David Chambers and Brian Pullan, *Venice: A Documentary History, 1450–1630* (Oxford, 1992); and Patricia Fortini Brown, *Venice and Antiquity: The Venetian Sense of the Past* (New Haven and London, 1996).

Some of Hakluyt's other associates have also become the subject of serious historical inquiry. For Sir Humphrey Gilbert see David B. Quinn, ed., *The Voyages and Colonising Enterprises of Sir Humphrey Gilbert*, 2 vols., Hakluyt Society, 2nd Ser., 83–84 (London, 1940). For Stephen Parmenius see David B. Quinn and Neil M. Cheshire, eds., *The New Found Land of Stephen Parmenius: The Life and Writings of a Hungarian Poet, Drowned on a Voyage from Newfoundland, 1583* (Toronto, 1972). For André Thevet see Roger Schlesinger and Arthur P. Stabler, eds., *André Thevet's North America: A Sixteenth-Century View* (Kingston and Montreal, 1986); Frank Lestringant, *Mapping the Renaissance World* (orig. publ. Paris, 1991), trans. David Fausett (Berkeley, Calif., 1994); Lestringant, ed., *André Thevet : Cosmographie de Levant*, Travaux d'Humanisme et Renaissance, 203 (Geneva, 1985) ; and Lestringant, *Le Huguenot et le sauvage: L'Amérique et la controverse coloniale, en France, au temps des guerres de religion* (Geneva, 2004). For Thevet's rival Jean de Léry, see his *History of a Voyage to the Land of Brazil*, trans. Janet Whatley (Berkeley, Calif., 1990).

I based the contents of this book almost entirely on documents produced by Hakluyt or his contemporaries, but such sources can be understood only in context. Although my argument differs substantially in places from other scholars, no one can wrestle with Hakluyt without immersion into the works that deal with the early modern Atlantic world, including the origins of the British Empire. Among the many works in these areas, see (in alphabetical order by author or editor) Kenneth R. Andrews, *Trade, Plunder, and Settlement: Maritime Enterprise and the Genesis of the British Empire, 1480–1630* (Cambridge, 1984); David Armitage, *The Ideological Origins of the British Empire* (Cambridge, 2000); Bernard Bailyn, *Atlantic History: Concept and Contours* (Cambridge, Mass., 2005); Philip L. Barbour, ed., *The Jamestown Voyages under the First Charter, 1606–1609*, 2 vols., Hakluyt Society, 2nd Ser., 136–137 (Cambridge, 1969); Nicholas Canny, *Making Ireland British, 1580–1650* (New York, 2001); Canny, ed., *The Origins of Empire* (Oxford, 1998); Joyce Chaplin, *Subject Matter: Technology, the Body, and Science on the Anglo-American Frontier, 1500–1676* (Cambridge, Mass., 2001); Leslie B. Cormack, *Charting an Empire: Geography at the English Universities, 1580–1620* (Chicago, 1997); Mordechai Feingold, "Science as a Calling? The Early Modern Dilemma," *Science in Context* 15 (2002): 79–119; Feingold, *The Mathematicians' Apprentice: Science, Universities, and Society in England, 1560–1640* (Cambridge, 1984); William W. Fitzhugh and Jacqueline S. Olin, eds., *Archaeology of the Frobisher Voyages* (Washington, D.C., 1993); Andrew Fitzmaurice, *Humanism and America: An Intellectual History of English Colonisation, 1500–1625* (Cambridge, 2003); Mary Fuller, *Voyages in Print: English Travel to America, 1576–1624* (Cambridge, 1995); Alison Games, *Migration and the Origins of the Atlantic World* (Cambridge, Mass., 1999); Richard Helgerson, *Forms of Nationhood: The Elizabethan Writing of England* (Chicago, 1992); Paul Hulton and David B. Quinn, *The American Drawings of John White, 1577–1590, with Drawings of European and Oriental Subjects*, 2 vols. (London, 1964); Harry Kelsey, *Sir Francis Drake: The Queen's Pirate* (New Haven and London, 1998); Karen Ordahl Kupperman, ed., *America in European Consciousness, 1493–1750* (Chapel Hill, N.C., 1995); Kupperman, *Indians and English: Facing Off in Early America* (Ithaca, N.Y., 2000); Malcolm Letts, ed., *Mandeville's Travels: Texts and Translations*, 2 vols., Hakluyt Society, 2nd Ser., 101–102 (London, 1935); James McDermott, *Martin Frobisher: Elizabethan Privateer* (New Haven and London, 2001); McDermott, ed., *The Third Voyage of Martin Frobisher to Baffin Island, 1578*, Hakluyt Society, 3rd Ser., 6 (London, 2001); Peter E. Pope, *Fish into Wine: The Newfoundland Plantation in the Seventeenth Century* (Chapel Hill, N.C., 204); David B. Quinn, *Explorers and Colonies: America, 1500–1625* (London, 1990); Quinn, ed., *The Roanoke Voyages, 1584–1590*, 2 vols., Hakluyt Society, 2nd Ser., 104–105 (London, 1955); Quinn, *Sir Francis Drake as Seen by His Contemporaries* (Providence, R.I., 1996); David Harris Sacks, *The Widening Gate: Bristol and the Atlantic Economy, 1450–1700* (Berkeley, Calif., 1991); Benjamin Schmidt, *Innocence Abroad:*

The Dutch Imagination and the New World, 1570–1670 (Cambridge, 2001); Carole Shammas, "The 'Invisible Merchant' and Property Rights: The Misadventures of an Elizabethan Joint Stock Company," *Business History* 17, no. 2 (1975): 95–108; William Sherman, *John Dee: The Politics of Reading and Writing in the English Renaissance* (Amherst, Mass., 1995); and J. A. Williamson, ed., *The Cabot Voyages and Bristol Discovery under Henry VII*, Hakluyt Society, 2nd Ser., 120 (Cambridge, 1962). In addition to considering works relating specifically to Hakluyt and his associates, it is crucial to understand that his efforts reflected early modern interests more generally, especially the desire (not limited to Europeans) to understand distant places. Travel narratives played a crucial role in the development of what we now call ethnography; see Margaret T. Hodgen, *Early Anthropology in the Sixteenth and Seventeenth Centuries* (Philadelphia, 1964). For a collection of travel narratives, including some published by Hakluyt, that sets European efforts into a global context see Peter C. Mancall, ed., *Travel Narratives from the Age of Discovery: An Anthology* (New York, 2006).

In addition to works focusing on the Atlantic context, understanding Hakluyt requires some attention to the expanding universe of print that he inhabited, as well as attention to the ways that information spread in media other than books. My thoughts on these issues have been shaped in particular by (again in alphabetical order by author) Elizabeth Eisenstein, *The Printing Press as an Agent of Change: Communications and Cultural Transformations in Early Modern Europe*, 2 vols. (Cambridge, 1979); Lucien Febvre and Henri-Jean Martin, *The Coming of the Book: The Impact of Printing, 1450–1800* (orig. publ. Paris, 1958), trans. David Gerard (London, 1976); Anthony Grafton, "The Importance of Being Printed," *Journal of Interdisciplinary History* 11 (1980): 265–286; Adrian Johns, *The Nature of the Book: Print and Knowledge in the Making* (Chicago, 1998); Harold Love, *Scribal Publication in Seventeenth-Century England* (Oxford, 1993); David McKitterick, *Print, Manuscript and the Search for Order, 1450–1830* (Cambridge, 2003); and Don R. Swanson, "Undiscovered Public Knowledge," *Library Quarterly* 56 (1986): 103–118.

Finally, since Hakluyt was too often reluctant to provide much information about the places he inhabited, I relied on others to provide the context, especially John Chamberlain and Pierre de L'Estoile. See Norman E. McLure, ed., *The Letters of John Chamberlain*, 2 vols., *Memoirs of the American Philosophical Society*, 12–13 (1939); Nancy Lyman Roelker, ed. and trans., *The Paris of Henry of Navarre as Seen by Pierre de L'Estoile* (Cambridge, Mass., 1958); and *Mémoires-Journaux de Pierre de L'Estoile*, ed. G. Brunet et al., 12 vols. (Paris, 1875–1896).

Abbreviations

Add. Mss.	Additional Manuscripts, British Library
BL	British Library
Cal. Foreign	*Calendar of State Papers, Foreign Series, of the Reign of Elizabeth*, 23 vols. (1863–1950)
Camden, *Annales* (1625)	[William Camden], *Annales: The True and Royall History of the famous Empresse Elizabeth, three books in one volume* (London, 1625)
Camden, *Annales* (1630)	[William Camden], *The Historie of the Most Renowned and Victorious Princesse Elizabeth . . . Composed by Way of Annals, four books in one volume* (London, 1630)
Camden, *Annales* (1635)	William Camden, *Annales: Or, The History of the Most Renowned and Victorious Princesse Elizabeth, 3d ed., trans. R.N., four books in one volume* (London, 1635)
Chamberlain, *Letters*	Norman E. McLure, ed., *The Letters of John Chamberlain*, 2 vols., *Memoirs of the American Philosophical Society*, 12, Parts 1 and 2 (Philadelphia, 1939)
Discourse	David B. Quinn and Alison M. Quinn, ed., *A Particuler Discourse Concerning the Greate Necessitie and Manifolde Commodyties That Are Like to Growe to This Realme of Englande by the Westerne Discoveries Lately Attempted*, Hakluyt Society, Extra Ser., 45 (London, 1993)
Divers Voyages	Richard Hakluyt, *Divers voyages touching the discoverie of America, and the ilands adjacent unto the same, made first of all by our Englishmen, and afterward by the Frenchmen and Britons* (London, 1582)
DNB	*Dictionary of National Biography*
Hak. Soc.	Hakluyt Society
"Hakluyt Chronology"	David B. Quinn and Alison M. Quinn, "A Hakluyt Chronology," in David B. Quinn, ed., *The Hakluyt Handbook*, 2 vols., Hakluyt Society, 2nd Ser., 144–145 (London, 1974), 1:263–331

Hakluyt Handbook	David B. Quinn, ed., *The Hakluyt Handbook,* 2 vols., Hakluyt Society, 2nd Ser., 144–145 (London, 1974)
Hakluytus Posthumus	Samuel Purchas, *Hakluytus Posthumus, or Purchas his Pilgrimes,* 5 books in 4 vols. (London, 1625)
HEH	Henry E. Huntington Library, San Marino, California
Howes, *Annales* (1631)	Edmund Howes, *Annales, Or, A Generall Chronicle of England. Begun by John Stow* (London, 1631)
Linschoten, *Discourse*	*John Huighen Van Linschoten his Discourse of Voyages unto ye Easte & West Indies* (London, 1598)
New American World	D. B. Quinn, ed., *New American World: A Documentary History of North America to 1612,* 5 vols. (New York, 1979)
ODNB	*The Oxford Dictionary of National Biography*
Principal Navigations (1598–1600)	Richard Hakluyt, *The Principal Navigations, Voyages, Traffiques and Discoveries of the English Nation,* 3 vols. (London, 1598–1600)
Principall Navigations (1589)	Richard Hakluyt, *The Principall Navigations, Voiages and Discoveries of the English nation* (London, 1589)
Stationers' Registers	Edward Arber, ed., *A Transcript of the Registers of the Company of Stationers of London, 1554–1640 A.D.,* 5 vols. (London and Birmingham, 1875–1877, 1894)
Stow, *Chronicles* (1580)	John Stow, *The Chronicles of England, from Brute unto this present yeare of Christ, 1580* (London, 1580)
Wood, *History and Antiquities*	Anthony à Wood, *The History and Antiquities of the University of Oxford,* trans. John Gutch, 2 vols. (Oxford, 1792–1796)
WMQ	*The William and Mary Quarterly*
Writings and Correspondence	E. G. R. Taylor, ed., *The Writings and Correspondence of the Two Richard Hakluyts,* 2 vols., Hakluyt Society, 2nd Ser., 76–77 (London, 1935)

N.B.: Hakluyt used similar titles for his major work. The distinction, though it may seem slight to modern readers, is crucial. The first edition is entitled *The Principall Navigations Voiages and Discoveries of the English Nation* (London, 1589); the second edition is entitled *The Principal Navigations, Voyages, Traffiques and Discoveries of the English Nation,* 3 vols. (London, 1598–1600). The notes in this book to Hakluyt's major work of 1584, the "Discourse on Western Planting," refer only to the Quinn and Quinn edition of 1993 (see above for bibliographic details).

Notes

CHAPTER 1. London, c. 1592

1. For a vivid European representation of Iceland in the 1590s, see the map in Abraham Ortelius, *Theatrum Orbis Terrarum* (Antwerp, 1595).

2. "A briefe note of the Morsse and the use thereof," in *Principal Navigations* (1598–1600), 3:191. The note is undated, but it is likely that Hakluyt wrote it in 1591 or 1592; see "Hakluyt Chronology," 1:305.

3. According to the records of the Stationers' Company of London, the bishop of London and an associate had indicated that they planned to publish *A ballad shewinge how a London womann falsely accused her self to be the kinge of Spaines daughter and beinge founde a lyer was for the same whipped through London the xiiijth of December 1592 beinge known to be a butchers daughter of London*; see *Stationers' Registers*, 3:294. For other books that year, see *Stationers' Registers*, 3:284ʳ (capture of the galley), 286ʳ (witchcraft), and 287ʳ (on cony catching). One enterprising printer also promised a tract on one of the murders; see *Stationers' Registers*, 3:289ʳ).

4. Howes, *Annales* (1631), 764–765; Camden, *Annales* (1635), 414.

5. Theodor de Bry, *Americae Tertia Pars Memorabilê provinciæ Brasiliæ Historiam Continês* (Frankfurt, 1592).

CHAPTER 2. London, 1568

1. Hakluyt never told the date of the meeting, though a letter he wrote in 1594 to the Dutch geographer Emanuel van Meteren implies that Hakluyt had been interested in the subject for "at least 26 years," which would mean that the visit took place in 1568, when Hakluyt was approximately sixteen. See Hakluyt to Van Meteren, December 6, 1594, in *Writings and Correspondence*, 2:419. For Sir Francis Drake's possible admission, see John Hutchinson, *A Catalogue of Notable Middle Templars, with Brief Biographical Notices* (London, 1902), 78–79.

2. [George Braun], *Civitas Orbis Terrarum*, 6 vols. (Cologne, 1593–1617), 1:sig. A; Roy Porter, *London: A Social History* (Cambridge, Mass., 1995), 61. For the Temple's founding, see John Stow, *A Survay of London, Conteyning the Originall, Antiquity, Increase, Moderne estate, and description of that City, written in the yeare 1598* (London, 1603), 401–405; and

George H. Cunningham, *London: A Comprehensive Survey of the History, Tradition and Historical Associations of Buildings and Monuments* (London, 1931), 714.

3. Stow, *Survay of London*, 403–404.

4. Cunningham, *London*, 709–710.

5. The contrast is most evident by comparing the maps and in Abraham Ortelius's *Theatrum Orbis Terrarum* (Antwerp, 1570). The map of England ("Angliae, Scotiae, et Hibernaie, sive Britannica") contains no representations of trees, whereas maps for France, Germany, and other parts of the Continent depict forests.

6. Stow, *Survay of London*, 404–405.

7. On the quality of the masters, see John Sargaunt, *Annals of Westminster School* (London, 1898), 51; on the queen's scholars, see John Richardson, *The Annals of London* (Berkeley, Calif., 2000), 97.

8. For the problems caused by butchers and earlier attempts to solve them (by banning slaughtering within the city and moving butchers further from dense settlements), see Richardson, *Annals of London*, 45, 47, 49, 50. As Keith Thomas observed, "There had been intermittent legislation against the pollution of the Thames" since the age of Richard II, but more persistent efforts to reduce the growing industrial pollution of London became more common in the seventeenth century; see Thomas, *Man and the Natural World: Changing Attitudes in England, 1500–1800* (London, 1983), 244–245. Londoners in the late seventeenth century, according to Thomas Babington Macaulay, used St. James's Square as "a receptacle for all the offal and cinders, for all the dead cats and dead dogs of Westminster"; see his *History of England*, ed. C. H. Firth, 6 vols. (London, 1913), 1:350.

9. Porter, *London*, 42, 64; Camden, *Annales* (1625), 1:99.

10. For Stow's most important work, see I. S. [John Stow], *The serpent of division* ([London], 1559); Stow, *The woorkes of Geffrey Chaucer, newly printed, with divers addicions whiche were never in printe before* (London, 1561); and Stow, *A summarie of Englyshe chronicles* (London, [1565]). For Grafton, see *An abridgement of the chronicles of England* [London, 1563]; and Grafton, *A Chronicle at large and meere History of the affayres of Englande* ([London], 1569), 2. Stow's response to Grafton quoted here is from *A Summarye of the Chronicles of Englande* (London, 1570), sig. [B]^v–Bi^r.

11. Howes, *Annales* (1631), 657–658.

12. Howes, *Annales* (1631), 659–660.

13. Howes, *Annales* (1631), 662.

14. Howes, *Annales* (1631), 662; Camden, *Annales* (1625), 2:410. On the need for immigration to sustain London's population and fuel its growth, see Porter, *London*, 42. On the importance of London as a human reservoir for migrants to early Virginia (and other destinations), many of whom had come from elsewhere in England before crossing the Atlantic, see James Horn, "Servant Emigration to the Chesapeake in the Seventeenth Century," in Thad Tate and David Ammerman, eds., *The Chesapeake in the Seventeenth Century: Essays on Anglo-American Society* (Chapel Hill, N.C., 1979), 66–74; Alison Games, *Migration and the Origins of the English Atlantic World* (Cambridge, Mass., 1999), 13–41; and Bernard Bailyn, *The Peopling of British North America: An Introduction* (New York, 1986), 24–25.

15. *Principall Navigations* (1589), sig. *2^r. Unless otherwise noted, the description of Westminster and London that follows here is from Stow, *Survay of London*, 451–465.

16. Stow, *Survay of London*, 459.

17. Royal Commission on Historical Monuments (England), *An Inventory of the Historical Monuments in London*, vol. 1, *Westminster Abbey* (London, 1924), 65.

18. Stow, *Survay of London*, 462–464. Stow actually described the route in the opposite direction.

19. Stow, *Survay of London*, 455–456.

20. Stow, *Survay of London*, 452–454.

21. Stow, *Survay of London*, 451–452.

22. *Principall Navigations*, sig. *2^r; John Dee, *The Mathematical Preface to the Elements of Geometrie of Euclid* (London, 1570), sig. b3^r; William Cuningham, *The Cosmographical Glasse, conteinyng the pleasant Principles of Cosmographie, Geographie, Hydrographie, or Navigation* (London, 1559), sig. Aiiij^r. On the antiquity of geography, see James S. Romm, *The Edges of the Earth in Ancient Thought* (Princeton, N.J., 1992). On the emergence of geography as a distinct scientific discipline in English universities in this period, see Leslie B. Cormack, *Charting an Empire: Geography at the English Universities, 1580–1620* (Chicago, 1997), esp. 17–47.

23. See, e.g., [John Honter], *Rudimentorum Cosmographicorum . . . Libri III* (Antwerp, [c. 1545?]), which includes a series of small maps, including a map of the world in which America appears like a thin wedge, similar to its representation on Martin Waldesmüller's map of 1507; Sebastian Münster, *Cosmographia Universalis Liber VI* (Basel, 1552). His cosmography was published in eight separate editions while he was alive, and then another thirty-five editions posthumously from the time of his death to 1628; see Elizabeth L. Eisenstein, *The Printing Press as an Agent of Change: Communications and Cultural Transformations in Early-Modern Europe* (orig. pub. in 2 vols., Cambridge, 1979; republished as 1 vol., Cambridge, 1980), 109. The title page of a French edition published that year had simpler iconography: two men, one using a sextant and the other a compass, stand on either side of a small landscape dotted with houses; see *La Cosmographie Universelle* (1552). For European knowledge of elephants, see Donald Lach, "Asian Elephants in Renaissance Europe," *Journal of Asian History* 1 (1967): 133–176.

24. [Andrew Borde], *The fyrst boke of the Introduction of knowledge* [London, 1562], title page (promise of its contents), sigs. Bi^1 (London), [Ciii^{r-v}] (Ireland); Cuningham, *Cosmographical Glasse;* the table of eclipses can be found at fols. 98–102.

25. See Valerie Flint, *The Imaginative Landscape of Christopher Columbus* (Princeton, N.J., 1992), 3–41; and William D. Phillips, Jr., and Carla Rahn Phillips, *The Worlds of Christopher Columbus* (Cambridge, 1992), 13–14.

26. Sebastian Münster, *Cosmographiæ Universalis Lib. VI* (Basel, 1572), n.p. The 1552 edition had 1,163 pages; the 1572 edition ran to 1,331 pages. As the historian Elizabeth Eisenstein has noted, these additions did not represent information that the cosmographer felt should be included; many of the later additions were the result of work within particular printers' establishments and efforts there to add detail even if it meant bowdlerizing the author's original intent. See Eisenstein, *Printing Press as an Agent of Change*, 109.

27. Martin Waldseemüller, "Universalis Cosmographia Secundum Ptholomaei Traditionem Et Americi Vespucii Aliorûque Lustrationes" (Strasbourg, 1507); Giacomo Gastaldi and Gerard de Jode, "Universalis Exactissima Atque Non Recens Modo" (Antwerp, 1555); Giacomo Gastaldi et al., "Cosmographia Universalis Et Exactissima Iuxta Postremam Neotericorum Traditionem" (Venice, c. 1561); Paolo Forlani, "Universale Descrittione Di Tutta La Terra Conosciuta Fin Qui" (Venice, 1562); Abraham Ortelius, "Nova

Totius Terrarum Orbis . . ." (Antwerp, 1564); Forlani, "Universale Descrittione Di Tutta
La Terra Conosciuta" (Venice, 1565); and Giovanni Francesco Camocio, "Cosmographia
Universalis Et Exactissima Iuxta Postremam Neotericorum Traditionem" (Venice, 1567).
Reproductions of each of these maps, and others from this period, are found in Rodney W.
Shirley, *The Mapping of the World: Early Printed World Maps, 1472–1700* (London, 1983),
28–31, 113–137. Gerard Mercator's most famous map, on which he displayed latitudes in
what became the modern sense (the Mercator projection), was published in 1569, and his
first world atlas did not appear until 1595, after the cartographer had died the previous
December; for details on all of Mercator's activities, see C. Koeman, *Atlantes Neerlandici,*
6 vols. (Amsterdam, 1967–1985), 2:281ff.

   28. Gastaldi, *La Universale Descrittione Del Mondo* (Venice, [1562]), sig. [A 10^r].

   29. *Principall Navigations* (1589), sig. *2^r.

   30. *Principall Navigations* (1589), sig. *2^r.

CHAPTER 3. Oxford, c. 1571

   1. William Camden, *Britannia: Or, A Chorographical Description of Great Britain and
Ireland, Together with the Adjacent Islands . . . Translated into English, with Additions and
Improvements. Revised, Digested, and Published, with large Additions, by Edmund Gibson,
D.D. Late Lord Bishop of London,* 3rd ed., 2 vols. (London, 1753), 1:303.

   2. R[obert] P[lot], *The Natural History of Oxford-Shire, Being an Essay toward the
Natural History of England* (Oxford, 1677), 24–25.

   3. P[lot], *Natural History of Oxford-Shire,* 158 (oak at Magdalen), 51–52 (lumber to
London), 51 (meadows and pastures); Camden, *Britannia,* 1:303.

   4. Lawrence Stone, "The Size and Composition of the Oxford Student Body, 1580–
1910," in Stone, ed., *The University in Society,* 2 vols. (Princeton, N.J., 1974), 1:91; Hugh
Trevor-Roper, *Christ Church Oxford* (Oxford, 1950), 11–13; Joseph Skelton, *Oxonia antiqua
restaurata,* 2 vols. (Oxford, 1823), pls. 27 and 124, frontispiece.

   5. "Hakluyt Chronology," 1:265–267.

   6. John J. Lambert, ed., *Records of the Skinners of London* (London, 1933), 373–374, 375;
George Bruner Parks, *Richard Hakluyt and the English Voyages* (New York, 1928), 60; Tom
Girton, "Mr. Hakluyt, Scholar at Oxford," *Geographical Journal* 119 (1953): 208–212;
Thomas Girton, *The Golden Ram: A History of the Clothworkers' Company, 1528–1958*
([London], 1958), 53–56; G. D. Ramsay, "Clothworkers, Merchants Adventurers and
Richard Hakluyt," *English Historical Review* 92 (1977): 504–521.

   7. [John Field], "An Admonition to Parliament" (1571[?]), and [Field], "A View of the
Popishe Abuses Yet Remaining in the Englishe Church, for which the Godly Ministers
have Refused to Subscribe,"reprinted in W. H. Frere and C. E. Douglas, eds., *Puritan
Manifestoes: A Study of the Origin of the Puritan Revolt* (London, 1954), 12, 21. As David
Armitage has noted, Hakluyt drew on John Foxe and John Bale (among others) in his
"Discourse on Western Planting" in 1584; see Armitage, *The Ideological Origins of the
British Empire* (Cambridge, 2000), 78. (See chapter 7, below, for an analysis of that
document.) In a Good Friday sermon published in 1570, for example, Foxe attacked the
pope and his followers yet nonetheless held out the hope that they would realize the errors
of their ways. See Foxe, *A Sermon of Christ Crucified* (London, 1570). Foxe's most famous
work, the so-called *Book of Martyrs,* provided ample evidence of the treacherous acts of

torture and murder carried out in Europe by agents of the Catholic Church; an edition possibly available to Hakluyt contained graphic illustrations along with lurid text. See Foxe, *The First Volume of the Ecclesiasticall history contayning the Actes and Monumentes of thyngs passed in every kyngs tyme in their Realme . . . from the primitiue tyme till the reign of K. Henry viii* (London, 1570), 699, 740, 754, 758, 762, 781, 782, 785, 786, 866–867. On Field's relation to the Clothworkers, see Ramsay, "Clothworkers, Merchant Adventurers and Richard Hakluyt," 514–517.

8. N. R. Ker, "Books at Christ Church, 1562–1602," in *The Collegiate University*, ed. James McConica, vol. 3 of *The History of the University of Oxford*, gen. ed. T. H. Aston, 8 vols. (Oxford, 1984–2000), 502–513; Mark H. Curtis, *Oxford and Cambridge in Transition, 1558–1642* (Oxford, 1959), 234–236. See also *DNB*, s.v. "Craddock, Edward," and "Savile, Henry"; and Craddock, *The Shippe of assured Safetie, wherein one may sayle towards the land of the living, promised to the True Israelites* ([London?], 1571). On Hakluyt and Thomas Savile, see Mordechai Feingold, *The Mathematician's Apprenticeship: Science, Universities and Society in England, 1560–1640* (Cambridge, 1984), 72, 131. Montagu, the fan of Savile, spent his career defending the Church of England in the early seventeenth century, believing that he needed to find others "to stand in the gap against puritanisme and popery, the Scilla and Charybdis of Ancient Piety." Mountagu [sic] to John Cosin, June 28, [1624], in *The Correspondence of John Cosin*, Publications of the Surtees Society, 52, pt. 1 (1868): 21.

9. Epistle Dedicatory to Walsingham, in *Principall Navigations* (1589), sig. *2^r.

10. Camden, *Annales* (1630), 123–124.

11. Wood, *History and Antiquities*, 2:170–171; Camden, *Annales* (1625), 2:266–267; Howes, *Annales* (1631), 667–668.

12. See *DNB*, s.v. "Cecil, William."

13. Hakluyt the elder to Lord Burleigh, February 28, 1571, in *Writings and Correspondence*, 1:90–91.

14. Guerau de Spes to Philip II, 1571, and Hakluyt the elder to Burleigh, November 7, 1571, both in *Writings and Correspondence*, 1:91–92, 93–95.

15. Unless otherwise noted, the material from Hawkes can be found in "A relation of the commodities of Nova Hispania, and the maners of the inhabitants, written by Henry Hawkes marchant," in *Principall Navigations* (1589), 545–553.

16. Hawkes's report, for example, was no match for the writings of the Huguenot missionary Jean de Léry, who described the Tupinambas of Brazil; Jan Huyghen van Linschoten (or John Huighen van Linschoten, as the English called him), whose epic travels included details about the peoples of India; and Thomas Harriot, who (with Hakluyt's help) later created one of the most enduring depictions of any Native American population when he returned from Roanoke in the mid-1580s. On the development of ethnography and the central role that early modern travelers played in it, see Margaret T. Hodgen, *Early Anthropology in the Sixteenth and Seventeenth Centuries* (Philadelphia, 1964), and Peter C. Mancall, ed., *Travel Narratives from the Age of Discovery: An Anthology* (New York, 2006), 3–14.

17. Hans Staden, *Warhafftige historia vnnd beschreibung einer landtschafft der wilden nacketen grimmigen menschfresser leuthen in der newen welt America* (Frankfurt, 1557[?]).

18. Wood, *History and Antiquities*, 2:171–172.

19. Wood, *History and Antiquities*, 2:173–179, 184–185. The man excommunicated,

William Noble, lying ill and fearing death, later apologized for his actions, and the excommunication was rescinded in 1576. Noble made an unexpected recovery and even became mayor of Oxford in 1581. See Wood, *History and Antiquities,* 2:185–186.

20. Camden, *Annales* (1625), 2:319–320. Well into the seventeenth century, English observers tried to understand the meaning of such celestial events. "Whatsoever was the materiall of this Comet, howsoever compact, and dissolved," John Bainbridge wrote about a comet that appeared in 1619, "I am enforced in conclusion of this Astronomicall part, to lie prostrate at the Almighties power in the globositie thereof, to admire his wisdome in the motion, and adore his goodnesse in the present apparition." See Bainbridge, *An Astronomicall Description of the late Comet* (London, 1619), 17.

21. Camden, born in 1551, had been educated in London before moving to Oxford, where he was at Magdalen College, Broadgates Hall (now Pembroke College), and then Christ Church, where he remained until he took a position at Westminister School in 1575. See *A Collection of Curious Discourses written by Eminent Antiquaries upon several heads in our English Antiquities,* 2 vols. (London, 1771), 2:425. This book was based on Thomas Hearne's book of the same title published in Oxford in 1720 and included material, including the brief biographical sketch of Camden, that did not exist in the first edition.

22. Camden, *Annales* (1625), 2:347–348.

23. "Hakluyt Chronology," 1:267; *Principall Navigations* (1589), sig. *2ʳ.

24. Camden, *Annales* (1625), 2:363–364.

25. Camden, *Annales* (1625), 2:364; Humphrey Gilbert, *A Discourse of a Discoverie for a new Passage to Cataia* (London, 1576). For a narrative of Martin Frobisher's first voyage, see James McDermott, *Martin Frobisher: Elizabethan Privateer* (New Haven and London, 2001), 120–152.

26. Camden, *Annales* (1625), 2:364–365.

CHAPTER 4. Oxford, 1577

1. Lists of tutors at Christ Church during this period are not extant, but as David Quinn has argued, such a position would have been logical for an individual in Hakluyt's position. The Clothworkers, who had already provided assistance, continued to support him with a pension that began in June 1578, though the company also supported another scholar; see "Hakluyt Chronology," 1:267–273.

2. See Penry Williams, "Elizabethan Oxford: State, Church, and University," in *The Collegiate University,* ed. James McConica, vol. 3 of *The History of the University of Oxford,* gen. ed. T. H. Aston, 8 vols. (Oxford, 1984–2000), 413.

3. Wood, *History and Antiquities,* 2:188–192.

4. There are conflicting accounts of the number who perished. Wood claimed 510 deaths; Camden believed that 300 died; Stow counted approximately 500. The numbers, including Ethryg's count, can be found in John Ward, "An Account of the Black Assizes at Oxford, from the Register of Merton College in that University," *Philosophical Transactions of the Royal Society,* 50, pt. 2, for 1758 (1759): 699–703. Lord Burghley reported that among the dead were "fiftie schollers and twenty townesmen." Burghley to the Earl of Shrewsbury, August 4, 1577, in William H. Turner, ed., *Selections from the Records of the City of Oxford* (Oxford, 1880), 392.

5. Charles Creighton, *A History of Epidemics in Britain, from AD 664 to the Extinction of Plague* (Cambridge, 1891), 125; Wood, *History and Antiquities,* 1:449–450; see also David

Herlihy, *The Black Death and the Transformation of the West*, ed. Samuel K. Cohn, Jr. (Cambridge, Mass., 1997).

6. J. F. D. Shrewsbury, *A History of Bubonic Plague in the British Isles* (Cambridge, 1970), 149, 39, 81; J. T. C. Nash, *Evolution and Disease* (Bristol, 1915), 10; Creighton, *History of Epidemics*, 288 (1503), 243 (1485), 247–248 (1517), 260 (1551), 339 (1571), 340 (1575); Wood, *History and Antiquities*, 1:660–661 (1503), 665 (1508), 2:13 (1517), 170 (1571), 179 (1575).

7. Thomas Elyot, *The Castle of Health, corrected, and in some places Augmented* (London, 1610), 137–140; Jhon Caius, *A boke, or counseill against the disease commonly called the sweate, or sweatyng sicknesse* ([London], 1552), quotation at fol. 7ᵛ; Konrad Gesner, *The newe Jewell of Health*, trans. George Baker (London, 1576), 170ʳ⁻ᵛ (bones and excrement), 174ʳ (frogs), 244ᵛ–245ʳ (gold). For herbals and apothecaries offering suggestions for specific symptoms but none with a cure for this kind of illness, see, e.g., Apulius Barberus (pseud.), *Herbarium* [Rome, c. 1483–1484]; *A boke of the propertyes of herbes the whiche is called an herbal* [London, 1539?]; [Anthony Askha[m]?], *A litle herball of the properties of herbes, newly amended & corrected, wyth certayn additions at the end of the boke, declaring what herbes hath influence of certain Sterres and constellations, wherby maye be chosen the best and most lucky tymes and dayes of their ministracion, according to the Moone beyng in the signes of heave[n] the which is daily appoi[n]ted in the Almanacke made in ... M.D.L.* [London, 1561]; William Turner, *The first and seconde partes of the herbal of William Turner Doctor in Phisick, lately oversene / corrected and enlarged with the Thirde parte / lately gathered / and nowe set out with the names of the herbes / in Greke Latin / English / Duche / Frenche / and in the Apothecaries and herbaries Latin / with the properties / degrees / and naturall places of the same* (Collen, 1568).

8. T[homas] B[rasbridge], *The Poor mans Jewell, that is to say, a treatise of the Pestilence. Unto the which is annexed a declaration of the vertues of the hearbes Carduus Benedictus, and Angelica: which are verie medicinable, both against the plague, & also against many other diseases. Gathered out of the Bookes of divers lerned Physicians* (London, 1578), sigs. [Aviʳ] (God's punishment), [Aviᵛ] (astronomers' warnings), [Aviiʳ]–Bʳ (pollution), Bᵛ (meat and drink), Biiiʳ (public and private sins), Cviᵛ–[Dviiᵛ] (Carduus Benedictus and Angelica), Ciiiiʳ–Cvᵛ (symptoms of plague). Brasbridge's belief that polluted air caused the epidemic fit prevailing clinical theories about plague, and even though the epidemic of 1577 was not plague itself, physicians proved as ill-equipped to treat it as if it were the return of plague.

9. Stow repeated the list of prominent victims and then offered his statistical summary. "There died in *Oxforde out of the newe founde worlde, wherein is declared the rare and singuler vertues of diverse and sundrie Hearbes, Trees, Oyles, Plantes, and Stones, with their applications, aswell for Phisicke as Chirurgerie . . . Englished by John Frampton* (London, 1577), sig. * ijᵛ–[* iijʳ], fol. 2ʳ.

10. E. A. Wrigley and R. S. Schofield, *The Population History of England, 1541–1871: A Reconstruction* (Cambridge, Mass., 1981), 332–340; Wood, *History and Antiquities*, 2:192. Even the deadliest months of July and August 1577, in which mortality soared in Oxford, had little obvious impact on national death rates; neither month represented an increase of even 10 percent of the national trend. See Wrigley and Schofield, *Population History of England*, 338–339.

11. Thomas Cogan, *The Haven of Health: Chiefely gathered for the comfort of Students, and consequently of all those that have a care of their health . . . With a short Censure of the late sicknes at Oxford* (London, 1584), 281.

12. [Francis Bacon], *Sylva Sylvarum, Or A Natural History in ten Centuries* (London,

1627), Century 10, 914; R[obert] P[lot], *The Natural History of Oxfordshire, Being an Essay toward the Natural History of England* (London, 1677), 23–25; comments by Thomas Birch in Ward, "An Account of the Black Assize at Oxford," 703; John Pringle, *Observations on the Diseases of the Army*, 7th ed. (London, 1775), 329–332. The inability to identify this epidemic is not unique: the so-called sweating sickness, which struck Britain periodically from 1485 to 1551, continues to defy modern diagnosis. See Alan Dyer, "The English Sweating Sickness of 1551: An Epidemic Anatomized," *Medical History* 41 (1997): 362–384; Guy Thwaites et al., "The English Sweating Sickness, 1485 to 1551," *New England Journal of Medicine* 336 (1997), 580–582; Mark Taviner et al., "The English Sweating Sickness, 1485–1551: A Viral Pulmonary Disease?" *Medical History* 42 (1998), 96–98; and E. Bridson, "The English 'Sweate' (Sudor Anglicus) and Hantavirus Pulmonary Syndrome," *British Journal of Biomedical Science* 58 (2001), 1–6. For the larger medical context, see Nancy G. Siraisi, *Medieval and Early Renaissance Medicine: An Introduction to Knowledge and Practice* (Chicago, 1990), 128–129.

13. [Nicholas Monardes], *Joyfull Newes out of the newe founde worlde, wherein is declared the rare and singuler vertues of diverse and sundrie Hearbes, Trees, Oyles, Plantes, and Stones, with their applications, aswell for Phisicke as Chirurgerie . . . Englished by John Frampton* (London, 1577), sig. *ij^v–[* iij^r], fol. 2^r.

14. [Monardes], *Joyfull Newes*, fols. 27^v, 35^r, 51^r, 76^v, 58^v–59^r, 100^r. For the appeal of tobacco at the time, see Peter C. Mancall, "Tales Tobacco Told in Sixteenth-Century Europe," *Environmental History* 9 (2004): 648–661; on Monardes, see Daniela Bleichmar, "Books, Bodies, and Fields: Sixteenth-Century Transatlantic Encounters with New World Materia Medica," in Londa Schiebinger and Claudia Swan, eds., *Colonial Botany: Science, Commerce, and Politics* (Philadelphia, 2004), 83–99.

15. John Parker, *Books to Build an Empire: A Bibliographical History of English Overseas Interests to 1620* (Amsterdam, 1965), 76, claims that Hakluyt had a longstanding interest in plants, but there is no evidence to demonstrate that he had developed this fascination by 1577.

16. Stow, *Chronicle*, 1190, 1193. For details about Frobisher's three expeditions, see the superb study by James McDermott, *Martin Frobisher: Elizabethan Privateer* (New Haven and London, 2001), as well as Thomas H. B. Symons, ed., *Meta Incognita: A Discourse of Discovery: Martin Frobisher's Arctic Expeditions, 1576–1578*, 2 vols. (Hull, Que., 1999).

17. Thomas Churchyard, *A Prayse, and Reporte of Maister Martyne Frobishers Voyage to Meta Incognita (A Name given by a mightie and most great Personage) in which praise and report is written divers discourses never published by any man as yet* (London, 1578), sigs. [Avi^v–Avii^r], Biii^v–Biiii^r. Maunsell's shop was one of many in the publishing heart of London; see Peter W. M. Blayney, *The Bookshops in Paul's Cross Churchyard*, Occasional Papers of the Bibliography Society 5 (London, 1990).

18. Churchyard, *Prayse, and Reporte*, sig. Biiii^v–Bv^v.

19. Churchyard, *Prayse, and Reporte*, sig. Bv^v–[Bvi^v].

20. Churchyard, *Prayse, and Reporte*, sig. Bvii^r–Bvii^v. The original drawing no longer exists. Perhaps White himself was on the expedition, though there is no clear evidence to indicate his presence other than the existence of a single painting. See Paul Hulton, *America in 1585: The Complete Drawings of John White* (Chapel Hill, N.C., 1984), 8.

21. Churchyard, *Prayse and Reporte*, sig. [Bvii^v–Bviii^r].

22. Churchyard, *Prayse, and Reporte*, sig. [Bviii^v]–Ci^r.

23. Churchyard, *Prayse, and Reporte*, sig. Ci^r–Cii^r.

24. Churchyard, *Prayse, and Reporte,* sig. Ciiiᵛ–Cvᵛ.

25. For an excellent analysis of two of the central texts, see Mary C. Fuller, "'Ravenous Strangers': The Argument of Nationalism in Two Narratives from Hakluyt's *Principal Navigations,*" *Studies in Travel Writing* 6 (2002): 1–28, esp. 3–8, 16–23.

26. This is not intended to suggest that the mere fact of printing meant that everyone had access to all printed texts on a certain subject. Then, as now, much knowledge was available to some individuals but for varied reasons—the unavailability of a certain book, a reader's inability to read certain languages—most people gained only limited access to the information that appeared in printed books. Historians, able to gather together many texts that contemporaries were probably unable to see, have the advantage of describing what one twentieth-century information scholar termed "undiscovered public knowledge"—the range of information on a topic that existed at a certain time but was not available to all equally. See Don R. Swanson, "Undiscovered Public Knowledge," *Library Quarterly* 56 (1986): 103–118. It is also necessary to recognize that the rise of print did not halt the continued spread of ideas in manuscript or by word of mouth; these forms of distributing information continued along with the growing volume of printed materials. On this phenomenon, see Harold Love, *Scribal Publication in Seventeenth-Century England* (Oxford, 1993); and David McKitterick, *Print, Manuscript and the Search for Order, 1450–1830* (Cambridge, 2003).

27. It was during Hakluyt's time that the English began to demonstrate new concerns for the nature and representation of knowledge, evident in the rise of double-entry bookkeeping and the discipline of chorography, which developed in response to the growth in travel accounts. See Mary Poovey, *A History of the Modern Fact: Problems of Knowledge in the Sciences of Wealth and Society* (Chicago, 1998), esp. 29–91, and Barbara J. Shapiro, *A Culture of Fact: England, 1550–1720* (Ithaca, N.Y., 2000), esp. 63–85.

28. Dionyse Settle, *A True reporte of the laste voyage into the West and Northwest regions, &c. 1577, worthily achieved by Capteine Frobisher of the sayde voyage the first finder and Generall. With a description of the people there inhabiting, and other circumstances notable* (London, 1577), sigs. Bᵛ, Biijᵛ, Bvʳ.

29. Settle, *True reporte,* sig. Bvᵛ–[Bviʳ], [Bviʳ⁻ᵛ].

30. Settle, *True reporte,* sig. [Bviᵛ–Bviiʳ].

31. Settle, *True reporte,* sig. [Bviiiᵛ], Cᵛ–Cijʳ.

32. Settle, *True reporte,* sig. Ciiijʳ–Cvʳ.

33. Settle, *True reporte,* sig. Cvʳ–[Diiiʳ].

34. Thomas Ellis, *A true reporte of the third and last voyage into Meta incognita . . . by Martine Frobisher* (London, 1578), sigs. Avʳ⁻ᵛ, Avᵛ–[Aviʳ].

35. Ellis, *True reporte,* sig. [Aviiʳ–Aviiiᵛ].

36. Ellis, *True reporte,* sig. Biiᵛ–Biiiʳ.

37. Ellis, *True reporte,* sig. Bvᵛ–[Bviʳ].

38. [George Best], *A True Discourse of the late voyages of discoverie, for the finding of a passage to Cathaya, by the Northwest, under the conduct of Martin Frobisher* (London, 1578), title page verso–sig. Aijʳ.

39. *New American World,* 4:191; Michael Lok, "The doynges of Captayne Furbusher; Amongest the Companyes busynes," in James McDermott, ed., *The Third Voyage of Martin Frobisher to Baffin Island, 1578,* Hak Soc., 3rd Ser., 6 (London, 2001), 71–102, quotation at 101; Camden, *Annales* (1625), 2:363–365.

40. Dodding's postmortem report and the record of the burials can be found in *New American World*, 4:216–218; see also Sir James Watt and Ann Savours, "The Captured 'Countrey People': Their Depiction and Medical History," in Symons, ed., *Meta Incognita*, 2:553–562. For the engravings, see *La navigation du capitaine Martin Forbisher* (La Rochelle, 1578); and *Beschreibung der schiffart des haubtmans Martine Forbissher* (Nuremberg, 1580).

41. Ookijoxy Ninoo's story is found in Susan Rowley, "Frobisher Miksanut: Inuit Accounts of the Frobisher Voyages," in William W. Fitzhugh and Jacqueline S. Olin, eds., *Archaeology of the Frobisher Voyages* (Washington, D.C., 1993), 27–40.

42. *Divers Voyages*, title page verso; *Principall Navigations* (1589), 615–641.

43. "Hakluyt Chronology," 1:268.

44. James O. Halliwell, ed., *The Private Diary of Dr. John Dee, and the Catalogue of His Library and Manuscripts* (London, 1892), 3; [John Dee], *General and Rare Memorials pertayning to the Perfect Arte of Navigation* [London, 1577], 7. This was not the first time Dee referred to such contacts in print; in his preface to Euclid's *Geometry* he praised Gilbert's efforts in Ireland. See *The Elements of Geometrie of the most auncient Philosopher Euclide of Megara. Faithfully (now first) translated into the Englishe toung, by H. Billingsley . . . With a very fruitfull Praeface made by M. I. Dee* (London, 1570), sig. Aj^r. The relationship between the lawyer and Dee continued to at least June 1578; see Halliwell, ed., *Private Diary of Dr. John Dee*, 4.

45. Thomas Churchyard, *A generall rehersall of warres, called Churchyardes Choise* (London, 1579), sig. Di^{r-v}.

46. Churchyard, *Generall rehearsall of warres*, sig. Dii^v–Diiii^r.

47. David Beers Quinn, ed., *The Voyages and Colonising Expeditions of Sir Humphrey Gilbert*, 2 vols., Hak. Soc., 2nd Ser., 83 (London, 1940), 1:188–194.

48. The older Hakluyt wrote this letter in 1578; the younger Hakluyt published it in *Divers Voyages* in 1582 (sig. K^r–Kiii^v).

49. See *New American World*, 3:199–210.

50. *Discourse*, 76.

51. *The order of prayer upon Wednesdayes and Frydayes, to avert and turne Gods wrath from us, threatned by the late terrible earthquake, to be used in al parish Churches.* (London, [1580]); *A Discourse containing many wonderfull examples of Gods indignation poured uppon divers people for their intollerable sinnes* (London, 1580), title page verso.

52. Thomas Churchyard, *A warning for the wise, a fear to the fond, a bridle to the lewde, and a glasse to the good. Written of the late Earthquake chanced in London and other places, the 6. of April 1580* (London, 1580). Within hours of the first tremor, printers were eager to publish books and pamphlets about the event. On April 8, three printers arrived at the Stationers' Company to register titles relating to the earthquake; one of them promised to produce a work (unfortunately no longer extant) entitled *comme from the plai, comme from the playe: the house will fall so people will saye: the earth quakes lett us hast[e] awaye.* Three days later two more titles entered the register, including Twyne's. By the end of June printers registered nine more titles, including one put forward by Ric Jones, who promised to publish a ballad entitled *quake quake yt is tyme to quake when towers and townes and all Doo shake.* Alas, no copies of that verse exist. See *Stationers' Registers*, 2:167^v–170^r. Twyne's book was published as T. T., *A shorte and pithie Discourse, concerning the engendring, tokens, and effects of all Earthquakes in Generall: Particularly applyed and conferred with that most*

strange and terrible worke of the Lord in shaking the Earth, not only within the Citie of London, but also in most partes of all Englande: Which hapned upon Wensday in Easter weeke last past, which was the sixt day of April, almost at sixe a clocke in the evening, in the yeare of our Lord God 1580 (London, 1580).

53. Churchyard, *Warning for the wise*, sig. [Aiv^v]–B^r.

54. Churchyard, *Warning for the wise*, sig. B^v.

55. Churchyard, *Warning for the wise*, sig. B^v–Bi^r.

56. Churchyard, *Warning for the wise*, sig. Ciiii^v.

57. [Gabriel Harvey], *Three Proper and wittie, familiar Letters: lately passed betweene two Universitie men: touching the Earthquake in Aprill last, and our English refourmed Versifying* (London, 1580), in Alexander Grosbart, ed., *The Works of Gabriel Harvey*, 3 vols. (London, 1884), 1:41ff.

58. T[wyne], *Shorte and pithie Discourse*, sigs. Aj^r–Aiiij^v (natural properties), B^{r-v} (signs and darkness), Bii^v–Biij^v (perceptions and damage).

59. T[wyne], *Shorte and pithie Discourse*, sig. Biij^v–C^v; Stow, *Chronicles*, 1210.

60. Wood, *History and Antiquities*, 199.

61. *Order of prayer*, title page, sig. [aii^v].

62. *Order of prayer*, title page verso (order of prayers in the service), sig. Dv^{r-v} (preface).

63. *A Discourse containing many wonderfull examples of Gods indignation poured uppon divers people for their intollerable sinnes: Al which ought of us to bee taken (as they are in deede) most fatherlie Admonitions, that by them we may be warned to amend our sinful lyves* (London, 1580), title page verso (description of the 1580 earthquake), sigs. Cij^r–Cij^v (biblical precedents), Ciij^{r-v} (other recent signs), Ciiij^r (God's purpose).

64. *Discourse containing many wonderfull examples of Gods indignation*, sig. F^v–Fiii^r.

65. Richard Willes, *The History of Travayle in the West and East Indies, and other countreys lying either way, towardes the fruitfull and rych Moluccas* (London, 1577), sig. iiii^r.

CHAPTER 5. Oxford, c. 1580

1. "Hakluyt Chronology," 1:272; Henry L. Thompson, *University of Oxford College Histories: Christ Church* (London, 1900), 35. Though the record is silent on the question, it is possible that Hakluyt sought ordination precisely so that he could retain his support at Oxford, which was available primarily to former students who were ordained (as well as some who studied law and medicine). If this were the case, it is possible that he had a change of heart, since he suggested in the dedication of the last volume of the revised *Principal Navigations* (London, 1600) that he was shifting his efforts away from geography and toward his clerical career. See Mordechai Feingold, "Science as a Calling? The Early Modern Dilemma," *Science in Context* 15 (2002): 79–119, esp. 86–87, 95–96.

2. Camden, *Annales* (1625), 2:409–410; Roy Porter, *London: A Social History* (Cambridge, Mass., 1995), 42–46, quotation at 42. For density of settlements, see, e.g., [Georg Braun], *Civitates Orbis Terrarum*, 6 vols. [1593–1618], 1:sig A^r–[Ai^r], HEH 180544; John Norden, *Speculum Britanniae. The first parte* ([London?], 1593), map following 26 (in HEH 18635).

3. Malcolm Letts, *Mandeville's Travels: Texts and Translations*, 2 vols., Hak. Soc.,2nd Ser., 101–102 (London, 1953), 101:xxxvii–xxxii, xxxv–xxxviii; C. W. R. D. Moseley, trans., *The Travels of Sir John Mandeville* (London, 1983), 9–10.

4. Edward Lynam, *The Mapmaker's Art: Essays on the History of Maps* (London, 1953), 1–3; see J. B. Harley, "Meaning and Ambiguity in Tudor Cartography," in Sarah Tyacke, ed., *English Map-Making, 1500–1650* (London, 1983), 22–45.

5. P. D. A. Harvey, *Maps in Tudor England* (Chicago, 1993), 7 (Shakespeare); Peter Eden, "Three Elizabethan Estate Surveyors: Peter Kempe, Thomas Clerke and Thomas Langdon," in Tyacke, ed., *English Map-Making*, 68–78 (mapping of estates); Valentine Leigh, *The Moste Profitable and commendable Science, of Surveiyng of Landes, Tenementes, and Hereditamentes* (London, 1578); Peter Barber, "England II: Monarchs, Ministers, and Maps, 1550–1625," in David Buisseret, ed., *Monarchs, Ministers, and Maps: The Emergence of Cartography as a Tool of Government in Early Modern Europe* (Chicago, 1992), 57–98 (cartography and the state). For technical advances, see David Woodward, "The Woodcut Technique," and Coolie Verner, "Copperplate Printing," in Woodward, ed., *Five Centuries of Map Printing* (Chicago, 1975), 25–75.

6. [Christopher Saxton], *Atlas of the County of England and Wales* (London, 1590?], HEH 82871.

7. George B. Parks, *Hakluyt and the English Voyages* (New York, 1928), 25–38, 238; Sir Lynden L. Macassey, *The Middle Temple's Contribution to the National Life* (London, [1930]), 21–29, 115; George Godwin, *The Middle Temple: The Society and Fellowship* (London, 1954), 144–146; John Hutchinson, *A Catalogue of Notable Middle Templars, with Brief Biographical Notices* (London, 1902), 78–79 (includes mention of Sir Francis Drake); Charles Henry Hopwood, ed., *Middle Temple Records*, 3 vols. (London, 1904), 1:100 (admission on May 26, 1555), 321 (notice of his death).

8. Hakluyt (lawyer) to Ortelius, 1567–1568, in *Writings and Correspondence*, 1:81–83. It should be noted here that this letter does not bear a date and that the two printed editions differ about when it was written. The standard collection of materials relating to Ortelius dated the letter to c. 1590, which suggests it could have been written by either of the two Hakluyts. By contrast, in *Writings and Correspondence*, the editor, E. G. R. Taylor, arrived at a date based on internal evidence within the letter and suggested that it was in all likelihood written in 1567 or 1568. (The situation is muddled by the fact that Taylor provided an incorrect citation to the letter.) The compelling logic for dating this letter to 1567 or 1568 is explained in *Writings and Correspondence*, 77–78n. For the earlier printing, which included a sketch of how the map should be designed, see Joannes Henricus Hessels, ed., *Ecclesiae Londino-Batavae archiuum; tomus primus; Abrahami Ortelli (geographi Antverpiensis) et virorum eruditorum ad eundem et ad Jacobum Colium Ortelianum (Abrahami Ortelii sororis filium) epistulae* (Cambridge, 1887), no. 172 (pp. 415–418). The Hakluyts were not the only scholars in England impressed by Ortelius's abilities; John Dee wrote to Ortelius in January 1577, praising the mapmaker's deep knowledge and the "immortal glory" of his name, and William Camden wrote to Ortelius later that year thanking him for meeting with him when Ortelius was in London. See Dee to Ortelius, January 16, 1577, and Camden to Ortelius, August 4, 1577, both in Hessels, ed., *Abrahami Ortelli*, 157–160, 167–169.

9. Hakluyt to Ortelius, 1567–1568, 1:81–83.

10. The material that follows here is from Anthony Parkhurst to Hakluyt (lawyer), November 13, 1578, in *Principall Navigations* (1589), 674–677.

11. See Peter E. Pope, *Fish into Wine: The Newfoundland Plantation in the Seventeenth Century* (Chapel Hill, N.C., 2004), 1–32.

12. Hakluyt to Morgan Hubblethorne, 1579, in *Principall Navigations* (1589), 454–455.

13. The material in this and the following paragraphs is taken from "A Pamphlet by Richard Hakluyt the Younger, 1579–80," in *Writings and Correspondence*, 1:139–146. As the literary critic Richard Helgerson has effectively argued, this pamphlet was only the first effort by Hakluyt to promote mercantile activity, an action that helped legitimize commerce as a motive for overseas expeditions; see Helgerson, *Forms of Nationhood: The Elizabethan Writing of England* (Chicago, 1992), 163–166. Hakluyt, it should be emphasized, was not the only author whose writings promoted mercantile endeavors. As the historian Laura Stevenson has demonstrated, concerns with merchants and their activities became a fixture in Elizabethan literature, a reflection of widespread changes in the culture and economy of England during her reign. See Stevenson, *Praise and Paradox: Merchants and Craftsmen in Elizabethan Popular Literature* (Cambridge, 1984), esp. 1–74.

14. In his summary of geographical knowledge printed two years later, La Popilinière also believed that the passage existed, as his map of the world made clear. See Lancelot-Voisin, sieur de La Popelinière, *Les Trois Mondes* (Paris, 1582), map opposite the first page of the "Premier Livre Des Tres Mondes."

15. "Note by Richard Hakluyt the Younger," in *Writings and Correspondence*, 1:163–164; cf. John Dee, *General and rare memorials pertaining to the perfect arte of navigation* (London, 1577).

16. The material that follows here can be found in "Notes in writing, besides more privie by mouth, that were given by M. Richard Hakluyt . . . To M. Arthur Pet, and to M. Charles Jackman," in *Principall Navigations* (1589), 460–466.

17. [Hans Weigel], *Habitus Præcipuorum Populorum, Tam Virorum Quam fæminarum Singulari arte depicti* (Nuremberg, 1577); *A Niewe Herball, or Historie of Plantes . . . first set foorth in the Doutche or Almaigne tongue, by that learned D. Rembert Dodoens, Physition to the Emperour*, trans. Henry Lyte (London, 1577).

18. For information about China then available in Europe, see Jonathan Spence, *The Chan's Great Continent: China in Western Minds* (New York, 1998), esp. 1–27.

19. Gerard Mercator to Hakluyt, July 28, 1580, in *Writings and Correspondence*, 1:159–162; see 161n for the details about the translation.

20. Camden, *Annales* (1625), 2:429–430.

21. Giovanni Battista Ramusio, *Terzo volume delle Navigationi et Viaggi* (Venice, 1556) ff. 435–453; *A Shorte and briefe narration of the two Nauigations and Discoueries to the Northweast partes called Newe France: First translated out of French into Italian, by that famous learned man Gio: Bapt: Ramusius, and now turned into English by Iohn Florio: Worthy the reading of all Venturers, Trauellers, and Discouerers* (London, 1580), sig. Aij^r. For the attribution to Hakluyt, see *Writings and Correspondence*, 1:164–168. In his study of *Divers Voyages* and the *Shorte and briefe Narration*, David B. Quinn noted that Hakluyt had "provided much of the material for Florio's address to his readers" in addition to making substantial changes to parts of the text." See Quinn, *Richard Hakluyt, Editor* (Amsterdam, 1967), 7.

22. The first account of Cartier's exploration to appear in print was his *Brief recit, & succincte narration, de la faicte es ysles de Canada, Hochelaga & Saguenay & autres, avec particulieres meurs, langaige, & ceremonies des hahitans d'icelles: forst delectable à veoir* (Paris, 1545). Cartier's journey of 1542–1544, the subject of his *Brief recit*, also played a minor role as the setting for part of the sixty-seventh story in Marguerite d'Angoulême's *Histoires des amas fortunez* (Paris, 1558), which began to be known by its modern name, *L'Heptaméron*, in 1559.

23. *Shorte and briefe narration,* sig. Bj^{r-v}.

24. *Shorte and briefe narration,* sig. Bj^{v}–Bij^{r}.

25. *Shorte and briefe narration,* sig. Bij^{r}.

26. *Shorte and briefe narration,* sig. Bij^{r-v}. Modern readers are often struck by the use of the term *reduce* in this context. Hakluyt and others used the term not in reference to indigenous cultures, which they found inferior and so in theory wanted to raise up to European standards, but instead in the sense that Native Americans possessed excessive wildness and needed to be tamed (reduced) to make them fit vessels for European colonization. See James Axtell, *The European and the Indian: Essays in the Ethnohistory of Colonial North America* (New York, 1981), 45–46.

27. *Shorte and briefe narration,* sig. Bij^{v}.

28. The original plan of Drake's voyage survives in fragment only, but enough remains to demonstrate his intent, the support he received, and his goals for his return; see E. G. R. Taylor, "The Missing Draft Project of Drake's Voyage of 1577–80," *Geographical Journal* 75 (1930): 46–47; and Harry Kelsey, *Sir Francis Drake: The Queen's Pirate* (New Haven and London, 1998), 172–174.

29. Camden, *Annales* (1625), 2:420–426. Fourteen years later an English author brought together current wisdom on bleeding in a detailed but small volume; see N[icholas] G[yer], *The English Phlebotomy: Or, Method and way of healing by letting of blood* (London, 1592). The best modern description of Drake's circumnavigation can be found in Kelsey, *Sir Francis Drake,* 93–204.

30. Camden, *Annales* (1625), 2:426–428.

31. Don Antonio de Padilla to Philip II, August 6, 7, 11, 16, 23, 31, and September 5, 1570, all in Zelia Nuttall, trans. and ed., *New Light on Drake: A Collection of Documents Relating to His Voyage of Circumnavigation, 1577–1580,* Hak. Soc., 2nd Ser., 34 (London, 1914), 400–405; "The Answer of the Spanish Ambassador," October 29, 1580, *Cal. Foreign,* 14:463–464; David B. Quinn, *Sir Francis Drake as Seen by His Contemporaries* (Providence, R.I., 1996), 5–6; La Popolinière, *Les Trois Mondes,* sig. ee iiij^{r-v}; Sir Edward Stafford to Sir Francis Walsingham, October 16, 1584, *Cal. Foreign,* 19:108.

32. Nicholas Breton, *A discourse in commendation of the valiant gentleman, maister Frauncis Drake, with a rejoysing of his happy adventures* (London, 1581); Quinn, *Drake as Seen by His Contemporaries,* 9–10; Stephen Parmenius, *De Navigatione illustris et magnanimi equities aurati Humfredi Gilberti* (London, 1582), trans. as "An Embarkation Poem for the voyage projected by the celebrated and noble Sir Humphrey Gilbert," in David B. Quinn and Neil M. Cheshire, eds., *The New Found Land of Stephen Parmenius: The Life and Writings of a Hungarian Poet, Drowned on a Voyage from Newfoundland, 1583* (Toronto, 1972), 103; W[illiam] B[urrough], *A Discours of the variation of the Cumpas, or Magneticall Needle* ([London], 1581), sig. [*iiij^{v}]; [Charles D'Ecluse], *Caroli Clusii Atreb. Aliquot Notæ in Garciæ Aromatum Historiam* (Antwerp, 1582), 9–10 (cocoanut), , 28–30 (cacao), 32–34 (*Drakena radix*); Queen Elizabeth to E. Tremayne, October 22, 1580, in Zuttall, ed., *New Light on Drake,* 429–430; Lewes Roberts, *The Merchants Mappe of Commerce* (London, 1638), 61.

33. See, e.g., Henry Haslop, *Newes Out of the Coast of Spaine. The true Report of the honourable service for England, perfourmed by Sir Frauncis Drake in the moneths of Aprill and May last past, 1587 . . . discoursed at large with everie severall exploit of their fortunate successe* (London, 1587); [Thomas Greepe], *The true and perfecte Newes of the woorthy and valiaunt exploytes, performed and doone by that valiant Knight Syr Frauncis Drake* (London, 1587);

[Walter Bigges], *A Summarie and True Discourse of Sir Frances Drakes West Indian Voyage* (London, 1589); David B. Quinn, "Early Accounts of the Famous Voyage," in Norman J. W. Thrower, ed., *Sir Francis Drake and the Famous Voyage, 1577–1580: Essays Commemorating the Quadricentennial of Drake's Circumnavigation of the Earth* (Berkeley, Calif., 1984), 33–34; *Principall Navigations* (1589), unpaginated section between 643 and 644; Sir Francis Drake, *The World Encompassed, Being his next voyage to that to Nombre de Dios formerly imprinted; Carefully collected out of the notes of master Francis Fletcher* (London, 1628).

34. William Bourne, *A Regiment for the Sea: Conteyning most profitable Rules, Mathematical experiences, and perfect knowledge of Navigation, for all Coastes and Countreys: most needefull and ncessarie for all Seafaring men and Travellers, as Pilotes, Mariners, Marchants, &c.* (London, [1574]), fol. 6ʳ. Bourne, who lacked a college education, wrote books on navigation, inventions, and gunnery; *Regiment for the Sea*, his most popular tract (a second edition appeared in 1580), drew on the work of others, notably Richard Eden's *Arte of Navigation* (London, 1561), a translation of Martin Cortés's *Breve compendio de la sphera y de la arte de navegar.*

35. *Divers Voyages,* title page.

36. *Divers Voyages,* [iᵛ–iiʳ], contain the list of authorities described in this and the next two paragraphs.

37. *Divers Voyages,* sig. qʳ.

38. *Divers Voyages,* sig. qʳ⁻ᵛ.

39. *Divers Voyages,* sig. opposite sig. q, q2ʳ⁻ᵛ. The original of the passage reads: *Magna tamet si pauca de nova Frobisheri navigatione seribis, quam miror ante mulotos annos no[n] fuisse attentatam. Non enim dubium est, quin recta & grevis via pateat in occidentem Cathaium usq. In quod regno[m] si recte navigationem instituunt, nobilissimas totius mundi merces colligent, & multis Gentibus adhuc idololatatros Christi nomen communicabunt.*

40. *Divers Voyages,* sig. q2ᵛ.

41. *Divers Voyages,* sig. q2ᵛ.

42. *Divers Voyages,* sig. q2ᵛ–4ʳ.

43. *Divers Voyages,* sig. Aʳ–A2ᵛ.

44. *Divers Voyages,* sig. A3ʳ–[A4ʳ].

45. *Divers Voyages,* sig. B3ᵛ–[D4ʳ]; Thorne's theory about the northern route to the Spice Islands is on sig. D2ʳ⁻ᵛ; the king's reaction is on sig. [D4ʳ].

46. *Divers Voyages,* sigs. B4ᵛ–Eʳ (Zeno), E2ʳ–G3ᵛ (Ribault). For specific details, see sigs. E2ᵛ (Cabot), F3ᵛ (mineral wealth), Gʳ–G2ʳ (environment), G2ᵛ (how to trade). When Zeno claimed that some northern residents found a way to grow herbs, flowers, and fruits even during the winter, Hakluyt called such a claim "a notable lye." See sig. C3ʳ.

47. *Divers Voyages,* sig. Aʳ–B4ʳ; the account of the rescue is at sig. A3ʳ; the speculations about religion are at sig. B4ʳ.

48. *Divers Voyages,* sig. Hʳ–[I4ᵛ], quotations at sigs. Hʳ (lawyer's directions), Kʳ–K3ᵛ (instructions). This was also not the first time that some of these works had been published. Ribault's account had appeared in Nicolas Le Challeux, *Discours de l'histoire de la Floride, contentant la trahison des Espagnols* (Dieppe, 1566), and, translated into English, as *A true and perfect description, of the last voyage . . . attempted by . . . French men into Terra Florida* (London, [1566]); shortly before *Divers Voyages,* material from Ribault had appeared in Lancelot-Voisin, sieur de La Popeliniere, *L'histoire de France . . . depute lan 1550 jusques a ce temps* ([La Rochelle], 1581). Zeno, as Hakluyt acknowledged, appeared in the

posthumously revised second edition of Ramusio's *Secondo Volume Delle Navigationi Et Viaggi* (Venice, 1574), fols. 222ʳ–225ᵛ (reprinted again in subsequent editions in 1583 and 1606); see George B. Parks, "The Contents and Sources of Ramusio's Navigationi," *Bulletin of the New York Public Library* (1955): 28–29.

49. *Divers Voyages*, sig. K4ʳ⁻ᵛ.

CHAPTER 6. Paris, 1583

1. Sir Edward Stafford to Sir Francis Walsingham, September 29, 1583, in *Cal. Foreign,* 18:117. There were various contemporary estimates for the size of Paris during the sixteenth century, but modern historians estimate that the city's population hit approximately 250,000 to 300,000 in the 1550s, declined during the wars of religion, rebounded during the time Hakluyt was there, and then lost inhabitants again due to wars by the early 1590s, when the population was approximately 200,000; see Jean-Pierre Babelon, *Nouvelle Histoire de Paris: Paris au XVIe siècle* (Paris, 1986), 159–166; and Barbara Diefendorf, *Beneath the Cross: Catholics and Huguenots in Sixteenth-Century Paris* (New York, 1991), 9–10.

2. Walsingham to Hakluyt, March 11, 1582, and Hakluyt to Walsingham, January 7, 1584, in *Writings and Correspondence,* 1:196–197, 206; "Hakluyt Chronology," 1:281.

3. For details on Gilbert's career and journey, see the excellent reconstruction of his life in Kenneth R. Andrews, *Trade, Plunder, and Settlement: Maritime Enterprise and the Genesis of the British Empire, 1480–1630* (Cambridge, 1984), 183–199. Marginal notes in one of the twenty-two surviving copies of *Divers Voyages* suggest, as one scholar put it, that "at least one reader seems to have been influenced (or was confirmed in his opinions) by it," since on the day after it was licensed (May 21, 1582), Sir Edmund Brudenell purchased a copy and subsequently joined Gilbert's expedition. See Anthony Payne, " 'Strange, remote, and farre distant countreys': The Travel Books of Richard Hakluyt," in Robin Myers and Michael Harris, eds., *Journey through the Market: Travels, Travellers, and the Book Trade* (New Castle, Del., 1999), 5. For Sir Philip Sidney's comment, see the apparently misdated letter of Sidney to Stafford, July 21, 1584, in Albert Feuillerat, ed., *The Prose Works of Sir Philip Sidney,* 4 vols. (Cambridge, 1962), 3:145; see also Pamela Neville-Sington, " 'A very good trumpet': Richard Hakluyt and the Politics of Overseas Expansion," in Cedric C. Brown and Arthur F. Marotti, eds., *Texts and Culture Change in Early Modern England* (London, 1997), 68. For Gilbert's dream, see Add. Mss. 36674, fol. 59ʳ. For the pamphlet, see John Derricke, *The Image of Ireland* (London, 1581; reprinted Edinburgh, 1883).

4. Camden, *Annales* (1625), 3:44.

5. See Seymour Phillips, "The Medieval Background," in Nicholas Canny, ed., *Europeans on the Move: Studies on European Migration, 1500–1800* (Oxford, 1994), 9–25; Richard C. Hoffman, "Economic Development and Aquatic Ecosystems in Medieval Europe," *American Historical Review* 101 (1996): 630–669, esp. 646–665; and Fernand Braudel, *The Mediterranean and the Mediterranean World in the Age of Philip II* (orig. publ. Paris, 1966), trans. Siân Reynolds, 2 vols. (New York, 1972), 1:290–312.

6. On the importance of knowledge about winds, see Alfred Crosby, *Ecological Imperialism: The Biological Expansion of Europe, 900–1900* (Cambridge, 1986), 105–131; on the arming of ships and its meaning, see Carlo M. Cipolla, *Guns, Sails, and Empires: Technological Innovation and the Early Phases of European Expansion, 1400–1700* (New York, 1965), 137–138; Fernand Braudel, *The Structures of Everyday Life: Civilization and*

Capitalism, Fifteenth-Eighteenth Century, trans Siân Reynolds, 3 vols. (New York, 1981), 1:409–415.

7. Konrad Gesner, *Historiae Animalium Liber IIII: qui est de Piscium & Aquatilium animantium natura* ([Zurich?], 1558), 245–252; Sebastian Münster, *Cosmographiae universalis lib. VI* ([Basel?], 1552), 850–854; Pierre Belon, *L'histoire naturelle des estranges poissons marins* (Paris, 1551), 20; Francisi Boussueti, *De Natural Aquatilium* (Lyon, 1558); Guillaume Rondolet, *L'Histoire Entiere Des Poissons,* 2 vols. (Lyon, 1558). Pliny's *Natural History,* kept alive through scribal publishing from antiquity through the Middle Ages, was first printed in Venice in 1469, with a major translation appearing in 1601; see *Pliny the Elder, Natural History: A Selection,* trans. John F. Healy (London, 1991), xxxvi–xl. The first English-language edition of any part of Münster's work appeared as *A Treatise of the Newe India* (London, 1553) and was followed by *A briefe collection and comendious extract of straunge and memorable thinges, gathered out of the Cosmographie of Sebastian Munster* (London, 1574), fol. 70ᵛ. The French geographer François de Belleforest, who had published his *L'histoire universelle du monde* in Paris in 1570, offered French readers a revised version of Münster's cosmogaphy in 1575. For Gesner's larger bibliographic project, see Elizabeth Eisenstein, *The Printing Press as an Agent of Change: Communications and Cultural Transformations in Early-Modern Europe* (orig. publ. in 2 vols., Cambridge, 1979; rpt. as 1 vol., Cambridge, 1980), 97–99. Conrad Gesner's forays into natural history had a decisive impact on the English naturalist Edward Topsell, who provided an updated version of Gesner's work in the early seventeenth century: *The historie of foure-footed beastes* (London, 1607) and *The historie of Serpents* (London, 1608).

8. Henry Lowood, "The New World and the European Catalog of Nature," in Karen Ordahl Kupperman, ed., *America in European Consciousness, 1493–1750* (Chapel Hill, N.C., 1995), 295–323; Jean de Léry, *Histoire d'un voyage faict en la terre du Bresil autrement dite Amerique* (Geneva, 1578) (sea creatures); C. R. Boxer, ed., *The Tragic History of the Sea, 1589–1622,* Hak. Soc., 2nd Ser., 112 (Cambridge, 1959), and Boxer, ed., *Further Selections from the Tragic History of the Sea, 1559–1565,* Hak. Soc., 2nd Ser., 132 (Cambridge, 1968) (shipwreck narratives); Peter Humfrey, *Painting in Renaissance Venice* (New Haven and London, 1995), 287–288 (mosaics). For one representation of the fantastic, see the exquisite marginal illustration of an unknown fourteenth-century artist who depicted the Norse explorer Olaf Tryggvason doing battle with a sea monster in a manuscript in the Arnamagnæan Institute in Reykjavik, reproduced in Fernand Braudel and Michel Mollat du Jourdin, eds., *Le Monde de Jacques Cartier: L'aventure aux XVIe siècle* (Montreal, 1984), 94.

9. For the spice trade see Giles Milton, *Nathaniel's Nutmeg, Or, The True and Incredible Adventures of the Spice Trader who Changed the Course of History* (New York, 1999), and Charles Corn, *The Scents of Eden: A History of the Spice Trade* (New York, 1999); for Cabral, see William B. Greenlee, ed., *The Voyages of Pedro Álvares Cabral to Brazil and India,* Hak. Soc., 2nd Ser., 81 (London, 1938): 47–48, 85.

10. Thomas Churchyard, *A Discourse of the Queenes Maiesties entertainement in Suffolk and Norffolk . . . Whereunto is adioyned a commendation of Sir Humfrey Gilberts ventrous iourney* (London, 1578), sig. kᵛ.

11. Nancy Lyman Roelker, ed., *The Paris of Henry of Navarre as Seen by Pierre de L'Estoile* (Cambridge, Mass., 1958), 91. On the famine in Seville, see Roger Bodenham to Walsingham, May 10/20, 1583, *Cal. Foreign,* 17:331–332.

12. Roelker, ed., *Paris of Henry of Navarre,* 92–96. For the king's walk to "Chartiers,"

see Nicholas Wilson to Walsingham, May 25, 1583, *Calendar of State Papers Foreign* 17:365.

13. Roelker, ed., *Paris of Henry of Navarre*, 96.

14. Roelker, ed., *Paris of Henry of Navarre*, 98.

15. [John Dee], *General and Rare Memorials pertaining to the Perfect Arte of Navigation* (London, 1577), 7 (reference to "R.H."), 79 (only one hundred copies to be printed). For an analysis of Dee's argument in the context of his other work, see William H. Sherman, *John Dee: The Politics of Reading and Writing in Renaissance England* (Amherst, Mass., 1995), esp. 152–171.

16. On Hakluyt's presumed influence on Christopher Carleill, see *Hakluyt Handbook*, 2:572.

17. Carleill, *A discourse upon the entended Voyage to the hethermoste partes of America*, quotations at sig. Aii^v and Aiii^v. For Bristol, see David Harris Sacks, *The Widening Gate: Bristol and the Atlantic Economy, 1450–1700* (Berkeley, Calif., 1991); and Peter E. Pope, *Fish into Wine: The Newfoundland Plantation in the Seventeenth Century* (Chapel Hill, N.C., 2004), 11–18.

18. Bartolomé de Las Casas, *The Spanish Colonie, or Briefe Chronicle of the Acts and gestes of the Spaniardes in the West Indies, called the newe World*, trans. M. M. S. (James Aliggrodo) (London, 1583), sig. q2^r. Before the English translation in 1583, the book had appeared most recently as *Historie admirable des horibles insolences, cruautez, & tryrannies excercees par les Espagnols es Indes Occidentale* (Geneva, 1582). After 1583, the text appeared in Samuel Purchas's *Hakluytus Posthumous*, 4 vols. (London, 1625), and again as *The Tears of the Indians* (London, 1656), and through these texts it became the basis for the so-called black legend of the Spanish conquest of the Americas. The text also directly affected Hakluyt, sharpening his critique of Spanish ambitions in the Americas and beyond; see Richard Helgerson, *Forms of Nationhood: The Elizabethan Writing of England* (Chicago, 1992), 183. See chapter 7, below, for Hakluyt's use of the text in "The Discourse on Western Planting."

19. Las Casas, *Spanish Colonie*, sig. q2^{r-v}, qq^v–qq2^r.

20. This information and what follows derives from Hakluyt's "Relation of Master Stephen Bellenger," Add. Mss. 14027, fols. 289–290^v, reprinted in David B. Quinn, *Explorers and Colonies: America, 1500–1625* (London, 1990), 296–300. For details about Bellenger's life, see Quinn, *Explorers and Colonies*, 286–288.

21. Quinn suggests a more probable sailing date of February 19; see *Explorers and Colonies*, 296n. The French often laid claim to a place by erecting a cross, though in this instance the flag of the cardinal of Bourbon presumably sufficed. For the ways that other French explorers demarcated their territory, see Patricia Seed, *Ceremonies of Possession in Europe's Conquest of the New World, 1492–1650* (Cambridge, 1992), 41–68.

22. See, e.g., Rondelet, *L'Histoire Entiere Des Poissons*, 2:176–181; this argument reached an English-language audience with the publication of Edward Topsell's *History of Foure-Footed Beastes* (London, 1607), 47–50.

23. Michel Eyquem de Montaigne, *Les Essais*, 2 vols. (Bordeaux, 1580), bk. 1, chap. 31; Belleforest, *Histoire des Prodigeuses Extraicts de Plusieurs Fameux Autheurs, Grecs & Latins, sacrez & prophanes, divisees en cinq Tomes. Le premier par P. Boaistuau: Le second par C. de Tesserant: le troisiesme par F. de Belle-Forest, Le quatriesme par Rod. Hoyer, & le cinquiesme traduit de nouveau par F. de Belleforest. Nouvellement augmente'es de plusieurs Histoires, & enrichies de leurs effigies outre les precedents impressions* (Paris, 1583), 44–49. Other books that

offered French readers information about the Americas in the early 1580s included Pierre Boaistuau, *Histoire Prodigeuses* (Paris, 1571, 1580, 1582); Jacques Gohary, *Instruction de la congnoisce . . . de lherbe Petun . . . et sur la racine Mechiocan* (Paris, 1572, 1580); Bernard Palissy, *Discours admirables de la nature des eaux et fontaines* (Paris, 1580), which included material on the cod fisheries in Newfoundland; and Lancelot Voisin, *L'histoire de France . . . depuis lan 1550 jusques a ce temps* ([La Rochelle], 1581). In addition, in the early 1580s translators produced French-language editions of the crucial accounts of Francisco López de Gómara (*Histoire generalle des Indes Occidentales et terres neuves* [Paris, 1580]), Las Casas (*Histoire admirable des horribles insolences, cruautez, & tyrannies excercees par les Espagnols es Indes Occidentales* [Geneva, 1582]), Conrad Gesner (*Quatre Livres des Secretes de medecine* [Paris, 1582]), and Abraham Ortelius (*Theatre de l'univers* [Antwerp, 1581]).

24. André Thevet dedicated his first major work to François, conte de la Rochefoucauld; see *Cosmographie de Levant* (Lyon, 1556), sig. a2ʳ. Doubts about Thevet's actual journeys started during his lifetime and continued afterward; see Roger Schlesinger and Arthur P. Stabler, eds., *André Thevet's North America: A Sixteenth-Century View* (Kingston, Ont., 1986), xvii, xxxiii–xl; Frank Lestringant, *Mapping the Renaissance World: The Geographical Imagination in the Age of Discovery* (orig. publ. Paris, 1991), trans. David Fausett (Berkeley, Calif., 1994), xii. On Thevet's relationship with Hakluyt, see Lestringant, *Le Huguenot and Le Sauvage: L'Amérique et la controverse coloniale, en France au temps des guerres de religion* (Geneva, 2004), 311–356. The English traveler Thomas Nichols wrote an undated report of the Canary Islands in part as a response to the "great untruths, in a booke called *The New found world Antarctike,* set out by a French man called Andrew Thevet"— an account that appeared in Hakluyt's *Principal Navigations* (2:bk. 2, 3).

25. Thevet, *Cosmographie de Levant* (Lyon, 1556), sigs. h1ᵛ–i1ʳ (Constantinople), i1ᵛ (picture of lion), i1ᵛ (tiger), i3ʳ (wild horse), 13ᵛ (elephant), k2ᵛ (camel), o[1]ʳ (Colosses de Rhodes), r[1]ʳ (hieroglyphics), s2ᵛ (crocodile), t3ʳ (pygmies). A map of Thevet's journey, as well as a facsimile of the Lyon, 1556, edition of the *Cosmographie de Levant,* can be found in Frank Lestringant, ed., *André Thevet: Cosmographie de Levant, Travaux d'Humanisme et Renaissance,* 203 (Geneva, 1985).

26. Thevet's method in the *Cosmographie* and his use of other sources are explored in depth in Lestringrant, *Mapping the Renaissance World,* esp. 32–41, 126–127. For the criticisms of Belleforest and subesequent readers, see Schesinger and Stabler, eds., *Thevet's North America,* xxxiii–xl.

27. Not all editions of Münster's work emerged with the same title. The Basel editions included *Cosmographia. Beschreibung aller Lender* in 1544, 1545, 1546, and 1548; *Cosmographei, oder beschreibung aller länder* in 1550, 1553, 1556, 1558, 1561, 1564, 1567, 1569, 1572, 1574, 1578, 1588, 1592, and 1598; *Cosmographiae universali lib. vi* in 1550, 1552, 1554, 1559, and 1572; *La Cosmographie universelle* in 1552, 1555, 1556, 1560, and 1565; and *Sei libri della Cosmografia universale* in 1558. Other editions included *A Treatise of the New India* (London, 1553); *Kozmograffia czeska* (Prague, 1554); and *Cosmographie universale,* published in Cologne and Venice in 1575. For publication details, see *European Americana,* vol. 1. For biographical details on Thevet, see Schlesinger and Stabler, eds., *André Thevet's North America,* xix–xvi; and Lestringant, *Mapping the Renaissance World,* 9–11.

28. Giuseppe Horologgi, *Historia Dell'India America Detta Altramente Francia Antartica* (Venice, 1561); André Thevet, *The New found worlde, or Antarctike,* trans. Thomas Hacket (London, 1568), title page, no sig. (sonnet).

29. Thevet, *The New found worlde, or Antarctike*, fols. 107ʳ–108ᵛ (island of rats), 131ᵛ (Canada); for Ralegh as a reader, see Stephen Greenblatt's foreword to Lestrigant, *Mapping the Renaissance World*, ix.

30. André Thevet, *La Cosmographie Universelle*, 2 vols. (Paris, 1575), 917ʳ, 927ᵛ, 930ᵛ (feasting and vomiting), 927ʳ (tobacco), 935ʳ (healing), 945ᵛ, 946ʳ (treatment of prisoners), 961ᵛ, 1002ʳ (succarath), 967ʳ (isle du rats), 975ᵛ (nighttime scene), 1011ʳ, 1019ᵛ (hunting boar in Canada).

31. Jean de Léry, *History of a Voyage to the Land of Brazil*, trans. Janet Whately (Berkeley, Calif., 1990), 53–54; for other criticisms of Thevet in this edition, see 89, 167.

32. Léry, *History of a Voyage to the Land of Brazil*, 226n11; Jean de Léry, *Histoire d'un voyage faict en la terre du Bresil, autrement dite Amerique, contenant la navigation & chose remarquables, veuës sur mer par l'auteur*, 3rd ed. (Geneva, 1585), sig. i2ʳ–i3ʳ, sig. i4ʳ⁻ᵛ.

33. *Divers Voyages*, [iᵛ–iiʳ]; Hakluyt to Walsingham, January 7, 1584, in *Writings and Correspondence*, 1:207. In *Divers Voyages*, Hakluyt listed individuals by year, not by work, so the date 1575 by Thevet's name indicates that Hakluyt recommended the *Cosmographie Universelle*, not any of his earlier work; in a following list he noted Thevet as one of a group of travelers who had written about their own voyages, providing the date of 1565, a year in which Thevet neither made a significant trip nor published any work. Hakluyt might have meant to note 1568, when Thomas Hacket's English translation of his *Singularitez* appeared as *The New found worlde, or antarctike*.

34. Stafford to Walsingham, November 17, 1583, *Cal. Foreign*, 18:218.

35. For Parmenius's travels, see David Beers Quinn and Neil M. Cheshire, eds., *The New Found Land of Stephen Parmenius: The Life and Writings of a Hungarian Poet, Drowned on a Voyage from Newfoundland, 1583* (Toronto, 1972), 6–7.

36. The poem, written in Latin, appears with an English translation in Quinn and Cheshire, eds., *Parmenius*, 140–155.

37. *De Navigatione*, in Quinn and Cheshire, eds., *Parmenius*, 77–79.

38. *De Navigatione*, 83–105 passim.

39. Parmenius to Hakluyt, 1583, in Taylor, ed., *Writings and Correspondence*, 198–202.

40. Sir G[eorge] P[eckham], *A True Reporte of the late discoveries and possession, taken in the right of the Crown of Englande, of the Newfound Landes: by that valiant and worthye gentleman, Sir Humphrey Gilbert knight* (London, 1583), quotation at sig. Fiiᵛ.

41. Raphael Holinshed, *Chronicles*, 3 vols. (London, 1587), 2:132–133 (also in *New American World*, 3:258–259).

42. Hayes, "A report of the voyage and success thereof, attempted in the yeere of our Lord, 1583, by Sir Humfrey Gilbert," in *Principall Navigations* (1589), 695, 692.

43. *Paean*, in Quinn and Cheshire, eds., *Parmenius*, 151–153.

CHAPTER 7. Paris and London, 1584

1. Hakluyt to Walsingham, January 7, 1584, in *Writings and Correspondence*, 1:206.

2. G. Brunet et al., eds., *Mémoires-journaux de Pierre de L'Estoile*, 11 vols. (Paris, 1875–1896), 2:146–150; Nancy Lyman Roelker, ed., *The Paris of Henry of Navarre as Seen by Pierre de l'Estoile* (Cambridge, Mass., 1958), 99–100.

3. Hakluyt to Sir Francis Walsingham, January 7, 1584, in *Writings and Correspondence*, 1:205–207.

4. Hakluyt to Walsingham, January 7, 1584, 1:207. A decade earlier Pena had cowritten one of Europe's most significant herbals. See Petro Pena and Mathia de Lobel, *Stirpium Adversaria Nova* ([London, 1571]), 251–252 (tobacco).

5. Hakluyt to Walsingham, January 7, 1584, 1:207.

6. "Hakluyt Chronology," 1:283; D. B. Quinn, "The Voyage of Étienne Bellenger to the Maritimes in 1583: A New Document," *Canadian Historical Review* 43 (1962): 339–342 (reprinted in David B. Quinn, *Explorers and Colonies: America, 1500–1625* (London, 1990), 285–300); *Discourse*, 87.

7. Hakluyt to Walsingham, April 1, 1584, in *Writings and Correspondence*, 1:208.

8. Hakluyt to Walsingham, April 1, 1584, 1:208–209.

9. Hakluyt to Walsingham, April 1, 1584, 1:209. Hakluyt was representative of a generation of scholars in Oxford and Cambridge who recognized the importance of mathematics to the advancement of knowledge; see Mordechai Feingold, *The Mathematicians' Apprenticeship: Science, Universities, and Society in England, 1560–1640* (Cambridge, 1984), esp. 45–85.

10. *The Latine Grammar of P. Ramus translated into English* (Cambridge, 1585); *The fyrst parte of Commentaries, Concerning the state of Religion, and the Common wealthe of Fraunce, under the reignes of Henry the second, Frauncis the second, and Charles the ninth*, trans. Thomas Tymme (London, 1573), sig. biij'; *The Logike of the Most Excellent Philosopher P. Ramus Martyr*, trans. M. Roll (London, 1581).

11. Hakluyt to Walsingham, April 1, 1584, 1:209–210.

12. Brunet et al., eds., *Mémoires-Journaux de L'Estoile*, 2:151–152, 155–158; Roelker, ed., *Paris of Henry of Navarre*, 100–102; [Walsingham] to Sir Edward Stafford, June 7, 1584, *Cal. Foreign*, 18:543; "An acccount of the funeral solemnities of the Duke of Anjou," *Cal. Foreign*, 18:562.

13. Jean-Pierre Babelon, *Nouvelle Histoire de Paris: Paris au XVIe siècle* (Paris, 1986), 171–176.

14. Pietro Bizarri to Walsingham, June 24, 1584, and Stafford to Walsingham, June 15 [25], 1584, both in *Cal. Foreign*, 18:551; Roelker, ed., *Paris of Henry of Navarre*, 101–102 (king at the window); "Account of the funeral solemnities," 562. For the friendship of the queen and the duke, see Camden, *Annales* (1625), 3:74.

15. As Ortel put it in his letter to Walsingham on July 5, the shot "lequell l'a touché du premier coup au coeur tout royde mort, sans que son Excellence encques parla parolle." For the reports circulating at this time, including the reports that Walsingham received, see George Gilpin to Walsingham, July 2, 1584; Gebhard Truchsess (Elector of Cologne) to the queen, July 1/11, 1584; Truchsess to Walsingham, July 1/11, 1584; "Torture and Execution of Balthazar Gérard"; Ortel to Walsingham, July 5, 1584; and Gilpin to Walsingham, July 6, 1584; all in *Cal. Foreign*, 18:578–581, 587–588, 592, 596. An official report of the assassination and further documentation can be found in M. Gachard, ed., *Correspondance de Guillaume Le Taciturne, Prince D'Orange* (Brussels, 1857), 126–246. The first letters about the assassination appeared on July 1 from people nearby. The news had reached London by July 6, when Walsingham wrote to Stafford that they had heard about the tragedy. The fact that Walsingham felt compelled to recount some of the details of the death scene to Stafford suggests that he did not know if the news had yet reached Paris. Walsingham to Stafford, July 6, 1584, *Cal. Foreign*, 18:594. For Orange's earlier activities, see Orange to Walsingham, May 7/17, 1584, *Cal. Foreign*, 18:486; for a history of the event, see Lisa

Jardine, *The Awful End of Prince William the Silent: The First Assassination of a Head of State with a Handgun* (New York, 2006).

16. Walsingham to Stafford, July 2, 1584, *Cal. Foreign,* 18:579; Camden, *Annales* (1625), 3:74.

17. "Instructions for William Herle," probably written by Walsingham, June 8, 1584, and W. Herle to the queen, July 22, 1584, *Cal. Foreign,* 18:547–548, 626–628; Roelker, ed., *Paris of Henry of Navarre,* 103–104.

18. See Geoffrey Parker, *The Grand Strategy of Philip II* (New Haven and London, 1998), 14, 134–135.

19. Walsingham to [William] Davison, July 12, 1584, *Cal. Foreign,* 18:607.

20. Stafford to Burghley, September 18, 1584, *Cal. Foreign,* 19:68.

21. André Thevet, *Vrais Pourtraits* (Paris, 1584), fols. 522–527 (Columbus), 528–529 (Magellan), 526–527 (Vespucci), 385–388 (Cortés), 374–78 (Pizarro), 641–643 (Atahualpa [Atabolipa]), 644–645 (Moctezuma [Motzume]), 661–662 (Quoniambec), 663–664 (Paraovsti Satovriana).

22. [Caradoc of Llancarvan], *The historie of Cambria, now called Wales: A part of the most famous Yland of Brytaine, written in the Brytish language above two hundreth yeares past,* trans. H. Lloyd, ed. David Powel ([London, 1584]).

23. [Caradoc of Llancarvan], *Historie of Cambria, now called Wales,* sig. qvv^v–[qvi^r].

24. [Caradoc of Llancarvan], *Historie of Cambria, now called Wales,* 227–228.

25. [Caradoc of Llancarvan], *Historie of Cambria, now called Wales,* 228–229.

26. *Discourse,* 8.

27. *Discourse,* 8.

28. *Discourse,* 11.

29. *Discourse,* 12–15.

30. *Discourse,* 15.

31. *Discourse,* 16–18; [Nicholas Monardes], *Joyfull Newes Out Of the newe founde worlde, wherein is declared the rare and singuler vertues of diverse and sundrie Hearbes, Trees, Oyles, Plantes, and Stones, with their applications, aswell for Phisicke as Chirurgerie,* trans. John Frampton, 2 vols. (London, 1577), 1:99–120.

32. *Discourse,* 16–20. For Norumbega, see Emerson Baker et al., eds., *American Beginnings: Exploration, Culture, and Cartography in the Land of Norumbega* (Lincoln, Nebr., 1994), xxv–xxxi; Hakluyt used part of Gonsalvo de Oviedo's work that had appeared in his *Summarye of the Weste Indies,* a work originally published in Venice in 1534; an English translation had appeared in Richard Wiles's translation of Peter Martyr D'Anghiera's work, published in London in 1577 as *History of travayle in the West and East Indies.* Hakluyt did not cite Ramusio here on this point, perhaps not knowing that Ramusio and Oviedo were business partners and that Ramusio was instrumental in circulating the reports of Oviedo's journeys. On the business arrangement between Ramusio and Oviedo, see the contract between them and Antonio Priuli (procurator of San Marco), December 20, 1537 (and accompanying testimonies), in Antonello Gerbi, *Nature in the New World from Christopher Columbus to Gonzalo Fernández de Oviedo* (orig. publ. Milan, 1975), trans. Jeremy Moyle (Pittsburgh, Pa., 1985), 411–416. On Europeans' understanding of Bartolomé de Las Casas, see E. Shaskan Bumas, "The Cannibal Butcher Shop: Protestant Uses of las Casas's *Brevísima relación* in Europe and the American Colonies," *Early American Literature* 35 (2000): 107–136. The Italian phrase quoted in Hakluyt was: "Gli

habitatori di questa terra sono genti trattabili, amichevoli, et piacevoli. La terra abondantissima d'omni frutto . . . [L]a terra è detta da paesani suoi Norumbega."

33. *Discourse,* 20–23.

34. *Discourse,* 23.

35. *Discourse,* 23–27.

36. *Discourse,* 27.

37. *Discourse,* 28. As one German traveler visiting London at the end of the sixteenth century realized, whenever the quarterly sessions court met, carts moved through the streets every day ferrying the twenty to thirty men and women destined for the gallows at Tyburn. See Clare Williams, trans., *Thomas Platter's Travels in England, 1599* (London, 1937), 174.

38. *Discourse,* 28.

39. *Discourse,* 28–32.

40. *Discourse,* 32.

41. *Discourse,* 35–36; Lancelot-Voisin, sieur de La Popelinière, *Les Trois Mondes* (Paris, 1582), bk. 2:fols. 35ʳ–40ᵛ (French account of hostilities); Stafford to Walsingham, April 2, 1584, *Cal. Foreign,* 18:446 (Moffet).

42. *Discourse,* 36–40. Taylor wrote that Hakluyt's phrasing here suggested that he did not yet know that the prince had been assassinated, only that there had been attempts on his life. Though such an interpretation is plausible, Hakluyt here could also be referring to the assassination of July 10. See *Writings and Correspondence,* 2:245n. It is also likely that Hakluyt and his readers knew about an earlier attempt on the prince's life, especially since a report of an earlier assault had been published in England. See *A True Discourse of the assault committed upon the person of the most noble Prince, William Prince of Orange, Countie of Nassau, Marquesse de la Vere &c. by John Laureguis Spaniarde* (London, [1582]). Five years before Hakluyt wrote the "Discourse," Philips Van Marnix, an avid student of religion and politics, published a lengthy screed under the title *The Bee hive of the Romishe Churche,* trans. George Gilpin (London, 1579). On the title page he warned that he was "a zealous Protestant, under the person of a superstitious Papist," who sought to "repell the grose opinions of Popery." In 1583, a year when Van Marnix served as a burgomaster in Antwerp, he published a short attack on the Spanish entitled *A pithie, And most earnest exhortation, concerning the estate of Christiandome, together with the meanes to preserve and defend the same* (Antwerp, 1583). Van Marnix did not come to these opinions lightly. Instead, his work reflected his deep reading in available books. His library, for which an auction catalog survives, contained books on theology, medicine, history, mathematics, philosophy, and music. Among his books were copies of works by Ortelius (*Theatrum Orbis* [Antwerp, 1575]), Mercator (*Chronologia* [Cologne, 1569]), and Thevet (*Cosmographie Universelle,* 2 vols. [Paris, 1575]). For the contents of his library, see *Catalogue of the Library of Philips Van Marnix Van Sint-Aldegonde Sold by Auction (July 6th), Leiden, Christophorus Guyot, 1599* (Nieuwkoop, 1964).

43. *Discourse,* 40.

44. *Discourse,* 40–44.

45. *Discourse,* 44–47. Hakluyt here referred to the story of Antigonus, who forced his men to realize that their enemies were "weakelinges and shrimps" clothed in "large apparell."

46. *Discourse,* 47–52.

47. *Discourse,* 51–52.

48. *Discourse,* 63–64.

49. *Discourse,* 64–71.

50. *Discourse,* 71–76, 79–80.

51. *Discourse,* 80–87. Ingram's book was purportedly published in 1582, but no copies survive. See chapter 8, below, for how Hakluyt used Ingram's information.

52. *Discourse,* 52; *The Spanish Colonie, or Briefe Chronicle of the Acts and gestes of the Spaniards in the West Indies, called the newe World . . . by the reverend Bishop Bartholomew de las Casas,* trans. M.M.S. (London, 1583).

53. *Discourse,* 52–60. This chapter also included material from Johannes Metellus Sequanus, another Catholic who had initially supported the Spanish but became horrified by what he saw. His views had been published in 1571 in the preface to what Hakluyt called Osorius's history *De rebus gestis Emanuelis* [Jerónimo Osório, *De rebus, Emmanuelis Regis Lysitananiæ invietissimi virtute et auspicio* (Lisbon, 1571)].

54. *Discourse,* 88–96. La Popelinière did argue that Cabot was the first European to discover the North American mainland, but for the territory that he called "Florida," La Popelinière actually credited the French. See *Les Trois Mondes,* bk. 2:fols. 25ʳ–26ʳ.

55. *Discourse,* 96–112, quotation at 96.

56. *Discourse,* 120–128, quotations at 124, 128, 127.

57. *Discourse,* 127.

58. For the complex relationship between commerce and politics, see Richard Helgerson's masterful invocation of the concept of "mercantile nationalism," which he argued is especially evident in Hakluyt's *Principal Navigations:* Helgerson, *Forms of Nationhood: The Elizabethan Writing of England* (Chicago, 1992), 163–187, quotation at 187. It should be noted that not all modern scholars have drawn the same conclusion from reading Hakluyt's "Discourse." Anthony Payne has suggested that the document "had no discernible political influence" and wonders if it might better be understood "as a physical emblem of Hakluyt's learning, of his sagacious counsel" and perhaps as "an element in the complex ritual of posturing and self-promotion" common among those seeking patronage in this era. See Payne, " 'Strange, remote, and farre distant countreys': The Travel Books of Richard Hakluyt," in Robin Myers and Michael Harris, eds., *Journeys through the Market: Travels, Travellers, and the Book Trade* (New Castle, Del., 1999), 4.

59. "Hakluyt Chronology," 1:286–287. Two copies of the manuscript survive: BL MSS Sloane 1982 and BL Royal MSS12. G. XIII. Recently this document has attracted more attention that it did for almost four hundred years. David Armitage has argued that the simultaneous presentation of both documents was crucial; the "Discourse" was "the greatest of all colonial tracts," and the analysis of Aristotle "supplied the political and moral context within which he expected Elizabeth and her counselors . . . to judge his proposals for English colonization." The analysis was also aimed "to frame English overseas activity within the context of classical civil philosophy" as well as an effort to solicit patronage. More recently Andrew Fitzmaurice has concurred, seeing Hakluyt's (and others') efforts to promote colonization in the Americas as part of "an extended discourse on the best form of a commonwealth." These interpretations minimize the role that religion, specifically the desire to spread Protestantism, played in Hakluyt's efforts—"Religion shaped little, if any, of Hakluyt's corpus, either generically or rhetorically" according to Armitage— though each recognizes the importance of colonization as a way to limit the spread of

Catholicism and the power of the Vatican. See Armitage, "Literature and Empire," in Nicholas Canny, ed., *The Origins of Empire: British Overseas Enterprise to the Close of the Seventeenth Century* (Oxford, 1998), 106–107 (quotation at 107); Armitage, *The Ideological Origins of the British Empire* (Cambridge, 2000), 72–92 (quotations at 71–73); and Fitzmaurice, *Humanism and America: An Intellectual History of English Colonisation, 1500–1625* (Cambridge, 2003), 50–51, 138,152–157. But religion quite likely played a more direct role in Hakluyt's efforts, evident in the "Discourse" and in his published writings; on this point, see esp. David Harris Sacks, "Discourses of Western Planting: Richard Hakluyt and the Making of the Atlantic World," in Peter C. Mancall, ed., *The Atlantic World and Virginia* (Chapel Hill, N.C., 2007). Hakluyt's treatment of the *Politics* itself does suggest, as Armitage has argued, that Aristotelian ideas shaped Hakluyt's understanding of America at this point in his career, but it makes no direct links between the ideal commonwealth envisioned by Aristotle and actual colonial enterprises. See Lawrence V. Ryan, "Richard Hakluyt's Voyage into Aristotle," *Sixteenth Century Journal* 12 (1981): 73–83, which focuses on what can be learned in Hakluyt's text and its place in the educational culture of Oxford.

CHAPTER 8. Paris and London, 1584 to 1589

1. For details about Walter Cope's life, see *DNB*. One eighteenth-century scholar of the Society of Antiquarians wrote that Stow "stiles this gentleman his worshipful friend" in his London survey, but "history hath not preserved any further account of him." See *A Collection of Curious Discourses written by Eminent Antiquaries upon several heads in our English Antiquities*, 2 vols. (London, 1771), 2:427. This volume was an expanded edition of a book by the same title by Thomas Hearne, who died in 1735 long before this note was added to an expanded edition of his *Collection of Curious Discourses*, which had first been published in Oxford in 1720. Stow mentions his "worshipfull frend, Walter Cope," but noted only that Cope had come into possession of a fine manuscript Bible written on vellum by an elderly priest. See John Stow, *A Survay of London, Conteyning the Originall, Antiquity, Increase, Moderne estate, and description of that City, written in the yeare 1598* (London, 1603), 366. The details about what was in Cope's cabinet come from Clare Williams, trans., *Thomas Platter's Travels in England, 1599* (London, 1937), 171–173.

2. Cope was not the only Elizabethan interested in insects capable of producing light; his contemporary Thomas Moffet devoted a section of his entomological masterpiece to such insects. See Tho[mas] Mouffet [Moffet], *The Theater of Insects, Or, Lesser living Creatures* (London, 1658), 975–981.

3. By the time Hakluyt had started to collect his accounts, learned Europeans at least had access to a wide variety of texts that described monsters and marvels. Given his extensive time in Paris, it is likely that Hakluyt at least would have known about the works of Ambroise Paré and Pierre Boaistuau. For contemporary views of such phenomena, see Lorraine Daston and Katharine Park, *Wonders and the Order of Nature, 1150–1750* (New York, 1998), esp. 173–214.

4. Ferrane Imperato, *Dell'historia naturale* (Naples, 1599); Silvio A. Bedini, *The Pope's Elephant* (Manchester, 1997). By Hakluyt's time the English had embraced the twinned cultures of collecting and printing, and London's naturalists maintained connections with explorers who traveled far and sent back samples of exotic goods, which then became described in books by such authorities as the entomologist Thomas Moffett and the

herbalist John Gerard; for the ways that this community functioned, see Deborah Harkness, *The Jewel House of Art and Nature: Elizabethan London and the Social Foundations of the Scientific Revolution* (New Haven and London, 2007).

5. Roger Schlesinger and Arthur P. Stabler, eds., *André Thevet's North America: A Sixteenth-Century View* (Kingston, Ont., 1986), xxii; *Principall Navigations* (1589), sig. *4ᵛ.

6. "The Letters Patents graunted . . . to Sir Humfrey Gilbert" and "The letters patents, graunted . . . to M. Walter Ralegh," both in *Principall Navigations* (1589), 677–679, 725–728, quotation at 725.

7. "First voyage made to the coastes of America," in *Principall Navigations* (1589), 728; Raphael Holinshed, *Chronicles* (London, 1587), 3:1369, reprinted in David B. Quinn, ed., *The Roanoke Voyages, 1584–1590*, 2 vols., Hak. Soc., 2nd Ser., 104–105 (London, 1955), 1:90–91.

8. "First voyage made to the coastes of America," 728–729.

9. "First voyage made to the coastes of America," 729–731.

10. "First voyage made to the coastes of America," 730–732.

11. Thus the report notes that Manteo and Wanchese, who are unnamed in the account, could provide evidence about the Carolina Algonquians' obedience to figures in authority. See "First voyage made to the coastes of America," 730.

12. Sir Edward Stafford to Sir Francis Walsingham, October 16, 1584, *Cal. Foreign,* 19:108.

13. G. Brunet et al., eds., *Mémoires-Journaux de Pierre de L'Estoile,* 11 vols. (Paris, 1875–1896), 2:172–173, 176; Nancy Lyman Roelker, ed., *Paris of Henry of Navarre as Seen by Pierre de L'Estoile* (Cambridge, Mass., 1958), 105–106.

14. Roelker, ed., *Paris of Henry of Navarre,* 106–107.

15. Roelker, ed., *Paris of Henry of Navarre,* 107–108; Brunet et al., eds., *Mémoires-Journaux de Pierre L'Estoile,* 2:181.

16. The Earl of Derby and Stafford to Walsingham, February 23, 1585, Captain George Fremyn to Walsingham, February 23, 1585, Stafford to Walsingham, March 1, 1585, and Stafford to Walsingham, March 1, 1585, all in *Cal. Foreign,* 19:295–296, 298, 310, 313. English officials across Europe knew that during Carnival comedies and festivals filled the air with music and laughter in Italy as cardinals joined others to celebrate. A bull ran through the Piazza San Marco in Venice, an ancient custom in Ramusio's hometown. See "News from Rome," and "Advertisements sent from Rome," both in *Cal. Foreign,* 19:304–306.

17. Hakluyt to Walsingham, April 7, 1585, in *Writings and Correspondence,* 2:343–345.

18. Hakluyt to Walsingham, April 7, 1585, 2:344.

19. The documents—"Inducements to the Liking of the Voyage intended towards Virginia in 40. and 42. degrees of latitude," and "Inducements to the lykinge of the voyadge intended to that pte of America wch lyethe betwene 34. and 36. degree of Septentrionall Latytude"—can be found in *Writings and Correspondence,* 2:327–343. E. G. R. Taylor made a similar suggestion relating to the two pamphlets, but the similarities between the entire texts make it at least as possible that the lawyer wrote one tract designed to encourage settlement to the region between 34 and 36 degrees North latitude and that John Brereton, eager to encourage settlement north of 40 degrees, adapted the then-deceased lawyer's prose for the published version. See *Writings and Correspondence,* 2:339n.

20. "Inducements . . . towards Virginia," 2:332.

21. "Inducements . . . towards Virginia," 2:330, 335, 336.

22. "Inducements . . . towards Virginia," 2:327; "Inducements . . . betwene 34. and 36. degree," 2:339; "Inducements . . . towards Virginia," 2:330.

23. "Hakluyt Chronology," 1:288–290; Hakluyt to Sir Walter Ralegh, December 30, 1586, in *Writings and Correspondence*, 2:353–356.

24. "An extract of M. Lanes letter, to M. Richard Hakluyt Esquire," in *Principall Navigations* (1589), 793.

25. Geffrey Whitney, *A Choice of Emblemes, and Other Devises, For the moste parte gathered out of sundrie writers, Englished and Moralized* (Leyden, 1586), 203.

26. [Thomas Cates], *A Summarie and True Discourse of Sir Frances Drakes West Indian Voyage. Wherein were taken, the Townes of Sant Jago, Sancto Domingo, Cartagena & Saint Augustine* (London, 1589), 1–3; Harry Kelsey, *Sir Frances Drake: The Queen's Pirate* (New Haven and London, 1998), 240–250.

27. Kelsey, *Sir Frances Drake*, 256–257; Camden, *Annales* (1625), 3:103–104 (celebration and pillage); [Cates], *Summarie and True Discourse*, 19–20; "The Discourse and Description of the Voyage of Sir Frawncis Drake & Master Frobisher," known as "The Primrose Journal," in Mary F. Keeler, ed., *Sir Francis Drake's West Indian Voyages*, Hak. Soc., 2nd Ser., 148 (London, 1981), 191 (two to three dead each day).

28. Camden, *Annales* (1625), 3:104–105; [Cates], *Summarie and True Discourse*, 35.

29. Juan de Posada to the Crown, September 2, 1586, in Irene A. Wright, ed., *Further English Voyages to Spanish America, 1583–1594*, Hak. Soc., 2nd Ser., 99 (London, 1951), 205–206; Kelsey, *Sir Frances Drake*, 257–279.

30. Camden, *Annales* (1625), 3:106–107; [Cates], *Summarie and True Discourse*, 48–50.

31. [Cates], *Summarie and True Discourse*, 50–51; Camden, *Annales* (1625), 3:107. Among the dead listed by Cates was Walter Digges himself, who had started the account that became the basis for the book. Kelsey calculated the losses at close to 40 percent (750 of 1,925 dead); see *Sir Francis Drake*, 280–281. For John White's presence among the settlers, see Paul Hulton and David B. Quinn, eds., *The American Drawings of John White, 1577–1590, with Drawings of European and Oriental Subjects*, 2 vols. (London, 1964), 1:15.

32. "Hakluyt Chronology," 1:289; see *Cal. Foreign, 1586–1588*, 53. As Basanier put it, "estant neantmois supprimee & esteinte ia par l'espace de vingt ans ou environ, ie l'ay tiree avec la diligence de Monsieur Hakluit, homme certainement bien verse en l'histoire geographique & ayant bonne part en la diversité des langues & sciences, comme du tombeau, où elle avoit ia si long temps inutille reposé pour la mettre où il m'a semblé par la frequente lecture d'icelle qu'elle se demandoit." M[artin] Basanier, *L'Histoire Notable de la Floride . . . par le Capitaine Laudonniere* (Paris, 1586), sig. aiij^v. For Antonio Espejo, see *Histoire des Terres Nouvellement Descouvertes . . . par Antonio de Espejo*, trans. M[artin] Basanier (Paris, 1586).

33. The exact date when Hakluyt received the Codex Mendoza is unclear, though Quinn plausibly suggests that the transfer occurred sometime in 1587. See "Hakluyt Chronology," 1:294–295. For the manuscripts that Thevet presumably offered to Hakluyt, see Schlesinger and Stabler, eds., *André Thevet's North America*, xxviii–xix.

34. *A Notable Historie containing foure voyages made by certayne French Captaynes unto Florida*, trans. R[ichard] H[akluyt] (London: 1587), sig. A^r–v.

35. *Notable Historie . . . unto Florida*, trans. H[akluyt], sig. [i^r].

36. *Notable Historie . . . unto Florida*, trans. H[akluyt], sig. [i^v].

37. *Notable Historie . . . unto Florida*, trans. H[akluyt], sig. [i^v–ii^r].

38. *New Mexico; Otherwise, The Voiage of Anthony of Espeio* (London, [1587]), title page, sig [B8ᵛ], sig. [iiiʳ⁻ᵛ]; *A Notable Historie . . . unto Florida*, trans. H[akluyt], sig. [iiʳ⁻ᵛ].

39. *Principall Navigations* (1589), 747–748.

40. Hakluyt to Ralegh, December 30, 1586, in *Writings and Correspondence*, 2:355.

41. *De Orbe Novo Petri Martyris Anglerii Mediolanensis, Protonotarij, & Caroli quinti Senatoris Decades octo, diligenti temporum observatione, & utilissimis annotationibus illustratæ, suóque nitori restitutæ, Labore & industria Richardi Hakluyti Oxoniensis Angli. Additus est in usum lectoris accuratus totius operis index* (Paris, 1587). As Ortelius put it: "In Catalago nundinarum Francofurtensium lego Haccletum vestrum edidisse Decades Petri Martyris, de nuper repertis insulis. nihil ne præter illas in eo? vel aliquid de suo addidit? aut quæ causa huius per Haccletum editionis? Placet de conchis lapideis dissertatio inter vos. Ego quid de ijs sentiam scire desideras." Abraham Ortelius to Jacobus Colius Oretlianus, May 15, 1589, in Johannes H. Hessels, ed., *Abrahami Ortelii et virorum eruditorum ad eundem et ad Jacobum Colium Ortelianum epistulae* (Cambridge, 1887), 394 (English translation on 393).

42. The comments here are based on a comparison of Hakluyt's edition with Pietro Martire d'Anghiera, *De Orbe Novo Decades* (Alcala, 1516); the "vocabulara Barbara" can be found in that edition on sig. [viʳ–viiiʳ].

43. Martyr, *De Orbe Novo* (Hakluyt ed.), 231–233.

44. Martyr, *De Orbe Novo* (Hakluyt ed.), sig. a ijʳ–aiijᵛ; translation in *Writings and Correspondence*, 2:362–364.

45. Martyr, *De Orbe Novo* (Hakluyt ed.), sig. aiijᵛ–aiiijʳ; translation in *Writings and Correspondence*, 2:365. ["Nam qui exterorum laudes proponit, suos, si non sunt stipites, provocat."]

46. Martyr, *De Orbe Novo* (Hakluyt ed.), sig. aiiijᵛ–[aivᵛ]; translation in *Writings and Correspondence*, 2:366–368.

47. Martyr, *De Orbe Novo* (Hakluyt ed.), sig. [avʳ⁻ᵛ]; translation in *Writings and Correspondence*, 2:368–369. The significance of this usage has been explored by David Harris Sacks in "Discourses of Western Planting: Richard Hakluyt and the Making of the Atlantic World," in Peter C. Mancall, ed., *The Atlantic World and Virginia* (Chapel Hill, N.C., 2007).

48. Martyr, *De Orbe Novo* (Hakluyt ed.), opp. sig. Aʳ.

49. Camden, *Annales* (1625), 3:221–222; Kelsey, *Sir Francis Drake*, 287–294.

50. Camden, *Annales* (1625), 3:222.

51. Roelker, ed., *Paris of Henry of Navarre*, 138–140; Brunet, ed., *Mémoires-Journaux* 3:119 (Paris); "Hakluyt Chronology," 1:294–298 (marriage); "Will of Richard Hackluyt, of Eyton," 1587, and Hakluyt to Burghley (Cecil), April 6, 1588, both in *Writings and Correspondence*, 2:370–371, 380. For de Bry's visit to England, see Hulton and Quinn, *The American Drawings of John White*, 25–26. Douglas Cavendish's relationship to Thomas Cavendish cannot be proved; see "Hakluyt Chronology," 1:298, and David Elisha Davy, "Suffolk Collections," xlvii, Add. Mss. 19122.

52. [John White], "The fourth voyage made to Virginia, with three shippes, in the yeere, 1587. Wherein was transported the second Colonie," in *Principall Navigations* (1589), 770–771.

53. [White], "Fourth voyage made to Virginia," 766.

54. [White], "Fourth voyage made to Virginia, 766.

55. [White], "Fourth voyage into Virginia," 766–767.

56. [White], "Fouth voyage into Virginia," 768.

57. [White], "Fourth voyage into Virginia," 768–770.

58. John White, "The first voyage intended for the supply of the Colonie planted in Virginia," in *Principall Navigations*, 771–772.

59. White, "First voyage intended for the supply of the Colonie," 772–773.

60. Camden, *Annales* (1625), 3:251–252.

61. Camden, *Annales* (1625), 3:285.

62. Camden, *Annales*, 3:286. Not everyone in England was so high-minded: Ralegh was concerned with the seizure and sale of wines hauled off Spanish ships. See Agnes Latham and Joyce Youings, eds., *The Letters of Sir Walter Ralegh* (Exeter, 1999), 46.

63. *Cal. Foreign*, 22:85; "Hakluyt Chronology," 1:300; Roelker, ed., *Paris of Henry of Navarre*, 157–158.

64. *The Historie of the great and mightie kingdome of China, and the situation thereof: Togither with the great riches, huge Citties, politike governement, and rare inventions in the same*, trans. R[obert] Parke (London, 1588), sig. q3ᵛ. Parke dated his dedication January 1, 1589, apparently after the title page had already been set.

65. Alison M. Quinn and David B. Quinn have provided a text-by-text breakdown of the works that appeared in the book; see Quinn and Quinn, "Contents and Sources of the Three Major Works," in *Hakluyt Handbook*, 2:341–377.

66. *Principall Navigations* (1589), title page. See Helen Wallis, "The Pacific," in *Hakluyt Handbook* 1:225–231; W. H. Ker, "The Treatment of Drake's Circumnavigation in Hakluyt's Voyages," *Papers of the Bibliographical Society of America* (1940): 281–302; Harry Kelsey, *Sir Francis Drake: The Queen's Pirate* (New Haven and London, 1998), 177–179.

67. *Principall Navigations* (1589), sig. *2ʳ⁻ᵛ.

68. *Principall Navigations* (1589), sig. 2ᵛ; translation from Pliny, *Natural History, Books 24–27*, trans. W. H. S. Jones (Cambridge, Mass., 1956), 137.

69. *Principall Navigations* (1589), sigs.*2ᵛ–*3ʳ (travels to East Asia), *3ᵛ (translations and cosmography), *4ᵛ, 3ᵛ (acknowledgments of assistance). In addition to his translation of Peter Martyr's *Decades*, Richard Eden also published a translated part of a popular cosmography under the title *A briefe collection and compendious extract of strange and memorable thinges: gathered out of the Cosmographye of Sebastian Münster* (London, 1574). Hakluyt took much of the first part of *Principall Navigations* from John Bale's *Scriptorum illustri[um] majoris Brytanniae, quam unc Angliam & Scotiam uocant: Catalogus*, 2nd ed., 2 vols. (Basel, 1557–1559). John Foxe's book had been published as *Actes and Monuments of matters most speciall and memorable, happenyng in the Church, with an Universall history of the same, whererin is set forth at large the whole race and course of the Church, from the primitive age to these latter tymes of ours, with the bloudy tymes, horrible troubles, and great persecutions agaynst the true Martyrs of Christ*, 2 vols. ([London], 1583).

70. *Principall Navigations* (1589), 1–2.

71. *Principall Navigations* (1589), 15–16.

72. *Principall Navigations* (1589), 515–516 (amanuensis), 517 (Thorne), 517–519 (Newfoundland).

73. *Principall Navigations* (1589), 25–77 (Mandeville's Latin text), 77 (warning to the reader, in Latin); for a translation of Hakluyt's "brevis admonitio ad Lectorem," see *Writings and Correspondence*, 2:395–396. For the number of Mandeville manuscripts, see C.

W. R. D. Moseley's introduction to the Penguin edition of *The Travels* (London, 1983), 9–10; for details about the manuscripts, see Malcolm Letts, ed., *Mandeville's Travels: Texts and Translations*, 2 vols., Hak. Soc., 2nd Ser., 101–102 (London, 1953), 101:xxvii–xxxii.

74. *Principall Navigations* (1589), 203–206 (sultan), 209 (goods in Babylon), 213–218 (weights and measures), 218 (shipping charges), 218–219 (location of goods), 219–222 (schedule of monsoons), 227–231 (dangers at sea).

75. *Principall Navigations* (1589), 243 (Arthur to Iceland), 245–248 (Edgar), 455–482 (eighteen expeditions), 460–466 (lawyer's instructions), 250–258 (Thorne), 500–501 (Ramusio and Mercator).

76. *Principall Navigations* (1589), 506–507 (Madoc), 515 (Columbus and Fabian).

77. *Principall Navigations* (1589), 517–519 (printed books), 520–545 (expeditions of the Hawkins family), 545–553 (Henry Hawkes's report), 615–622 (account of Frobisher's first expedition), 622–630 (Settle's account of the second expedition), 630–635 (Ellis's account of the third expedition), 764–770 (White report), 770–771 (names of colonists in Roanoke). Hakluyt took material from [Edward Hall], *The Union of the two noble and illustre famelies of Lancastre & Yorke* ([London], 1548), who wrote about Henry VIII sending out two ships "to seke strange regions" (fol. clvii^v), and from [Richard Grafton], *A Chronicle at large and meere History of the affayres of Englande and Kinges of the same* ([London?], 1569), who provided the same brief information (see 1149). The only printed material that Hakluyt used for Hawkins and Hawkes was Hawkins's *A true declaration of the troublesome voyage of M. John Haukins to the parties of Guynea and the west Indies, in the yeares of our Lord 1567 and 1568* (London, 1569), which he copied for his description of what happened on Hawkins's epic journey to Guinea, the West Indies, and New Spain (see *Principall Navigations* [1589], 553–556). William Hawkins's report included Henry Hawkes's description of Mexico, given to the lawyer several years earlier (*Principall Navigations* [1589], 545–553.) Hakluyt printed a brief report by Thomas Wiars, who had been a passenger on Martin Frobisher's last voyage of 1578, at the end of Thomas Ellis's account (*Principall Navigations* [1589], 635).

78. Hawkins, "The 3. vnfortunate voyage made with the Iesus, the Minion, and foure other shippes," in *Principall Navigations* (1589), 556–557. The manuscripts related to Ingram's journey are collated in David B. Quinn, ed., *The Voyages and Colonizing Enterprises of Sir Humphrey Gilbert*, 2 vols., Hak. Soc., 2nd ser., 83–84 (London, 1940), 2:283–296.

79. "Relation of David Ingram," in *Principall Navigations* (1589), 557, 561–562. One manuscript version of the account notes the place of origin as "Camina"; see Esmond Wright, ed., *Elizabethans' America* (Cambridge, Mass., 1966), 285. The river is identified as "Rio de mnynas" in Sloane 1447, fol. ^r, and as "Rio de minas" in Tanner Ms. 79, both in BL.

80. "Relation of David Ingram," 559 (gold, fertile fields, value of plants), 560 (fauna), 562 (Northwest Passage).

81. "Relation of David Ingram," 557–558 (whiteness), 558 (nakedness), 558–559 (conflicting views of Americans). On the importance of these early contacts, see James Axtell, "At the Water's Edge: Trading in the Sixteenth Century," in Axtell, *After Columbus: Essays in the Ethnohistory of Colonial North America* (New York, 1988), 144–181.

82. "Relation of David Ingram," 562.

83. "Relation of David Ingram," 561; Thomas Harriot, *A briefe and true report of the new found land of Virginia* (Frankfurt, 1590), 25. On the significance of the color black to the Elizabethans; see Winthrop Jordan, *White Over Black: American Attitudes toward the Negro, 1550–1812* (Chapel Hill, N.C., 1968), 40–43.

84. "Relation of David Ingram," 561. Hakluyt was not the only observer to rely on Ingram's tale; see G[eorge] P[eckham], *A True Reporte of the late discoveries . . .* (London 1583), sig. Ciii^v.

CHAPTER 9. London, 1590 to 1600

1. The Latin title: *Admiranda narratio fida tamen, de commodis et incolarum ritibus Virginiae;* the German title: *Wunderbarliche, doch warhafftige Erklärung, von der Gelegenheit und Sitten der Wilden in Virginia, welche newlich von den Engelländern, so im Jar 1585 . . . ist erfunden worden;* the French title: *Merveilleux et estrange rapport, toute fois fidele, des commoditez que se trouvent en Virginia.* On Hakluyt's involvement with the project, see the comment about his role translating the text from Latin ("The True Pictures and Fashions") and "To the gentle Reader" (unpaginated), *A briefe and true report of the newfound land of Virginia* (Frankfurt, 1590).

2. See, e.g., Sebast. Munstere, *La Cosmographie Universelle* [Basel, 1552], 1359–1360. For European knowledge about Asia, see Donald F. Lach, *Asia in the Making of Europe,* vol. 1, *The Century of Discovery* (Chicago, 1965), bk. 1, 204–217. Among the pictures available in printed books was a depiction of an enormous celebration of Brazilians timed to commemorate the visit of King Henri II to Rouen in 1551. See *C'est la deduction du sumptueux ordre plaisantz spectacles et megnifiques thatres Dresses, et exhibes par les citoiens de Rouene ville* (Paris, 1551; facs. reprint, Amsterdam, n.d.), sig. [Ki^r–Ki^v].

3. "Hakluyt Chronology," 1:303–304; Jean-Pierre Babelon, *Nouvelle Histoire de Paris: Paris au XVIe siècle* (Paris, 1986), 460; [Albertus Meier], *Certaine briefe, and speciall Instruc-tions for Gentlemen, merchants, students, souldiers, mariners, &c. Employed in services abrode, or anie way occasioned to converse in the kingdoms, and governments of forren Princes,* trans. Philip Jones (London, 1589), sig. B^r (list of twelve attributes of foreign societies), A3^v.

4. Harriot, *Briefe and true report,* 7–8 (flax, hemp, silk), 8–9 (*materia medica,* trees, grapes), 11–12 (dyestuffs), 20 (game and fowl), 10–11 (iron, pearls).

5. Harriot, *Briefe and true report,* 12 (latitude), 22–24 (forest products).

6. Harriot, *Briefe and true Report,* 13–14 (maize and other crops), 16–17 (roots), 18–19 (fruits and nuts), 20–21 (products of the sea and river).

7. Harriot, *Briefe and true report,* 13–15.

8. Harriot, *Briefe and true report,* 16.

9. Hans Stade (Staden), *Warhafftige historia vnnd beschreibung einer landtschafft der wilden nacketen grimmigen menschfresser leuthen in der newen welt America* (Frankfurt, 1557?); Michel de Montaigne, *Essais,* 2 vols. (Bordeaux, 1580) 1:299–330; Jean de Léry, *Histoire d'un voyage faict en la terre du Bresil autrement dite Amerique* (Geneva, 1578).

10. Harriot, *Briefe and true report,* 24–25.

11. Harriot, *Briefe and true report,* 25.

12. Harriot, *Briefe and true report,* 25–26; *Principal Navigations* (1598–1600), 3:277.

13. Harriot, *Briefe and true report,* 26.

14. Harriot, *Briefe and true report,* 26.

15. Harriot, *Briefe and true report,* 26–27.

16. Harriot, *Briefe and true report,* 27.

17. Harriot, *Briefe and true report,* 27.

18. Harriot, *Briefe and true report,* 27–28.

19. Harriot, *Briefe and true report,* 28–29.

20. Harriot, *Briefe and true report*, 29.

21. Harriot, *Briefe and true report*, 29. For a discussion of how Harriot understood what he was hearing—or even if he was understanding what the Americans were telling him—see Joyce E. Chaplin, *Subject Matter: Technology, the Body, and Science on the Anglo-American Frontier, 1500–1676* (Cambridge, Mass., 2001), 29–34.

22. Harriot, *Briefe and true report*, 31–32.

23. As modern scholars have revealed, the de Bry engravings differed in some ways from White's original watercolors; see, e.g., Paul Hulton, *America, 1585: The Complete Drawings of John White* (Chapel Hill, N.C., 1984), 18.

24. As Mary C. Fuller has argued, there was confusion about Americans within European intellectual circles, with some of the information appearing in Hakluyt's *Principal Navigations* conflicting with other accounts; see Fuller, "'Ravenous Strangers': The Argument of Nationalism in Two Narratives from Hakluyt's *Principal Navigations*," *Studies in Travel Writing* 6 (2002): 22–23.

25. For Bristol and its connections to the wider Atlantic community, see David Harris Sacks, *The Widening Gate: Bristol and the Atlantic Economy, 1450–1700* (Berkeley, Calif., 1991); and Peter E. Pope, *Fish into Wine: The Newfoundland Plantation in the Seventeenth Century* (Chapel Hill, N.C., 2004).

26. Abraham Ortelius to Jacob Cool, August 25, 1590, in Joannes Henricus Hessels, ed., *Ecclesiae Londino-Batavae archiuum; tomus primus; Abrahami Ortelli (geographi Antverpiensis) et virorum eruditorum ad eundem et ad Jacobum Colium Ortelianum (Abrahami Ortelii sororis filium) epistulae* (Cambridge, 1887), trans. F. C. Francis, 442–443.

27. "A letter of M. Henrie Lane to M. Richard Hakluit, concerning the first ambassage to our most gracious Queene Elizabeth from the Russian Emperour anno 1567," in *Principal Navigations* (1598–1600), 1:374–375, quotation at 374; "A voyage made with the shippes called the Holy Crosse, and the Mathew Gonson, . . . about the yeere 1534," and "Another voyage made to the Iles of Candia and Chio made by the shippe the Mathew Gonson, about the year 1535," both in *Principal Navigations* (1598–1600), 2:bk. 1, 98.

28. *Principal Navigations* (1598–1600), 2:sig*4^r. According to E. G. R. Taylor, Hakluyt also received the maps found on the ship as well as a register of the East Indies; see *Writings and Correspondence*, 1:59.

29. "An excellent treatise of the kingdome of China, and of the estate and government thereof," in *Principal Navigations* (1598–1600), 2:bk. 2:88 (spaciousness), 90–91 (mineral wealth and exports).

30. "An excellent treatise of the kingdome of China," 89 (towns and wall), 89–90 (longevity and living conditions), 92 (gunpowder and printing), 92–93 (literature and education), 95 (the king's idolatry), 96–97 (Chinese religious practices), 98 (Christianity).

31. "Hakluyt Chronology," 1:306, dates the christening at June 3, 1593, whereas *Writings and Correspondence*, 1:53, puts it as January 3. Even the genealogy of Douglas's family provided no details about her age when she married Hakluyt; see Davy's Suffolk Collections, vol. 46, Add. Mss. 19122, fol. 350. Hakluyt married Douglas in either 1587 or 1588. If they were a typical first-time couple, he would have been twenty-seven or twenty-eight and she would have been twenty-five or twenty-six. He was approximately thirty-five at that time, and over forty when their son was born. If Douglas was a typical first-time bride, she would have been about thirty-one or thirty-two when she gave birth. For infant mortality estimates, see C. G. A. Clay, *Economic Expansion and Social Change: England,*

1500–1700, 2 vols. (Cambridge, 1984), 1:6; on the age of marriage, see David Cressy, *Birth, Marriage, and Death: Ritual, Religion, and the Life-Cycle in Tudor and Stuart England* (Oxford, 1997), 285; on the approximate dating of their marriage, see "Hakluyt Chronology," 298.

32. John White to Hakluyt, February 4, 1593, in *Principal Navigations* (1598–1600), 3:287–288.

33. Harvey, *Pierces Supererogation, Or A New Prayse of the Old Asse* (London, 1593), 48–49; "A briefe note concerning the voyage of M. George Drake of Apsham to the Isle of Ramea in . . . 1593," in *Principal Navigations* (1598–1600), 3:193; "A voyage with three tall ships . . . begunne by M. George Raymond, in the yeare 1591," in *Principal Navigations* (1598–1600), 2:bk. 2, 102–110.

34. Hakluyt to Emanuel van Meteren, December 6, 1594, in *Writings and Correspondence*, 2:418–420.

35. Van Meteren to Jacob Valcke, December 15/25, 1594, in *Writings and Correspondence*, 2:417–418.

36. William Camden, *The Historie of the Life and Reign of that Famous Princesse Elizabeth* (London, 1634), 37–38.

37. "Will of Richard Hackluyt, of Eyton," 1587, in *Writings and Correspondence*, 2:370–371.

38. For Thomas Cavendish, see Camden, *Historie of the Life and Reigne of that Famous Princesse Elizabeth*, 59, which notes his death in 1591, and Davy's Suffolk Collections, vol. 46, Add. Mss. 19122, fol. 350, which refers to his drowning in 1592; for Martin Frobisher, see Camden, *Historie of the Life and Reigne of that Famous Princesse Elizabeth*, 108–109; for Hawkins and Drake, see "The voyage truely discoursed, made by Sir Francis Drake, and Sir John Hawkins . . . in the yeere 1595," in *Principal Navigations* (1598–1600), 3:584 (death of Hawkins), 588 (death of Drake).

39. Camden, *Historie of the Life and Reigne of that Famous Princesse Elizabeth*; John Norden, "Notes on London and Westminster, 1592," in William B. Rye, ed., *England as Seen by Foreigners in the Days of Elizabeth and James the First* (London, 1865), 93–100, quotations at 95–96.

40. See Van Meteren to Valcke, January 18/28, February 8/18 and 14/24, 1595, all in Gerrit de Veer, ed., *Reizen van Willen Barents, Jacob van Heemskerck, Jan Cornelisz: Rijp en anderen naar het Noorden* ('s-Gravenhage, 1917), 204–210, quotation at 205. These letters were translated by Anne Goldgar with advice from Katy Kist. See also P. A. Tiele, ed., *Mémoire bibliographique sur les journaux des nagivateurs néerlandais* (Amsterdam, 1867), 299–301. For the West Indies account, see "A voyage of the honourable Gentleman M. Robert Duddeley, now knight, to the Isle of Trinidad, and the Coast of Paria," in *Principal Navigations* (1598–1600), 3:574.

41. W[alter] Ralegh, *The Discoverie of the Large, Rich, and Bewtiful Empyre of Guiana, with a relation of the great and Golden Citie of Manoa (which the Spanyards call El Dorado) And of the Provinces of Emeria, Arromaia, Amapaia, and other Countries, with their rivers, adjoyning* (London, 1596), [1]–2.

42. Ralegh, *Discoverie of Guiana*, 5–8.

43. Ralegh, *Discoverie of Guiana*, 9 (towns and treasure), 10 (son to Peru), 11–14ff. (Spanish reports), 21–22 (chart and fear of the French).

44. Ralegh, *Discoverie of Guiana*, 22–24.

45. Ralegh, *Discoverie of Guiana*, 27–28, 13 (geography), 33–34 (Spanish efforts), 61 (armadillo), 69–71 (other marvels), quotation at 70.

46. Ralegh, *Discoverie of Guiana*, 99–101.

47. Levinus Hulsius, *Brevis & admirando descriptio Guianæ, Avri Abundantissimi, in America* (Nuremberg, 1599); *Kurke Wunderbare Zeschreibung. Def Goldreichen König* (Nuremberg, 1599). To understand the relationship between Ralegh's and Hulsius's agendas and the nature of their books, see Benjamin Schmidt, "Reading Ralegh's America: Texts, Books, and Readers in the Early Modern Atlantic World," in Peter C. Mancall, ed., *The Atlantic World and Virginia* (Chapel Hill, N.C., 2007).

48. *Principal Navigations* (1598–1600), 3:652 (marginal notes), 662–666 (supporting documents); Lawrence Keymis, "A Relation of the second Voyage to Guiana, performed and written in the yeere 1596," in *Principal Navigations* (1598–1600), 3:687–689. Keymis's book had first appeared as *A Relation of the Second Voyage to Guiana* (London, 1596); see sig. [F4^r]–G2^r for the table.

49. "The antiquitie of the trade with English ships," in *Principal Navigations* (1598–1600), 2:bk. 1, 96; "A note drawen out of a very ancient booke remaining in the hands of the right worshipfull M. Thomas Tilney," in *Principal Navigations* (1598–1600), 2:bk. 1, 29; "A briefe note concerning an ancient trade of the English Marchants to the Canarie-ilands," in *Principal Navigations* (1598–1600), 2:bk. 2:3. For a modern edition of some of these texts, with corrections to Hakluyt's original versions, see C. Raymond Beazley, ed., *The Texts and Versions of John de Plano Carpini and William de Rubruquis*, Hak. Soc., Extra Ser., 13 (London, 1903). Hakluyt printed them in the Latin original and then followed with a translation. For John de Plano Carpini, see *Principal Navigations* (1598–1600), 1:21–53 (Latin), 53–71 (English); for William de Rubruquis, see *Principal Navigations* (1598–1600), 1:71–92 (Latin), 93–117. Lord Lumley's library became one of the foundations of the British Library and as a result has attracted much interest. A catalog made shortly after his death enumerates 2,609 titles in the collection; see Sears Jayne and Francis R. Johnson, eds., *The Lumley Library: The Catalogue of 1609* (London, 1956). Hakluyt's *Principal Navigations* is no. 1436, where it is cataloged among other historical works; works of geography and cosmography are numbered from 2485 to 2517.

50. "A voyage with three tall ships . . . to the East Indies," in *Principal Navigations* (1598–1600), 2:bk. 2, 102–110.

51. John Pory, trans., *A Geographicall Historie of Africa, Written in Arabicke and Italian by John Leo a More, borne in Granada, and brought up in Barbarie* (London, 1600), dedication (no sig.), 57.

52. "Hakuyt Chronology," 1:309.

53. Abraham Hartwell, trans., *A Report of the Kingdome of Congo, a Region of Africa. And of the Countries that border rounde about the same . . . Drawen out of the writinges and discourses of Odoardo Lopez a Portingall, by Philippo Pigafetta* (London, 1597), opp. sig. *.

54. Hartwell, trans., *Report of the Kingdome of Congo*, sig. *^{r}.

55. Hartwell, trans., *Report of the Kingdome of Congo*, sig.*^{r}.

56. Hartwell, trans., *Report of the Kingdome of Congo*, sig.*^{v}–*2 ^{r}.

57. *Itinerario, Voyage ofte Schipvaert van Jan Huygen van Linschoten naer eost ofte Portugaels Indien* (Amsterdam, 1596); [Linschoten], *The Description of a voyage made by certaine Ships of Holland into the East Indies. With their adventures and successe*, trans. W[illiam] P[hillip] (London, 1598), sig. A2^{r-v}.

58. The smaller version was the *Description of a Voyage;* the larger was published as *John Huighen Van Linschoten. his Discours of Voyages into ye Easte & West Indies* (London, [1598]); quotations at sigs. A^{r-v}, A3^{r} (Hakluyt's recommendation), 141 (marginal note to Hakluyt). The illustrations appear together between pages 78 and 79. See "Hakluyt Chronology," 1:311, for the identification of Phillip as the translator of this volume.

59. *Principal Navigations* (1598–1600), 1:sig. *2^{r}.

60. *Principal Navigations* (1598–1600), 1:sig. *3^{r-v}; [Edmund Wright], trans., *The Haven-Finding Art, Or The Way to Find any Haven or place at sea, by the Latitude and variation* (London, 1599), sig. A2^{r}.

61. *Principal Navigations* (1598–1600), 1:sig. [*4^{r}].

62. *Principal Navigations* (1598–1600), 1:sig. [*4^{r-v}].

63. *Principal Navigations* (1598–1600), 1:sig. [*4^{v}].

64. *Principal Navigations* (1598–1600), 1:sig. [*4^{v}–5^{r}].

65. *Principal Navigations* (1598–1600), 1:sig. [*5^{r-v}].

66. *Principal Navigations* (1598–1600), 1:sigs. [*5^{v}–6^{r}] (antiquity of London's merchants), [6^{v}], 187–208 (commodities), **2^{r} (thanks to others), ** [1]^{r-v} (authenticity of manuscripts), **2^{v} (Iceland), **2^{r-v} (Armada).

67. *Principal Navigations* (1598–1600), 1:sig. **3^{r-v}, translated by Anthony Corbeill.

68. "Hakluyt Chronology," 1:312.

69. *Principal Navigations* (1598–1600), 2:sigs. *4^{r-v} (dedication), *2^{v} (contents).

70. *Principal Navigations* (1598–1600), 2:sig. *3^{r}.

71. For mention of these islands, see, e.g., *Principal Navigations* (1598–1600), 2:bk. 2:22–23, 120–121.

72. *Principal Navigations* (1598–1600), 3:sig. (A2)^{v}. On the positions, see the contents of the letter from the Privy Council to the archbishop in *Acts of the Privy Council of England*, n.s., 30 (for 1599–1600) (London, 1905): 330–331; and "Hakluyt Chronology," 1:313.

73. David Beers Quinn, *Set Fair for Roanoke: Voyages and Colonies, 1584–1606* (Chapel Hill, N.C., 1985), 341–378.

74. *Principal Navigations* (1598–1600), 3:sig. (A2)^{r} ("new world"), 2–4 (Columbus and the English).

75. *Principal Navigations* (1598–1600), 3:sig. A2^{v}–A3^{r}.

76. *Principal Navigations* (1598–1600), 3:sig. A2^{v}–A3^{r}.

77. *Principal Navigations* (1598–1600), 3:sig. A3^{r}. George Wateson had recently published *The Cures of the Diseased in remote regions* (London, 1598), a brief work that included references to exotic plants (such as tobacco, manioc, and pineapples). Wateson's book was published twice in London that year, but never again, perhaps a sign that Hakluyt was not the only person skeptical about its contents.

78. *Principal Navigations* (1598–1600), 3:sig. A3^{v}. As Pory's modern biographer has noted, despite Hakluyt's hopes that Pory would follow him, he produced only one more book after his translation of Leo Africanus, a translation of Ortelius published as *An Epitome of Ortelius His Theatre of the World, wherein the principal regions of the earth are described in smalle Mappes* (London, 1602). For the extent of Pory's publications and his relationship with Hakluyt, see William S. Powell, *John Pory, 1572–1636: The Life and Letters of a Man of Many Parts* (Chapel Hill, N.C., 1977), 9–25.

79. *Principal Navigations* (1598–1600), 3:sig. A3^{v}.

80. By 1598, editions of Mandeville had been published in German (at both Augsburg and Basel in 1481), Italian (at Milan in 1480), Dutch (at Gouda in 1475), and Spanish (at Valencia in 1521), as well as in various Latin editions; for the publication history, including the survival of translations in English, see Malcolm Letts, ed., *Mandeville's Travels: Texts and Translations*, 2 vols., Hak. Soc., 2nd Ser., 101–102 (London, 1953), 1:xxvii–xxxviii. The existence of Amazons in the Americas also would not have been surprising given that Duarte Lopez's report on Africa—the book Hakluyt had urged Abraham Hartwell to translate into English—reported that they lived and fought there. See Pigafetta, *Report of the Kingdome of Congo*, 195, 205.

81. Hakluyt had translated Álvar Núñez Cabeza de Vaca's account, though his translation was published by Purchas in 1625; see George Parks, "The Contents and Sources of Ramusio's *Navigationi*," *Bulletin of the New York Public Library* 59 (1955): 306. Hakluyt also referred to the journey in the preface that he wrote for the translation of Soto's account, published as *Virginia Richly Valued by the description of the maine land of Florida her next neighbour* (London, 1609); see Hakluyt's "Epistle Dedicatorie" in Don Ferdinando de Soto, *The Discovery and Conquest of Terra Florida*, ed. William B. Frye, Hak. Soc., 1st Ser., 9 (London, 1851), 1–2.

82. The account was originally published as *The Rare Travailes of Job Hartop, an Englishman, who was not heard of in three and twentie yeares space* (London, 1591); Hakluyt entitled it "The travailes of Job Hortop" and included it in *Principal Navigations* (1598–1600), 3:487–495. For Purchas's comments see *Purchas his Pilgrimage. Or Relations of the World and the Religions Observed in all ages and Places discovered, from the Creation unto this Present* (London, 1613), 648; and *Purchas His Pilgrimage. Or Relations of the World and the Religions Observed in All Ages and Places Discovered, from the Creation unto this Present . . .*, 2nd ed. (London, 1614), 777. See also B. F. DeCosta, "Ingram's Journey through North America in 1567–68," *Magazine of American History* 9 (1883): 170.

83. It should be noted that modern scholars have been equally dismissive. See Rayner Unwin, *The Defeat of John Hawkins: A Biography of the Third Slaving Voyage* (New York, 1960), 293–312; Percy G. Adams, *Travelers and Travel Liars, 1660–1800* (Berkeley, Calif., 1962), 133; Gordon M. Sayre, *Les Sauvages Américains: Representations of Native Americans in French and English Colonial Literature* (Chapel Hill, N.C., 1997), 94; James A. Williamson, *Hawkins of Plymouth*, 2nd ed. (London, 1969), 106.

84. Michel de Montaigne, *The essayes or morall, politike and millitarie discourses*, trans. John Florio (London, 1603), 101.

85. Clare Williams, trans., *Thomas Platter's Travels in England, 1599* (London, 1937), 226–227. Twenty years after Platter saw the ship, it looked, in the opinion of Venice's ambassador to England, "exactly like the bleached ribs and bare skull of a dead horse." By 1662 there was almost nothing left. See John Hampden, ed., *Francis Drake, Privateer: Contemporary Narratives and Documents* (University, Ala., 1972), 246. According to the annalist John Stow, the *Golden Hind* was one of the English ships that battled the Spanish Armada in 1588; see Stow, *The Annales of England* (London, [1601]), 1262.

CHAPTER 10. London, 1609

1. John Chamberlain to Dudley Carleton, January 23, 1609, in Chamberlain, *Letters*, 1:282–283. Of Chamberlain's letters to Carleton 452 survive, providing remarkable insight

into the world of a man who traveled in similar circles as Hakluyt (he was an associate of Camden's, for example). For an overview of his life (and Carleton's), see *ODNB*.

2. Chamberlain to Carleton, December 30, 1609 (ships), January 10, 1609 (Ralegh's loss of his estate), March 3, 1609 (smallpox), all in Chamberlain, *Letters,* 1:292, 280, 288. In a letter of April 20, Chamberlain refers specifically to smallpox but does not indicate if that was the illness that had spread the previous month; see Chamberlain to Carleton, April 20, 1609, in Chamberlain, *Letters,* 1:289.

3. Scholars have begun to debate the precise impact of print, challenging the one-time prevailing view that the advent of the printing press signaled a revolution in the circulation of ideas. Although print was of course crucial to the spread of information, as Hakluyt knew, scribal publishing remained important, as did the circulation of information in manuscripts not intended for publication. Rather than print supplanting manuscripts, the two forms of communication existed simultaneously and complemented each other. See David McKitterick, *Print, Manuscript and the Search for Order, 1450–1830* (Cambridge, 2003), and Harold Love, *Scribal Publication in Seventeenth-Century England* (Oxford, 1993). See also Lucien Febvre and Henri-Jean Martin, *The Coming of the Book: The Impact of Printing, 1450–1800* (orig. publ. Paris, 1958), trans. David Gerard (London, 1976); Elizabeth L. Eisenstein, *The Printing Press as an Agent of Change: Communications and Cultural Transformations in Early-Modern Europe* (orig. pub. in 2 vols., Cambridge, 1979; republished as 1 vol., Cambridge, 1980); Adrian Johns, The *Nature of the Book: Print and Knowledge in the Making* (Chicago, 1998); and Anthony Grafton, "The Importance of Being Printed," *Journal of Interdisciplinary History* 11 (1980): 265–286.

4. "Notes drawn up by Richard Hakluyt, 1601," in *Writings and Correspondence,* 2:476n; William Warner, *Albions England. Or Historicall Map of the Same Island* (London, [1586]), sig. [a.iiijᵛ].

5. Wolfgang Schivelbusch, *Tastes of Paradise: A Social History of Spices, Stimulants, and Intoxicants* (orig. publ. Munich, 1980), trans. David Jacobson (New York, 1992), 3–14; Charles Corn, *Scents of Eden: A Narrative of the Spice Trade* (New York, 1998). On the later tortures of the English by the Dutch, see the broadside "Newes out of East India: Of the Cruell and Bloody Usage of our English Merchants and others at Amboyna" (photostat at HEH 398531).

6. "A Voyage with three tall ships . . . written from the mouth of Edmund Barker of Ipswich . . . by Richard Hakluyt," in *Principal Navigations* (1598–1600), 2:bk. 2, 102–110, quotation at 107.

7. "A brief note of a voyage to the East Indies . . . by Henry May," in *Principal Navigations* (1598–1600), 3:571–574.

8. The notes on Hakluyt's address, which are the source for the material in the following paragraphs, can be found in *Writings and Correspondence,* 2:476–482. One measure of Ramusio's influence is that his lengthy work appeared in multiple editions. The first edition of volume one appeared in 1550 and was followed by a second edition in 1554 and three posthumous editions (of 1563, 1588, and 1613, as well as a 1606 reprinting of the edition of 1588); the second volume, the source for the material that Hakluyt used in his comments to the East India Company, appeared posthumously in 1559, with a second edition in 1574, a third edition in 1583, and a fourth edition in either 1606 or 1613.

9. "Notes of information one the behaulfe of the Merchaunts entending trade to the Easte Indies," HEH EL 2360; the text, including a transcript, can be found in Heidi

Brayman Hackel and Peter C. Mancall, "Richard Hakluyt the Younger's Notes for the East India Company in 1601: A Transcription of Huntington Library Manuscript EL 2360," *Huntington Library Quarterly* 67 (2004): 423–436.

10. John Stow, *The Annales of England, Faithfully collected out of the most autenticall Authors, Records, and other Monuments of Antiquitie* (London, [1601]), sig. a^{r–v}; John Pory, *A Geographical Historie of Africa* (London, 1600), dedication to Robert Cecil sig. [A1^r] (Pory's praise of Hakluyt), 57 (Hakluyt's praise of Pory). The exact date of the publication of the last volume of *Principal Navigations* remains unknown ("Hakluyt Chronology," 1:314), though Pory dated the dedication in which he referred to Hakluyt on January 15, 1601 (new style).

11. William S. Powell, *John Pory, 1572–1636: The Life and Letters of a Man of Many Parts* (Chapel Hill, N.C., 1977), 16–17; Ben: Jonson, *The Characters of Two royall Masques* (London, [1608]), in C. H. Herford Percy and Evelyn Simpson, eds., *Ben Jonson*, 11 vols. (Oxford, 1925–1952), 7:167–180, reference to Leo Africanus at 169. As Winthrop Jordan has noted, Leo Africanus's text, along with the work of Jean Bodin, "helped pattern initial English perceptions" of Africans; see Jordan, *White Over Black: American Attitudes toward the Negro, 1550–1812* (Chapel Hill, N.C., 1968), 33–35, quotation at 35.

12. Leo Africanus's history was the first text to appear in the second volume of Ramusio's work: "Della descritione dell'Africa et delle cose notabili che quivi sono," in Ramusio, *Primo volume, & Seconda editione Delle Navigationi et Viaggi* (Venice, 1554), 1–103. On the ways that Europeans translated the text, see Natalie Zemon Davis, *Trickster Tales: A Sixteenth-Century Muslim between Worlds* (New York, 2006), 153–156.

13. David B. Quinn, "Thomas Harriot and the Virginia Voyages of 1602," *WMQ*, 3rd Ser., 27 (1970): 273–274; William Camden, *Remaines of a Greater Worke, Concerning Britaine* (London, 1605), sig. B^r, 170. Harriot did not identify Hakluyt as the author, though as Quinn has suggested this is the only likely text that Harriot would have recommended at the time, especially given the recent publication of the third volume of *Principal Navigations*.

14. Walter Cope's suggestion and Hakluyt's subsequent plan of action can be found in Antonie Galvano [António Galvão], *The Discoveries of the World from their first originall unto the yere of our Lord 1555 . . . Corrected, quoted, and not published in English by Richard Hakluyt* (London, 1601), sig. [A2^r].

15. Galvano, *Discoveries of the World*, sig. [A2^v].

16. Galvano, *Discoveries of the World*, sig. [A2^v–A3^r].

17. Galvano, *Discoveries of the World*, sig. [A3^r].

18. Galvano, *Discoveries of the World*, sig. [A3^v]. Hakluyt did not mention the title of the book he sought, but presumably it was Galvão, *Tratado . . . dos diversos & desvayrados caminhas* (Lisbon, 1563).

19. Galvano, *Discoveries of the World*, sig. [A3^v–A4^r].

20. Galvano, *Discoveries of the World*, 1–20 (ancient discoveries), 20–29 (Portuguese discoveries), 29–97 (primarily Spanish discoveries, but including Portuguese and other expeditions from 1492 to 1553). João de Barros produced three books on the subject: *Asia . . . dos fectos que os Portugueses fizeram no descobrimeno & conquista dos mares & terres do Orienta* (Lisbon, 1552); *Segunda decade da Asia* (Lisbon, 1553); and *Terceira decade da Asia* (Lisbon, 1563).

21. Galvano, *Discoveries of the World*, 12 (mermaids), 85 (snorting fish), 24–25 (papal indulgence and slavery), 19–20 (Macham's voyage), 43, 4 (bells and penises). For Machim's

alleged journey see *ODNB*, s.v. "Machin, Robert"; for the excommunication of Elizabeth, see Wallace MacCaffrey, *Elizabeth I* (London, 1993), 327–328.

22. *The Journall, or Dayly Register, containing a true manifestation, and Historical declaration of the voyage, accomplished by eight shippes of Amsterdam,* trans. William Walker (London, 1601), sig. q2ʳ.

23. *Journall, or Dayly Register,* trans. Walker, sig. q2ᵛ.

24. *Journall, or Dayly Register,* trans. Walker, sig. p3ᵛ–q3ᵛ. Walker, imitating Hakluyt's editorial methods, noted the link to the *Principal Navigations* in the margins of his own work; see *Journall, or Dayly Register,* trans. Walker, sig. q2ᵛ.

25. On Smythe's career, see *ODNB*, s.v. "Smythe [Smith], Sir Thomas."

26. C. S. Knighton, ed., *Acts of the Dean and Chapter of Westminster, 1543–1609,* 2 vols. (Woodbridge, Suffolk, 1999), 2:199–214, 218–232 passim, bell ringer (207–208), inventory (220), dearth times (231), plague (203, 205). For the complete list of dates when Hakluyt's signature appears in Westminster's record, see "Hakluyt Chronology," 1:317–318.

27. Howes, *Annals* (1631), 797 (lightening, earthquake), 804 (bonfires, ear chopping), 812 (priest's execution); Camden, *Annales* (1635), 559 (prisoners), 563–[571] (Ireland). The epidemic of 1603 was much more severe than any other that Hakluyt would have experienced in the city—notably the plague of 1578, which killed 3,568 (out of a population of 101,000) and the epidemic of 1593, with 10,675 dead (in a city of 125,000). See Paul Slack, *The Impact of Plague in Tudor and Stuart England* (London, 1985), 151.

28. John Brereton, *A Briefe and true Relation of the Discoverie of the North part of Virginia; being a most pleasant, fruitfull and commodious soile* (London, 1602), 14 (notice of Mace's journey), 3–4 (sailing dates), 4–5 (fish), 6 (plants and animals), 10–11 (natives), 12 (return).

29. Brereton, *Briefe and true Relation,* 17–18

30. Brereton, *Briefe and true Relation,* 19–20 (relations with natives), 20–23 (trade).

31. "A Voyage set out from the Citie of Bristoll . . . for the discoverie of the North part of Virginia, in the yeere 1603, under the command of me Martin Pring," in *Hakluytus Posthumus,* 4:1654.

32. Pring, "A Voyage set out from . . . Bristoll," 4:1654–1656. The text, as Purchas printed it, notes that the French had brought their furs to Europe in 1604, a year after Pring returned, suggesting that someone—Pring, Hakluyt, and Purchas all could be implicated—had added this detail to let readers know just how valuable such furs could be. Purchas did not provide the title of any herbals that mentioned how sassafras might be used to heal plague victims. English readers could have already learned about the healing properties of sassafras from Monardes's study of American plants or from Hakluyt, who spoke of its value for the crew of Jacques Cartier; see Nicholas Monardes, *Joyfull Newes out of the newe founde worlde,* trans. John Frampton, 2 vols. (London, 1577), 1:99–120; *Principal Navigations* (1598–1600), 3:227.

33. Camden, *Annales* (1635), 584.

34. Camden, *Annales* (1635), 585, 584; Chamberlain to Carleton, [March 30, 1603], in Chamberlain, *Letters,* 1:188–190; Howes, *Annales* (1631), 812. For a more sentimental account of the queen's final days, see *Memoirs of Robert Cary, Earl of Monmouth* (Edinburgh, 1808), 115–123.

35. Stow, *Annales,* 812–813; Chamberlain to Carleton, [March 30, 1603], 1:189; Camden, *Annales,* 586.

36. William Camden [?], *The Funeral Procession of Queen Elizabeth* (London, 1791?), HEH 601835.

37. Howes, *Annales*, 815; Johann Jacob Grasser, "Notes on England, circa 1606," in William B. Rye, ed., *England as Seen by Foreigners in the Days of Elizabeth and James the First* (London, 1865), 127; [William Camden], *Reges, Reginæ, Nobiles, Et alij in Ecclesia Collegiata B. Petri Westmonasterij sepulti* (London, 1606), 25.

38. Pring, "A Voyage set out from . . . Bristoll," 4:1654.

39. "Notes attributed to Richard Hakluyt, 1603," in *Writings and Correspondence*, 2:487–488; the notes refer to "his majestie," which put it after the death of Queen Elizabeth on March 24, 1603.

40. "Notes attributed to Richard Hakluyt," 488.

41. Ralegh, *Historie*, 1614, bk. 2, chap. 3, sec. 8; *Hakluytus Posthumus*, 1:1122; "A note of Australia del Espiritu Santo. Written by Master Hakluyt," in *Hakluytus Posthumus*, 4:1432 (meetings); "A Letter written from Valladolid by Ludovicus Tribaldus Toletus to Master Richard Hakluyt," in *Hakluytus Posthumus*, 4:1565–1567.

42. *Sir Thomas Smithes Voyage and Entertainment in Russia* (London, 1605), sigs. B^r, D3^v, Ii^r; details from Jerome Horsey's journey can be found in *Principal Navigations* (1598–1600), 1:468–473. Robert Stafforde's text recommends that readers consult "the discourse of Master *Harriot,* and Master *Hackant,*" a misspelling of Hakluyt. It should be noted that Stafforde's recommendation of Hakluyt followed his assertion that the native peoples of Terra Florida ate the captives taken in their many wars, did not marry until they were forty years old, suckled their children until they were twelve, and "live mostly upon Serpents & worms." [Robert Stafforde], *A Geographicall and Anthologicall description of all the Empires and Kingdomes, both of Continent and Ilands in this terrestriall Globe* (London, 1607), 62.

43. Peter C. Mancall, "Tales Tobacco Told in Sixteenth-Century Europe," *Environmental History* 9 (2004): 648–678.

44. George Chapman, Ben Jonson, and John Marston, *Eastward Hoe as it was playd in the Black-friers by The Children of her Majesties Revels* (London, 1605), quotation at sig. E^v.

45. *ODNB*, s.v. "Hall, Joseph" (distemper); Mercurio Britannica [Joseph Hall], *Mundus Alter et Idem sive Terra Australis ante hac semper incognita longis itineribus pergorini Academici nuperimme Lustrata* (London, 1605), translated by John Millar Wands as *Another World and Yet the Same: Bishop Joseph Hall's Mundus alter et idem* (New Haven and London, 1981), xxv–xxvi (dystopia), xliv–xlvi (on the relation of the text to travel literature).

46. Neither Hall nor Healey had their names on the book or its translation, but scholars have long agreed that Hall was the primary author and Healey the translator; see Wands, ed., *Another World and Yet the Same*, xiii–xvii; Joseph Hall, *The Discovery of a New World (Mundus Alter et Idem)*, ed. Huntington Brown (Cambridge, Mass., 1937), xxvii–xxxi.

47. [Joseph Hall], *The Discovery of a New World or A Description of the South Indies*, trans. [John Healey] ([London, 1613 or 1614]), 24–25 (Eat-allia), 67–68 (Drink-allia, quotation at 68), 97–98 (Shee-landt), 111 (Ile Hermophradite), 137–138 (Fooliana), 116–117 (Shrewesbourg). For analysis of the sources of Hall's work, see Hall, *Discovery of a New World*, ed. Brown, xxiii–xxvi.

48. "Letters Patent to Sir Thomas Gates and Others, April 10, 1606," in Philip L. Barbour, ed., *The Jamestown Voyages under the First Charter, 1606–1609*, 2 vols., Hak. Soc., 2nd Ser., 136 (Cambridge, 1969), 24–25; [Stafforde], *Geographicall and Anthologicall description*, 31.

49. "Letters Patent to Gates," 25.

50. "Letters Patent to Gates," 25–29.

51. "Letters Patent to Gates," 29–31.

52. "Letters Patent to Gates," 31–33; "Instructions for Government," November 20, 1606, in Barbour, ed., *Jamestown Voyages*, 1:34–44.

53. Unless otherwise noted, the material relating to this plan are from "Instructions for the Virginia Colony of 1606," in *Writings and Correspondence*, 2:492–496.

54. "Dispensation for Richard Hakluyt and Robert Hunt," November 24, 1606, in Barbour, ed., *Jamestown Voyages*, 1:62–64.

55. Michael Drayton, "Ode 11," in Drayton, *Poemes Lyrick and pastorall* (London, [1606?]).

56. Hakluyt was at Westminster on December 5, 1606, and May 4, 1607; see "Hakluyt Chronology," 1:322.

57. For details about the book's publication, see Philip L. Barbour, ed., *The Complete Works of Captain John Smith (1580–1631)*, 3 vols. (Chapel Hill, N.C., 1986), 1:5–7.

58. *A True Relation of such occurrences and accidents of noate as hath hapned in Virginia since the first planting of that Collony* (London, 1608), sig. A3ʳ–A4ᵛ.

59. *True Relation*, sig. B1ʳ; Carville Earle, "Environment, Disease, and Mortality in Early Jamestown," in Thad Tate and David Ammerman, eds., *The Chesapeake in the Seventeenth Century: Essays on Anglo-American Society* (Chapel Hill, N.C., 1979), 96–125.

60. *True Relation*, sigs. B3ʳ (abundance of game birds and speculation about the river's source), [B4ʳ] (compass).

61. *True Relation*, sigs. [B4ʳ] (Robinson's body), [B4ᵛ] (letter), C2ʳ (region, cannibals), C2ᵛ (Smith and Powhatan).

62. Smith, *True Relation*, sigs. C3ᵛ–[C4ʳ] (Smith and Powhatans), E3ᵛ–[E4ʳ] (Pocahontas), [E4ᵛ] (return to England).

63. "A Journall of the third Voyage to the East Indies . . . by William Keeling," in *Hakluytus Posthumous*, 1:iii, 188.

64. Gerrit de Veer, *A True Description of Three Voyages by the North-East towards Cathay and China*, trans. William Phillip, ed. Charles T. Beke, Hak. Soc., 1st Ser., 13 (London, 1853), sig. [A2ʳ].

65. De Veer, *Three Voyages by the North-East*, sig. [A2ʳ⁻ᵛ].

66. Knighton, ed., *Acts of the Dean and Chapter of Westminster*, 2:231; Gentleman of Elvas, *Virginia richly valued, By the description of the maine land of Florida, her next neighbour*, trans. Richard Hakluyt (London, 1609), sig. A 2ʳ.

67. Gentleman of Elvas, *Virginia richly valued*, sig. A 2ʳ–3ʳ.

68. Gentleman of Elvas, *Virginia richly valued*, sig. A3ʳ.

69. Gentleman of Elvas, *Virginia richly valued*, sig. A3ʳ–[A4ʳ].

70. Gentleman of Elvas, *Virginia richly valued*, sig. [A4ʳ].

71. Gentleman of Elvas, *Virginia richly valued*, sig. [A4ᵛ].

72. "Hakluyt Chronology," 1:323–324. Hakluyt himself was listed (as "Richard Hacklewt") as one of the "Adventurers to Virginia" in a list possibly dating from 1618, and again (as "Master Richard Hackleuit") on a June 22, 1620, list of the adventurers who had paid Sir Thomas Smythe (Smith) for their shares; see Susan M. Kingsbury, ed., *Records of the Virginia Company of London*, 4 vols. (Washington, D.C., 1906–1935), 3:84, 326.

CHAPTER 11. Wetheringsett and London, 1614

1. Samuel Purchas, *Purchas his Pilgrimage. Or Relations of the World and the Religions Observed in All Ages and Places discovered, from the Creation unto this Present* (London, 1613); Samuel Purchas, *Purchas his Pilgrimage. Or Relations of the World and the Religions Observed in All Ages and Places discovered, from the Creation unto this Present* (London, 1614), sig. [q5ᵛ–6ʳ].

2. Purchas, *Purchas his Pilgrimage* (1613 ed.), sig. q2ᵛ–[q3ʳ], sig. [q4ʳ].

3. Purchas, *Purchas his Pilgrimage* (1613 ed.), 625–626 (Parkhurst et al.); Purchas, *Purchas his Pilgrimage* (1614 ed.), sig. [A5ʳ] (Ramusio and Hakluyt), 782 ("Admirall"). Hakluyt had not transferred all of his papers yet since he was still collecting information about the East Indies and English efforts to establish commercial links there; some of those papers perhaps reached Purchas after Hakluyt died. For a later letter, see Thomas Roe to Lord Carew, January 17, 1616 (later published by Purchas), in William Foster, ed., *The Embassy of Sir Thomas Roe to the Court of the Great Mogul, 1615–1619*, 2 vols., Hak. Soc., 2nd Ser., 1–2 (London, 1899), 1:110–114.

4. Joseph Hodskinson, *The County of Suffolk* (London, 1783; rpt. Suffolk Records Society, 1972), pl. 8. For Hodskinson's efforts to improve the efficiency of farming with particular attention to such matters as drains and fences, see *The Farmer's Guide; Or, An Improved Method of Management of Arable Land, with Some Hints upon Drainage, Fences, and upon the Improvement of Turnpike and Cross Roads* (London, [1794]). William Dowsing kept an accurate count of the icons he smashed, dashing through the country "like a Bedlam breaking glasse windowes," as one contemporary described him; see "The Journal of William Dowsing, Parliamentary Visitor, Appointed to Demolish Church Ornaments, etc., within the County of Suffolk, 1643–1644," in *Proceedings of the Suffolk Institute of Archaeology and Natural History* 6 (1888): 264 (inventory at Wetheringsett); and *Mercurius Rusticus: Or, The Countries Complaint of the barbarous Outrages committed by the Sectaries of this late flourishing Kingdom. Together with A Brief Chronology . . . to the 25th of March, 1646* (London, 1685), 197. For the history of the building, see Roy Tricker, *All Saints Church Wetheringsett-Cum-Brockford* (n.p., 1998).

5. Hakluyt never wrote about Suffolk, but extensive surveys in the nineteenth century documented early human occupation through surviving artifacts, revealed the presence of the Roman road, and cataloged the county's fauna; see William Page, ed., *The Victoria County History of the County of Suffolk* (London, 1911), 1:257 and 263 (Neolithic remains at Coddenham and Wetheringsett), 303 (Roman road at Coddenham), 177–214 (survey of birds), and 215–233 (survey of mammals).

6. Hugo Grotius, *The Free Sea,* trans. Richard Hakluyt, ed. David Armitage (Indianapolis, Ind., 2004), 3 (law of nations), 5 (Dutch rights). All subsequent citations to Grotius's *Free Sea* are to this edition.

7. Grotius, *Free Sea,* xxii (translation), 11 (navigation, Seneca).

8. Grotius, *Free Sea,* 13 (tribute), 16–17 (pope's bull), 19–20 (Dutch actions).

9. Grotius, *Free Sea,* 26, 27 (limits on claims to the sea), 31 (fishing rights), 31–32 ("unmeasurable and infinite"), 32 (passage did not confer rights), 34 (Columbus), 35 (Dutch predecessors), 37 (limits to Portuguese claims).

10. Grotius, *Free Sea,* 38 (pope not lord of the seas), 39 (effort to minimize strife), 48–49 (other Europeans' journeys), 49–51 (classical authorities), 52 (limits of papal power).

11. Grotius, *Free Sea*, 55–56.

12. David Armitage reprints the core criticisms made by the mathematician and civil lawyer William Welwod in a treatise first published in England in 1613, which elicited a response from Grotius; see Grotius, *Free Sea*, xxiii–xxiv, 65–130.

13. As Grotius put it (in Hakluyt's translation): "And although title be not sufficient for dominion, because possession is also required": Grotius, *Free Sea*, 13.

14. Purchas, *Purchas His Pilgrimage* (1614 ed.), 766–767.

15. George Percy, "Observations gathered out of a Discourse of the Plantation of the Southerne Colonie in Virginia by the English," in *Hakluytus Posthumus*, 4:1685–1690; the fatalities are reported on 1690. Though Purchas did not always record when he received a text from Hakluyt, in this instance (as in many others) he marked the text with an "H" to tell of its immediate provenance; see *Hakluytus Posthumus*, 3:sig A2ʳ.

16. Percy, "Observations," 1690.

17. Carville Earle, "Environment, Disease, and Mortality in Early Virginia," in Thad Tate and David Ammerman, eds., *The Chesapeake in the Seventeenth Century: Essays on Anglo-American Society* (Chapel Hill, N.C., 1979), 96–125 (illnesses); Frederic Gleach, *Powhatan's World and Colonial Virginia: A Conflict of Cultures* (Lincoln, Nebr., 1997) (tensions); *A True Declaration of the Estate of the Colonie in Virginia* (London, 1610) (propaganda); Edmund Morgan, *American Slavery, American Freedom: The Ordeal of Colonial Virginia* (New York, 1975), 73 (cannibalism).

18. See John Chamberlain to Dudley Carleton, January 23, 1609, July 9, 1612, and August 1, 1613, all in Chamberlain, *Letters*, 1:282–283, 367, 471. For Chamberlain's holdings in the Virginia Company, see his will at 2:635.

19. On Edmond, see "Hakluyt Chronology," 1:326; Hakluyt's will is reprinted in *Writings and Correspondence*, 2:506–509.

20. *Writings and Correspondence*, 2:482 (interpreter); "Extracts taken out of two Letters of Josias Logan from Pechora, to Master Hakluyt Prebend of Westminster," in *Hakluytus Posthumus* 3:546–547 (Logan's letters).

21. *Calendar of State Papers, Colonial: East Indies, China and Japan, 1513–1616* (London, 1862), 272. The minutes record the discussion at a meeting on January 22, 1614.

22. *Dialogues in the English and Malaian Languages: Or, Certaine Common Formes of Speech, First Written in Latin, Malaian, and Madagascar tongues, by . . . Gotardus Arthusius*, trans. August Spalding (London, 1614), sig. q aʳ⁻ᵛ. It is impossible to know Hakluyt's precise role in the production of this text in English. According to F. M. Rogers, "Hakluyt translated Gothard Arthus' Malayan dialogues into English": Rogers, "Hakluyt as Translator," in *Hakluyt Handbook*, 1:45.

23. *Dialogues*, 1–2.

24. *Dialogues*, 2–4.

25. *Dialogues*, 5–6.

26. *Dialogues*, 7–10.

27. *Dialogues*, 10–13, quotations at 13 (trade at the docks), 13–18, quotations at 15 and 17 (bartering), 25 (shopkeeper).

28. *Dialogues*, 19 (lost in the woods), 27–33 (credit and directions), 33–38, quotations at 36–37 (weighing rituals), 38–55 (feast), 66–71, quotations at 68–69 (preparations for sea), 71–73 (Madagascar).

29. "An Abstract of the Journall of Master Henry Hudson, for the Discoverie of the

North-west Passage," and "A larger Discourse of the same Voyage . . . written by Abacuk Pricket," both in *Hakluytus Posthumus*, 3:596–605; "A true report of a Voyage Anno 1615 for Discoverie of the Seas, Lands, and Ilands, to the Northwards; as it was performed by Robert Fotherbie," in *Hakluytus Posthumus*, 3:728–731 (quotation at 731); William Baffin, "A Journall of the Voyage made to Greenland, with sixe English ships and a Pinnasse, in the yeere 1613," in *Hakluytus Posthumus*, 3:716–720; Baffin, "A true Relation of such things as happened in the fourth Voyage for the Discoverie of the North-west Passage, performed in the year 1615," in *Hakluytus Poshumus*, 3:836–842 (the effort to establish longitude is at 839–840). For a complete listing of the reports that Hakluyt passed to Purchas, see C. R. Steele, "From Hakluyt to Purchas," in *Hakluyt Handbook*, 1:84–96.

30. "Master Bartholomew Gosnolds Letter to his Father, touching his first Voyage to Virginia, 1602," in *Hakluytus Posthumus*, 4:1646; George Percy, "Observations gathered out of a Discouse of the Plantation of the Southerne Colonie in Virginia by the English, 1606," and William Strachey, "A true repertory of the wracke, and redemption of Sir Thomas Gates, Knight; upon, and from the Ilands of the Bermudas," in *Hakluytus Posthumus*, 4:1685–1690, 1734–1758 (see 1735–1737 for a description of the storm and the wreck); "A Letter of Samuell Argoll touching his Voyage to Virginia and Actions there: Written to Master Nicholas Hawes, June 1613," in *Hakluytus Posthumus*, 4:1764–1765.

31. Bartholomew Pitiscus, *Trigonometry: Or The Doctrine of Triangles*, trans. Ra[lph] Handson (London, [1614]), [bk. 2]:1, [bk. 1]:sig. A2^v.

32. Anthony Farrington, ed., *The English Factory in Japan, 1613–1623*, 2 vols. (London, 1991), 2:983 (order to Saris); "A Discourse of the Kingdome of China, taken out of Ricius and Trigautius, contayning the Countrey, People, Government, Religion, Rites, Sects, Characters, Studies, Arts, Acts; and a Map of China," in *Hakluytus Posthumus*, 3:401 (map of China); Purchas, *Purchas his Pilgrimage* (1614 ed.), 782–783 ("greatest Benefactor"); Edmund Scott, "A Discourse of Java, and of the first English Factorie there, with divers Indian, English, and Dutch occurrents . . . from the eleventh of Februarie, 1602 till the sixt of October, 1605," in *Hakluytus Posthumus*, 1:164–185 (quotation at 167); Walter Payton, "A Journall of all principall matters passed in the twelfth Voyage to the East-India," in *Hakluytus Posthumus*, 1:488–500.

33. "Hakluyt Chronology," 1:329–330.

34. "Omitted men and named Men, and Lands (not here, indeede, / So written of as they serve) at large in Hakluit reede": William Warner, *Albions England* (London, 1612), 294–295; Thomas Edge; "A briefe Discoverie of the Northerne Discoveries of Seas, Coasts, and Countries," in *Hakluytus Posthumus*, 3:464 (on Hudson); William Gourdon, "A Voyage made to Pechora 1611," in *Hakluytus Posthumus*, 3:531. For the number of books in which Hakluyt was involved and the identification of his printers, see Anthony Payne, "'Strange, remote, and farre distant countreys': The Travel Books of Richard Hakluyt," in Robin Myers and Michael Harris, eds., *Journeys through the Market: Travels, Travellers, and the Book Trade* (New Castle, Del., 1999), 19, and *Hakluyt Handbook*, 2:461–575; on the importance of translating books for the English market, see William H. Sherman, "Bringing the World to England: The Politics of Translation in the Age of Hakluyt," *Transactions of the Royal Historical Society* 14 (2004): 199–207.

35. "A true report of a Voyage Anno 1615 for Discoverie of Seas, Lands, and Ilands, to the Northwards; as it was performed by Robert Fotherbie," in *Hakluytus Posthumus*, 3:730; "Hakluyt Chronology," 1:330; "A briefe and true Relation of Journall, containing such

accidents as happened in the fift[h] voyage, for the discoverie of a passage to the North-west . . . performed in the yeere of our Lord 1616," in *Hakluytus Posthumus*, 3:846–847.

36. The map is labeled "Poli Arctici, et Circumiacentum Terrarum Desciptio Novissima," and appears (unpaginated) in the chapter entitled "The Pole Arctique," in Gerardi Mercatoris et I. Hondii, *Atlas, Or A Geographicke description of the Regions, Countries, and Kingdomes of the world, through Europe, Asia, Africa, and America, represented by new and exact maps* (Amsterdam, 1636), 43–44; N. Sanson d'Abbeville, "Amerique Septentrionale," (Paris, 1650), G. De L'Isle, "L'Amerique Septentrionale" (Paris, 1700), and Guilaume De l'Isle, "Carte du Canada ou de la Nouvelle France et des Descouvertes qui y ont été faites" (Paris, 1703) in HEH 109496, fols. 21, 23, 39; John Ross, A *Voyage of Discovery . . . for the Purpose of Exploring Baffin's Bay, and Inquiring into the Probability of a North-West Passage* (London, 1819), frontispiece: "A General Chart shewing the Track and Discoveries of H. M. Ships Isabella & Alexander to Davis's Straits & Baffins Bay" (walls of ice).

37. See, e.g., Chamberlain to Carleton, May 12, 1614, in Chamberlain, *Letters*, 1:529.

38. Counseil for Virginia, *A Briefe Declaration of the present state of things in Virginia, and of a Division to be now made* [London, 1616], 2–3.

39. Counseil for Virginia, *Briefe Declaration*, 3–4.

40. Counseil for Virginia, *Briefe Declaration*, 5–8.

41. Chamberlain to Carleton, June 22, 1616, in Chamberlain, *Letters*, 2:12. Chamberlain continued to pay close attention to occurrences in Virginia and remained suspicious of the actions of English settlers there; he even blamed the Powhatan attack of 1622 on the "supine negligence" of the colonists, whose dispersed settlements (set up as if they lived in England) made them easy victims of the Americans. "The disgrace and shame is as much as the losse," he wrote when he heard the news, "for no other nation wold have ben so grossely overtaken." Chamberlain to Carleton, July 13, 1622, in Chamberlain, *Letters*, 2:446.

42. There is no reference in the records of the Stationers' Company indicating when the pamphlet was registered, if it ever was.

43. Details of the society's history and a complete list of its publications can be found in R. C. Bridges and P. E. H. Hair, eds., *Compassing the Vast Globe of the Earth: Studies in the History of the Hakluyt Society, 1846–1996*, Hak. Soc., 2nd Ser., 183 (London, 1996).

44. Joseph Hall, *Quo Vadis? A Just Censure of Travell as it is commonly undertaken by the gentlemen of our nation* (London, 1617), 87–88; *ODNB*, s.v. "Hall, Joseph."

45. Hall, *Quo Vadis?* 1–4, quotations at 3–4.

46. Hall, *Quo Vadis?* 70 (anti-Catholicism), [97] (misnumbered as 91; better to stay home); *The Works of Joseph Hall* (London, 1647), 633–658.

47. E[dmund] G[ardiner], *The Triall of Tobacco* (London, 1610); William Barclay, *Nepenthes; Or The Vertues Of Tabacco* (Edinburgh, 1614), sigs. [A7ᵛ] (use by Barclay and the French man), [A8ʳ] ("abusers"), Bʳ (brains); C. T., *An Advice How to Plant Tobacco in England* (London, 1615), sigs. [C4ʳ] (youthful abuse), A3ʳ⁻ᵛ (costs), [A4ʳ⁻ᵛ] (tainted), Cᵛ (dog cure), Bᵛ–[B4ʳ] (tending the plant). Gardiner used Hakluyt not to discuss tobacco but to demonstrate that individuals in other parts of the world often lived extraordinarily long lives, including the king of Ballobaom, who lived to the age of 160, according to the account printed by Hakluyt; see *Triall of Tobacco*, fol. 8ʳ. For Trinadadian tobacco, see fols. 8ᵛ–9ʳ. For his reference to key authorities, see his use of Thevet (fol. 5ʳ⁻ᵛ), Monardes (fol. 9ʳ⁻ᵛ), and the English botanist John Gerard, whom Gardiner called "the most learned

Herbalist of this age" and "a man of unreproochable authoritie" (fol. 49^r–50^r, quotations at 49^r and 50^r). C. T. pointed out that it was Phillip II, the "Catholike King" of Spain, who had poisoned the dog to test the therapeutic powers of tobacco and that the tainting of the plant was done by the Spanish, not by native Americans, whose tobacco was purer and thus healthier (see sig. B^r).

48. [Joshua Sylvester], "Tobacco Battered; & The Pipes Shattered," [1616] in Sylvester, *The Maidens Blush* (London, 1620), 101 (growth), 106 (intellect), 107 (memory), 108–109 (sociopaths), 102–103 (addictive), 109–110 (expensive), 82–83 (Americans), 93 ("lewdeth" et al), 116 (scandalous to Christendom); [John Deacon], *Tobacco Tortured, Or, The Filthie Fume of Tobacco Refined* (London, 1616), 10 (negative traits of other peoples), 80 (Trojan horse), 175 (threat to the state); *Jack Drums Entertainement, Or The Comedie of Pasquil and Katherine* (London, 1616), sig. B3^v. The king's views on tobacco appeared in his *Counterblaste to Tobacco* (London, 1604).

49. Barnabe Rich, *The Honestie of This Age* (London, 1614), 25–29; Rich, *My Ladies Looking Glasse* (London, 1616), 22–27, quotations at 26 (impoverishing tendencies), 25 (devil). Rich condemned alehouses, too, for the social pathologies they bred but hinted that he had been to them when he wrote that "for *Tobacco Houses* and *Brothell Houses*, (I thanke God for it) I doe not use to frequent them"; see *Honestie of This Age*, 28. Rich was not the only observer to notice the unpleasant public behavior of those who used tobacco. An epigram by a contemporary author identified only as H. P. included the following: "*Trocus* in Tavernes twice a day must bowze it, / And belch Tobacco on his Clients Purses: / No matter *Trocus*, 'tis thy place allowes it, / Though like the Foxe 'canst not escape from curses." [H. P.], *The Mastive, Or Young-Whelpe of the Olde Dogge* (London, 1615), sig. E^r.

50. For Edmond's sale, see the records of a meeting held by the Virginia Company on June 13, 1621, and "Shareholders in the Virginia Company from 1615 to 1623," in Susan M. Kingsbury, ed., *The Records of the Virginia Company of London*, 4 vols. (Washington, 1906–1935), 1:497, 3:63.

51. Samuel Purchas, *Purchas his Pilgrimage, Or Relations of the World* (London, 1617), sig. A4^r–[8^v] (catalog of authors; Hakluyt's name is the first under the letter "H" on sig. [5^v]), 930 (repeating praise); and see the marginal notes alongside the texts describing America (e.g., at 913, 922, 929, 938, 939, 948, 949, 958); *Hakluytus Posthumus*, 1:sig. [q4^v] (1625 observations).

52. *Hakluytus Posthumus*, 1:sig. [a2^r] ("corrected" accounts of circumnavigations); marginal note to Antonio De Herrera, "A Description of the West Indies" [1601], in *Hakluytus Posthumus*, 3:855. For Purchas's reputation, see Steele, "From Hakluyt to Purchas," 74–75.

53. For the list of these works, see *Hakluytus Posthumus*, 1:sig. [a2^v–a3^r].

A Note on Method and Sources

1. *Athenæ Oxonienses. An Exact History of all the Writers and Bishops who have had their Education in the most ancient and famous University of Oxford*, 2 vols. (London, 1691), 1:349.

2. [Albertus Meier], *Certaine briefe and speciall Instructions for Gentlemen, merchants, students, souldiers, mariners, &c. Employed in services abrode, or anie way occasioned to converse in the kingdoms, and governementes of forren Princes*, trans. Philip Jones (London, 1589), [22]; for Hakluyt's urging, see sig. A3^v.

Acknowledgments

Richard Hakluyt knew how to thank his patrons. He used his most famous dedication (to the *Principall Navigations* in 1589) to thank his benefactor and to tell his own life story. Such writings seem a relic from a long-lost age. But Hakluyt was modern in one key respect: he recognized that his work could progress only through extensive personal connections and financial support. Without Sir Francis Walsingham he would have never made it to France and might instead have drowned, as Stephen Parmenius did, on a ship foundering in the waters off Newfoundland. Without André Thevet he would not have seen the manuscripts from Jacques Cartier's journeys to Canada nor would he have obtained the Codex Mendoza, which now can be found in the Bodleian Library at Oxford. Without Abraham Ortelius's connections to the lawyer, Hakluyt might never have gained such a sure grasp on geography. Without the Skinners' and Clothworkers' companies he might have never made it to Christ Church, despite the talent he had shown in getting a scholarship to Westminster School. Without the East India Company he might have never recognized the benefit of the *Malaian Dialogues*. Without Lady Stafford he might have never received a clerical position in Wetheringsett, an appointment close enough to his heart that he apparently wrote much of his work nearby and buried one of his wives there. And without his cousin the lawyer, this book would in all likelihood not exist because he might not have set off on the course of study that led him to become one of the most important scholars of his age.

Four hundred years later, scholars are entangled in similar webs of financial and intellectual support, as I well know. I could not have completed this book without support provided by the National Endowment for the Humanities, the Henry E. Huntington Library, the Library Company of Philadelphia, the College of Letters, Arts, and Sciences at the University of Southern California, the USC–Huntington Early Modern Studies Institute, and the Hall Center for the Humanities and the College of Liberal Arts and Sciences at the University of Kansas. I also thank the institutions that provided permission to reproduce images in their collections: the Henry E. Huntington Library, Houghton Library of Harvard College Library, English Heritage/National Monuments Record, and the British Library. During my years of research and writing I accumulated important debts to many scholars who commented on the manuscript. Among the many who provided assistance and suggestions I thank Malcolm Baker, Daniela Bleichmar, Trevor Burnard, Nicholas Canny, Luis Corteguera, Jon Earle, Heidi Brayman Hackel, Eric Hinderaker, Richard Jenkyns, Beth LaDow, Steve Pincus, Martha Robinson, Alison Sandman, Ann Schofield, Carole Shammas, Kevin Sharpe, Leslie Tuttle, Marta Vicente, and Don Worster. Matthew Day graciously sent me a copy of a vital Hakluyt manuscript from the British Library; Anne Goldgar, Tony Corbeill, and Siobhan McElduff provided crucial translations; and Luca Mola went well beyond the call of duty to provide assistance in the Venetian archives. I have benefited immeasurably from discussions with a cluster of sixteenth-century scholars, notably Mary Fuller, Deb Harkness, David Sacks, and Ben Schmidt, all of whom shared their not-yet published work with me. I also thank the staffs of the Library Company of Philadelphia, which provided valuable support early in this project; the Biblioteca Marciana, the Archivio di Stato Venezia, and the Vatican Library, where I caught glimpses of Ramusio; Christ Church, where I sought traces of Hakluyt; the John Carter Brown Library, whose treasures include Thevet's *Cosmographie Universelle*; and especially the Huntington Library, where I wrote and revised this book. Like all scholars fortunate enough to spend time there, I will forever be in debt to Roy Ritchie, who has nurtured and shaped the most exciting early modern research center in the world.

In addition, I thank those who read the manuscript or parts of it. Whatever faults this book still possesses cannot be blamed on Moti Feingold, Mary Fuller, Alison Games, Elliott Mancall, Lou Masur, and the anonymous readers for Yale University Press. My incomparable agent, Deirdre Mullane, shaped this book more than she can know, as did Bernard Bailyn, who has provided enormous support since the early 1980s. My editors, Chris Rogers, Ellie Goldberg, and Laura Jones Dooley, skillfully shepherded this book through production and made substantial improvements to it in the process. Last, as always, I thank Lisa Bitel. For everything.

Index

Page numbers in *italics* indicate illustrations